A HEINRICH SCHÜTZ READER

A Heinrich Schütz Reader

LETTERS AND DOCUMENTS IN TRANSLATION

Edited by Gregory S. Johnston

OXFORD
UNIVERSITY PRESS

Oxford University Press is a department of the University of Oxford.
It furthers the University's objective of excellence in research, scholarship,
and education by publishing worldwide.

Oxford   New York
Auckland   Cape Town   Dar es Salaam   Hong Kong   Karachi
Kuala Lumpur   Madrid   Melbourne   Mexico City   Nairobi
New Delhi   Shanghai   Taipei   Toronto

With offices in
Argentina   Austria   Brazil   Chile   Czech Republic   France   Greece
Guatemala   Hungary   Italy   Japan   Poland   Portugal   Singapore
South Korea   Switzerland   Thailand   Turkey   Ukraine   Vietnam

Oxford is a registered trademark of Oxford University Press
in the UK and certain other countries.

Published in the United States of America by
Oxford University Press
198 Madison Avenue, New York, NY 10016

© Oxford University Press 2013

First issued as an Oxford University Press paperback, 2016

All rights reserved. No part of this publication may be reproduced, stored in a
retrieval system, or transmitted, in any form or by any means, without the prior
permission in writing of Oxford University Press, or as expressly permitted by law,
by license, or under terms agreed with the appropriate reproduction rights organization.
Inquiries concerning reproduction outside the scope of the above should be sent to the
Rights Department, Oxford University Press, at the address above.

You must not circulate this work in any other form
and you must impose this same condition on any acquirer.

Library of Congress Cataloging-in-Publication Data
Schütz, Heinrich, 1585–1672.
[Works. Selections. English]
A Heinrich Schütz reader: letters and documents in translation/edited by Gregory S. Johnston.
   pages cm
ISBN   978-0-19-981220-2 (hardcover : alk. paper); 978-0-19-062847-5 (paperback : alk. paper)
1. Schütz, Heinrich, 1585–1672.   2. Composers—Germany—Biography.
I. Johnston, Gregory S., 1955–, editor.   II. Title.
ML410.S35A25   2013
782.2'2092—dc23
[B]
2012011188

To my family

Contents

Preface xvii
Acknowledgments xxiii
Bibliographical Abbreviations xxv
Illustrations xxvii

1. Youth and Early Manhood (1611–27) 1

    1. *Il primo libro de madrigali* (Venice, 1611): Title Page and Dedication (1 May 1611) (Original language: Italian) 1

    2. Johann Georg I, Elector of Saxony, to Moritz, Landgrave of Hesse-Kassel (27 August 1614) 3

    3. Johann Georg I to Moritz of Hesse-Kassel (25 April 1615) 4

    4. Moritz of Hesse-Kassel to Johann Georg I (27 April 1615) 5

    5. Schütz to Christoph von Loss, Privy Councillor and Marshal of the Court (23 September 1616); Johann Georg I's reply (30 September 1616) 6

    6. Moritz of Hesse-Kassel to Johann Georg I (1 December 1616) 8

    7. Christoph von Loss to Johann Georg I (11 December 1616) 8

    8. Johann Georg I to Moritz of Hesse-Kassel (13 December 1616) 10

    9. Schütz to Moritz of Hesse-Kassel (16 December 1616) 11

    10. Moritz of Hesse-Kassel to Schütz (23 December 1616) 12

11. Dresden Court to Schütz (? July 1617) 13

12. Schütz to Heinrich Posthumus Reuss (9 December 1617) 16

13. Schütz to Johann Georg I (15 April 1618) 21

14. Moritz of Hesse-Kassel to Johann Georg I (11 January 1619) 22

15. Johann Georg I to Moritz of Hesse-Kassel (25 January 1619) 23

16. *Psalmen Davids* (Dresden, 1619): Title Page and Dedication 24

17. *Psalmen Davids* (1619): Title Page and Preface from the Basso Continuo Partbook 26

18. Schütz to the City Council of Frankfurt am Main (17 July 1619) 28

19. Schütz's Poem on the Occasion of Georg Schütz's Wedding (9 August 1619) 29

20. Schütz to Ludwig Wilhelm Moser, Court Chamber Secretary (3 July 1621) 29

21. Schütz's Text to *Syncharma musicum* (3 November 1621) (Original language: Latin) 31

22. Schütz's Text to *Teutoniam dudum belli* (3 November 1621) (Original language: Latin) 32

23. *Historia der Auferstehung Jesu Christi* (Dresden, 1623): Title Page and Preface (25 March 1623) 33

24. Schütz to Wilhelm Ludwig Moser (25 May 1624) 35

25. Schütz to Wilhelm Ludwig Moser (30 December 1624) 36

26. *Cantiones sacrae* (Freiberg, 1625): Title Page and Dedication (1 January 1625) (Original language: Latin) 37

27. *Cantiones sacrae* (Freiberg, 1625): Foreword to the Reader (Original language: Latin) 39

28. Schütz to the Attention of Johann Georg I (before 17 March 1625) 40

29. Schütz to Johann Georg I (28 March 1625) 41

30. Dresden Court Musicians to Johann Georg I (11 June 1625) 41

31. Schütz to Johann Georg I (22 September 1626) 42

32. Schütz to Johann Georg I (9 May 1627) 44

33. Schütz to the Dresden Court (after 26 May 1627) 46

34. Schütz to Johann Georg I (2 August 1627) 47

35. Schütz to the Dresden Court (? September 1627) 48

36. *Da pacem, Domine* for the Electoral Assembly in Mühlhausen (4 October to 5 November 1627): Dedication and Performance Instructions (Original language: Latin and German) 50

37. Schütz to an Unnamed Person (October/November 1627) 51

38. Johann Georg I to Johann Sautor, Court Chamberlain (15 November 1627) 52

39. Johann Sautor to Johann Georg I (11 December 1627) 53

40. Johann Georg I to Johann Sautor (18 December 1627) 54

2. *Middle Age (1628–44)* 55

41. Schütz to Georg Pflugk, Marshal of the Palace (early 1628) 55

42. Dresden Court Musicians Directed to Johann Georg I (Palm Sunday, 6 April 1628 [Julian Calendar]) 56

43. Schütz to Johann Georg I (22 April 1628) 57

44. Schütz to Johann Georg I (10 July 1628) 58

45. Schütz to Georg Pflugk (14 July 1628) 59

46. Schütz to Johann Georg I (3 November 1628) 60

47. *Becker Psalter* (Freiberg, 1628): Title Page and Dedication to Electress Hedwig, Duchess of Saxony (6 September 1627) 62

48. *Becker Psalter* (Freiberg, 1628): Preface to the Reader 64

49. *Becker Psalter* (Freiberg, 1628): Two Memoranda to the Reader 65

50. Schütz to Johann Georg I (29 June 1629) 66

51. *Symphoniae sacrae I* (Venice, 1629): Title Page and Dedication (19 August 1629) (Original language: Latin) 69

52. Schütz to Johann Georg I (24 August 1629) 71

53. Excerpt from Philipp Hainhofer's Travelogue (27 October 1629) 72

54. Schütz to Georg Pflugk (late 1629) 73

55. Schütz to the Dresden Court (late 1629 or early 1630) 74

56. Schütz to Johann Georg I (22 April 1630) 75

57. Schütz Directed to Johann Georg I (mid 1630?) 76

58. Schütz's Elegy on the Death of Johann Hermann Schein (†19 November 1630) (Original language: Latin) 77

59. Schütz to the Dresden Court (presumably January 1631) 78

60. Schütz to the Dresden Court (presumably Janurary 1631) 79

61. Schütz to Georg Pflugk (28 February 1631) 81

62. Schütz to Philipp Hainhofer (23 April 1632) 82

63. Schütz to Friedrich Lebzelter (6/16 February 1633) 85

64. Schütz Directed to Johann Georg I (9 February 1633) 87

65. Friedrich Lebzelter to Christian (V), Prince-Elect of Denmark (15 February 1633) 90

66. Friedrich Lebzelter to Christian (V), Prince-Elect of Denmark (13 November 1633) 91

67. Memorandum Regarding Preparations for Schütz's Appointment to the Danish Court (late 1633) 92

68. Schütz's Entry in Joachim Morsius's *Stammbuch* (21 January 1634) (Original language: Latin) 93

69. Zacharias Hestius Directed to Johann Georg I (23 April 1634) 94

70. Christian IV, King of Denmark, to Johann Georg I (25 May 1635) 95

71. Danish Travel Pass Issued to Schütz (25 May 1635) 95

72. *Musicalische Exequien* (Dresden, 1636): Title Page and Dedication 96

73. *Musicalische Exequien* (Dresden, 1636): Elegy on the Death of Heinrich Posthumus Reuss 98

74. *Musicalische Exequien* (Dresden, 1636): Memoranda and Instructions for Performance 101

75. Schütz to Johann Georg I (9 August 1636) 104

76. Schütz to the Dresden Court (after 9 August 1636) 105

77. *Kleine geistliche Concerte I* (Leipzig, 1636): Title Page and Dedication (29 September 1636) 105

78. Schütz Directed to Georg Pflugk (1 February 1637) 107

79. Printing Patent Granted Schütz by Emperor Ferdinand III (3 April 1637) 108

80. Danish Travel Pass Intended for Schütz (16–31 March 1639) 109

81. *Kleine geistliche Concerte II* (Dresden, 1639): Title Page and Dedication to Friedrich III, Duke of Schleswig-Holstein-Gottorp (2 June 1639) 110

82. Dresden Court Musicians to the Court Privy Councillor (21 October 1640) 112

83. Schütz to Johann Georg I (7 March 1641) 113

84. Schütz to Johann Georg II, Electoral Prince of Saxony (14 September 1641) 115

85. Schütz to Ferdinand III, Holy Roman Emperor (25 April 1642) 117

86. Schütz's Second Appointment to the Royal Danish Court (3 May 1642) 118

87. Schütz to the Dresden Court (15 July 1642) 119

88. Schütz to Sophie Elisabeth, Duchess of Brunswick-Lüneburg (22 October 1644) 120

3. Old Age (1645–56) 123

89. Schütz to the Wolfenbüttel Court (early 1645) 123

90. Schütz to Sophie Elisabeth of Brunswick-Lüneburg (17 March 1645) 125

91. Schütz Directed to Johann Georg I (21 May 1645) 126

92. Schütz Directed to Johann Georg I (28 September 1645) 127

93. Johann Klemm to Johann Samuel Schein (9 March 1646) 130

94. Schütz to the Dresden Court (24 May 1646) 131

95. Schütz Directed to Jacob Weller, Senior Court Chaplain (30 July 1646) 133

96. Schütz to Christian Schirmer (7 September 1646) (Original Language: Latin) 137

97. Heinrich II Reuss to Schütz (22 October 1646) 138

98. Schütz to Martin Knabe (30 October 1646) 139

99. Bautzen Town Council to Schütz (5 March 1647) 140

100. Schütz to the Bautzen Town Council (14 March 1647) 141

101. Bautzen Town Council to Schütz (11 April 1647) 142

102. Schütz to the Bautzen Town Council (28 April 1647) 142

103. *Symphoniae sacrae II* (Dresden, 1647): Title Page and Dedication (1 May 1647) 144

104. *Symphoniae sacrae II* (Dresden, 1647): Preface to the Reader 146

105. *Symphoniae sacrae II* (Dresden, 1647): Appended List of Published Works 148

106. Schütz Directed to Johann Georg I (between 20 June and 22 July 1647) 149

107. Schütz to Christian Reichbrodt, Privy Chamber Secretary (21 September 1647) 153

108. Johann Georg II to Johann Georg I (29 September 1647) 154

109. Schütz to August, Duke of Saxe-Weissenfels (28 December 1647) 155

110. Schütz to Wilhelm IV, Duke of Saxe-Weimar (6 January 1648) 157

111. August of Saxe-Weissenfels to Schütz (18 January 1648) 159

112. Schütz to an Unnamed Person (early 1648) (Original language: Latin) 160

113. Johann Georg II to Giovanni Sansoni (29 March 1648) (Original Language: Italian) 161

114. *Geistliche Chor-Music* (Dresden, 1648): Title Page and Dedication (21 April 1648) 162

115. *Geistliche Chor-Music* (Dresden, 1648): Preface 164

116. Schütz to the Dresden Court (7 July 1648) 166

117. Alexander Hering to the Bautzen Town Council (30 August 1648) 170

118. Johann Georg Hofkontz to Johann Georg I (16 May 1649) 171

119. Schütz to Burkard Berlich (3 July 1649) 174

120. Schütz to Heinrich von Taube, Marshal of the Court (between December 1649 and February 1650) 176

121. Schütz to the Dresden Court (11 February 1650) 176

122. *Symphoniae sacrae III* (Dresden, 1650): Title Page and Dedication (29 September 1650) 177

123. *Symphoniae sacrae III* (Dresden, 1650): Preface from the *Bassus ad Organum* Partbook 179

124. *Symphoniae sacrae III* (Dresden, 1650): Appendix to the *Bassus ad Organum* Partbook 180

125. Schütz to Johann Georg I (14 January 1651) 181

126. Schütz Directed to the Dresden Court (21 February 1651) 186

127. Schütz to Christian Reichbrodt (11 April 1651) 188

128. Schütz and Johann Georg Hofkontz to Christian, Duke of Saxony (14 August 1651) 189

129. Schütz to Christian Reichbrodt (19 August 1651) 191

130. Schütz to Christian Reichbrodt (4 February 1652) 194

131. Schütz to Christian Reichbrodt (28 May 1652) 196

132. Schütz to Heinrich von Taube (26 June 1652) 197

133. Schütz to Heinrich II Reuss (16 June 1653) 199

134. Schütz's Endorsement of Caspar Ziegler's *Von den Madrigalen* (Leipzig, 1653/1685) (11 August 1653) 201

135. Schütz to Heinrich von Taube, Jacob Weller, and Christian Reichbrodt (21 August 1653) 202

136. Schütz to Johann Georg I (21 August 1653) 203

137. Schütz to Johann Georg II (21 August 1653) 204

138. Schütz to Johann Georg I (21 September 1653) 206

139. Schütz to the Dresden Court (undated, probably 1653 or 1654) 208

140. Schütz to Johann Georg I (29 May 1655) 209

141. Sophie Elisabeth of Brunswick-Lüneburg to Schütz (22 June 1655) 211

142. Schütz to Johann Georg I (21 July 1655) 212

143. Schütz to Sophie Elisabeth of Brunswick-Lüneburg (24 July 1655) 213

144. Schütz's Contract as Kapellmeister in Wolfenbüttel *in absentia* (23 August 1655) 216

145. Sophie Elisabeth of Brunswick-Lüneburg to Schütz (10 November 1655) 218

146. Schütz to Sophie Elisabeth of Brunswick-Lüneburg (27 November 1655) 219

4. Last Years (1657–72) 222

147. *Zwölf geistliche Gesänge* (Dresden, 1657): Title Page and Christoph Kittel's Preface 222

148. *Zwölf geistliche Gesänge* (Dresden, 1657): First Memorandum in the Basso Continuo Partbook 224

149. *Zwölf geistliche Gesänge* (Dresden, 1657): Second Memorandum in the Basso Continuo Partbook 224

150. Schütz's Appraisal of Constantin Christian Dedekind's *Aelbianische Musenlust* (Dresden, 1657) (21 September 1657) 225

151. Johann Jacob Löwe von Eisenach to Schütz (5 May 1660) 226

152. Schütz to August the Younger, Duke of Brunswick-Lüneburg (10 April 1661) 227

153. *Becker Psalter*, Second Edition (Dresden, 1661): Title Page and Preface to the Reader 229

154. *Becker Psalter*, Second Edition (Dresden, 1661): Schütz's Remarks in the Basso Continuo Partbook 231

155. *Becker Psalter*, Second Edition (Dresden, 1661): Schütz's Afterword to Organists in the Basso Continuo Partbook 233

156. Schütz's Receipt for Payment from the Wolfenbüttel Court (21 May 1663) 233

157. Schütz to the Zeitz Court (14 July 1663) 234

158. Schütz to Moritz, Duke of Saxe-Zeitz (29 September 1663) 237

159. Catalog of Schütz's Published Works Sent to Wolfenbüttel (undated, probably September 1663) 238

160. Schütz to August of Brunswick-Lüneburg (10 January 1664) 240

161. *Historia von der Geburt Jesu Christi* (Dresden, 1664): Title Page and Memorandum to the Reader 241

162. Schütz Directed to Johann Georg II (3 May 1666) 244

163. Schütz to the Superintendent at Zeitz (after 1667) 245

164. Schütz to Christoph Bernhard (1670) 248

165. Constantin Christian Dedekind's Poem Commemorating the Completion of Schütz's Tomb (2 September 1670) 248

166. *Schwanengesang* (1671): Proposed Title Page of Schütz's Unpublished Setting of Psalm 119 249

167. Schütz's *Curriculum Vitae* Written by Martin Geier for the Composer's Funeral (17 November 1672) 250

168. Christoph Bernhard's Rhymed Psalm 150 from the *Geistreiches Gesang-Buch* (Dresden, 1676) 256

169. Anonymous Genealogy of the Schütz Family (1761) 258

Glossary 263
Bibliography 265
Index 271

Preface

HEINRICH SCHÜTZ (1585–1672), the long-serving Kapellmeister at the illustrious electoral Saxon court in Dresden, was described by his contemporaries as the "Orpheus of our times"[1] and "the father of our modern music."[2] In 1690, eighteen years after the composer's death, Wolfgang Caspar Printz (1641–1717) wrote of Schütz in the first major German history of music that "around the year 1650 he was considered to be the very best German composer."[3] Printz identified him as one of the "three famous S's,"[4] along with Johann Hermann Schein (1586–1630) and Samuel Scheidt (1587–1654). Schütz was the first German composer to enjoy an international reputation, and is generally acknowledged as the most important German composer of the seventeenth century. Today his music is widely admired, frequently heard in performance and on recordings, but the composer himself and the cultural climate in which he lived continue to be largely unfamiliar outside his native Germany.

There may be any number of reasons as to why English-language studies of Schütz have had difficulty finding purchase within the discipline of musicology. The principal barrier,

---

1. "O Du Orpheus vnsrer Zeiten" is both the opening and closing lines to Martin Opitz's consolatory poem addressed to Schütz on the death of the composer's wife, Euphrosyne, in 1625. Opitz, *Weltliche Poëmata. Der Ander Theil*, 155–56. Martin Opitz (b. 23 Dec. 1597; d. 20 Aug. 1639) was the leading German poet in his day and is significant historically as an influential literary reformer. He was the librettist for Schütz's *Dafne*, which was staged at Schloss Hartenfels in Torgau in 1627.
2. Elias Nathusius (b. 1628; d. 29 Nov. 1676) applied for the position of Thomaskantor at Leipzig following the death of Tobias Michael in 1657, saying in his application that he feared no musician but Schütz as *"Parentem musicae nostrae modernae."* Cited in Moser, *Heinrich Schütz: Sein Leben und Werk*, 2nd ed., 201.
3. "Um das Jahr Christi 1650. ist er für den allerbesten Teutschen Componisten verhalten worden." Printz, *Historische Beschreibung der Edlen Sing- und Kling-Kunst*, 136.
4. "Drey berühmte S. aber seyn gewesen Schütz/Schein/Scheit [*sic*]" ("three famous S's were Schütz, Schein, Scheidt"). Printz, *Historische Beschreibung*, 137.

xvii

arguably, is a linguistic one. For native speakers of English working in the area of baroque music, the comparative ease of reading seventeenth-century Italian and French has contributed to the formation of a substantial body of secondary literature. This corpus in turn has created a foundation, a momentum, and academic currency for new research and a broader understanding of those repertoires. A reading knowledge of German, however, does not adequately prepare one for dealing with German of the seventeenth century: its lack of a standardized orthography, its arcane and obsolete vocabulary, the exceedingly complex grammatical constructions, the courtly rhetoric, and the archaic handwriting, which even native speakers of German can find daunting. These characteristics, collectively and to varying degrees individually, have impeded the formation of a canon of secondary literature in English upon which new scholarship might be based. There can be no real substitute for acquiring the necessary linguistic skills to engage the original documents, but making a selection of primary texts available in English may offer an initial footing and incentive to embark on research into the music of Schütz and his compatriots. And for those whose main interest may not be in musicological research per se, for students making their first foray into the music of the baroque, these readings will add a new dimension to an informed enjoyment of his music.

Seventeenth-century German is a highly rhetorical language, a language at times fully conscious or even self-conscious of its style. It poses all sorts of challenges to a translator trying to strike a judicious balance and tone between style and content. The present translations strive foremost for accuracy, but they attempt, too, to preserve and reflect something of the historical style—the luxuriant language typical of printed dedications, the courtly rhetoric of Schütz's letters to the Elector and other authorities, the moderate yet formal style of writing used in communications to his peers or assistants, and the completely unadorned language used in notes, memoranda, and directives. The repetitive and formulaic addresses and salutations, for example, often omitted in modern translation, were in fact essential to court protocol and are thus retained here, the better to capture the rhetorical etiquette of the day. An attempt to modernize or overly familiarize the language, I think, is more likely to obscure than reveal the true nature of these writings.

There are, of course, advantages to including the original text along with translations, but there are a number of reasons for resisting that here. First, pairing the translations with the original text would either double the length of the book or reduce at least by half the number of documents that could be included. Second, it would be impractical to attempt an edition of handwritten German documents from the seventeenth century, some of which are scribbled drafts on scraps of paper full of emendations, additions, and deletions. Third, for those who are particularly interested in making comparisons between texts, many of the documents translated here are available in the original language, in whole or in part, in published sources cited in the present volume. There are, however, exceptions to the rule. Poetic texts in German and Latin have been reproduced in the original language as well as in translation in order to avoid giving up completely the poetry to the prose. Adages or maxims in Latin and German, in addition to terms that are foreign to the German text, are generally retained in square brackets for the sake of greater clarity as well as to impart a better sense of how these early-modern authors used language in their communications. In some cases, where terms have multiple denotations in German (sometimes to be comprehended simultaneously)—for instance, *Herr* and *Music*—words have been left in the original language in the text and explained in the glossary. Court and noble titles, currency and coinage, and certain other words without ready equivalents in English have likewise been retained in the documents and defined in the glossary.

Over the years, various transcriptions of Schütz documents have appeared in print, and the present volume is indebted to those contributions. Until very recently, much Schütz scholarship relied on the seminal but famously flawed transcriptions by Erich Müller von Asow,[5] which first appeared in 1931. Other scholars since then have discovered new documents periodically and augmented this core of primary literature.[6] In a few cases, where the original documents have been lost or destroyed, scholars have had to rely entirely on earlier, sometimes incomplete, transcriptions, such as those found in Moritz von Fürstenau's *Zur Geschichte der Musik und des Theaters am Hofe zu Dresden* of 1861.[7] The present volume also includes translations of several manuscripts that have not yet been published in facsimile, transcription, or translation in any language.[8] Work on this book was largely completed prior to the appearance of the first installment of *Schütz Dokumente*, a research project begun long ago by Wolfram Steude and finally brought to light by Michael Heinemann in 2010.[9] Though it is far more comprehensive, reliable, and authoritative than the Müller in terms of Schütz's own writings, readers will note immediately that *Schütz Dokumente* contains only those documents actually authored by the composer. Contemporary writings about Schütz are missing, letters or communications addressed to Schütz are omitted, and any exchange between Schütz and his correspondent is oddly one-sided. Nevertheless, this collection of transcriptions has been useful as a cross-reference and may even serve as a companion to the present translations. Another important work worth mentioning here is a collection of poetry and prose pertaining to Schütz assembled and edited by Eberhard Möller, Friederike Böcher, and Christine Haustein (2003).[10] Regardless of the source of earlier transcriptions consulted for the present volume, all the translations here were done in close consultation with the original documents.

Miscellaneous translations of Schütz documents can occasionally be found elsewhere. When there are alternative translations to the ones included in this volume, they are

---

5. Müller von Asow, *Heinrich Schütz. Gesammelte Briefe und Schriften*.
6. Complete citations of these works can be found in the bibliography and footnotes.
7. See Bibliography for full citation.
8. A number of documents are first mentioned in Wade, *Triumphus nuptialis danicus: German Court Culture and Denmark: The "Great Wedding" of 1634*.
9. Heinemann, ed., *Schriftstücke von Heinrich Schütz*, Schütz-Dokumente, vol. 1.
10. See Bibliography for full citation.

cited in the bibliography and referred to in the footnotes, sometimes to call attention to factual errors or omissions in the translations, sometimes merely to direct the reader to the existence of other translations. The prefaces to the printed works have been translated for the most part, usually in modern editions of the composer's works and occasionally in other places.[11] The annotated translations by Gina Spagnoli (1990) of forty-five Schütz documents were an important addition to the literature, based on her doctoral dissertation and focused for the most part on the last fifteen or so years of Schütz's life.[12] Translations of complete documents have also appeared in work by Robin A. Leaver (1973/74, 1984), Piero Weiss and Richard Taruskin (1984), and Mary E. Frandsen (2000, 2006, 2008).[13] Carl F. Pfatteicher's 1959 translation of Hans Joachim Moser's monumental life and works biography of Schütz contains a wide range of complete and excerpted documents by the Kapellmeister and his contemporaries.[14] A good deal of what we have in English by and about Schütz is abridged, excerpted, and integrated into contextual or biographical studies, often leaving the reader to wonder just how much was left out. In 1985, Joshua Rifkin undertook to create a character portrait of Schütz to mark the quadricentennial celebration of the composer's birth, revisiting and drawing liberally on the original documents to flesh out a portrayal of the composer in his own words.[15]

A primary aim of this Reader is to let the original authors speak for themselves as much as possible, partly by keeping editorial interference of the translations to a minimum. At the same time, I hope to bring the reader as close to the author as possible. Consequently, the footnotes and annotations are not intended to interpret what the original writers have to say, but rather to provide clarification, to offer complementary information, and to anticipate some of the initial questions a researcher or casual reader might have upon reading a document. In the footnotes one will find biographical detail; explanations of professional relationships and ancestral lines; information on geographic regions, domains, cities, courts, and institutions; references to biblical, classical, and contemporary literary sources, and suchlike. The footnote commentary is intentionally referential rather than critical, though it is hoped the objective approach taken will in turn enhance the book's overall usefulness as a reliable research tool for future scholarly studies.

In the end, the present collection of translations must be understood to be, as the title suggests, *A Heinrich Schütz Reader* and not *The Heinrich Schütz Reader*. It does not and cannot make claims toward comprehensiveness, but it does contain in translation for

---

11. See Strunk, *Source Readings in Music History*, vol. 4, *The Baroque Era*; MacClintock, trans. and ed., *Readings in the History of Music in Performance*; Buelow, "A Schütz Reader: Documents of Performance Practice," 1–35.
12. Spagnoli, *Letters and Documents of Heinrich Schütz 1656–1672: An Annotated Translation*.
13. See Bibliography for full citations.
14. Moser, *Heinrich Schütz: His Life and Works*. The first edition of Moser's work was pubished in 1936.
15. Rifkin, "Towards a New Image of Henrich Schütz," Pts. 1 and 2.

the first time between two covers all the main documents associated with Schütz, and a good many more. It is hoped that these firsthand accounts from the seventeenth century will give a personal dimension to Heinrich Schütz in the same way that translations of letters have done for other composers, from Hildegard von Bingen to Elliott Carter. The book will be of interest and use not only to students and scholars in the discipline of musicology, but also to those in such related and overlapping fields as cultural and social history, church history, Germanic studies, and, most important, to all lovers of Baroque music.

Acknowledgments

THE INITIAL RESEARCH for this book was funded by a three-year grant from the Social Sciences and Humanities Research Council of Canada, and I am grateful for its financial support. It afforded me the invaluable opportunity of examining documents firsthand, to acquire copies of manuscripts, and to employ graduate students to assist in the research.

This project would have been impossible without the generous cooperation and assistance of the various institutions that house the documents. For their help on so many levels I would like to thank Det Kongelige Bibliotek in Copenhagen, the Herzog Anton Ulrich Museum in Brunswick, the Herzog August Bibliothek in Wolfenbüttel, the Hessisches Staatsarchiv in Marburg, the Institut für Stadtgeschichte (Karmeliterkloster) in Frankfurt am Main, the Landeshauptarchiv Sachsen-Anhalt in Magdeburg (Zweigstelle Wernigerode), the Morgan Library & Museum in New York City, the Niedersächsische Staats- und Universitätsbibliothek in Göttingen, the Niedersächsisches Landesarchiv—Staatsarchiv in Wolfenbüttel, the Österreichisches Staatsarchiv, Abt. Haus-, Hof- und Staatsarchiv in Vienna, the Rigsarkivet—Danish National Archives in Copenhagen, the Ratsschulbibliothek in Zwickau, the Sächsische Landesbibliothek—Staats- und Universitätsbibliothek in Dresden, the Sächsisches Hauptstaatsarchiv in Dresden, the Staats- und Universitätsbibliothek Hamburg Carl von Ossietzky in Hamburg, the Stadtarchiv in Bautzen, the Stadtarchiv in Chemnitz, the Stadtarchiv in Gera, the Stadtbibliothek in Lübeck, the Thüringisches Staatsarchiv in Greiz, and the Thüringisches Hauptstaatsarchiv in Weimar. I would also like to thank the University of Toronto Libraries, and in particular the staff of the University of Toronto's Faculty of Music Library.

I am deeply indebted to a wide range of scholars with even wider ranging expertise, without whose help this work could not have been completed. I should like to thank Jeffrey Kurtzman and Michael Sherberg for their help with Schütz's Italian, and I am grateful to Tina Marshall and Andrew Hicks for their marvelous work on the Latin texts. For their help with deciphering some extremely difficult German handwriting and their suggestions on interpreting some particularly stubborn texts, I owe a debt of gratitude to Jill Bepler, Mary E. Frandsen, Eberhard Möller, Arne Spohr, Mara R. Wade, and especially to Gerhard Dünnhaupt. Others who provided assistance at various stages along the way and whose support is greatly appreciated include Lawrin Armstrong, Adam Cohen, Graham Freeman, Frederick K. Gable, Roseen Giles, Molly Morrison, Jürgen Neubacher, Bjarke Moe, Rebecca Möllemann, Anna Rutledge, Suzanne Ryan, Angela Strauß, and Janette Tilley.

Finally I would like to thank my colleagues, friends, and family who have generously given their support over the years.

Bibliographical Abbreviations

LIBRARIES AND ARCHIVES

A-Whh	Österreichisches Staatsarchiv, Abt. Haus-, Hof- und Staatsarchiv, Vienna
CDN-Tu	Music Library, University of Toronto
D-BAUs	Stadtarchiv Bautzen
D-Dl	Sächsische Landesbibliothek—Staats- und Universitätsbibliothek Dresden
D-Dla	Sächsisches Hauptstaatsarchiv Dresden
D-Fsa	Institut für Stadtgeschichte Frankfurt/Main (formerly Stadtarchiv Frankfurt/Main)
D-Gs	Niedersächsische Staats- und Universitätsbibliothek Göttingen
D-GZsa	Thüringisches Staatsarchiv Greiz
D-Hs	Staats- und Universitätsbibliothek Carl von Ossietzky, Hamburg
D-KARr	Stadtarchiv Chemnitz
D-MGha	Hessisches Staatsarchiv Marburg
D-LÜh	Stadtbibliothek Lübeck
D-StA-Ge	Stadtarchiv Gera
D-W	Herzog August Bibliothek, Wolfenbüttel
D-Wa	Niedersächsisches Landesarchiv—Staatsarchiv, Wolfenbüttel
D-WERa	Landeshauptarchiv Sachsen-Anhalt, Zweigstelle Wernigerode
D-WR1	Thüringisches Hauptstaatsarchiv, Weimar
DK-K	Det Kongelige Bibliothek, Copenhagen
DK-RA	Rigsarkivet—Danish National Archives, Copenhagen

I-Bc   Civico Museo Bibliografico Musicale, Bologna
US-NYpm Pierpont Morgan Library & Museum, New York

BOOKS AND RESOURCES

ADB *Allgemeine deutsche Biographie.* Hrsg. durch die Historische Commission bei der Königl. Akademie der Wissenschaften. Vols. 1–56. Leipzig: Duncker & Humblot, 1875–1912.

DWB Grimm, Jakob, and Wilhelm Grimm. *Deutsches Wörterbuch.* 16 vols. in 32. Continued and revised by Moriz Heyne, Rudolf Hildebrand, Karl Weigand…[et al.] Leipzig: S. Hirzel, 1854–1960.

Grove-Mus *Grove Music Online.* Edited by Deanne Root. http://www.grovemusic.com.

NDB *Neue deutsche Biographie.* Hrsg. von der Historischen Kommission bei der Bayerischen Akademie der Wissenschaften. Vols. 1–24. Berlin: Duncker & Humblot, 1953–.

NSA Schütz, Heinrich. *Neue Ausgabe sämtlicher Werke.* Herausgegeben im Auftrag der Internationalen Heinrich-Schütz-Gesellschaft. Vols. 1–40. Kassel: Bärenreiter Verlag, 1955–2008.

RISM Répertoire International des Sources Musicales. Series A. Kassel: Bärenreiter, 1971–81.

SA Schütz, Heinrich. *Sämtliche Werke.* Edited by Philipp Spitta. 16 vols. Leipzig: Breitkopf & Härtel, 1885–94.

Sachs-Chronik Schäfer, Wilhelm. *Sachsen-Chronik für Vergangenheit und Gegenwart, oder Magazin für Ansammlung und Mittheilung der allseitigen Eigenschaften, Schicksale und Verhältnisse der sächsischen Gesammtlande.* Erste Serie. Dresden: Julius Blochmann jun., 1854.

Schütz-Dokumente Heinemann, Michael, editor. *Schriftstücke von Heinrich Schütz.* Schütz-Dokumente, Vol. 1, edited by Heinrich Schütz-Archiv der Hochschule für Musik Carl Maria von Weber Dresden. Köln: Verlag Dohr, 2010.

Schütz-GBr Müller von Asow, Erich H. *Heinrich Schütz. Gesammelte Briefe und Schriften.* Regensburg: Gustav Bosse, 1931.

Spagn. Spagnoli, Gina. *Letters and Documents of Heinrich Schütz 1656–1672: An Annotated Translation.* Studies in Music, 106. Edited by George J. Buelow. Ann Arbor: UMI Research Press, 1990.

SSA Schütz, Heinrich. *Stuttgarter Schütz-Ausgabe. Sämtliche Werke.* Edited by Günter Graulich and Paul Horn. Neuhausen-Stuttgart: Hänssler 1971–.

SWV *Schütz-Werke-Verzeichnis (SWV). Kleine Ausgabe.* Edited by Werner Bittinger. Kassel: Bärenreiter, 1960.

Illustrations

All illustrations are located between pages 122 and 123

1. Heinrich Schütz. Engraving by Augustus John, 1627–28.
2. Moritz, Landgrave of Hesse-Kassel. Engraving by unknown artist.
3. Johann Georg I, Elector of Saxony. Painting by Frans Luycx (b. 1604; d. after 1656).
4. The Electoral Palace in Dresden. Engraving by Anton Weck (1623–80), ca 1680.
5. Michael Praetorius. Woodcut by unknown artist from 1604 printed in *Musae Sioniae* (Regensburg, 1605).
6. Samuel Scheidt. Engraving by unknown artist from *Tabulatura nova* (Hamburg: Michael Hering, 1624).
7. Johann Georg II, Elector of Saxony. Engraving by unknown artist, before 1656.
8. Johann Hermann Schein. Painting by unknown artist, 1620.
9. Draft of a travel and security pass issued to Schütz by the Danish Court, 1635.
10. Sophie Elisabeth, Duchess of Brunswick-Lüneburg. Engraving by unknown artist.
11. August the Younger, Duke of Brunswick-Lüneburg. Engraving by Konrad Buno, 10 April 1662.
12. Title page from the 1661 edition of Schütz's *Becker Psalter*, containing Schütz's autograph and presented to Duke August the Younger at Wolfenbüttel.
13. Organ galleries in the Dom St. Peter and Paul, the palace church in Zeitz.
14. Schütz's handwritten letter to Duke August the Younger of Brunswick-Lüneburg from 10 January 1664.
15. Heinrich Schütz. Engraving by Christian Romstet (1640–1721) from the printed funeral sermon of 1672.
16. The interior of the Dresden Hofkapelle, with Schütz directing at the music desk, engraving by Conrad David (1604–81), from Christoph Bernhard's *Geistreiches Gesangbuch* of 1676.

Illustrations are reproduced by kind permission of the following, and may not be reproduced without permission: Ratsschulbibliothek Zwickau (fig. 1); Herzog Anton Ulrich-Museum Brunswick (figs. 2, 10, and 11); Sächsische Landesbibliothek—Staats- und Universitätsbibliothek Dresden, Deutsche Fotothek (figs. 3, 5, 6, 7, and 15); Herzog August Bibliothek Wolfenbüttel (figs. 4, 12, 14, and 16); Bjarke Moe (fig. 9); Gregory S. Johnston (figs. 8 and 13).

A HEINRICH SCHÜTZ READER

I

Youth and Early Manhood (1611–27)

1. *IL PRIMO LIBRO DE MADRIGALI* (VENICE, 1611): TITLE PAGE AND DEDICATION (1 MAY 1611) (ORIGINAL LANGUAGE: ITALIAN)

[Title page]

Canto
*Il primo libro
de madrigali* [The First Book of Madrigals]
by the German
Heinrich Schütz
in Venice, 1611.
Printed by Angelo Gordano & Sons.[1]

[Dedication]

To the Most Serene
Prince and Lord,
Lord Moritz, Landgrave
of Hesse, Count of Katzenelnbogen, Dietz, Ziegenhain,
and Nidda, etc.
My Most Clement Prince and Lord.

---

1. SWV 1–19; RISM A/I/8 S 2272; *SA* 9; *NSA* 22; *SSA* 1.

It is a sea, Your Serene Highness, I know not whether more of virtue or of munificence, well worthy of such a prince, which caused me to sing of it. I recognize you as such when I see you water the ground with your most esteemed name, while exultant rivers spread over the earth, only that devoted tributaries bearing that quality which they usually take from their riverbed may return to you. I call myself blessed to number among these, even more so since from your court where, from my tender years I was kindly nourished by your clemency, it fell to me in particular to leave for Italy, and there to unite with that wave which illuminates all Italy, with a murmuring similar more than any other to Heavenly Harmony. He is the most famous Gabrieli,[2] who shared with me the wealth of his shores, so rich in this kind of studies, that they can envy neither Tagus nor Pactolus.[3] Do not disdain, then, Your Most Serene Highness, my small tribute of gratitude, but great in sentiment, of these, my first madrigals, which I offer you with the most resolute spirit, to open out one day into your sea (should God grant me the favor), not as a small stream, but as an ocean of devotion, that mingles with the depth of your royal favor, to which, in conclusion, I dedicate and consecrate my whole being.

From Venice, the first of May, 1611.
Your Most Serene Highness's
most devoted and obliging servant,
Heinrich Schütz.

>
> Vast Sea, in whose bosom
> Concordant winds
> Make suave harmony
> Of Greatness and Virtue,
> These devoted accents
> My Muse offers you,
> You, great Moritz, take pleasure in them,
> And in so doing, you will make harmonious my uncouth song.

---

2. Giovanni Gabrieli (b. ca. 1554–57; d. 12 Aug. 1612) was one of the principal figures in establishing the Venetian style of the late sixteenth and early seventeenth centuries. He spent several years in Munich under Orlande de Lassus (b. 1530/32; d. 14 Jun. 1594) at the court of Albrecht V, Duke of Bavaria (b. 29 Feb. 1528; d. 24 Oct. 1579), and by 1584 was in Venice where he filled in as organist for Claudio Merulo (b. 8 Apr. 1533; d. 4 May 1604) who had vacated the post. Gabrieli's position became permanent the following year, and he retained this post for the rest of his life.

3. The Tagus is the longest river on the Iberian Peninsula (1038 km), running across much of Spain, along part of the border between Spain and Portugal, and across all of Portugal before emptying into the Atlantic Ocean. The Pactolus is a river in modern-day Turkey, said to be the river in which King Midas of Greek mythology washed away the curse of the golden touch. It was a rich source of gold deposits in the ancient world.

[Original text]

Vasto MAR, nel cui seno
Fan soaue armonia
D'Altezza, e di Virtu, con cordi venti,
Questi deuati accenti
T'offre la Musa mia
Tu Gran Mauritio lor gradisci, e in tanto
Farai di rozo armonioso'l canto.

2. JOHANN GEORG I, ELECTOR OF SAXONY, TO MORITZ, LANDGRAVE OF HESSE-KASSEL (27 AUGUST 1614)

Letter requesting Schütz's services as organist at the Dresden Court

[D-MGha: Bestand 4 f Kursachsen Nr. 210 "Die von Kurfürst Johann Georg I. von Sachsen gewünschte Überlassung von Heinrich Schütz," 1614–17, fols. 1r–2v]

[Address]

To the Most Noble Prince, our Gracious Beloved Cousin, Father, and Godfather,[4] Lord Moritz, Landgrave of Hesse, Katzenelnbogen, Dietz, Ziegenhain, and Nidda

[Text]

Our benevolent offices and favors to the best of our ability and means, first and foremost, Most Noble Prince, gracious beloved Cousin, Father, and Godfather. We write to inform Your Dilection that we have arranged the Christian baptism of our God-given young son for this coming September 18.[5] We understand that Your Dilection has at present an organist by the name of Heinrich Schütz. Believing as we do that Your Dilection will be suspending your music for a time owing to the mourning that has set in, we should very much like to hear him, and therefore request that you kindly allow the aforementioned organist to come here for the indicated date, and a few days prior, and to stay with us for a while. Should he not be hampered by obligations, we understand accordingly that Your Dilection shall not refuse us in this matter, and we should like not to leave

---

4. It was not uncommon among the German nobility of the seventeenth century to address one another using terms that suggested a kinship or close relationship. *Sohn*, *Vetter*, *Vater*, and *Gevatter* can often be seen in salutations of the time, even when there were no actual family ties between correspondents.

5. August, Duke of Saxe-Weissenfels (b. 13 Aug. 1614; d. 4 Jun. 1680) was the second son of Elector Johann Georg I (b. 5 Mar. 1585; d. 8 Oct. 1656). He was the Administrator of the Diocese of Magdeburg, to which position he was named at the age of thirteen in 1628. He spent his time in Halle, which flourished culturally during this period. August was married 23 November 1647 to Anna Maria (b. 1 Jul. 1627; d. 11 Dec. 1669), daughter of Adolph Friedrich, Duke of Mecklenburg-Schwerin (b. 15 Dec. 1588; d. 27 Feb. 1658).

undeclared to you our inclination to render corresponding friendly and cousinly service at any time, commending you together with your beloved family to divine protection. Dated at Dresden, 27 August 1614.

By grace of God, Johann Georg, Duke of Saxony, Jülich, Cleves and Berg, Grand Marshal of the Holy Roman Empire and Elector, Landgrave of Thuringia, Margrave of Meissen, Burgrave of Magdeburg, Count of the Mark and Ravensberg, Lord of Ravenstein.
  Johann Georg, Elector.[6]

3. JOHANN GEORG I TO MORITZ OF HESSE-KASSEL (25 APRIL 1615)

Letter requesting Schütz's services at the Dresden Court for a period of two years

[D-MGha: Bestand 4 f Kursachsen Nr. 210 "Die von Kurfürst Johann Georg I. von Sachsen gewünschte Überlassung von Heinrich Schütz," 1614–17, fols. 4r–6v]

[Address]

To the Most Noble Prince, our gracious beloved Cousin, Father, and Godfather, Lord Moritz, Landgrave of Hesse, Katzenelnbogen, Dietz, Ziegenhain, and Nidda

[Text]

Our benevolent offices and favors to the best of our ability and means, first and foremost, Most Noble Prince, gracious beloved Cousin, Father, and Godfather. Your Dilection last year allowed your organist, Heinrich Schütz, to come here for a period of time, for which we are once more grateful to Your Dilection. We ought now to expect nothing more of Your Dilection beyond such willingness, it is true, even if the qualities of the aforesaid Schütz pleased us very well, and he with his art has been agreeable to us. We labor now under a lack of such a subject, and thus we did not want to forbear approaching Your Dilection in regard of him once more, and to entreat you kindly and cousinly herewith, that you would show us fatherly good will, and graciously allow the aforesaid Schütz to come for a couple of years and reside here until such time as we shall secure those persons whom we sent away to Italy and to other places to learn this art. We are ever grateful to Your Dilection for rendering this favor and acceding to our wishes: thus you shall not have us petition in vain in this case, but rather demonstrate in practice once again your

---

6. Signed by the Elector. The second son of Christian I (b. 29 Oct. 1560; d. 25 Sept. 1591), Johann Georg I (b. 5 Mar. 1585; d. 8 Oct. 1656) became Elector of Saxony upon the death of the heirless Christian II, who succumbed to his excesses at the age of twenty-seven on 23 June 1611. A faithful Lutheran, Johann Georg was forced to shift political and military allegiances several times during the course of the Thirty Years' War in his attempt to protect Saxony variously from Calvinists, Catholics, and Swedes, which ultimately led the electorate into fiscal ruin. The *Hofkapelle* both flourished and suffered greatly during his reign.

good affection felt toward us, that we in return benevolently requite Your Dilection in similar and other ways, to whom we are also ready and devoted otherwise to offer corresponding, obliging services always.[7] Dated at Langensalza, 25 April 1615.

By grace of God, Johann Georg, Duke of Saxony, Jülich, Cleves and Berg, Grand Marshal of the Holy Roman Empire and Elector, Landgrave of Thuringia, Margrave of Meissen, Burgrave of Magdeburg, Count of the Mark and Ravensberg, Lord of Ravenstein.

[now in Johann Georg's hand]

Your Dilection's faithful Cousin, Son, and Godfather,
Johann Georg, Elector.

4. MORITZ OF HESSE-KASSEL TO JOHANN GEORG I (27 APRIL 1615)

Letter acceding to the Elector's request but stressing the two-year limitation on Schütz's appointment

[D-MGha: Bestand 4 f Kursachsen Nr. 210 "Die von Kurfürst Johann Georg I. von Sachsen gewünschte Überlassung von Heinrich Schütz," 1614–17, fol. 9r]

[Text]

What Your Dilection kindly intended and requested of us once more in regard to our organist and dear, loyal Heinrich Schütz, dated at Langensalza the twenty-fifth of this month, we have understood well from the same communication, among other things. Inasmuch as we would part with the aforementioned Schütz from our *Music* for such a long time with great difficulty, his position moreover cannot now be suitably reassigned. However, so that we in fact prove our friendly and cousinly affection toward Your Dilection, thus in obliging favor to you would we graciously give leave to our aforementioned organist, Schütz, that he might reside and most humbly serve for a couple of years at Your Dilection's Court, with the firm assurance that Your Dilection shall not detain him longer, but rather discharge him at the end of these two years, to be taken once more into service by us most graciously, as we agreed by our earlier arrangement, and remain willing and devoted to Your Dilection in other desired services and more, graciously commending us together to divine protection. Dated at Kassel, 27 April 1615.

---

7. According to *Sachs-Chronik* (507), there was a line in the draft that was not included in the actual letter. In the draft, the last sentence before the date reads: "Da E. L. hinwieder sich eines oder des andern unserer Diener gebrauchen können, soll Ihr derselben nicht versagt werden." ("Inasmuch as Your Dilection can make use of one or another of our servants in return, you shall not be denied.")

Handwriting of the ruler[8]

God willing, should I have the good fortune that Your Dilection should sometime surprise your faithful *Herr* Father in Hesse, I would devote myself to showing you every fatherly office and ministration to the best of my ability and means.

5. SCHÜTZ TO CHRISTOPH VON LOSS, PRIVY COUNCILLOR AND MARSHAL OF THE COURT (23 SEPTEMBER 1616); JOHANN GEORG I'S REPLY (30 SEPTEMBER 1616)

Letter concerning a runaway Kapellknabe, *and Johann Georg I's response*

[*Sachs-Chronik*, 519–20, fn. 10. Original document is lost.]

[*Address*]

To the Lord Imperial Treasurer, Christoph von Loss auf Schleinitz[9]

[*Text*]

Noble Worship, Lord Imperial Treasurer etc., my most indebted and obedient services.

With the present insignificant letter of mine, I have been unable to avoid soliciting Your Honor, to whom I herewith most obediently report, in what manner Bruno[10] arrived here on Thursday past, brother of the *Knabe* who ran away unbeknownst to his father, as we finally received confirmation. After we readily admitted him here and retained him for a period of time for his brother's sake, we finally exhorted him to pack up and to return to his father. Upon his departure, however, he was caught by chance in the act of stealing, and was found to have packed to take along with him a number of linen goods and additional things from me and others in the establishment. Thus we upbraided him, expelled him from the establishment, and further threatened that he should get out of town and not dwell here any longer to his brother Bruno's disgrace. This was of no avail, however, and the wretch, as I understood it from others, still lived as ever here in very dissolute company, until finally yesterday, Sunday, after I came home from church service,

---

8. At this point in the manuscript draft of the letter, it reads *ma: princip*, suggesting that the first part of the letter would be written in fine by a scribe and that Landgrave Moritz would then add his personal note to the Elector at the end.
9. Christoph von Loss auf Schleinitz (b. 13 Apr. 1574; d. 17 Aug. 1620) came from an old and influential Saxon noble family. Christoph was simultaneously Privy Councillor and Marshal of the Court (*Hofmarschall*) to Elector Christian II of Saxony. See Schattkowsky, *Zwischen Rittergut, Residenz und Reich*.
10. Biographical information on Bruno is sketchy. According to *Schütz-GBr* (320) he was the son of one Hans Bruno, a French instrumentalist who in 1606 was employed in the Dresden *Hofkapelle*. The young Bruno appears eventually to have become organist in Hamburg, and according to a letter by Michael Praetorius was brought to Halle in 1616. *Schütz-GBr* cites La Mara, *Musikerbriefe aus fünf Jahrhunderten*, vol. 1, 57; and Fürstenau, *Beiträge zur Geschichte der königlich-sächsischen musikalischen Kapelle*, 39.

I noticed that Bruno himself, the *Knabe* assigned to me, was missing. I was very much surprised by this, mainly because I had admonished him that very morning that he should go to church, and we in the establishment discussed it at length. In particular, most were of the opinion that he might have gone along part of the way with his brother in order to put him on the right road, in order to get rid of him. In sum: he has not yet been found, and we do not know where he might have gone. But I see and sense, in fact, that this apple does not fall far from the tree, and believe there is in this entire family not much of worth, as far as can be seen. The rascal had a pleasant life, even though I may well have scolded him from time to time (as a case in point, eight days ago when he went to confession and promised with tears in his eyes that he would behave himself properly: *sed lupus pilos mutat, animum non*).[11] I can however swear before God that I never once beat him, so Your Noble Worship can therefore rest assured that he did not run away either out of fear or otherwise for want. Consequently I blame his reckless brother for luring him away and stirring all this up. With that I obediently await what Your Noble Worship now wants to order or command in this case. For my part, since we have heard that the two of them may have set out on their way to Meissen, I have gone to the district treasurer here and asked him whether he might send a scout after them so that one might stand them before His Electoral Grace and thus settle the matter.[12] He willingly took this upon himself and had them pursued. Whether they may be found and again brought hither, time will tell.

Recently both I and the *Knaben* entrusted to me have been assailed in a short time by all manner of illnesses, and I look forward to better days ahead. Caspar [Kittel] has almost completely recovered, praise God, and is going out again.[13] I am also expecting to use him again next Sunday. Johann [Vierdanck] is a fine, virtuous fellow; he has made a very good and solid beginning in composition, so that we can expect to hear something from him in the near future.[14]

I dutifully beg Your Noble Worship for forgiveness, that with all other business […]

[the transcription ends here]

Dresden, 23 September 1616.
Heinrich Schütz.

---

11. "But the wolf changes its coat, not its character."
12. At this time the District Administrator was August Cracau, who had become a tax collector (*Schosser*) in 1608.
13. Caspar Kittel (b. 1603; d. 9 Oct. 1639) likely began his musical career as a Dresdner *Kapellknabe*. With financial support from the court, Kittel studied in Italy from 1624 until 1629. He returned to Dresden from Italy with Schütz in 1630, and there taught theorbo, served as instrument inspector in 1632 and later as court organist. He studied composition with Schütz and was one of the first German imitators of Giulio Caccini (b. 8 Oct. 1551; d. 10 Dec. 1618), as can be seen in his *Arien und Kantaten* of 1638. See Kittel, *Arien und Kantaten: Dresden 1638*.
14. Johann Vierdanck (b. ca. 1605; d. Mar. 1646) was a German composer, organist and instrumentalist who, by 1616, was one of the *Kapellknaben* at the Dresden court. He studied composition under Schütz, and was an instrumentalist at the court 1630–31. He later served as violinist at the Güstrow court (1631–32), and traveled to Lübeck and Copenhagen. From 1635 until his death, Vierdanck was organist at the Marienkirche in Stralsund.

[Johann Georg's reply]

Regarding the young Bruno, we regret to hear that he has again run away and is not to be found. Now, should his brother be guilty in this, he would not be unduly punished on account of it, so that the young Bruno might have an example and warning. Chemnitz Palace, 30 September 1616.

Johann Georg, Elector.

6. MORITZ OF HESSE-KASSEL TO JOHANN GEORG I (1 DECEMBER 1616)

Letter requesting Schütz's immediate return to the Kassel Court

[D-MGha: Bestand 4 f Kursachsen Nr. 210 "Die von Kurfürst Johann Georg I. von Sachsen gewünschte Überlassung von Heinrich Schütz," 1614–17, fol. 14r]

Most Noble Prince, benevolent, beloved Cousin, Son, and Godfather, we do not doubt at all that Your Dilection shall still remember in good measure what you petitioned of us, dated at Langensalza, 25 April 1615, in regard to our appointed *Musicus* and organist Heinrich Schütz, and what we, on the twenty-seventh of the same, declared thereupon, among other things, and particularly in regard of the requested two years. Although this term has not yet expired completely, but rather extends a few months still, such things befall us now, for the arrangements of which we cannot dispense of him, Schütz, without exceptional difficulty for us. Thus our inescapable need has required that we kindly request of Your Dilection herewith that you might not object to discharging him, the aforesaid Schütz, most graciously so that he might be taken anew into service here by us at the earliest opportunity and humbly serve us. And since we are bent on using him now toward our, praise God, maturing young Lordships and their princely education and training, and moreover do not doubt Your Dilection is sufficiently endowed with others of his equal, thus are we all the more confident Your Dilection shall not refuse us but rather kindly take to heart this our Christian, princely, and fatherly purpose, for which accordingly we then kindly and cousinly petition herewith once more, and in return remain utterly devoted to Your Dilection for all corresponding, possible services. Dated at Kassel, 1 December 1616. Moritz.

7. CHRISTOPH VON LOSS TO JOHANN GEORG I (11 DECEMBER 1616)

Communication in response to Moritz's request, and advice to the Elector as to why Schütz should not be released from service

[*Sachs-Chronik*, 512–14]

Most Gracious Elector and Lord.

I forward to Your Electoral Grace most humbly the enclosed letter sent by His Princely Grace, Lord Landgrave Moritz of Hesse, which was received in Privy Council and opened there, and from which one is most graciously given to understand, among other things, what the aforesaid Lord Landgrave kindly has directed to you concerning Heinrich Schütz. The aforesaid Schütz through a similar writing has been called to Kassel in such a way that he should let nothing short of an act of God prevent him from entering without fail into service there for the new year. Now it resides truly with Your Electoral Grace's most gracious instruction how you would have this matter administered in this case. It is however evident to Your Grace that, if the *Musica* in the church and at table should be appointed and maintained in the manner as has occurred up to the present, one absolutely cannot dispense with such a person, who must be especially highly skilled in composition, knowledgeable of instruments, and experienced in concerted music, in which I, in my humble assessment, know of no one better currently than the aforesaid Schütz, who has shown up to now what he is capable of presenting to Your Electoral Grace's particular renown. I fear on the other hand that if one should lose him in this way, it would be difficult to acquire such a subject to take his place. Although Your Electoral Grace's *Herr* [Michael] Praetorius still holds an appointment,[15] you know indeed most graciously that he now serves *in absentia*, and cannot always free himself from the princely Brunswick Kapelle. Thus in his absence (since there would not be Heinrich Schütz) there would be no concerted music [*Concert*] in the church; all the rehearsals would be discontinued entirely, whereby then your *Musik* would suffer not a little harm. Thus I worry in truth that, if this change is not averted, one shall soon become aware of the damages in this place.

At Your Electoral Grace's most gracious pleasure I have prepared in fact the enclosed reply to the aforementioned Lord Landgrave in your name, which you also receive herewith, to consider at your pleasure whether you wish to execute it in this manner or however else you might have it done. I also have this reply directed in a way that said Schütz might be fully relinquished to Your Electoral Grace so that you never again have to be at risk of suchlike recalls in future. And as Otto von Starschedel is still in the region,[16] as I recently spoke with him in regard to the aforesaid Schütz at the wedding in Borna,[17] he also offered to apply all possible diligence to assist, in order that he [Schütz] remains wholly in service to Your Electoral Grace. Thus would I be resolved to go to him, insofar as it graciously pleases Your Electoral Grace, to discuss all this necessarily once again with him and to ask him to direct the matter to that end, according to Your Electoral Grace's most gracious wishes, so that the Lord Landgrave's Princely Grace might be persuaded away from his present purpose and he, Schütz, might remain with us. This could however occur with greater and better effect if Your Electoral Grace would command of me to

---

15. Michael Praetorius (b. ca. 15 Feb. 1571; d. 15 Feb. 1621) was best known as a prolific composer, and in particular for his versatile treatment of Protestant hymns. He is also significant historically for the three volumes of his *Syntagma musicum* (1614/15 and 1618). For most of his career Praetorius was appointed to the ducal court of Brunswick-Wolfenbüttel, though he also spent considerable periods of time at other noble courts.
16. Otto von Starschedel was first Court Advisor in Altenburg, Co-founder of the Ducal Saxon Fraternity against the Vice of Cursing (1590), and Privy Councillor to Landgrave Moritz. See *Sachs-Chronik*, 513.
17. The town of Borna lies approximately 30 km south of Leipzig.

discuss this matter with him, Starschedel. I duly await your most gracious resolution in one way or another, and am obliged and ever willing to perform for you most humble, most obedient and faithful services all my life. Dated at Dresden, 11 December 1616.

PS. Moreover, Most Gracious Elector and Lord, so that the Lord Landgrave graciously perceives that this matter is of concern to Your Electoral Grace (thus it rests at your most gracious pleasure), should you wish this reply forwarded via one of your chamber-servants to Kassel, it would first have to come here in order for it to be given to Otto von Starschedel's copyist. *[Datum] ut in litteris.*[18] Christoph von Loss.

8. JOHANN GEORG I TO MORITZ OF HESSE-KASSEL (13 DECEMBER 1616)

Letter commenting on Schütz's late arrival, and the ban on music owing to public mourning at the Dresden Court

[D-MGha: Bestand 4 f Kursachsen Nr. 210 "Die von Kurfürst Johann Georg I. von Sachsen gewünschte Überlassung von Heinrich Schütz," 1614–17, fols. 16r–17v]

[We pledge] our benevolent offices and favor to the best of our abilities and means, first and foremost, Most Noble Prince, benevolent, beloved Cousin, Father, and Godfather. Your Dilection's letter dated at Kassel, the first day of this December, was received safely and in good order by us, and we have also understood from it, among other things, what you kindly addressed to us regarding your organist, Heinrich Schütz. And we still remember well how Your Dilection at our previous request graciously permitted the aforementioned Schütz to enter into our service for a couple of years, and to put our *Music* into a sound state and order.

As we appreciate Your Dilection's kindness with particular gratitude, we did not intend to hinder you in your princely plans, rather on the contrary to voice our indebted willingness to be ready to help you as much as we are ever able; hence we know well that we should duly spare Your Dilection from further petitions in this matter.

All the same, inasmuch as he, Schütz, could not immediately enter into service with us here after Your Dilection's kind declaration to us in regard of him, rather at that time first had to put his affairs in order in Kassel, thus it delayed his entrance into service somewhat. Beyond this, because of the unexpected death of our late, beloved brother, Duke August of Saxony, Jülich, Cleves and Berg of blessed memory,[19] we were not able to make

---

18. "Dated as above."
19. Duke August (b. 7 Sept. 1589; d. 26 Dec. 1615), as the youngest son of Christian I, was the youngest brother of Duke Johann Georg I and Duke Christian II. August was married 1 January 1612 to Elisabeth (b. 23 Jun. 1593; d. 25 Mar. 1650), the daughter of Heinrich Julius, Duke of Brunswick-Wolfenbüttel (b. 15 Oct. 1564; d. 30 Jul. 1613). Childless at the time of August's death at the age of twenty-six, she remarried in 1618 to Johann Philipp, Duke of Saxe-Altenburg (b. 25 Jan. 1597; d. 1 Apr. 1639).

use of his services for almost an entire year, and in addition to that we do not know where we would so easily obtain another from another place.

Having set aside all those things which lay in our way in this case, we did not want to refrain from requesting this once more, as follows, and direct to you our most diligent petition, may it please you in extraordinary friendship to us, that you commit the aforementioned Schütz to us completely in order to reform our *Music* for glory and honor; and hereby to continue in future the loyal cousinly and fatherly affection you previously showed toward us in many ways to our particular satisfaction. In particular consideration that Your Dilection, as in addition to other noble princely virtues, is highly skilled in music as well, and hence has achieved renown before one and all, and (more than others) has worthy, well-qualified subjects of the kind in sufficient number, you can thereby easily fill this position and realize no less your intended princely, honorable, and praiseworthy aims stated in your letter. Your Dilection shall not take amiss this our request which flows out of genuinely good, cousinly, and filial trust, but much rather, as has occurred in many other cases in your domain and city, help us thereby to our full satisfaction. You will certainly see that we will not forget all that which Your Dilection might kindly do for us, but rather that we shall make every effort so that you in fact notice that this benevolent compliance affords us utmost pleasure and is not misplaced. We remain moreover entirely willing to render corresponding, obliging services at any time. Dated at Sitzeroda, 13 December 1616.

By Grace of God, Johann Georg, Duke of Saxony, Jülich, Cleves and Berg, Grand Marshal of the Holy Roman Empire and Elector, Landgrave of Thuringia, Margrave of Meissen and Burgrave of Magdeburg, Count of the Mark and Ravensberg, Lord of Ravenstein,

[in the Elector's hand]

Your Dilection's faithful Cousin, Son, and Godfather,
Johann Georg, Elector.

9. SCHÜTZ TO MORITZ OF HESSE-KASSEL (16 DECEMBER 1616)

Letter of apology as to why he is unable to return immediately to the Kassel Court

[D-MGha: Bestand 4 f Kursachsen Nr. 210 "Die von Kurfürst Johann Georg I. von Sachsen gewünschte Überlassung von Heinrich Schütz," 1614–17, fols. 35r–v, 36v][20]

[Address]

To the Serene, Most Noble Prince and Lord, Lord Moritz, Landgrave of Hesse, Count of Katzenelnbogen, Dietz, Ziegenhain, and Nidda, etc. My Gracious Prince and Lord[21]

---

20. The entire letter is in Schütz's hand. Transcribed in *Schütz-Dokumente*, Nr. 7.
21. Written below the address in a second hand is the date of receipt at the court: Kassel, 22 December 1616.

[Text]

Serene, Most Noble Prince, Gracious Lord, Your Princely Grace, in addition to wishes of worldly and eternal welfare, I pledge my wholly willing, humble, and most obedient service to the best of my abilities and means always, first and foremost.

Most Noble Prince, Gracious Lord, Your Princely Grace's recently forwarded gracious command to me was received safely and most humbly, and I understood sufficiently from it as well the gracious recall and summons of my insignificant person from here back to Kassel. For my part, even though it would have been for me an especially great joy indeed, that in accordance to the gracious command obtained from Your Princely Grace, I would thus have immediately obeyed most humbly, and as I might duty bound present myself obediently. To that end, however, His Electoral Grace of Saxony has thus most graciously given me to understand, that until further notice of Your Princely Grace's gracious resolution, I should not expect a dismissal. Without doubt too it is for those reasons that His Electoral Grace, on account of the imminent holidays, and in the absence of Michael Praetorius as the appointed Kapellmeister *in absentia* here, would not gladly dispense of my modest services. I am of no doubt that it will most graciously please His Electoral Grace after the holidays, that I might humbly obey this Your Princely Grace's issued command, and present myself as soon as possible in Kassel, to which end I, for my part, shall work with all possible diligence. In the meantime may it please Your Princely Grace to construe this my delay in grace and not to misunderstand that, barring an act of God, I would not shun for a moment your gracious command, provided that I would have been able to defer His Electoral Grace with his permission for a leave of absence. I live humbly however in the comforting and undoubted confidence that, for this one time, Your Princely Grace shall graciously be content with this my apology, and remain now as before with the customary clemency shown toward me hitherto. And to Your Princely Grace and to your laudable princely house, as all natural and divine laws exhort me, I am as desirous as duty bound to attend and to perform all possible humble services all my life. Appealing herewith to Almighty God for Your Princely Grace, your beloved Consort, young Princely Lordship and Ladyship, that He shall, in addition to a blissful and joyous New Year, abundantly bestow upon you a reign blessed by fortune, complete physical health, together with every welfare of body and soul. Dated at Dresden, the sixteenth day of December 1616.

Your Princely Grace's
humble, willing, and obedient servant,
Heinrich Schütz.

10. MORITZ OF HESSE-KASSEL TO SCHÜTZ (23 DECEMBER 1616)

Letter concerning Schütz's continuation of service at the Dresden Court

[D-MGha: Bestand 4 f Kursachsen Nr. 210 "Die von Kurfürst Johann Georg I. von Sachsen gewünschte Überlassung von Heinrich Schütz," 1614–17, fol. 37r]

Moritz, by the Grace of God, Landgrave of Hesse, Count of Katzenelnbogen, etc.

Dear faithful [Schütz], the Noble Prince, *Herr* Johann Georg, Duke of Saxony, Jülich, Cleves and Berg, Grand Marshal of the Holy Roman Empire and Elector, our amicable beloved Cousin, Son, and Godfather, requested of us in writing that for the better appointment of His Dilection's *Music* we would relinquish your person [to him] completely. As we know of no compelling reasons herein not to accede, thus have we indeed conceded out of particular honor and favor to His Dilection that you might yet reside for a period of time in Dresden and be ready to serve him, which you are to observe accordingly. And as it is required of you particularly that you should elevate the *Music* there to a completely and properly serviceable state, the sooner you are able to bring this to completion, the sooner we might again have sway over you.

We did not wish to forbear informing you of this, and remain graciously disposed toward you. Dated at Kassel, 23 December 1616.

11. DRESDEN COURT TO SCHÜTZ (? JULY 1617)

Memorandum from the Marshal of the Court (Christoph von Loss) regarding the Imperial visit to Dresden, 25 July to 13 August 1617

[D-Dla: Oberhofmarschallamt, F, Nr. 1, fols. 20r–22r]

Ordinance, upon the extraordinary decree of the Elector of Saxony and Burgrave of Magdeburg, our Most Gracious Lord, how His Electoral Grace's *Musica* shall be employed and arranged for the visit of the Roman Imperial Majesty,[22] the Royal Majesty of Bohemia,[23] and the Archduke Maximilian of Austria.[24]

1. First and foremost, Heinrich Schütz, as the appointed Director, shall make the necessary arrangements so that all instruments to be used during this time are in good repair and well tuned, and that no deficiency occurs on that account.

2. He [Schütz] shall convey earnestly to all His Electoral Grace's instrumental and vocal musicians that they diligently attend at their duties to which each might be called upon and employed; be available at all times; behave soberly, modestly, and moderately; and to be remiss in nothing, on pain of our above-mentioned Lord's punishment and displeasure.

---

22. Matthias (b. 24 Feb. 1557; d. 20 Mar. 1619) was Holy Roman Emperor (1612–19), King of Bohemia (1611–17), King of Hungary (1608–19).
23. Archduke Ferdinand II (b. 9 Jul. 1578; d. 15 Feb. 1637) was elected King of Bohemia at the Bohemian Diet, 5 June 1617, and then succeeded Matthias as Holy Roman Emperor in 1619.
24. Maximilian, Archduke of Austria (b. 12 Oct. 1558; d. 2 Nov. 1618), was the son of Emperor Maximilian II von Habsburg (b. 31 Jul. 1527; d. 12 Oct. 1576) and Maria von Habsburg, *Infanta de España* (b. 21 Jun. 1528; d. 26 Feb. 1603).

3. When the Imperial Majesty shall keep open table, he [Schütz] should be mindful of an appropriate, well-chosen selection of music; in addition to this to employ not too many of His Electoral Grace's musicians, nonetheless the best and those who are secure of and have full command of their material; not to perform a great deal of grand material but rather pleasant music in different styles, and to alternate them; and thus in every respect arrange it so that His Electoral Grace might derive glory and honor from it.

4. And since in all likelihood a princely table shall be kept in addition to the imperial one, he [Schütz] shall form a separate body from the remaining musicians not employed in the imperial dining room, and likewise from the youths proficient in music. [He shall] then organize the same and enjoin them to serve diligently in the same chamber where the princely table is arranged, abstain from all excessive drinking and running back and forth, but rather discharge their services as well as possible, as is their duty.

5. Should it so happen that the Royal Majesty or Archduke Maximilian of Austria would eat separately in his chamber and to that end desire music: a suitable musical ensemble of a few persons shall be assigned to one or the other chamber, in that case, to provide the service diligently.

6. Would the Imperial Majesty however eat alone, and our Most Gracious Lord keep table with the Royal Majesty, Archduke Maximilian, and other lords, the entire *Musica* serves in that case before His Electoral Grace. A number of them would be required then for the Imperial Majesty; and they would duly attend the same and, moreover, must be the best.

7. He [Schütz] shall also enquire early on, or have enquiries made, of the Lord Marshal of the Court each time as to how one shall deal with the dining at one or the other location, so that he [Schütz] can attend accordingly to the appointment and arrangement of the various music.

8. And inasmuch as a dance might be held in the great hall, he [Schütz] should earnestly enjoin all the instrumentalists to serve diligently and to play suitable dances, and they should be remiss in nothing in this respect on pain of our Most Gracious Lord's commensurate punishment and displeasure.

Finally he, Heinrich Schütz, shall apply all possible diligence to ensure there is no want of good *concertos* and fine music in the church on the customary sermon days. In particular, however, he shall employ something occasionally for voices or instruments alone with organ accompaniment, as much as it permits and is seemly, and thus in every way see to it that His Electoral Grace might derive honor and glory from his *Music* amongst the visitors.

Register of those musicians which, for the arrival of the Roman Imperial Majesty, the newly crowned King in Bohemia, and Archduke Maximilian of Austria, could be employed in Pirna as well as on the way down to Dresden:

Anthonius Colander with the *Instrument* [i.e., regal or harpsichord]

Johann Nauwach ⎫
                ⎬ Theorbists
Hans Christoph Traubell ⎭

Adolph Weisshahn
Ernst Trost
Augustus Tax[25]
Sebastian Hirnschrötl
Hans May
Caspar ⎫
        ⎬ Discantists[26]
Hans   ⎭

Ten persons

In accordance with the most gracious decree of the Elector of Saxony and Burgrave of Magdeburg, the following persons could be positioned with wind instruments in the balcony above the outer-most castle gate for the approach of the Imperial Majesty:

Thomas Tax
Wilhelm Günther
Johann Köckeritz
Gregor Hoyer
Hans Klee
Andreas Voigt
Hans Werner
Nicoll Hauptvogel
Thomas Simson ⎫
              ⎬ both Schaumburg instrumentalists[27]
Nicolaus   ⎭

Ten persons

---

25. Augustus Tax was trained around 1610 under the Augsburg instrumentalist Jacob Baumann (b. ca. 1571; d. ca. 1653) at the expense of the Elector of Saxony. In 1612, he was an instrumentalist in the Dresden *Hofkapelle* with a salary of 150 *gulden*. He was still in Dresden in 1632, and in 1641 became the director of the instrumental music in the *Kurprinzliche Capella* (Kapelle of the Electoral Prince) with an additional stipend of 50 thalers.
26. Schütz is referring to the two *Kapellknaben* in his care: Caspar Kittel and Johann Vierdanck.
27. Schaumburg is a district in north-central Germany through which the Weser River runs. Dynastically, the county was broken up during the Thirty Years' War when there was no male heir following the death of Count Otto V in 1640.

12. SCHÜTZ TO HEINRICH POSTHUMUS REUSS (9 DECEMBER 1617)

Appraisal of the musical establishments of the Church, Court, and Town of Gera

[D-GZsa: n. Rep. Gera/K, Kap. LIX, 1 Nr. 1, fols. 77r–85v][28]

Deliberations of the Director of the Electoral Saxon Court Musicians at Dresden, on the church, court and city music here [in Gera], together with other additional points, etc.

Noble Gracious Lord.[29]

In reference to Your Grace's proposals [*Propositiones*] charged to me on the matter of your praiseworthy *Music*, I submit to Your Grace most humbly, Christianly, and duly herewith my modest judgment graciously desired by you. Your Grace's entire musical body [*corpus musices*] consists of three parts: 1) its court music, 2) the school music, 3) town musicians or domestics.

Court Music.

Gracious Lord, although Your Grace's Court Music is already sufficiently appointed with fine, appropriate and, to me, very pleasing voices, I do wish to comment humbly to Your Grace, in particular with regard to the instrumentalists necessary for a serviceable *Music*:

I.
Court Organists.

Your Grace, for this expansive, distinguished musical body [*corpus musicum*], two organists are necessary, at the very least. Then, should something be performed with multiple choirs, the organists must maintain the foundation [*Fundament*] such that each choir all but deserves to have its own organist. Nevertheless, two organists diametrically across from each other [*e diametro*], on their organ or regal, can accompany the choir standing beside them so that the fundament can be heard in the church at all times. In my opinion, no fewer [than two] organists, at the very least, are required for Your Grace's *Music*, and indeed one can even employ one or two for the embellishment of the choirs without the principals [*minus principales*], which I otherwise

---

28. Copyist's hand. See transcription in Jung, "Ein neuaufgefundenes Gutachten von Heinrich Schütz aus dem Jahre 1617," 241–47, and *Schütz-Dokumente*, Nr. 9.

29. Heinrich Schütz and Heinrich Posthumus Reuss (b. 10 Jun. 1572; d. 3 Dec. 1635) enjoyed an enduring personal and professional relationship which spanned at least the two decades before Reuss's death in the winter of 1635. Posthumus, so called because he was born two months after the death of his father, ruled over a small dominion centered at Gera, a town some 65 km southwest of Leipzig. Schütz, who came from Köstritz (now Bad Köstritz), was by birth a subject of the Reuss domain, and though he was destined to spend his life in the service of other courts, he always maintained strong bonds of loyalty to his birthplace and to the Reuss family. Posthumus was beloved as a *Herr*, and esteemed widely as a musician and patron of the arts. It was for his funeral in 1636 that Schütz composed the *Musicalische Exequien* (SWV 279–81).

call *Kapellen* or adjunct choirs [*choros adjunctos*]. It is my opinion, however, that the aforesaid [organists] are required necessarily if one composes or performs in the current style [*manier*] with fine ripostes—that is, when two discantists, Alto, Tenor, and Bass should respond to one another more or less.

And Your Grace can very well accomplish this to your satisfaction in many different ways, that the same organists shall equally support other of Your Grace's court musicians, as shall follow.

Your Grace already discussed with me *in specie* with regard to my brother, Valerius.[30] In that Your Grace benevolently declares to that end that my aforementioned youngest brother might be brought in among your praiseworthy young lordships,[31] and given board, lodging, and supervision, I am entirely of the undoubted opinion that my beloved father Christoph Schütz will welcome this in humble, grateful favor and singular grace. And, in particular, because my dear parents are desirous that he should continue with his studies, I address to Your Grace my humble petition to promote him graciously to that end, as I am undoubted and humbly confident you shall.

2.

Lutenist.

Gracious Lord, with regard to the lutenist, it would be my humble advice, as previously discussed humbly with Your Grace, that Your Grace assign to him, the said lutenist, a second duty [*Officium*]. He would not support himself from the *Music* alone or from his lute, and the likes of him can still be acquired easily by respectable people. Also in this case I humbly defer to Your Grace's suggestion with regard to the person in question, and have begun giving him all possible assistance, and am humbly, faithfully intent upon applying myself to and helping this person to your satisfaction, God willing.

3.

Discantist.

Noble Gracious Lord, because of Your Grace's travels which occur from time to time, it is not possible for this discantist to study. Although this really does not matter, other classes must also be supported. May it graciously please Your Grace accordingly, in regard of this point, after informing the parents of the boy, to appoint someone who can supervise him simply and solely in his singing and writing, in which he can be most readily promoted. If he is so inclined and by nature disposed toward it, the said *Knabe* can also perhaps

---

30. Little is known about of Heinrich Schütz's younger brother, Valerius (1601–32), other than that he was killed in a duel. At the time, victims of duels were classed as suicides and thus denied a Christian burial in sacred ground. According to Martin Gregor-Dellin, however, Valerius was granted a funeral at Erfurt's Barfüsserkirche, 16 December 1632. See Gregor-Dellin, *Heinrich Schütz: Sein Leben, Sein Werk, Seine Zeit*, 188. Valerius must have been mortally wounded and lived long enough to confess his sins, in which instances a Christian burial could not be denied. This was likewise the case for one Johann Friedrich Günther, who died at Dresden in 1668. D-W: Stolberg Leichenpredigtsammlung, Nr. 3510, 61ff.

31. Reuss promoted the Gymnasium in Gera by having his own children study there.

learn other instruments from Your Grace's court instrumentalists who shall reside there, as shall follow, and hence can feel confident of advancement.

4.
Two Instrumentalists.

Regarding the two instrumentalists, Gracious Lord, there is no doubt Your Grace will always be able to have charge of them, as I have sufficiently seen support of them already. Your Grace may wish graciously to give them both, each of them specifically, their expenses, livery, and as well, in my opinion, have granted to them from 20 to around 30 *gulden* in cash, according to Your Grace's considered discretion. I expect that pious, honest journeymen will undoubtedly aspire to comparable conditions at any time.

5.
Vocalists at the Court.

Gracious Lord, with regard to these persons Your Grace can graciously rejoice that they not only possess fine qualities in singing, but rather in this case also bear especial inclination toward and pleasure in gratifying Your Grace in the promotion of the *Music*. I can think of nothing to mention in this instance.

6.
School Music.

In the aforementioned passage, Gracious Lord, many particulars are advanced which for the most part have been proposed and discussed by von Machwitz and my own unworthy person in the presence of the Rector and Cantor,[32] as Your Grace can graciously see not only from our propositions presented to them and their responses, but rather from your own protocol as well, that it does not appear necessary in this case for me to repeat at length. What can be humbly mentioned by me is the following:

1. It does not seem to me that this member of Your Grace's *Music*, i.e., the school music, can attain proper success if the Rector lives in disagreement with the Cantor—not to mention those other teachers who can be reined in by the Rector; otherwise they would also have to be included in this passage. For this reason Your Grace benevolently shall want to have particular and gracious attention paid to both these persons, since these two conduct the *Directorium* over the other members of all Your Grace's *Music*, as shall be reported in the conclusion—in particular, not only because the Rector has absolute

---

32. Peter Neander (1575–1645) was *Cantor figuralis* and head of the *Quarta* class at the Gera Rutheneum from the time it was founded in 1608 by Heinrich Posthumus Reuss. In addition to his musical duties, Neander also taught Latin to students of the *Tertia* and *Quarta* classes. Neander was the principal musical liaison between musical establishments of Gera and the Reuss Court. It was most likely Neander who directed the first performance of Schütz's *Musicalische Exequien* (SWV 279–81) at Heinrich Posthumus's funeral in early February 1636. Hippolyte Hubmeier (b. 1576; d. 9 Dec. 1637) arrived from Göttingen and was Rector of the Gymnasium from 1611 until 1621. Hubmeier had strong musical opinions and in his *Disputationes quaestionum illustrium, philosophicarum, musicarum* (Jena, 1609) aggressively attacked the bocedization system of sight-singing promoted by the Leipzig Thomaskantor, Sethus Calvisius (b. 21 Feb. 1556; d. 24 Nov. 1615), in his *Exercitationes musicae duae* (Leipzig, 1600). Calvisius countered later that year in his *Exercitatio musica tertia* (Leipzig, 1609).

authority over all the school teachers, but also for his part in terms of music is sufficiently and, to my mind, eminently qualified. By what means this concord is to be preserved, Your Grace has not only made a mercifully good beginning, in that you have inquired, discussed, and settled everything through von Machwitz and my unworthy person, and that Your Grace also has moreover in this case gracious and suitable means about which I myself heard from you and have taken into consideration.

I nonetheless address my humble petition to Your Grace that you might in this case graciously mandate von Machwitz, my most benevolent young nobleman and adjoined in this commission, since it is well known to me that His Reverence shall not shy away from slipping into the chancel unexpectedly from time to time and to pass through incidentally, just so that all school attendants might see Your Grace's mercifully stern resolve that they should live strictly and diligently according to the existing memorandum.

2. According to this solid union, Gracious Lord, the rehearsal with the pupils must be methodically arranged, in which I am in complete agreement with the opinion of the *Herr* Rector, so that the little tyros or beginners in the *Music* might be placed in separate rooms from the adults or accomplished musicians [*Perfectioribus*] and the rehearsal be held with each of them separately, and especially with those who have durable, good voices.

3. The manner in which Your Grace can have the scholars [*Stipendiaten*] shepherded separately to the *Music* at the appropriate time into the church and where otherwise needed, Your Grace has in your protocol and Nr. 2.[33]

4. As regards the two *Tischknaben* who shall be provided for, Gracious Lord, it is my opinion that Your Grace can reasonably base the entire foundation of your *Music* hereupon, since the same shall be in part supported completely *gratis*, as I also understand from Your Grace, and they shall be required consequently to accommodate themselves totally to Your Grace's wishes [*ad nutum*]. And if this Your Grace's intention should be implemented hereafter, the same *Knaben* all—be there few or many—must necessarily be instructed by the Cantor in singing and by Your Grace's court instrumentalists on bowed instruments, and on other instruments, such as cornetti and trombones, according to the inclination and pleasure of the *Knaben*, wherein Your Grace, God willing, shall himself produce appropriate ordinances. I, too, for my part will always gladly advise according to my ability and means, should God grant me life, etc.

7.
Civic Music or Domestics.

Gracious Lord, this company shall undoubtedly be ever sustained by a merciful, most-wise Council of the Town of Gera, with God's help, as up to the present and thus in future as well. Thus I should not neglect to mention the following:

1. That Your Grace devise a means that might be applied to them so that they are bound at all times to attend rehearsal.

---

33. This protocol does not seem to exist.

2. That on certain days and times they might come up to Your Grace's castle and rehearse with your instrumentalists, in order that all members of Your Grace's *Music* might be kept in practice.

Beyond the Abovementioned Instrumental Civic Music.

I am pleased that Your Grace is graciously inclined as well to establish a musical company and consortium amongst the citizenry, for this will be a positive and convenient medium for all of those who are innately musical to be honored and cherished all the more, as we have seen to be the case [*hoc probatur ab exemplis*]. Wherever such consortia and companies are found, a good *Music* is also found for the most part, as one might otherwise reasonably expect. As to the common things [*quo ad communia*] which are necessary, how this company is perhaps to be initiated and ratified resides primarily with Your Grace and an honorable and most-wise Town Council of Gera.

With regard to the regulations [*Leges*] which would have to be presented to this company, Gracious Lord, Your Grace can have *Herr* Melchior Fintzsch, Clerk of the Treasury, draft the same according to the circumstances of the times and occasion of this place, on which I am unable to pass judgment. However, in considering how the rehearsal could be maintained in this company, it seems to me, Gracious Lord, that in your regulations [*Legibus*] the three high feasts in particular and then other feast-days too might be specified to them, whereupon they would be obliged to appear both at the preceding rehearsals and then also in the church.

In the event more festivities might then occur, or should they have to provide service between certain specified holidays, they would have to be referred to Your Grace's previous command to the Cantor.

Director of Music.

Gracious Lord, since it will be necessary for all the aforementioned members to assist the Cantor, and he for his part shall have in this case earnest, total obedience; Your Grace ultimately shall want above all to keep a watchful eye so that all the aforementioned members might assist him, the Cantor; and to dismiss duly and apply a Christian gravity to those who shall willfully disobey Your Grace's highly esteemed, gracious command.

I have absolutely no doubt Your Grace shall appoint a highly distinguished *Music*, for the Glory of Almighty God especially, and then for the everlasting fame of Your Grace himself and his beloved family. I hope most sincerely and with unceasing praise that Your Grace as my gracious and dear Lord, in whose praiseworthy domain I was born and raised to glorify God and my fatherland, makes this his aim, which glorious and gracious intention Almighty God in Grace shall undoubtedly fulfill, here in this world and there in eternity.

Carried out [*Actum*] at Gera, 9 December 1617.

Your Grace's most humble, loyal, and most dutiful [servant],

as long as I live,
Heinrich Schütz,
at present, Electoral Saxon Kapellmeister.

13. SCHÜTZ TO JOHANN GEORG I (15 APRIL 1618)

Petition for the first of three electoral printing patents prior to publication

[D-Dla:[34] Loc. 10 757,[35] Privilegia, Bd. 2, 1618–1628, fol. 85r–v]

Most Serene, Illustrious Elector, Most Gracious Lord.

Your Electoral Grace will most graciously yet recall that some time ago I most humbly informed you regarding the planned publication of some of my modest compositions. Not only did Your Electoral Grace meet my intention at that time with most gracious favor but rather beyond that lent me most gracious support in the purchase of new and elegant music here in Your Electoral Grace's printing-house (for which I am most humbly thankful). Inasmuch as I would now gladly take up the work and make a start on it as soon as possible, I am yet afraid that, upon completion of the work, experienced booksellers and printers perhaps might immediately undertake to publish it, reprint anew, and then sell it. Consequently my copies might then remain unsold and cause me significant and considerable losses.

Hence I can see no way to avoid petitioning Your Electoral Grace most humbly, and submit herewith to you my utmost humble petition, may it please Your Grace, in order to avert such losses, to bestow on me an electoral patent: That for a period of ten years, on pain of Your Electoral Grace's punishment, which shall be determined according to your most gracious pleasure, no one in Your Electoral Grace's electorate, institutions, and lands might undertake to reprint, without my foreknowledge and permission, the musical works I am planning and which I might decide to publish with God's help—this, so that I might enter upon this work without impediment, begin, and complete it successfully, and recover all the more quickly from the trouble and quite considerable expense. To Your Electoral Grace, in most humble honor of whom and whose famed *Music* I entered upon this work, I once again am grateful, for all my life, with my most humble service to the utmost of my ability and means. Herewith I commend you to Almighty God for continuing good health, and blessed reign together with all worldly and spiritual well-being.

---

34. Copyist's hand. This document could not be released for viewing owing to its deteriorated condition. The text of the petition is reproduced in Kobuch, "Neue Sagittariana im Staatsarchiv Dresden," 88–90, and more recently in *Schütz-Dokumente*, Nr. 11.
35. Kobuch (88) gives the incorrect shelf number Loc. 10 754.

Dated at Dresden, 15 April 1618.
Your Electoral Grace's most humble and obedient
Heinrich Schütz.

14. MORITZ OF HESSE-KASSEL TO JOHANN GEORG I (11 JANUARY 1619)

Letter urgently requesting Schütz's return to the Kassel Court owing to the death of Kapellmeister Georg Otto

[*Sachs-Chronik*, 517–18]

Our benevolent service etc. [...] We do not wish to conceal from Your Dilection that our former Kapellmeister Georg Otto passed away recently and it is now upon us that we would readily fill his vacant position with another suitable and well-qualified person, the sooner the better.[36]

As we are able to find no one currently in our music establishment or otherwise in these regions whom we might suitably employ hereto, we are thus obliged kindly to request of Your Dilection (which accordingly we do herewith most diligently and earnestly) that you would show us the great and gracious kindness, and as we previously entrusted to you our former alumnus Heinrich Schütz for that prior occasion out of friendly and cousinly affection, you would now allow him to return to us and for the purpose indicated (and whereas Your Dilection since then will undoubtedly be sufficiently provisioned with others of his equal).

And we expect of Your Dilection all the more an obliging, accommodating answer, that our aforementioned Kapellmeister Georg Otto of blessed memory was likewise a native of Torgau from the territory of Meissen,[37] and thus it appears as though it has become a long-standing custom for our *Musica* to be governed and guided by its subjects.

We assure Your Dilection herewith that, as you shall confer upon us a singularly great kindness and favor through the favorable gratification of our request, we will acknowledge it all our life with grateful heart and apply ourselves earnestly to reciprocate in similar and other ways to the utmost of our ability and means. We thus await your favorable resolution hereupon, faithfully commending us all to God's gracious care. Dated in our City and Fortress, Kassel, 11 January 1619.

---

36. Georg Otto (b. 1550; bur. 30 Nov. 1618) was born in Torgau, served as Cantor in Langensalza from 1569, and from 1586 until his death in 1618 as *Hofkapellmeister* to Wilhelm IV, Landgrave of Hesse-Kassel (b. 24 Jun. 1532; d. 25 Aug. 1592), where he taught the Landgrave's heir, Moritz. As a composer Otto wrote primarily sacred works.

37. Torgau is situated on the Elbe approximately 90 km northeast of Dresden. The town's imposing Renaissance castle, Schloss Hartenfels, became the property of the Albertine line of the House of Wettin following the Schmalkaldic War (1546–47) and continued to be used after the electoral family moved its principal residence to Dresden. It was notably the location of the performance of Schütz's *Dafne* in 1627.

Moritz, Landgrave of Hesse,
Your Dilection's obliging, loyal Cousin and Father.

15. JOHANN GEORG I TO MORITZ OF HESSE-KASSEL (25 JANUARY 1619)

Letter informing the Landgrave that Schütz is to remain permanently in Dresden

[*Sachs-Chronik*, 518–19]

Your Dilection's letter dated at Kassel the eleventh day of January of this year 1619 was received in good order and safely by us, from which we then understood, among other things, what you kindly request of us in regard to the restitution of our appointed Kapellmeister, Heinrich Schütz. We will certainly see to it for Your Dilection, and we are entirely disposed to accede to you favorably in every possible way. You will however undoubtedly recall for what reasons we earlier requested before Your Dilection his, Schütz's, outright transfer and also received to our particular satisfaction. On the strength of that, we have appointed him in such a way to our continuing service, provided him with comforts of every kind, and committed and entrusted to him the direction of our entire musical establishment [*chorus musicus*], whereby he has proven himself up to the present such that we in grace can be truly satisfied with him and thus do not see—insofar as we are not endowed with the likes of this subject among our appointees in the profession with which to fill this post—how we can relinquish or dismiss him without harm to our *Musik*, especially as our old, former Kapellmeister, now at an advanced age and without physical strength, is incapacitated such that we can no longer use him for service in the church or at table.[38]

In addition to that, the aforementioned Schütz, despite our repeated admonitions, has engaged himself to be married here,[39] and in consequence of which must oblige himself then, on account of his future bride, parents, and friends, not to turn away from this place and our service, but rather to continue and to remain in them. From all this Your Dilection sufficiently realizes we cannot do without him, Schütz—also in consideration of his own interests—that he is now firmly attached here, and thus we entreat most kindly that you will not think any worse of us for not complying with your request. We are and remain otherwise ready to offer you corresponding service always. Dated at Dresden, 25 January 1619.

Johann Georg, Elector.

---

38. Originally from Holland, Rogier Michael (b. ca. 1552; d. after 25 Jan. 1619) was a singer and composer who trained in the *Hofkapelle* in Graz and subsequently in Italy from 1569 to 1572. He spent the years 1572–74 as a singer in the *Hofkapelle* of Georg Friedrich, Margrave of Brandenburg-Ansbach (b. 5 Apr. 1539; d. 25 Apr. 1603) before taking up a position at the Electoral Court in Dresden. He was promoted to Kapellmeister in 1587, which title he retained until his death, though he was assisted from 1613 on by the likes of Michael Praetorius and Heinrich Schütz.

39. On 1 June 1619, Schütz married Magdalena Wildeck, the eighteen-year-old daughter of Christian Wildeck, the Bookkeeper for Land and Beverage Tax at the Electoral Court.

16. PSALMEN DAVIDS (DRESDEN, 1619): TITLE PAGE AND DEDICATION

Title page from the Cantus *partbook of* Chor I *and dedication of the work to Johann Georg I*

[Title page]

Psalmen Davids [Psalms of David],[40]
including
sundry motets and *concertos*
with eight and more voices
together with two other Kapellen, so that a number of them
can be performed with three and four choirs,
at one's discretion,
as well
with added *Basso Continuo* for the organ,
lutes, chitarrone, etc.
Composed by
Heinrich Schütz,
Electoral Saxon Kapellmeister.
CANTUS I. CHORI.
Anno M.DC.XIX
Published by the author.
Dresden,
[Printed] in [the] Electoral Saxon Publishing House by Gimel Berg.

[Dedication]

To the Most Serene, Illustrious
Prince and Lord, Lord Johann Georg,
Duke of Saxony, Jülich, Cleves, and Berg,
Grand Marshal of the Holy Roman Empire,
Elector, at present Vicar
in the Lands of the Saxon Law
and in parts of the same Empire belonging to that Vicariate,
Landgrave of Thuringia,
Margrave of Meissen, Burgrave of Magdeburg,
Count of the Mark and Ravensberg, Lord of Ravenstein &c.

---

40. SWV 22–47; RISM A/I/8 S 2275; *SA* 2–3; *NSA* 23–26.

To my Most Gracious Elector and Lord.

Most Serene, Illustrious Elector: to Your Electoral Grace, I pledge my most humble and obedient service, unsparing diligence always, first and foremost.

Most Gracious Elector and Lord, Your Electoral Grace remembers without doubt and most graciously how you appointed, received, and accepted me into your service some three years ago, and conferred upon me the directorship [*Directorium*] and office of Kapellmeister in your splendid, distinguished, and far-famed *Music*, which office up to now I have faithfully and diligently administered, without boasting inappropriately, according to the abilities which the Almighty graciously granted me.

For this and other noble electoral favor shown toward my unworthiness in my continuing service I am duly most humbly thankful. Hence from the bottom of my heart I would not desire more and greater, were it thus within my power, that I should be able to prove obediently to Your Electoral Grace my indebted, most humble gratitude in deeds. But if I find myself much too minor and insignificant for this, yet would I rather do something than to neglect completely to show any sign of gratitude.

And inasmuch as I composed before this sundry German psalms in the Italian manner in which I was diligently instructed by my dear and world-famous teacher, Giovanni Gabrieli, while I stayed with him in Italy, and upon earnest entreaty from various distinguished people, I undertook to publish the same. I resolved at the same time to dedicate this most humbly to Your Electoral Grace, and hereby not only to confirm both my most humble affection and lofty desire—at least to have appear a small spark of my indebted, most obedient gratitude (since my inability at present does not allow me to do more, however strong is my desire to do it)—but also the practice which is customary in suchlike publication.

I recognize in truth the imperfection and insignificance of this my work, and consider it entirely unworthy of Your Electoral Grace's eminent Electoral Person. But because great potentates, among which you justly hold one of the most distinguished positions, as though it were in their nature, in such instances as this do not so much direct their most gracious attention to the conspicuousness of the gift as to the spirit of him who offers it. I therefore live in the most humble hope that Your Electoral Grace might be pleased at least by this attempt of mine and the great desire, which exists only in some measure as thanks for such exceedingly eminent electoral favor received by me, and have this slight work of mine recommended to your most gracious protection, until by the grace of God something better might soon follow. Accordingly then I also ask for this in complete obedience.

I hereby commend faithfully and most humbly Your Electoral Grace, together with all your electoral family, to Almighty God for continuing good health, enduring prosperous rule, and all electoral well-being, and myself to you for continuing favor. Dated at Dresden, 1 June, in the year of Christ our one Savior and Redeemer, 1619.

Your Electoral Grace's
most humble and obedient servant, as I live,
Heinrich Schütz.

17. PSALMEN DAVIDS (1619): TITLE PAGE AND PREFACE FROM THE BASSO CONTINUO PARTBOOK

[Title page]

BASSO CONTINUO
for the organ, lute, chitarrone, etc.,
of the
Psalmen Davids [Psalms of David],
including
sundry motets and concertos
with eight and more voices,
together with two other Kapellen, so that a number of them
can be used with three and four choirs at one's discretion,
set by
Heinrich Schütz,
Electoral Saxon Kapellmeister.
Anno M.DC.XIX
Published by the author.
Dresden
[Printed] in [the] Electoral Saxon Publishing House by Gimel Berg.

[Preface]

To all those skilled in music my greetings and service first and foremost.

Although I consider it all but unnecessary to write anything on the disposition of these psalms and other compositions of mine, since prudent Kapellmeister are at liberty to arrange them according to the circumstances of each *Capella* and the qualifications of the personnel [i.e., musicians], I call to mind the following few items to which one should principally pay attention so that they, who have requested to know the opinion of the *Author* [i.e., composer] on the matter, might also be satisfied.

1. The *Cori Favoriti* must be well distinguished from the *Capellen*. The *Cori Favoriti* are what I call those choir[s] and voices which the Kapellmeister should most favor and employ in the best and most pleasing ways. The *Capellen*, on the other hand, are introduced for a full sound and for splendor. The organist should therefore be alert to these terms as they appear in the basso continuo [partbook], and stop the organ judiciously, now quietly, now forcefully.

2. In the disposition and arrangement of the *Capellen* for two choirs [i.e., antiphonally], one can take care that the choirs are set up across from each other, and that *Capella 1* is next to the second *coro favorito* and, conversely, *Capella 2* next to the first [*coro favorito*]. Thus shall the *Capellen* achieve the desired effect.

3. *Psalm:* "Ich hebe meine Augen auf," *Psalm:* "Der Herr is mein Hirt," *Concerto:* "Lobe den Herren, meine Seele" (to which *Canzon:* "Nun lob, mein Seel, den Herren" can be added as well if one wishes to omit the instrumental *Capellen* and [perform it] only with eight voices).[41] In the aforementioned pieces, *coro secondo* is used for one *Capella*, and hence strongly voiced, whereas *Coro 1* which is a *coro favorito*, on the contrary, lightly [voiced] and [comprised] of only four singers. It is left to the discretion of each whether he would make a copy from the aforesaid *Coro 1*, [beginning] where it reads *Capella* after the small stroke, and thus employ a second *Capella* separately. Thus shall a better balance [*Proportion*] of the choirs occur.

4. The *Capellen*, which are scored for high voices, are for the most part intended for cornetti and other instruments. However, if it is possible for one to have singers on hand as well, so much the better. In this case, from the low *Bass* parts with the F on the fifth line, which are convenient for the large viol, bass trombone,[42] and bassoon, one might copy out other bass parts with the proper range [*Ambitus*] for the bass singers, with the F on the fourth line.

5. Where suchlike instrumental *Capellen* with high clefs [*Clavibus*] are found, it is easy to see that the *cori favoriti* must conversely be appointed with singers, which are meant to sing then for the most part of this entire work, up to the aforesaid *motets, concertos, etc.* Nevertheless, some of the psalms—such as 1. "Herr, unser Herrscher," 2. "Wohl dem, der nicht wandelt," 3. "Wie lieblich [sind deine Wohnungen]," 4. "Wohl dem, der den Herren fürchtet"[43]—also adapt themselves very nicely when the higher choir is comprised of cornetti and violins, the lower one with trombones or other instruments, and one voice sings alongside in each gallery.

6. Because I have also set the present psalms of mine in *stylo recitativo* (virtually unknown in Germany up to now), which in my opinion almost no style is better suited to the composition of psalms, in that one recites continually without frequent repetitions owing to the large amount of text. I kindly request of those who have no knowledge of this method [*modi*] that they will not to want to hurry the beat too much in the performance of my aforementioned psalms, but rather keep to a middle path, so that the text will be clearly recited by the singers and understood. Otherwise a very unpleasant harmony will grow out of it—nothing but a *Battaglia di Mosche*, or "battle of flies"—contrary to the intentions of the author.

7. The basso continuo is in fact only intended for the psalms. From the motet, "Ist nicht Ephraim,"[44] on to the end of the work, diligent organists will take the trouble transcribing into score [*Partitur*], and know furthermore how to extract the bass [lines] from the psalms in case more than one organ is to be used.

---

41. *Psalm:* "Ich hebe meine Augen auf" (Nr. 10, SWV 31); *Psalm:* "Der Herr ist mein Hirt" (Nr. 12, SWV 33); *Concerto:* "Lobe den Herren, meine Seele" (Nr. 18, SWV 39); "Nun lob, mein Seel, den Herren," *Canzon* (Nr. 20, SWV 41).

42. *Quartposaune*, which is also called the *Trombone majore, grando*, or *grosso*. See Praetorius, *Syntagma musicum III*, 131.

43. 1. "Herr, unser Herrscher" (Nr. 6, SWV 27); 2. "Wohl dem, der nicht wandelt" (Nr. 7, SWV 28); 3. "Wie lieblich sind deine Wohnungen" (Nr. 8, SWV 29); 4. "Wohl dem, der den Herren fürchtet" (Nr. 9, SWV 30).

44. Nr. 19, SWV 40.

I would thus give this for the information of well-intentioned musicians [*Musicis*], and commend myself to them with this slight work of mine until something better follows in future, with God's help, and finally to their favorable services.

Heinrich Schütz.

18. SCHÜTZ TO THE CITY COUNCIL OF FRANKFURT AM MAIN (17 JULY 1619)

Letter accompanying the composer's presentation copy of the Psalmen Davids

[Copy in Institut für Stadtgeschichte Frankfurt/Main, *Rats-Supplikationen* 1619 tom. III (= August bis Dezember), fols. 12r–v, 16v][45]

[Address]

To the Noble, Right Honorable, Great and Most Learned, Most Wise *Bürgermeister* and Council of the City of Frankfurt am Main, my Most Benevolent Lords

[Text]

Noble, Right Honorable, Great and Most Learned, Most Reverend, and Most Benevolent Lords.

I write dutifully to inform Your Lordships and Graces that I have set to music a few psalms of the King and Prophet David, as they in their forms were conceived by him out of singular devotion to praise God, to which end each one in his profession is duty bound to direct and prepare everything first and foremost, and now made ready in print upon the request and entreaties of a good many devout souls and Christians.

Inasmuch as Your Lordships and Graces are much acclaimed and celebrated owing to your benevolent inclination toward music, this is demonstrated evidently in deed in that you cultivate and practice at great expense all manner of instrumental and vocal music in your well-appointed churches and schools.

As I live in the undoubted confidence Your Lordships and Graces would find favor in these and similar sacred concertos primarily, and no disinclination or displeasure in this my work [*opus*], I address to you the presentation of the aforesaid and enclosed copy of my work [*opus*] herewith, and request with utmost humility that you receive and accept it with generous spirit, and commend me ever to your affection, whereas I will avow myself duly to ever-willing service.

---

45. Transcribed in *Schütz-Dokumente*, Nr. 16. An entry in the Frankfurt *Bürgermeisterbuch 1619* from Thursday, 5 August 1619 (fol. 59v) reads: "In that Heinrich Schütz, Electoral Saxon Kapellmeister in Dresden, presented to the Honorable Council sundry sacred psalms composed for several voices, one shall give him an honorarium of 6 thalers." *Schütz-Dokumente*, 76.

Dresden, 17 July 1619.
Your Lordships'
most dutiful
Electoral Saxon Kapellmeister thereat,
Heinrich Schütz.

19. SCHÜTZ'S POEM ON THE OCCASION OF GEORG SCHÜTZ'S WEDDING (9 AUGUST 1619)

Dedicatory poem on the composition of Psalm 133, written on the occasion of his brother Georg's marriage

[The only traceable exemplar was housed in the University Library in Königsberg (Kaliningrad), presumed destroyed in 1944][46]

I have sung many psalms with sweet-sounding modulation, psalms which the Teutonic land may have as a gift. This is owed to you alone, germane brother; since a single faith has united our two hearts. I pray that this very faith, which joined us from our mother's womb, remain firm in eternity.

[9 August 1619]

[Original]

Dulcisono cecini plures modulamine Psalmos,
Quos sibi donatos Teutonis ora habeat.
Hic tibi debetur soli GERMANE; *quia una*
Univit nostrûm pectora bina FIDES,
Ista FIDES, *quæ nos matris conjunxit ab alvo,*
Æterno perstet tempore firma, precor.

20. SCHÜTZ TO LUDWIG WILHELM MOSER, COURT CHAMBER SECRETARY (3 JULY 1621)

Letter regarding an order of steel strings from Nuremberg

[D-Dla: Loc. 7327/1, Kammersachen Anno 1621, Vorgang 70, fols. 166r–v;[47] Bl. 70 in *Schütz-GBr* (298)]

---

46. Georg Schütz (1587–1637) was Heinrich's favorite brother. They were together in Marburg at the University (1609), and continued throughout their lives to have close contact with each other. Georg married Anna Grosse at Leipzig on 9 July 1619, and until his death in 1637 was a member of the Supreme Court of the Judicature (*Oberhofgerichtsadvokat*) in Leipzig. *Schütz-GBr*, 321. See also *Schütz-GBr*, Nr. 7; *Schütz-Dokumente*, Nr. 17.
47. The document is in Schütz's hand. Transcribed in *Schütz-GBr*, Nr. 9; *Schütz-Dokumente*, Nr. 19.

Right Honorable, Highly Respected, Most Learned, especially Most Benevolent Lord and Most Venerable Friend, I pledge my entirely willing services together with wishes for every welfare of body and of the soul from God in the highest, first and foremost.

On account of this urgent matter, I cannot neglect, with the present letter, to importune and humbly advise my Most Benevolent Lord Chamber Secretary that some money was recently remitted from the Electoral Treasury here to Nuremberg for strings that should have been purchased for the Electoral *Music* from a wire-drawer there by the name of Jobst Meuler,[48] who makes excellent steel instrumental strings, the likes of which are not to be found anywhere.

Now the aforementioned wire-drawer has in fact written to me that he would most willingly gratify us and manufacture the strings, but he would not be allowed by other of his fellow-masters of the trade to make something more remarkable and better than they—unless perhaps a small dictate might be sent off by our Most Gracious Lord to the Nuremberg City Council. In that case, he would certainly be given permission.

Most Benevolent Lord Chamber Secretary, since good strings are of no less importance to me and my colleagues in our profession than is a pair of good pistols or other weapons to a soldier, you would not take it amiss then that I trouble you with this.

And my most humble request is herewith directed to you, that you might kindly obtain a small dictate of this sort in regard to the aforementioned Jobst Meuler, from our Most Gracious Lord to the City Council of Nuremberg, that he [Meuler] [manufacture] as many of the best instrumental strings for the electoral household as one might wish to order, and have it forwarded to me at the earliest opportunity (since a messenger acquainted with these matters shall set out for there in a few days in any event).

This is done not only to the best advantage of the entire *Music*, rather also in the interests of our Most Gracious Elector and Lord insofar as we receive quality goods for the money. I in return am ready to repay such favor to my Most Benevolent Lord Chamber Secretary, to the best of my ability and means, when the occasion presents itself. Finally, with utmost diligence, I commend you to divine protection herewith. Dated at Dresden, the third day of July, 1621.

My Most Benevolent Lord
Chamber Secretary's
most dutiful
Heinrich Schütz,
Kapellmeister, in his own hand.

---

48. Jobst Meuler, according to *Schütz-GBr* (321), was described as a *Scheibenzieher* (wire-puller or wire-drawer) and descended from an old Nuremberg family of craftsmen, which was already referred to as early as 1534. He was buried 11 December 1632.

21. SCHÜTZ'S TEXT TO *SYNCHARMA MUSICUM* (3 NOVEMBER 1621) (ORIGINAL LANGUAGE: LATIN)

SYNCHARMA
MUSICUM [Musical Felicitation],[49]
set for three choirs,
&
for the celebrated princes
& estates of Silesia,
so that peace is restored to them
through intervention of the Most Serene
Elector of Saxony,
Lord Johann Georg etc.,
in the year MDCXXI [1621],
dedicated most humbly
by
Heinrich Schutz,
Electoral Kapellmeister.

Behold, a new guest succeeds in the Elysian fields, a Saxon duke, sword-bearer of the Roman empire, in order that he may bring the rewards of the longed-for peace to the region and bind its subjected members into the faith of the emperor; in order that with the defeat of the enemies, the work of religion and the honorable beauty of justice may flourish in all the city. O Silesia, rejoice in your fortune so great, and sing your pious prayers to the incoming duke: greetings, love of peace, greetings, Duke Johann Georg: you offer help to us, we venerate you.

[3 November 1621]

[Original text]

SYNCHARMA
MUSICUM
tribus Choris adornatum
&

---

49. SWV 49; RISM A/I/8 S 2276; *SA* 15; *NSA* 38. Schütz's text to SWV 49 is dedicated to Johann Georg I, marking the ceremonies in Breslau (Wrocław, Poland) on 3 November 1621 at which the Silesian estates proclaimed their loyalty to Emperor Ferdinand II following the imperial victory at the Battle of the White Mountain, 8 November 1620. Schütz and sixteen members of the Kapelle accompanied the Saxon Elector to Breslau for the ceremonies and performance of this work and possibly his *Teutonium dudum belli* (SWV 338). Johann Georg I helped negotiate the peace between the estates and Emperor Ferdinand II, and subsequently served as the emperor's envoy at the formal declaration, 3 November. According to *Schütz-GBr* (299), a complete printed copy of the work is housed in the Stadtbibliothek Breslau/Wrocław.

inclytis Silesiae Principibus
& Ordinibus,
Cum iisdem interventu Serenissimi
Saxoniae Electoris,
D. JOHANNIS GEORGII &c.
pax redderetur,
Anno Ep. Chr., MDCXXI.
D.D.
ab
HENRICO SCHÜTZIO
Electoralis Capellae Magistro

En novus Elysiis succedit sedibus hospes
Dux Saxo, Romani Ensifer Imperii,
Ut ferat optatae Regioni munera pacis
Caesaris inque fidem subdita membra liget.
Hostibus ut pulsis omni florescat in urbe
Relligionis [sic] opus Iustitiaeque decus.
O tibi fortunam gratare Silesia tantam
Et pia ventanti concine vota Duci:
Salve pacis amor, salve Dux Jane Georgi:
Tu nobis praestas, nos veneramur opem.

22. SCHÜTZ'S TEXT TO *TEUTONIAM DUDUM BELLI* (3 NOVEMBER 1621)
(ORIGINAL LANGUAGE: LATIN)

[Printed in Ambrosius Profe's *Ander Theil Geistlicher Concerten und Harmonien* (Leipzig, 1641)][50]

Long have war's dark dangers disturbed Germany—O may good peace bring a thousand joys to all. Let citizens rejoice in the open, all the world's people rejoice at the new prosperity in the sweet fatherland. Let all Silesia, all Budorgis resound—O may good peace bring a thousand joys to all.[51] Let the people celebrate their new son with new songs, let Apollo strike the resonant ivory with golden plectrum, let the Graces cry out here and there, and venerable men—O may good peace bring a thousand joys to all.

---

50. SWV 338; *NSA* 38. Schütz's *Teutoniam dudum belli* (SWV 338) was quite possibly composed for and performed at the declaration of loyalty of the Silesian estates in 1621, along with his *En novus Elysiis* (SWV 49). Twenty years later, the composition was included in Ambrosius Profe's *Ander Theil geistlicher Concerten und Harmonien*... (Leipzig, H. Köler, 1641). RISM B/I/1 1641³.

51. Budorgis was the old Silesia before the introduction of Christianity.

[Original text]

Teutoniam dudum belli atra pericla molestant,
Omnibus a bona pax gaudia mille ferat.
Laetentur cives patulo, gens omnis in orbe
In patria dulci prosperitate nova.
Tota Slesis resonet jam iota Budorgis:
Omnibus o bona pax gaudia mille ferat.
Turba novem filium nova cantica cantet,
Apollo aureolo resonum pectine pulset ebur,
Exclamant passim Charites, hominesque venusti:
Omnibus o bona pax gaudia mille ferat.

23. HISTORIA DER AUFERSTEHUNG JESU CHRISTI (DRESDEN, 1623): TITLE PAGE AND PREFACE (25 MARCH 1623)

[Title page]

HISTORIA
of the Joyous and Triumphant
Resurrection of our one Savior and
Redeemer Jesus Christ,[52]
suitable for performances in princely chapels and rooms
at Easter, for spiritual Christian recreation,
set to music
by
Heinrich Schütz,
Electoral Saxon Kapellmeister.
VOX EVANGELISTAE
[Printed at] Dresden by Gimel Berg,
1623.

[Preface]

To the Reader, my
greetings and devotion.
Whoever wishes to perform my present composition, the *Historia* of the Joyous and Triumphant Resurrection of our Lord God, Savior and Redeemer, Jesus Christ, must attend to and appoint two choirs, namely:

---

52. SWV 50; RISM A/I/8 S 2277; *SA* 1; *NSA* 3; *SSA* 4.

1. The Choir of the Evangelist
2. The Choir of the Speaking Characters

It is left to the discretion of each, however, depending on the location and the musicians, whether to leave both choirs together in one place or to separate them from each other.

Concerning the Choir of the Evangelist

1. The [role of the] Evangelist can be sung to an organ, *positif* [positive organ], or to a harpsichord [*Instrument*], lute, bandora, etc., according to preference, and for which reason then the Evangelist's text has been included under the basso continuo.[53] The organist who wishes to represent his [the Evangelist's] character well should note here that, as long as the *falsobordone* continues on one tone,[54] he on the organ or harpsichord [*Instrument*] always play beneath it elegant and appropriate runs or *passaggi*, which imparts to this work, as with all other *falsobordoni*, the proper manner. Otherwise they do not achieve their proper *effect*.

2. But when it is possible to do so, it is better that the organ and others be omitted here, and instead of them only to have four violas da gamba [*viole da gamba*] employed (which parts are also included here) to accompany the character of the Evangelist.

3. It will be necessary, however, for the four viols [*viole*] to practice very diligently with the character of the Evangelist in the following way: the Evangelist takes his part and recites it without measure,[55] as it seems comfortable to him, and moreover does not hold a syllable longer than one is otherwise accustomed to do in normal, slow, and comprehensible speech.

Similarly, the viols should not pay heed to the beat, but rather only to the text which the Evangelist recites and which is written in their parts under the *falsobordone*. In this way one cannot go wrong. It might also be possible for one viol in the ensemble to play *passagi*, as is customary in *falsobordone* and produces a good effect.

4. It is also to be noted that the basso continuo of the Speaking Characters has been included in the four parts for the viols, in order that they might have an indication of when they should enter again with the character of the Evangelist, so that the work is orderly and proceeds without confusion.

5. The final chorus *à 9* is also copied at the end of the partbooks for the violas da gamba, so that they might be able to play along if they wish.

---

53. In his translation of this document, George J. Buelow omits instruments (e.g., bandora), misidentifies others (harpsichord), and treats Schütz's "etc." as "or some similar instrument." Buelow, "A Schütz Reader," 13.
54. *Falsobordone* is a chordal recitation based on root position triads, usually of a psalm tone or similar liturgical chant, though it was also applied to various sacred and secular genres of music throughout much of Europe well into the seventeenth century.
55. Buelow (13) translates "ohne einigen tact" as "in a completely free rhythm," which is not quite accurate.

Concerning the Choir of the Speaking Characters

1. This choir must be near the organ, because all these *actiones* must be performed to a very quiet *gedackt* [stop], so that one can understand clearly the singers' delivery.

2. The Kapellmeister, or whoever conducts the work, can also tend to this choir and provide it with a suitable, slow, appropriate beat (in which exists, as it were, the soul and life of all music).

3. In the larger book, in which this choir is written, the text of the Evangelist is also found in order that the [Speaking] Characters can see from it when they should enter.

4. On the occasion when only one person speaks in the *Historia*—that is, the Lord Christ, Mary Magdalene, etc.—I have written a *Duo*, and in particular the character of the Lord Christ, with an alto and a tenor. Both voices can be sung, or just one, with the other played instrumentally or possibly left out altogether if desired.

5. Where [the word] *Chorus* is indicated before a verse, it means that the same can be sung by the full choir [*pleno choro*].

For reference I wish to specify the parts which belong to this *Historia*:

1. One large book in which one finds the Speaking Characters
2. One book for the voice-part of the Evangelist
3. Four books for the four violas da gamba
4. The basso continuo

It would also be very much worth noting to what extent this *Historia* could be performed with better grace [*gratia*] or elegance, specifically if the Evangelist alone were visible, and the other characters and suchlike [i.e., the chorus and instrumentalists] were hidden. I wanted to go over this carefully, but confidently refer it to the judgment of prudent musicians that, if they should wish to take up the work, they will give themselves to understand everything of the space and other circumstances of the place. In the meantime, however, may they take notice of this aforementioned slight account of mine in the best spirit, and have me commended to their kind affection. Dated at Dresden, on the day of the Annunciation of Mary [March 25], 1623.

Heinrich Schütz, Author.

24. SCHÜTZ TO WILHELM LUDWIG MOSER (25 MAY 1624)

Memorandum to the Chamber Secretary concerning the organ builder, Gottfried Fritzsche

[D-Dla: Loc. 7328/1 Kammersachen Ao. 1624, Vorgang 80, fol. 161r–v;[56] Bl. 80 in *Schütz-GBr* (299)]

---

56. The document is in Schütz's hand. Transcribed in *Schütz-GBr*, Nr. 13; *Schütz-Dokumente*, Nr. 28.

Memorandum to the Electoral Saxon Privy Councillor and Chamber Secretary, *Herr* Wilhelm Ludwig Moser,[57] regarding the organ builder, Gottfried Fritzsche.[58]

Most Benevolent Lord Chamber Secretary, you will remember, the manner in which our Most Gracious Elector and Lord wrote to his appointed organ builder, Gottfried Fritzsche (who once again resides in Wolfenbüttel in the employ of the Duke of Brunswick), that for the construction of a new organ in the electoral church in Torgau, he should proceed there as quickly as possible. The good man apologizes, just now in a communication to me, that he would gladly obey most humbly the command of our Gracious Lord and present himself, but would be prevented lest one begrudge paying him for his work [in Wolfenbüttel], and that he would therefore suspend [this work] at great loss to himself; and though he would gladly leave there at the earliest possible date, he would surely worry that he might not ever be paid afterwards.

Most Generous Lord Chamber Secretary, since we are very much in need of the aforementioned organ builder, not only on account of the organ construction in Torgau but also for the inspection of the palace instrument in this place, I should like for my part to request that our Most Gracious Lord have a brief missive drafted to the Duke of Brunswick for the dismissal of said organ builder, as well as a stern command to the organ builder himself. Although he would still scarcely be able to present himself before Michaelmas [29 September], I fear that we otherwise would still not have him here for a year or more. I will however leave everything to the discretion of my most generous *Herr*, to whom I make this suggestion with good intentions, and would at the same time commend myself to his services.

Dresden, 25 May 1624.

My Most Benevolent Lord's

ever most obliging

Heinrich Schütz, in his own hand.

25. SCHÜTZ TO WILHELM LUDWIG MOSER (30 DECEMBER 1624)

Formal appraisal of organ music submitted to the Dresden Court by Samuel Scheidt (30 December 1624)

[D-Dla: Loc. 7328/2 Kammersachen Ao. 1625, fol. 4r–v][59]

---

57. Wilhelm Ludwig Moser (b. 5 Mar. 1557) was appointed Chamber Secretary in 1594. *Schütz-GBr*, 323.
58. Gottfried Fritzsche (Frietzsche) (b. 1578; d. 1638) was the Electoral Saxon Court organ-builder, and father-in-law of the poet, Johann Rist (b. 8 Mar. 1607; d. 31 Aug. 1667). Fritzsche built not only the organ in the Dresden palace chapel (1614), there are also organs by him in the Freiberg Petrikirche (rebuilt 1614), Trinitatiskirche in Sondershausen (1615), in the Stadtkirche in Bayreuth (inaugurated by Scheidt, Praetorius, and Schütz), the Ulricikirche in Brunswick (1626), the St. Maria Magdalena Church in Hamburg (1630), Torgau *Schlosskapelle* (1631), Hamburg's Katharinenkirche (1634), and Jacobikirche (rebuilt 1636). The organ in Wolfenbüttel's *Hauptkirche* Beatae Mariae Virginis was built 1619–23, and is still there. Also dating from around this time is the organ at Schloss Harbke (1621), still largely in its original state, and located midway between Wolfenbüttel and Magdeburg. See Bruch, "Fritzsche, Gottfried," 213–14; and Frandsen, "Gottfried Fritzsche (Frietzsche) at the Dresden Court, 1628–29."
59. Schütz's autograph memorandum is preceded in the archival file by Scheidt's presentation letter, fols. 2r–3v. Transcribed in La Mara, 68–69; *Schütz-GBr*, Nr. 14; *Schütz-Dokumente*, Nr. 29.

Memorandum presented in regard to musical items by Samuel Scheidt, Kapellmeister at Halle.[60]

Most Honorable, Most Learned, Most Benevolent Lord Chamber Secretary: upon your request for an accurate report concerning the presented musical items by Samuel Scheidt, Kapellmeister at Halle, and my judgment of it, I respectfully submit to you for your information the present work (two books in folio format bound in white leather with gilt border, speckled edges, each book with a thickness of three finger-widths) comprises organ works in the Netherlandish *manier*, and in his, Scheidt's, style sound very good indeed. The first of these two books, with a separate previously printed preface, is dedicated to our Most Gracious Elector and Lord. Beyond this, however, may it please my Most Benevolent Lord Chamber Secretary perhaps still to recall, the aforementioned Samuel Scheidt presented yet two other works prior to this one,[61] the letter for which, when I once was called to my duty, had been accidentally misplaced by one of the [choir] boys. Those works, however, were not dedicated to our Most Gracious Lord but rather merely presented. They are also still at hand, but have not yet been entered into the book catalog because no recompense has yet been made for them. With regard to the present dedication at this time, it would therefore be my most humble opinion that our Most Gracious Elector and Lord settle most graciously with him [i.e., Scheidt] once and for all, and to pay him his due. In my humble estimation (and at the pleasure of my Most Benevolent Lord Chamber Secretary) it seems to me that a goblet filled with 30 or 35 thalers, or instead of that, since he has dedicated a part of the work, should it better please our Most Gracious Lord, a goblet of 20 thalers together with His Electoral Grace's portrait, would be sufficient for the reputation of our Most Gracious Lord. It rests ultimately with our Most Gracious Lord and my Most Benevolent Lord Chamber Secretary to do as you please, and to whose divine protection I commend myself. 30 December 1624.

My Most Benevolent Lord Chamber Secretary's
most dutiful
Heinrich Schütz.

26. *CANTIONES SACRAE* (FREIBERG, 1625): TITLE PAGE AND DEDICATION (1 JANUARY 1625) (ORIGINAL LANGUAGE: LATIN)

[Title page]

Cantiones sacrae [Sacred Songs][62]
for four voices

---

60. The presentation under consideration was mostly likely Scheidt's *Tabulatura Nova, Parts 1 & 2* (Hamburg, 1624).
61. The works referred to here could be *Cantione sacrae* (Hamburg, 1620); *Paduana, galliarda, courante, alemande, intrada, canzonetto…* (Hamburg, 1621); *Pars prima concertuum sacrorum…adiectis symphoniis et choris instrumentalibus* (Hamburg, 1622); or *Ludorum musicorum secunda pars* (Hamburg, 1622).
62. SWV 53–93; RISM A/I/8 S 2279; *SA* 4; *NSA* 8–9.

with *basso ad organum*
by
Heinrich Schütz,
Kapellmeister to the Most Serene
Elector of Saxony
CANTUS
Freiberg[63]
Printed by Georg Hoffmann,
1625.

[Dedication]

To the Most Illustrious and Highest Prince and Lord, Lord Johann Ulrich, Prince and Lord in Krumau[64] and Eggenberg, Count in Adelsberg, Ruler of Pettau,[65] Ernhausen and Stras, Knight of the Golden Fleece, Director of the Privy Council of His Holy Imperial Majesty, and Master of the Supreme Imperial Court, and President of the Provinces of Styria and Croatia, my Most Clement Prince and Lord.[66]

Most Illustrious and Highest Prince, after I applied my mind to the study of music, that excellent branch of knowledge agreeable and pleasant to God and mortals, I directed the greatest care and all my industry toward the following goal: namely, that in this matter, my study and all my labors might yield first indeed to the glory of the divine Spirit; secondly, that they might be pleasing to men, especially princes—indeed, in my opinion, deservedly so. Since all music, or rather all our actions more generally, ought to be uniquely directed to celebrating the praises of immortal God, the noblemen especially, as they in their dignity approach God all the more closely, are even more worthy of this than are other people, and music should be greatly occupied in honoring and pleasing them beyond other men. Truly, I myself did not find that this opinion was altogether without foundation: years ago, on the occasion of the assembly of the two most unconquerable emperors Matthias and Ferdinand, at the court of the Most Serene Elector of Saxony, my Most Clement Lord, when, as director (however unworthy) of the musical establishment [*chorus musicus*] of the Saxon Court, I saw that these most glorious princes, as also Your Highness, kindly took pleasure in my music.

---

63. The word *Hermundororum* is added to the Latin *Fribergae* in the original print to make clear the reference to Freiberg in Saxony. The Hermundori were an early German people who lived in what became Saxony and Thuringia.
64. Český Krumlov, Czech Republic.
65. Ptuj, Slovenia.
66. Johann Ulrich von Eggenberg (b. Jun. 1568; d. 18 Oct. 1634) was born in Graz into a Protestant noble family, converted to Catholicism in 1600, and subsequently became one of most politically influential men of his day as a result of his close and richly rewarded cooperation with Emperor Ferdinand II and the Habsburgs.

And so, from that very time, when I came to know Your Highness and your obvious heroic virtues and ones worthy of such a great prince, but especially your great enthusiasm for the discipline of music—from that time, I say, I was constantly wishing for and seeking again and again an opportunity to augment and preserve Your Highness's clemency toward me (which has been seen so often before), and it happened to me most opportunely, as if by a miraculous *deus ex machina*, that I completed certain sacred songs that I had begun long ago, a slight work containing pieces of various kinds, varying constantly with my age and my years, for indeed they partake partly of the old and partly of the new manner of singing. Hence, having been asked by friends and supporters of music to publish the work, I consented in order to give back to God, the most generous author and bestower of this art, what He had imparted to me, and to show some sign of a grateful spirit to Your Highness, since the testimonies of your kindness toward me were abundantly clear.

For these reasons I humbly offer and dedicate this musical work to Your Highness, praying with due obedience, that you accept my labors with kindness now, when I am absent, just as then, when I was present, you declared that my musical endeavors were not displeasing to the Holy Imperial Majesty, nor to you yourself. May the good and great God long keep Your Highness safe and prosperous for the public good of the Christian world. Dated at Dresden, from my musical library, on the first of January, in the year 1625.

Your Highness's most humble and devoted
Heinrich Schütz,
Kapellmeister to the Most Serene Elector of Saxony.

27. *CANTIONES SACRAE* (FREIBERG, 1625): FOREWORD TO THE READER (ORIGINAL LANGUAGE: LATIN)

To the Benevolent Reader.

The publisher, thinking that this slight work would be more agreeable [to the public], wrested this basso continuo from me; and he provided the opportunity that I should furthermore add, at the end, one or two pieces suited to basso continuo.[67] I would beg the organists who wish to satisfy more delicate ears, however, not to spare the pains of writing out all the parts in score or so-called tablature.[68] Should you wish to accompany, in the usual manner, solely from the continuo part, I should find it misguided and clumsy. Farewell.

H.S.

---

67. Nr. 18 "Turbabor, sed non perturbabor" (SWV 70); Nr. 32 "Ecce advocatus meus apud te Deum Patrem" (SWV 84); Nr. 33 "Domine, ne in furore to arguas me" (SWV 85); Nr. 34 "Quoniam non est in morte" (SWV 86), Nr. 35 "Discedite a me omnes" (SWV 87).
68. See Johnston, "Polyphonic Keyboard Accompaniment in the Early Baroque," 51–64.

28. SCHÜTZ TO THE ATTENTION OF JOHANN GEORG I (BEFORE 17 MARCH 1625)

Memorandum regarding Johann Peltz's request for instrumental study in Berlin

[D-Dla: Loc. 7424, Registratur über Universitäts-, Konsistorial- und geistliche Sachen, 1624–1627, fol. 223r; address on unpaginated verso of a page between numbered fols. 228/3 and 228/4][69]

[Address]

Memorial regarding the former *Kapellknabe*, Johann Peltz,[70] who wishes to study the small cittern [*Citherlein*] in Berlin[71]

[Text]

It is most humbly inquired of our Most Gracious Elector and Lord, in regard to Johann Peltz, the former *Kapellknabe*, whether His Electoral Grace is most graciously disposed toward sending him, Peltz, along with the Berlin musicians here at present, to study the small cittern for one year with the one [musician]. It would be fitting to advise His Electoral Grace, in consideration of which, that this place shall nonetheless incur expenses.

In the event that this might most graciously please His Electoral Grace:

1. To spare boarding expenses (which Walter, the Berlin musician, also advises), a letter of recommendation to His Electoral Grace[72] in Berlin could be given to Peltz to take along, not only that he might have unrestricted admission to the court but also free board there, and be able to serve alongside in accordance with his skills.

2. For room and board, laundering expenses, etc., the Englishman Kitt wants 120 thalers for the year in which he proposes to teach Peltz everything, and that this might be paid to him after the year has passed when he sends Peltz back.

3. For Peltz's departure, he would need a livery and an additional 30 thalers so that he would be able to acquire shoes and other necessities for the year.

---

69. The unsigned document appears to be in Schütz's hand. Transcribed in *Schütz-Dokumente*, Nr. 32.
70. Johann Peltz was sent to Berlin in order to learn to play the small cittern under the "English musician" by the name of Kitt. Peltz had returned to Dresden by 1627, and died sometime before 1633.
71. The wire-strung, quill-plucked cittern was a popular instrument of the Renaissance and Baroque. The small *Citherlein* referred to in the present document may well be of the kind mentioned by Praetorius in *Syntagma musicum II* (Wolfenbüttel, 1619), 55. The diminutive instrument had only made its way to Germany from England some three years earlier, and was then being practiced by various prominent lutenists.
72. Georg Wilhelm von Hohenzollern (b. 13 Nov. 1595; d. 1 Dec. 1640) became Elector of Brandenburg in 1619.

His Electoral Grace's most gracious resolution in all this is most humbly awaited by Peltz, who earnestly requests this.

29. SCHÜTZ TO JOHANN GEORG I (28 MARCH 1625)

Memorandum regarding a cash advance for Johann Peltz's journey to Berlin

[D-Dla: Loc. 8687/1, Kantoreiordnung so Kurfürst Moritz...1548, fol. 71r–v][73]

Memorandum regarding Johann Peltz.

Most Serene, Illustrious Elector, Most Gracious Lord: Inasmuch as I note that Peltz, who for his journey to Berlin ordered some clothing, boots, and other items, is unable to leave the city, Your Electoral Grace is herewith most humbly entreated to command most graciously that, of the allowance of 30 thalers deputed to him, he would like to have 18 thalers now. I submit everything, however, to Your Electoral Grace's most gracious pleasure. 28 March 1625.

Your Electoral Grace's most humble,
most obedient,
Heinrich Schütz, in his own hand.

[On the verso side and written in another hand]

20 *gulden*, 12 *groschen* to the instrumentalist Johann Peltz [Hans Peltzen] to give on account, for his departure to Berlin, 28 March 1625.

30. DRESDEN COURT MUSICIANS TO JOHANN GEORG I (11 JUNE 1625)

Petition to the Elector for payment of outstanding salaries

[D-Dla: Loc. 33 655, Schuldforderungen an die Kammer, Bd. 30, Nr. 207^h, fols. 1r–2v][74]

[Address]

To the Most Serene, Noble-Born Prince and Lord, Lord Johann Georg, Duke of Saxony, Jülich, Cleves and Berg, Grand Marshal and Elector of the Holy Roman Empire, Landgrave in Thuringia, Margrave of Meissen, and Burgrave of Magdeburg, Count of the Mark and Ravensberg, Lord of Ravenstein, and our Most Gracious Elector and Lord

---

73. Transcribed in *Schütz-GBr*, Nr. 17; *Schütz-Dokumente*, Nr. 33.
74. The document is in a copyist's hand except for *Capellmeister, sämtliche Vocalisten vndt Instrumentisten*, which is in Schütz's hand. Transcribed in *Schütz-Dokumente*, Nr. 34.

[Text]

Most Serene, Illustrious Elector.

We write in supplication most humbly to inform Your Electoral Serenity herewith out of direst need, according to which (as Your Electoral Serenity is probably aware) we are now entering the seventh quarter that we have not been paid.

It is true we live at present in the most humble hope and confidence that Your Electoral Serenity would most graciously take pity on us and our wives and poor little children, with whom the majority of us must endure much suffering. And despite our confidence this [payment] has once again failed to come, God have mercy on us. For that reason we do not know how in future we shall provide for ourselves and our dear ones, who should eat and who hunger, since we are losing everything hereby—household furniture and goods sold and pawned, credit lost, and great, insuperable debts incurred. For most of us it has also reached the point where the townspeople, with whom we live and board, neither want to house nor board us any longer, because we cannot keep up with payments or come to suitable terms with them.

Most Gracious Lord, the misery, moans, and lamentation of us and of our poor wives and children are so great, it seems impossible that this should be further endured by us.

May Your Electoral Serenity, out of innate electoral clemency and virtue, and for God's sake, take to heart our most humble, most ardent supplication and prayer, have most gracious pity on us and our dear ones, and issue a command so that we indeed, one of these days, get what is ours and which might be disbursed at the coming St. John's Fair [ca. 24 June], where one can come by everything pertaining to housekeeping for considerably less than afterwards. And thus the great misery, sighs, groans, and moans (whereby Your Electoral Serenity is little served) might be set aside and the Divine Service be celebrated by us with joy, and not with sighs and groans.

Almighty God shall richly reward Your Electoral Serenity in turn, and we remain willing and devoted, to beseech with our devout prayers for God's intercession in Your Electoral Serenity's continued good health, as well to extend our most humble, most obedient services.

Dresden, 11 June 1625.

Your Electoral Serenity's

most humble and obedient

Kapellmeister, singers, and instrumentalists.

31. SCHÜTZ TO JOHANN GEORG I (22 SEPTEMBER 1626)

Letter concerning the acquisition of property near Weissenfels and request for arrears

[D-Dla: Loc. 33 659, Schuldforderungen an die Kammer, Bd. 39, Nr. 216°, fols. 1r–v, 2v][75]

---

75. The document is in Schütz's hand. Transcribed in *Schütz-Dokumente*, Nr 39.

[Address]

To the Most Serene, Noble-Born Prince and Lord, Lord Johann Georg, Duke of Saxony, Jülich, Cleves and Berg, Grand Marshal and Elector of the Holy Roman Empire, Landgrave in Thuringia, Margrave of Meissen, and Burgrave of Magdeburg, Count of the Mark and Ravensberg, Lord of Ravenstein, and my Most Gracious Elector and Lord

[Text]

Most Serene, Noble-Born Elector.

To Your Electoral Serenity I plege my most humble, most obedient services to the best of my ability first and foremost, Most Gracious Lord, that Your Electoral Serenity, through your highly ordained Lord Councillor of the Treasury and Mines, Johann Georg von Osterhausen, accorded me most gracious promise of compensation and electoral clemency upon my repeated, most humble petitions and in consideration of my more than ten years of faithfully rendered service (without wishing to boast), and also especially on account of the losses heretofore specified by me in the previous costly years of supporting nearly all the *Kapellknaben*. Insofar as means could be made available, I am most grateful for it in most humble obedience.

If indeed I had reservations of importuning Your Electoral Serenity with the present petition of mine at this time, thus my most pressing need induced me to bring to the attention of Your Electoral Serenity with appropriate, proper, most humble devotion a solution about which my people notified me: namely, a few days ago in my homeland, a half mile from Weissenfels,[76] Hans Georg von Stahr, then his wife and his only son, and subsequently other co-feoffees but for a single brother, Hans Christoff von Stahr, still unmarried, died suddenly of the currently raging pestilence. Thus in these perilous times could this property easily become completely uninhabited and pass to Your Electoral Serenity.

To Your Electoral Serenity I submit herewith in most humble obedience anew, together with which I most humbly petition, that in the event of a vacancy Your Electoral Serenity would see me favorably in respect of the aforesaid Storkau property, which is valued at 6,000 *gulden* and said to carry a mortgage of 3,000 *gulden*, thus present this to me out of customary electoral generosity so that no person might be favored or preferred to me, and have delivered to me most gracious written assurance in this regard. In such a way it might perhaps come to pass that, without further trouble to Your Electoral

---

76. Weissenfels is situated on the River Saale, approximately 30 km south of Halle. It became a ducal residence with the establishment of the Saxe-Weissenfels line in 1656 on the death of the Saxon elector, Johann Georg I. August, for whose baptism Schütz was first called to Dresden in 1616, became the first Duke of Saxe-Weissenfels. It was also in Weissenfels that Moritz, Landgrave of Hesse-Kassel, recognized Schütz's uncommon musical talent, and the future Kapellmeister maintained strong ties to the town for the rest of his life.

Serenity, I might become entitled and participant in the promise of electoral, and to me of quite urgent, clemency.

Leaving everything once more to Your Electoral Serenity's most gracious pleasure, on which I pledge myself ready and duty bound to attend and to serve most humbly, together with the entire most praiseworthy Electoral House of Saxony, all my life to the best of my ability and means.

Dresden, 22 September 1626.
Your Electoral Serenity's
most humble, most obedient
Heinrich Schütz, Kapellmeister, in his own hand.

Moreover:
Most Serene, Noble Elector, Most Gracious Lord.

I humbly and not without urgency implore Your Electoral Serenity that, of my extraordinary stipend, which was added following the deaths of both the Kapellmeister Michael Praetorius and Rogier Michael of blessed memory, 250 *gulden* of it still owed to me might be paid out by your chamberlain at the current fair in Leipzig. In this way I could get by with my ordinary salary all the better. I in return remain beholden to serve Your Electoral Serenity with most humble diligence always.

Dated as above, 22 September 1626.
Your Electoral Serenity's
most humble and obedient
Heinrich Schütz, in his own hand.

32. SCHÜTZ TO JOHANN GEORG I (9 MAY 1627)

Letter requesting leave for travel to Italy

[D-Dla: Kurfürstliche Befehliche (Spezialreskripte), 1627–1628 [1627], fols. 330r–v, 335v][77]

[Address]

To the Most Serene, Noble-Born Prince and Lord, Lord Johann Georg, Duke of Saxony, Jülich, Cleves and Berg, Grand Marshal and Elector of the Holy Roman Empire, Landgrave in Thuringia, Margrave of Meissen, and Burgrave of Magdeburg, Count of the Mark and Ravensberg, Lord of Ravenstein, and my Most Gracious Elector and Lord

[Text]

Most Serene, Noble Elector.

---

77. The document is in Schütz's hand. Transcribed in *Schütz-Dokumente*, Nr. 41.

To Your Electoral Serenity, together with God's blessing for every beneficial welfare of the body and soul, I pledge my most humble and obedient services to the best of my abilities and means, first and foremost.

Most Gracious Lord. Your Electoral Serenity shall perhaps most graciously be able still to recall, how not only previously and in Christoph von Loss's lifetime, but rather again not long ago through our current inspector, the Lord Chief Councillor of the Treasury, I most humbly requested and made application in regard to a journey to Italy for six months. Most Gracious Elector, I have undertaken this plan not in any way out of frivolousness and wanderlust, but rather for various satisfactory reasons, foremost among them: previously I had been only a pupil in Italy, and heard no music anywhere as remarkable as in Venice, but now, with better developed understanding, I trust myself to draw from such a journey many lessons which shall be of use and benefit to me in my profession for my entire life. My mind thus induces me once again most submissively to approach Your Electoral Serenity with the present most humble letter of mine, may it please you to put this plan of mine into effect, most graciously to give me leave in this convenient springtime. And because I for my part do not intend to importune Your Electoral Serenity in this case with future expenses, thus do I live in the most humble, confident hope, on the other hand, that you nonetheless grant the continuation of my appointment in the interim and, from that which is owed me up to now, have 300 *gulden* disbursed for the journey and as much again next Michaelmas [Feast of St. Michael, 29 September], and remitted to the exchange.

And as Your Electoral Serenity, in as long as I have most humbly served you up to the present, will have perceived in me (as is hoped) nothing other than most humble sincerity and loyalty, I also solemnly pledge to you once again herewith: provided that my, in truth, modest services might also please Your Electoral Serenity in future, neither lord nor place nor anything else outside of an act of God shall deter me from appearing and presenting myself again obediently and honorably in my office at a determined time. Also everything good I shall have learned on this journey, I will always apply in service and for the reputation of Your Electoral Serenity, to the best of my most humble ability.

I most humbly await official, most gracious resolution, and am also disposed to present myself most humbly in person for an audience (in the case that Your Electoral Serenity is inclined toward entitling me to do so, as I hope) and to pick up the actual order myself, in accordance with which I will arrange my journey.

Finally, with utmost diligence, I commend anew Your Electoral Serenity, together with your dearly beloved family, to divine protection for every electoral well-being.

Dated at Dresden, 9 May 1627.
Your Electoral Serenity's
most humble and obedient
Heinrich Schütz, in his own hand.

33. SCHÜTZ TO THE DRESDEN COURT (AFTER 26 MAY 1627)

Memorandum regarding the Kapellknaben *Martin Zehm and Gabriel Günther following the death of Michael Möhlich*

[D-Dla: Loc. 8687/1, Kantoreiordnung so Kurfürst Moritz...1548, fol. 49r–v][78]

Memorandum.

I

Regarding the late Michael Mölich's two *Kapellknaben* left behind.[79]

These have both undergone voice changes and are of little or no use to the *Music*, except for the one with the little English cittern [*Citherlein*] which he is learning to play somewhat. If then both actively petition for promotion, our Most Gracious Lord's decision will be awaited as to whether His Electoral Serenity is satisfied [as follows]:

1. That Martin Zehm,[80] one of the two, would like to go to the Electress at Lichtenburg,[81] since she is somewhat well-disposed toward him and would wish to employ him in her service and to lend most gracious support for him to learn the lute.

2. That the second, namely, Gabriel Günther,[82] the lackey's son, set out with one of the nobility from Lusatia named Christoph von Hoym[83] on a journey to the imperial court for a half year, to listen to its music and perhaps then to grasp in some measure the style of singing. The same will be taken along by the nobleman, and in fact at his [i.e., the latter's] expense. Perhaps it may become evident in the meantime whether this boy, his voice having broken, might once again obtain to a good one, as I hope might happen, so that one can make use of him permanently.

In the meantime these two *Knaben* positions have been made vacant.

---

78. The manuscript bears no date, though *Schütz-GBr* (301) proposes 1625 as a possible year. Transcribed in *Schütz-GBr*, Nr. 23; *Schütz-Dokumente*, Nr. 42.

79. By 1587, Michael Mölich was as an instrumentalist and citharist at the *Hofkapelle* in Dresden, and later sent at the elector's expense to Italy, returning to the Saxon Court in July 1594. He was made second organist in 1620, and appears to have died either 26 or 27 May 1627. *Schütz-GBr*, 327–28.

80. There is no further information available on Martin Zehm, according to *Schütz-GBr*, 328.

81. The Princess Hedwig (b. 5 Aug. 1581; d. 26 Nov. 1641) was the daughter of Frederik II, King of Denmark, and became Electress of Saxony upon her marriage in 1602 to the Saxon Elector Christian II (b. 23 Sept. 1583; d. 23 Jun. 1611; reg. 1591–1611). Her brother was the long-ruling Christian IV, King of Denmark (reg. 1588–1648), her sister was the consort of James I, King of England, and her brother-in-law Johann Georg I, became Elector of Saxony after Christian II's death. As Electress Dowager, Hedwig was an independent, strong-willed, and influential figure.

82. There is no further information available on Gabriel Günther, apart from the fact that he was shot to death sometime before 1633. *Schütz-GBr*, 328.

83. Christoph von Hoym was appointed in 1647 as *Oberaufseher* (Chief Overseer) to the *Grafschaft* (Earldom or County) Mannsfeld.

2

Out of all the *Kapellknaben*, Wilhelm Günther's boy has a superior talent for music,[84] and is entirely and humbly at our Most Gracious Lord's disposal.

That His Electoral Serenity, through Friedrich Lebzelter or someone else,[85] have the said boy recommended to the imperial cornettist Giovanni Sansoni and transferred there [i.e., Vienna] for a couple of years.[86] His Electoral Serenity will make a musician of him, who on his own will be of greater value than several others combined.

3

Regarding the *Kapellknaben*

[The document ends here.]

34. SCHÜTZ TO JOHANN GEORG I (2 AUGUST 1627)

Petition for the second of three electoral printing patents

[D-Dla: Loc. 10 757, Privilegia, Bd. 2, 1616–1628, fol. 590r, 591v, 592r][87]

[Address]

To the Most Serene, Noble-Born Prince and Lord, Lord Johann Georg, Duke of Saxony, Jülich, Cleves and Berg, Grand Marshal and Elector of the Holy Roman Empire, Landgrave in Thuringia, Margrave of Meissen, and Burgrave of Magdeburg, Count of the Mark and Ravensberg, Lord of Ravenstein, and my Most Gracious Elector and Lord

[Text]

Most Serene, Most Noble Elector.

To Your Electoral Serenity, I pledge my most humble and obedient, most diligent services, first and foremost. Most Gracious Lord, to Your Electoral Serenity I submit herewith most humbly for your information how I heretofore composed some simple, new melodies on Dr. Cornelius Becker's psalms and set them to music

---

84. Wilhelm Günther, a Dresdner, was sent at the elector's expense to Italy in 1596. In 1604 he was favored with a house, and in 1611 received a pension of 200 thalers. In 1632, he was still in office. *Schütz-GBr*, 325.
85. Friedrich Lebzelter had the title of *Geheimer Cammerdiener* (Privy Chamber Servant), an agent of the Electoral Court, who in addition to fulfilling certain political duties was the purchaser of art objects for the court. According to *Schütz-GBr* (328), he was the brother-in-law of the Kreuzkantor Christoph Neander (1589–1625). He was active in Hamburg from 1632 to 1634, and died probably at the beginning of 1640.
86. Giovanni Sansoni (Johann Samson) (b. 1593; d. 15 Nov. 1648) was a famous virtuoso on the bassoon and cornetto, who from 1619 until the time of death was an instrumentalist in the Viennese court *cappella*. In addition to being the highest paid instrumentalist by far at the imperial court, Sansoni enjoyed a great reputation as a teacher, as numerous students came to him from various countries to study.
87. Fine, unsigned court copy. The petition includes a draft of the title page of the psalter, transcribed in *Schütz-Dokumente*, Nr. 43.

[i.e., harmonized] for the morning and evening prayer of those *Kapellknaben* committed to my care. But after these fell time and again into the hands of other people, I was counseled and exhorted repeatedly to carry on with this work I had commenced. Thus, Most Gracious Elector and Lord, upon the request and in the opinion of many pious, kind-hearted Christians, I have now completed this work by the Grace of God, as can be seen in detail from the enclosed title page. It is now at the printers and shall be published and appear for the coming Michaelmas fair [i.e., September 29], God willing.

But I am also afraid that this might someday be reprinted or republished anew. Thus it is my most humble petition submitted to Your Electoral Serenity, should it please you most graciously, to endow me with a patent. To receive this from Your Electoral Serenity, I remain most humble and indebted.

Dated at Dresden, 2 August 1627.
Your Electoral Serenity's
most humble
Heinrich Schütz.

35. SCHÜTZ TO THE DRESDEN COURT (? SEPTEMBER 1627)

Proposed index of musicians to accompany Johann Georg I to the Electoral Assembly in Mühlhausen

[D-Dla: Loc. 8687/1, Kantoreiordnung so Kurfürst Moritz...1548, fol. 53r–v][88]

Register of those persons from the [company of] musicians who could be taken along to Mühlhausen both for attendance on days with church services and at table.[89]

Full Register.

1. Heinrich Schütz, Kapellmeister.

Instrumentalists.
2. Wilhelm Günther
3. Augustus Tax
4. Carlo Farina[90]

---

88. The document is in Schütz's hand. Transcribed in *Schütz-GBr*, Nr. 21; *Schütz-Dokumente*, Nr. 44.
89. The Electoral Assembly, or *Kollegtag*, was held from 4 October to 5 November 1627, for which occasion Schütz composed the *Da pacem, domine* (SWV 465).
90. Carlo Farina (b. ca. 1600; d. ca. 1640) was a native of Mantua. From 1627 to 1628, Farina was employed as violinist in the Dresden *Hofkapelle*, and from 1636 to 1637 as municipal musician (*Ratsmusiker*) in Danzig. He spent the remainder of his life in the service of Empress Eleonora Gonzaga (b. 23 Sept. 1598; d. 27 Jun. 1655) in Vienna. As a composer, Farina produced five books of dances, published in Dresden between 1626 and 1628. *Schütz-GBr*, 326.

5. Johann Köckeritz
6. Ernst Trost[91]
7. Friedrich Sultz

Singers.
8. Johann Hasselt,[92] provided he returns home from his travels as expected
9. Sebastian Hirnschrötl[93]
10. Philipp [Jacob] Nusser
11. Johann Kramer,[94] bass

Organist.
12. Johann Müller[95]

Beyond this, the following could be included:

13. Johann Nauwach[96]
14. [Johann] Peltz, with the small English cittern.

Two Discantists

Three Instrumentalist *Knaben*

Two coaches would be needed, and a traveling carriage for the instruments and baggage, as well as for the *Knaben*.

---

91. Next to nothing is known about the trombone player, Ernst Trost, other than that he died before 1633. *Schütz-GBr*, 326.
92. Little is known about Johann Hasselt. He married in 1625, at which time he is identified as a chamber musician at the Dresden Court. His name is no longer mentioned in the register after 1632. *Schütz-GBr*, 326.
93. Sebastian Hirnschrötl was born in Ingolstadt, and from 1 January 1605 to 1610 was employed as an alto in the imperial court in Vienna with an annual salary of 60 *gulden*. In 1612, he was a member of the Dresden *Hofkapelle* where, in 1632, he is described as a tenor. He was still at the Saxon court as late as 1651. *Schütz-GBr*, 327.
94. Johann Kramer, according to the dedication in Samuel Scheidt's *Padouanen* of 1621, was at that time a bass in the archiepiscopal Kapelle in Halle. He may have been a member of the Dresden Kapelle in 1627, but is absent from the register of 1632. *Schütz-GBr*, 327.
95. According to *Schütz-GBr* (327), Johann Müller was born in Dresden and at some point in his career studied under Marco Giuseppe Peranda (b. ca. 1625; d. 12 Jan. 1675).
96. Johann Nauwach (b. ca. 1595; d. ca. 1630) was one of the first German composers to follow in the footsteps of Caccini. He was born in Brandenburg, and went to Dresden as a *Kapellknabe* in 1607. He was sent by Johann Georg I to Carlo Emanuele I, Duke of Savoy (b. 12 Jan. 1562; d. 26 Jul. 1630), for two years in 1612, and from there to Florence to study lute with Lorenzo Allegri (b. 1567; d. 1648). In 1625, he was named electoral Saxon chamber musician, and died probably around 1630. His most important works are: *Libro primo di arie passaggiate a una voce per cantar e sonar* (Dresden, 1623) and *Erster Theil teutscher Villanellen* (Dresden, 1627), which was occasioned for the same wedding in Torgau as Schütz's *Dafne*. Nauwach's 1627 publication is the first German collection of continuo *Lieder*.

Greatly abbreviated register of the above-mentioned persons.

1. Heinrich Schütz, Kapellmeister

Instrumentalists.
2. Augustus Tax
3. Wilhelm Günther
4. Carlo Farina
5. Ernst Trost

Singers.
6. Bastian [i.e., Sebastian Hirnschrötl]
7. [Hans] Hasselt, provided he returns home
8. [Johann] Kramer

Organist.
9. Johann Müller
10. Johann Nauwach

Two Discantists

Two Instrumentalist *Knaben*

One cannot, however, make too many alterations without running into difficulty, and should it please our Most Gracious Lord to decide forthwith in favor of the full register, I think it advisable that we should have space together at a large table if an *ordinance* could be given to the caretaker of the house to set it up all the more stoutly. Beyond this: two or three meals for the fellows.

36. *DA PACEM, DOMINE* FOR THE ELECTORAL ASSEMBLY IN MÜHLHAUSEN (4 OCTOBER TO 5 NOVEMBER 1627): DEDICATION AND PERFORMANCE INSTRUCTIONS (ORIGINAL LANGUAGE: LATIN AND GERMAN)

[According to *Schütz-GBr*, 301, the work was available only in manuscript in the Gottholdschen Bibliothek in Königsberg (Kaliningrad), and thus probably destroyed in 1944.][97]

---

97. *NSA* 38. The text of *Da pacem, Domine* (SWV 465) is found in Philipp Spitta's edition of the work in *SA* 15, which edition is used as the principal source for Werner Bittinger's edition in the *NSA*.

[Latin]

Grant peace, Lord. And long live Ferdinand, the most unconquerable emperor: the most holy men of Mainz, Trier, Cologne: the most glorious men of Bavaria, Saxony, Brandenburg: the Electors of the Holy Roman Empire—seven most august men, gods of our Germany, blessed tutelary deities, bringers of peace![98]

Heinrich Schütz, Kapellmeister of the Most Serene Elector of Saxony, wishes, and expresses his wish with nine voices, that these men may, with the protection and help of God most high and everlasting, with the Temple of Janus firmly closed,[99] establish and secure altars of peace and liberty in imperial Mühlhausen.

[German]

Ordinance of this piece:

Primus Chorus for five voices [*5. Vocum*], can be performed by five viols, and to which one or two voices can sing quietly [*submissè*]:

Secundus Chorus is for four singers which articulate the text with elegant grace [*gratiâ*], and otherwise sing fully. It is also possible to have this choir set up separately from the first one.

37. SCHÜTZ TO AN UNNAMED PERSON (OCTOBER/NOVEMBER 1627)

Itemized list of unpaid salary following the deaths of Michael Praetorius and Rogier Michael

[D-Dla: Loc. 33 659, Schuldforderungen an die Kammer, Bd. 39, Nr. 216°, fol. 13r][100]

What is owed to me of my increased salary following the deaths of Praetorius and Rogier Michael:

1625	Quarter year,	*Crucis*	[Feast of the Cross, September 14]	50 *gulden*
	Quarter year,	*Lucia*	[Feast of St. Lucy, December 13]	50 *gulden*
1626	Quarter year,	*Reminiscere*	[Second week of Lent]	50 *gulden*
	"	*Trinitatis*	[Trinity]	50 *gulden*
	"	*Crucis*		50 *gulden*
	"	*Lucia*		50 *gulden*

---

98. The main reason for the assembly of this Electoral Diet, 4 October to 5 November 1627, was to find a way through compromise out of the political and military turmoil that was tearing apart central Europe. The assembly was largely unsuccessful and the war continued for another two decades.
99. The lost Temple of Janus stood in the Roman Forum and had doors at either end and a statue of Janus inside. When the doors of the temple were opened, Rome was at war; when they were closed, peace prevailed.
100. The document is in Schütz's hand. Transcribed in *Schütz-Dokumente*, Nr. 47.

1627	Quarter year,	*Reminiscere*	50 *gulden*
	"	*Trinitatis*	50 *gulden*
	"	*Crucis*	50 *gulden*
	"	*Lucia*	50 *gulden*
Total			350 [sic] *gulden*

Nota bene: What I, to my knowledge, have received from all claims:

100 *gulden* from the Lord Chamberlain prior to the wedding in Torgau,
100 *gulden* for the present Electoral Assembly in Mühlhausen.

38. JOHANN GEORG I TO JOHANN SAUTOR, COURT CHAMBERLAIN (15 NOVEMBER 1627)

Memorandum concerning Schütz's distressed financial circumstances

[D-Dla: Loc. 33 659, Schuldforderungen an die Kammer, Bd. 39, Nr. 216°, fol. 9r][101]

By the Grace of God, Johann Georg, Duke of Saxony, Jülich, Cleves and Berg, Elector. Loyal and Beloved Subject.

We have been most humbly solicited by our Kapellmeister and dear, faithful Heinrich Schütz that, since he has a considerable amount to claim from our treasury in salary, stipend, and monetary expenses for the *Kapellknaben*, this claim of his might be disbursed to him at two or three different fairs.

He stated that he was in debt to his relative Michael Hartmann,[102] the bookkeeper. Thus we most graciously desire that you would not only correctly balance accounts with the aforesaid Kapellmeister, but rather enquire of the bookkeeper regarding his [Schütz's] debts and circumstances as well, and together with him consider by what means he may be most conveniently satisfied and paid at various appointed times. Most humbly inform us of this in writing for future resolution. This is our ruling.

Dated at Weissensee,[103] 15 November 1627.

Johann Georg, Elector.[104]

---

101. The fine scribal copy is signed by Johann Georg I.
102. In the document, Hartmann is described as Schütz's *Schwager*, which in its strictest sense means "brother-in-law." At the time, however, as with the Latin *affini*, *Schwager* (m.) or *Schwägerin* (f.) (from the verb *verschwägern*) meant only that one individual was related to another through marriage.
103. Weissensee is located roughly 55 km east of Mühlhausen and approximately 30 km north of Erfurt. Johann Georg and his retinue were likely traveling home to Dresden following the Assembly of Electors in Mühlhausen.
104. Signed by the Elector.

39. JOHANN SAUTOR TO JOHANN GEORG I (11 DECEMBER 1627)

Report detailing the nature of Schütz's debts and strained finances

[D-Dla: Loc. 33 659, Schuldforderungen an die Kammer, Bd. 39, Nr. 216°, fols. 11r–12r][105]

Most Gracious Elector and Lord.

In most humble accordance with Your Electoral Serenity's most gracious command issued to me, I had a statement of account prepared of arrears owed to your Kapellmeister Heinrich Schütz in salary, stipend, and expense money for the *Kapellknaben*, which Your Electoral Serenity hereby most graciously recommends, as this claim runs to 1534 *gulden*, 3 *groschen*, 6 *denarii* [*pfennige*]. Thus on Your Electoral Serenity's aforesaid most gracious command I have discussed with the tax bookkeeper, Michael Hartmann, how he could be assisted in this matter. I was then informed by him that indeed he for his part advanced him [Schütz] several hundred *gulden* and stood security for him in connection to [loans from] others as well. He is urgently in need not only of his share, but also the creditors of theirs, and was exhorted by them for payment.

Therefore, with the aforementioned bookkeeper, I devised a plan, since we note that Your Electoral Serenity would gladly see him, Schütz, as a distressed servant, assisted in this matter: that Your Electoral Serenity, at your most gracious pleasure, issue a command to the main office for collecting taxes to see that Your Electoral Serenity's revenue-department pay such a sum of money as he is entitled to in *denarii*, advanced from outstanding taxes to be collected at various times, and afterwards deduct it from the chamber budget, so that he, the Kapellmeister, could receive his payment.

What Your Electoral Serenity now most graciously rules on this matter shall be most obediently carried out by me. I duly pledge myself to your most humble, faithful service always.

Dated at Dresden, 11 December 1627.

Extract:

What remains to be paid to the Kapellmeister Heinrich Schütz from the Electoral Saxon revenue-department:

1004 *gulden*, 3 *groschen*, 6 *pfennige*	Salary according to Georg Lehmann's statement [of account]
350 *gulden*	Stipend added to the Salary
180 *gulden*	Money for boarding in regard to the two *Kapellknaben*, according to Christian Schweissken's statement [of account]

Sum total
1534 *gulden*, 3 *groschen*, 6 *pfennige*.

---

105. Unsigned document.

40. JOHANN GEORG I TO JOHANN SAUTOR (18 DECEMBER 1627)

Command that Schütz be paid arrears to his income

[D-Dla: Loc. 33 659, Schuldforderungen an die Kammer, Bd. 39, Nr. 216°, fol. 8r][106]

By the Grace of God, Johann Georg, Duke of Saxony, Jülich, Cleves and Berg, Elector.

Loyal and Beloved Liege.

Your report and the enclosed account statement were most humbly placed before us, concerning our Kapellmeister and dear, faithful Heinrich Schütz, of arrears to his salary, stipend, and boarding expenses for the *Kapellknaben*, which up to the present quarter including the Feast of St. Lucy[107] [13 December] runs in total to 1534 *gulden*, 3 *groschen*, 6 *denarii*.

We thus issue a command to the chief collectors for the amount suggested by you and the bookkeeper in the tax office. We desire most graciously that you should act next in accordance to it. This is our ruling.

Dated at Pforta,[108] 18 December 1627.

Johann Georg, Elector.[109]

---

106. This document is written in a copyist's hand, signed by Johann Georg I.
107. Also, Saint Lucia.
108. Pforta, about 5 km west of Naumburg, was a Cistercian monastery founded in 1137 and became one of three princely schools (*Fürstenschulen*) established by the Protestant Elector Moritz, Duke of Saxony in 1543. The schools accepted only the most promising, literate students between the ages of eleven and fifteen regardless of background, and provided room, board, and education for six years in preparation for university studies. The schools in Pforta, Meissen, and Grimma provided the primary education for some of the land's best administrators, scientists, philosophers, poets, and musicians. Pforta alone counts among its alumni: the musicians Johann Hermann Schein (b. 20 Jan. 1586; d. 19 Nov. 1630) and Erhard Bodenschatz (b. 1576; d. 1636), the poet Friedrich Gottlieb Klopstock, and the philosophers Johann Gottlieb Fichte and Friedrich Nietzsche.
109. Signed by the Elector.

2
Middle Age (1628–44)

41. SCHÜTZ TO GEORG PFLUGK, MARSHAL OF THE PALACE (EARLY 1628)

Memorandum regarding violins ordered from Cremona and a request for money for Caspar Kittel's return from Italy

[D-Dla: Loc. 8687/1, Kantoreiordnung so Kurfürst Moritz...1548, fol. 52r][1]

Memorandum of what to mention to the Lord Marshal of the Palace on matters [pertaining to] the musicians.[2]

1. The enclosed communication might be registered with Friedrich Lebzelter regarding the manufacture of two discant violins and three tenor violins in Cremona insofar as previously, during the late Osterhausen's lifetime,[3] he [Osterhausen] was already instructed to order the same from Italy for the support of the *Music*, inasmuch as such good instruments as these will not be obtained in any other place in such quality, should the present old master pass away.

2. Since Caspar Kittel, who has resided in Italy now into his fourth year, should come back next Easter, it would thus be most necessary that perhaps 50 crowns [*Cronen*] (which amounts to approximately as many Spanish thalers) be remitted to him herein

---

1. The document is in Schütz's hand. Transcribed in *Schütz-GBr*, Nr. 24; *Schütz-Dokumente*, Nr. 48.
2. Georg Pflugk (d. 12 Mar. 1642) was Marshal of the Palace from 1628.
3. Johann Georg von Osterhausen was Marshal of the Palace from 1611 until his death in 1627.

for the purchase of various, suitable musical compositions, of which rather little has been procured up to now and indeed ought to be in our Kapelle. These compositions will remain in use for a long time thereafter and shall be a model of instrumental [composition] in the catalog of books.

An Ordinance must also be given to Lebzelter in this instance.

3. With regard to Martin Zehm, one of the youths of the late Michael Mölich, a certificate must be issued and the old one should be taken back from him.

42. DRESDEN COURT MUSICIANS DIRECTED TO JOHANN GEORG I (PALM SUNDAY, 6 APRIL 1628 [JULIAN CALENDAR])

Memorandum requesting payment on behalf of the musicians at the Dresden Court

[D-Dla: Loc. 8687/1, Kantoreiordnung so Kurfürst Moritz...1548, fol. 56r]⁴

The Most Serene, Noble Elector of Saxony, Burgrave of Magdeburg, our Most Gracious Lord, is most humbly reminded by the undersigned that little has been given to them up to now in settlement of their salary, in particular to those who were not present in Mühlhausen and Torgau,⁵ indeed not much more than a month's worth in the space of a year, and thus the distress is quite great.

They petition most humbly that His Electoral Serenity would most graciously have them provided with something against the approaching Easter feast. They are willing to forbear, and to repay this most obediently with diligent service. Dresden, Palm Sunday [6/16 April], 1628.

His Electoral Serenity's
most humble, most obedient
Instrumentalists
and
Singers.

---

4. The document is in Schütz's hand. Transcribed in *Schütz-GBr*, Nr. 25; *Schütz-Dokumente*, Nr. 49.
5. Schütz may have been referring to the wedding celebrations in Torgau, which took place in the spring of 1627. These were extended festivities celebrating the marriage of the Elector's daughter, Sophie Eleonore, Duchess of Saxony (b. 23 Nov. 1609; d. 2 Jun. 1671) to Georg II, Landgrave of Hesse-Darmstadt (b. 17 Mar. 1605; d. 11 Jun. 1661), which ceremony took place on 1 April. Schütz and the Kapelle spent a month in Torgau at Schloss Hartenfels to prepare for and participate in the lavish entertainments and services. On 13 April, Schütz's staged the pastoral tragic-comedy *Dafne* at the castle, based on Martin Opitz's (b. 23 Dec. 1597; d. 20 Aug. 1639) adaptation of a libretto by Ottavio Rinuccini (b. 20 Jan. 1562; d. 28 Mar. 1621). The other event to which Schütz refers is the *Kurfürstentage* (Electoral Diet), 4 October to 5 November 1627, which involved the Protestant Electors of Brandenburg and Saxony. For the occasion Schütz composed his *Da pacem, Domine* [SWV 465].

43. SCHÜTZ TO JOHANN GEORG I (22 APRIL 1628)

Memorandum repeating his request for permission for leave to travel to Italy

[D-Dla: Loc. 8687/1, Kantoreiordnung so Kurfürst Moritz...1548, fols. 57r, 67v][6]

[Address]

Most humble memorandum, to
His Electoral Serenity of Saxony,
His Most Gracious Lord

[Text]

Most Illustrious, Most Noble Elector, Most Gracious Lord. This most humble, brief and respectful memorandum appears before Your Electoral Serenity in most obedient devotion, as I await your most gracious, venerable, and ultimate decision concerning my intended and fully prepared travel to Italy. For if those who would gladly increase their worldly goods do their utmost repeatedly in connection to Your Electoral Serenity, why should I not also strive more than once, most humbly, to gain that which serves me in the advancement of my learned liberal art, and in other virtues as well?

As Your Electoral Serenity will undoubtedly understand the not unapparent usefulness of my journey, so on the other hand I remain in the certain hope that Your Electoral Serenity will not refuse my request perhaps for lesser reasons or possibly because of smaller dangers along the way (from which no man is safe, even in his own home), inasmuch as I intend in this case to take good care of myself and to set out in a large company, which in part is known to me.

I would remind Your Electoral Serenity most humbly of this: that if someone out of supposed good affection should appear to oppose me before Your Electoral Serenity, this would certainly not satisfy my mind in any way but only perturbs my well-disposed thoughts, and shamefully robs me of the time in which indeed I could have made more than one useful journey such as this.

But in the end I submit myself completely to Your Electoral Serenity's superior discretion, with the most humble declaration that I came upon these bold ideas for your sake (I would, for God's sake, take up and acknowledge herein) and how from the start not in any way out of frivolousness, for the sake of pleasure alone, or wanderlust, but rather out of the impulse of perhaps attaining to a better spirit. Thus I shall hope that Almighty God may indeed not dispose and turn Your Electoral Serenity's heart unkindly toward this undertaking of mine. Therefore I appeal to divine omnipo-

---

6. The document is in Schütz's hand. Transcribed in *Schütz-GBr*, Nr. 26; *Schütz-Dokumente*, Nr. 50.

tence in the meantime, and in profound humility commend myself to your hitherto customary electoral favor.

Dresden, 22 April 1628.
Your Electoral Serenity's
ever most humble, most obedient
Heinrich Schütz, in his own hand.

44. SCHÜTZ TO JOHANN GEORG I (10 JULY 1628)

Request for a travel pass for his journey to Venice and for a letter of introduction

[D-Dla: Loc. 9217/1, Kriegswesen im Reich, 81. Buch, 1628, fol. 179r–v][7]

Most Serene, Illustrious Elector.

To Your Electoral Serenity, I pledge my most humble and obedient services in faithful diligence always, first and foremost.

Most Gracious Lord. Insofar as Your Electoral Serenity has decided most graciously in favor of my most humble request and petition, and most graciously consented to the carrying out of my planned journey [to Italy], I am once again most humbly thankful.

In addition to this then I am very much in need of valid documentation. My most humble petition is therefore directed to Your Electoral Serenity, should it most graciously please you, to show me as your unworthy servant and native subject the great kindness, as well as for better and more secure travel there and back, of issuing a passport. Should Your Electoral Serenity have no objections, I would also then most humbly request to have issued to me likewise a small letter of recommendation addressed to the Grand Duchess of Florence,[8] as I hope by this means to have assured admission to her court. To earn this in most humble obedience from Your Electoral Serenity, I pledge myself most dutifully and willingly. Dated at Dresden, 10 July 1628.

Your Electoral Serenity's
most humble and obedient servant,
Heinrich Schütz.

---

7. The document is in a copyist's hand, signed by Schütz. Transcribed in *Schütz-Dokumente*, Nr. 51.
8. The Grand Duke of Tuscany at this time was Ferdinando II de' Medici (b. 14 Jul. 1610; d. 23 May 1670) who was still a minor at the time of the death of his twenty-year-old father, Cosimo II (d. 28 Feb. 1621). Consequently, a regency government was established with the young Grand Duke's mother, Maria Magdalena of Austria (b. 7 Oct. 1589; d. 01 Nov. 1631) and her mother-in-law, the real power behind the throne, Christina (Chretienne) of Lorraine (b. 16 Aug. 1565; d. 19 Dec. 1637).

45. SCHÜTZ TO GEORG PFLUGK (14 JULY 1628)

Memorandum concerning the individual circumstances of four musicians at the Dresden Court

[D-Dla: Loc. 8687/1, Kantoreiordnung so Kurfürst Moritz...1548, fols. 60r-v, 64v][9]

[Address]

Memorandum on matters pertaining to musicians, dated 14 July 1628

[Text]

Memorandum of what appears necessary to discuss in matters pertaining to musicians.

1.

That the Electoral Saxon Lord Marshal of the Palace might intercede with our Most Gracious Lord by way of a most humble letter of recommendation on behalf of the matured *Kapellknabe*, Johann Vierdanck, who until now has resided with Wilhelm Günther, in order that he [Vierdanck] might obtain and bring along with him a most gracious command to Friedrich Lebzelter from His Electoral Serenity, so that he might be able to continue his studies with the imperial cornettist Sansoni.

2.

Inasmuch as the Electress Our Most Gracious Lady[10] has permitted her former discantist Gabriel Günther, who heretofore lived with the late Michael Mölich, to undertake a journey to Gudeborn with a member of the nobility, namely, Christoph von Hoym, it is necessary that instructions in this instance be sent to the treasury and that the aforementioned *Knabe* be discharged, as of the last Feast of St. John [24 June] 1628 until further notice of his return.

3.

Accordingly too, I, Heinrich Schütz, as per Michael Mölich's testimony which I have in my possession, upon her earnest command, took the one discantist, by the name of Martin Zehm, to me for board, accommodation, etc., immediately following Michael Mölich's death. To the aforementioned Marshal of the Palace I thus direct my dutiful petition to have a brief written command issued to the treasury in this matter and to credit me for the said *Knabe*, so that the customary allowance is remitted to me for that

---

9. The document is in Schütz's hand. Transcribed in *Schütz-GBr*, Nr. 27; *Schütz-Dokumente*, Nr. 52.
10. Magdalena Sibylle of Prussia (b. 31 Dec. 1586; d. 12 Feb. 1659), the daughter of Albrecht Friedrich, Duke of Prussia (b. 29 Apr. 1553; d. 27 Apr. 1618), became Electress of Saxony upon her marriage to Johann Georg I at Torgau on 19 July 1607.

period from the Feast of St. Lucy [13 December] 1627 up to 14 July 1628, and after which this *Knabe's* position might be completely stricken.

4.

The former trumpeter[11] and apprentice instrumentalist by the name of Michael Fischer, who until now resided with Christian Scheffer,[12] and indeed whose surname appeared at the past Feast of St. John [June 24], to have from that same time stricken [from the register] in the treasury.

5.

With regard to Johann Kramer, the bass, I mention by virtue of my office, that in view of the urgency of the matter, and that he is the best in his profession here, it would be a mistake to allow him to be lost for the sake of minor arrears in [his] salary. This man would certainly obtain an employer again, though I doubt that we would again acquire the likes of him for this money. He is moreover a pious, gentle, and peaceable man, and I for my part beg that if the Lord Marshal of the Palace were able to retain him with an assurance from the Lord Chamberlain, he should not neglect to do so.

46. SCHÜTZ TO JOHANN GEORG I (3 NOVEMBER 1628)

Letter regarding his late arrival in Venice and a request for additional funding from the Dresden Court

[D-Dla: Loc. 8687/1, Kantoreiordnung so Kurfürst Moritz…1548, fols. 62r–v, 63v][13]

[Address]

To the Most Serene, Noble-Born Prince and Lord, Lord Johann Georg, Duke of Saxony, Jülich, Cleves and Berg, Grand Marshal and Elector of the Holy Roman Empire, Landgrave in Thuringia, Margrave of Meissen, and Burgrave of Magdeburg, Count of the Mark and Ravensberg, Lord of Ravenstein, and my Most Gracious Elector and Lord

[Text]

Most Serene, Most Noble Elector, to Your Electoral Serenity, together with my personal desire for every highest, most blessed welfare of soul and body from God, I pledge my most obedient services to the best of my ability and means, first and foremost.

---

11. *Schütz-GBr* (94) transcribes the original text as *Trommeler*, read *Trommeter*.
12. *Schütz-GBr* (94) suggests perhaps *Schossern* or *Schaffern*, but Schütz's handwriting clearly has the name as *Scheffern*. Christian Scheffer was instrumentalist and trumpeter at the Saxon court, and died before 1633. *Schütz-GBr*, 329.
13. Transcribed in *Schütz-GBr*, Nr. 28; *Schütz-Dokumente*, Nr. 53.

Middle Age (1628–44)

Most Gracious Lord, out of indebted, most humble duty, I have not wanted to neglect notifying Your Electoral Serenity most obediently herewith, that, indeed, in accordance with your most gracious permission granted me, I set about and departed as quickly as possible from Dresden on my intended journey to Italy. However, on account of the closed passes, partly in Germany and partly at the Italian borders, I was not able to reach Venice until just a few days ago. My Most Gracious Lord, I live now in the confident hope once more that, with God's help, this journey of mine shall be in many respects decidedly beneficial to me in acquiring additional knowledge in my, in truth, modest profession. Hence it is no less my ardent desire, and I am most humbly and fully confident, Your Electoral Serenity shall not look upon my absence in the interim with displeasure, neither occupy nor invest my position with anyone else, which up to now I have served according to my most humble ability, but rather to leave it open for and to me until my earliest return, which shall always follow without delay and most obediently upon Your Electoral Serenity's most gracious command, barring an act of God.

Beyond this, Most Gracious Elector and Lord, I am also most humbly thankful, not without due cause, that Your Electoral Serenity nonetheless in my absence has most graciously approved and granted the continuation of my established salary, through which means I was indeed fortunately able to undertake and, up to now, continue my travel. But since, according to the urgency of the matter, carrying through this plan of mine at my expense alone will of necessity weigh very heavily and painfully upon me; in consideration that the way here, which dragged on into ten weeks, already cost me a considerable amount; moreover for the purchase additionally of many new, beautiful musical compositions, there will be increased expenses. Inasmuch as I perceive that the entire situation has changed greatly since the time when I was first here in these parts, and that the music which is practiced at princely tables, comedies, ballets, and similar representations, has now markedly improved and progressed, thus I dare say I have pressing reason to petition Your Electoral Serenity most humbly that you, as a potentate blessed by God and to whom it will be an insignificant expense, at your most gracious pleasure, might this once have something additional [*extraordinare*] ordered into the exchange here, to put me your loyal and most humble servant in good stead. In return I assure Your Electoral Serenity with due devotion that this, like my purpose in these places here, is intended and undertaken by me for nothing other than your reputation alone and for the better qualification of my own person in your most humble service. Hence in future too, and as long as God grants me life, I shall show and demonstrate in return, always to the best of my ability and means, my indebted, due gratitude to Your Electoral Serenity more in deed, through my most humble service, than now with broad diffusion of words, God willing.

To Your Electoral Serenity on this most important point (especially now abroad), I commend myself with utmost and foremost diligence, and with absolute loyalty, to your most gracious, venerable resolution, you, however, together with all the most praiseworthy Electoral House, to divine protection. Dated at Venice on 3 November of the new calendar, 1628.[14]

Your Electoral Serenity's
most humble, most obedient servant,
Heinrich Schütz, in his own hand.

47. *BECKER PSALTER* (FREIBERG, 1628): TITLE PAGE AND DEDICATION TO ELECTRESS HEDWIG, DUCHESS OF SAXONY (6 SEPTEMBER 1627)

[Title page]

Psalms of David[15]
heretofore made into German verse
by Dr. Cornelius Becker
and now,
with one hundred and
three original melodies, among them
ninety-two new and
eleven old ones,
according to common contrapuntal style in
four voices, set
by
Heinrich Schütz,
Electoral Saxon Kapellmeister,
together with two appended
registers at the end, the one according to the alphabet, the
other to the old familiar melodies to
which each psalm
can be sung.
With special patent of the Elector of Saxony
Printed at Freiberg, in Meissen
at Georg Hoffmann's,
Anno 1628.

---

14. The Gregorian Calendar (New Style, NS), our modern civil calendar, was introduced by Pope Gregory XIII in 1582. The new calendar was intended to address a problem with the Julian Calendar (Old Style, OS) whereby a miscalculation of the vernal equinox caused Easter celebrations to appear progressively earlier. By the time the Gregorian Calendar (NS) was introduced, the Julian system (OS) had slipped some ten days behind the New Calendar. Protestant countries, however, wary of Rome's motives and concerned about appearances, were particularly slow to adopt the new calendar, and as a consequence it is not uncommon to see documents from this period dated according to both Old Style and New Style.
15. SWV 97a–256a; RISM A/I/8 S 2282; *NSA* 40; *SA* 16.

[Dedication]

To the Most Serene, Noble Princess and
Lady, Lady
Hedwig
Born of the Royal House of Denmark,
Electress, also Duchess
of Saxony, Jülich, Cleves and Berg, Landgravine of Thuringia, Margravine of Meissen,
Burgravine of Magdeburg, Countess of the Mark and Ravensberg, Lady of Ravenstein,
and Dowager, my Most Gracious Electress and Lady.

Most Serene, Noble Electress, to Your Electoral Serenity, I offer my most humble, most obliging services with most indebted diligence, first and foremost.

Most Gracious Lady, the little psalm book of the late Dr. Cornelius Becker, with its old melodies, has now become all but universal in many regions, countries, and towns as the Christian foundation in churches, schools, and homes. Hence a devout mind might perhaps deem it unnecessary or even inappropriate that I should now wish to provide the same with new and thus hitherto unknown melodies. Indeed, in the first place, with regard to the old, traditional melodies which have now been in use for almost a hundred years in the special promotion of the Gospel Truth, I have not just left them as they are, but rather for my part, much more than that, would publicly praise and testify that I consider several of them to have been more likely conceived by the heavenly seraphim in praise of their creator than by men: just as these old melodies together with the pious text to which they were originally composed are duly retained unaltered and collectively commended in the present psalm booklet. Thus, on the other hand, and as my second point, it did not seem appropriate to me that such old melodies by Doctor Luther and songs by other pious Christians (primarily psalms and *Lieder* which otherwise are customarily only sung in certain seasons) should be reproduced without identifying them in the present psalter book, and thereby to have these blessed, equally pious songs and text by the late Dr. Becker appear and be heard in Christian assemblies as if in borrowed clothing.

In consideration of which, I heretofore set for my domestic music, and for morning and evening prayers for the *Kapellknaben* committed to my care, several simple new melodies to the inspirited psalms of Dr. Becker. After these fell time and again into the hands of other people, I was variously exhorted [by others], both in writing as well as in person, to continue and complete this work. And though in fact owing to other work at hand, and then also considering that he is all but no *Musicus* who might not be able to compose a melody, this would probably have been delayed yet longer, it pleased Almighty God, according to His infinite wisdom and gracious will, through a particular family grief and through the sudden death of my late beloved wife, Magdalena Wildeck, to bring to a halt such other work I was planning and put into my hands this little psalter, as it were, so that I could derive more comfort from it in my sorrow. I thus set about this task most willingly, without further thought of myself, as a comforter in my sorrow, and finally prepared this small work, as it is presented here, with God's help.

Accordingly, now that this comes to light through public print, I esteem no one to whom it will be more fittingly dedicated than Your Electoral Serenity, of whom it is sufficiently known to me that you harbor, in addition toward other sacred songs, also toward this small book of psalms by Dr. Becker, a special fondness and attachment, and have also caused this to be practiced most diligently and sung daily in Your Electoral Residence and Palace Church. Beyond this I remember besides, not unduly, of the abundant favor bestowed upon me by Your Electoral Serenity, and especially the benefit which you previously conferred most graciously for the purchase of my present residence, and never hesitated that this book, under Your Electoral Serenity's most venerable name and protection, shall remain sheltered from grudgers and sophists, and preserved from repression and ruin.

For my part, next to the praise of God, whither all Christian work is duly directed above all else, this work is also intended as testimony and token of my most humble devotion and most indebted gratitude, and is herewith most humbly set forth, submitted, and dedicated to Your Electoral Serenity. May it please Your Electoral Serenity to accept and to receive from me with most gracious hands this slight gift in consideration of my person and, should you find something in it that might please you, to use this together with other sacred melodies in your most praiseworthy Christian devotion. For you, finally, I most humbly and most faithfully wish, of God the Most High, to all the electoral family good fortune and prosperous physical and spiritual well-being. Also for continuing electoral favor I do commend myself with most humble diligence to the best of my ability. Dated at Dresden, 6 September 1627.

Your Electoral Serenity's
most humble,
most obedient
Heinrich Schütz.

48. *BECKER PSALTER* (FREIBERG, 1628): PREFACE TO THE READER

To the Kind-Hearted Reader.

Although these new melodies of mine on the little psalm book of Dr. Cornelius Becker are not of great art or accomplishment, nonetheless it was not completed without difficulties.

First of all, since I had to conform to the manner of the old church songs, and yet also adjust in accordance with today's music, and thus not always make use of breves [*Breven*] and semibreves [*Semibreven*], but rather mostly of minims [*Minimen*], semiminims [*Semiminimen*], and *fusae* [*Fusen*], so that the song is not only more animated, but rather too that the text might not be much too prolonged, be better understood, and a psalm more likely to be sung to the end, principally because these faster notes take away nothing from the dignity of the song if one sings them to a proper measure or beat [*Tact*] after the current manner. Indeed, even though the old church songs themselves are already written out in slower note values, they are still sung to a faster measure or beat [*Tact*] in Christian assembly.

Secondly, instead of the pauses [*Pausen*], I have made use of small strokes at the end of each poetic line,[16] because the pauses [*Pausen*] in suchlike compositional genres, after all, are not actually observed. Indeed these *Arias* or melodies can also be sung much more gracefully without a beat [*Tact*], in accordance with the text. Should, however, some of these melodies strike anyone as too secular, or rather if a composer or organist should wish to provide a chorale above it [i.e., Becker's text], he [would] set apart the *Discant* (which carries the choir [melody] or principal part) with the long notes and inserted *Pausen*, and will be satisfied as is to be hoped.

Now, Dear Reader, should this work of mine please you, make use of it in praise of the Most High God. Should one or another melody displease you, however, use instead the old, familiar melodies, which the register located in the conclusion of this book refers to you, or rather help to encourage that better ones be composed by someone else and published for the magnification of God's honor and glory.[17] God be with you.

H. S.

49. *BECKER PSALTER* (FREIBERG, 1628): TWO MEMORANDA TO THE READER

Two Memoranda to the Kind-Hearted Reader.

I.

Benevolent dear Reader, when the present small work was already in press and almost the half of it ready, a Latin songbook entitled *Cithara Davidica Luthero-Becceriana* by Valentinus Cremcovius,[18] the rector at Magdeburg, was dispatched to me by my dear brother in Leipzig, Georg Schütz, doctor of laws, etc. And in consequence, I feel that these new melodies of mine agree no less with the same text and can thus be used fittingly with the Latin as well. Hence I have all the less cause to regret this work of mine, which I

---

16. The stroke that Schütz refers to is a vertical line right through the staff to indicate the end of one line of poetic text, or what he calls a *Versslein*.
17. At the back of the book, between the register of psalms and the two memoranda is "Register der alten melodeyen auff welche D. Beckers Psalm=Büchlein gesungen wird: Die vorangesetzten Wort bedeuten die Weise/ vnd die nachgesetzten Ziffern die Psalmen/so darauff gesungen warden." ("Register of the old melodies to which Dr. Becker's Psalter is sung: the text placed at the beginning indicates the melody, and the number after it indicates the psalms which are sung to them.")
18. Valentinus (Valens) Cremcovius came from Gardelegen, north of Magdeburg, and in 1603 was schoolmaster at Salza. He later appears to have been employed at the Gymnasium in Magdeburg.

wanted to communicate in this place, should it please anyone to perform the aforementioned *Arias* in this way.

II.

Beyond the preceding registers, the concordances of the Psalms with the Epistles of the Evangelists which one reads on Sundays and named feast-days throughout the entire year in particular should have been added and printed to this small work as well. I have however had to leave out not only these but other introductory remarks as well, and the summaries too, so that the book would be more manageable for binding.[19] The kindhearted reader in this case is referred back and directed to editions previously published in Leipzig, primarily because it was never my intention through this work to deprive others of their praise and usefulness.

May the true God, in these afflicted times of late, let His holy, pure, true Word live abundantly in the churches, the schools, and with each father in his home, through pure devout teachings, as also through spiritual and consolatory songs and psalms, until the longed for future of His beloved son, our Savior and Redeemer, that we might await Him in love, patience, and joyous hope, and be found always ready for that time. Amen.

Glory to God alone.

50. SCHÜTZ TO JOHANN GEORG I (29 JUNE 1629)

Letter concerning his late return from Venice, travel documentation for Caspar Kittel, and appraisals of the violinists Tobias Grünschneider and Francesco Castelli

[D-Dla: Loc. 8687/1, Kantoreiordnung so Kurfürst Moritz...1548, fols. 90r–91v][20]

[Address]

To the Most Serene, Noble-Born Prince and Lord, Lord Johann Georg, Duke of Saxony, Jülich, Cleves and Berg, Grand Marshal and Elector of the Holy Roman Empire, Landgrave in Thuringia, Margrave of Meissen, and Burgrave of Magdeburg, Count of the Mark and Ravensberg, Lord of Ravenstein, my Most Gracious Elector and Lord

[Text]

Most Serene, Noble Elector, to Your Electoral Serenity, together with my wishes for every welfare of body and soul from God, I pledge my most obedient services to the best of my ability and means, first and foremost.

---

19. As it is, this small volume is just over 600 pages in length.
20. The document is in Schütz's hand. Transcribed in *Schütz-GBr*, Nr. 29; *Schütz-Dokumente*, Nr. 55.

Most Gracious Lord, I live in most humble, confident hope that Your Electoral Serenity will look upon and perceive my recent and continued absence beyond the allotted time in no other way than in electoral grace. I comfort myself greatly down here in the protection of the Lord Marshal of the Palace, and he shall report most humbly, in one thing and another, how this undertaking of mine is intended no way other than in loyal service to Your Electoral Serenity. Accordingly, with God's help, that for which I set out to do I have now accomplished as wished. I have collected together a considerable store of various musical compositions and have already sent these away together with some instruments to Leipzig. I most humbly await the Lord Marshal of the Palace's formal letter and final ordinance in regard to Caspar Kittel so that he too might be able to set out together with me, with the intention then of not losing any more time but rather setting out for home as early as possible, and to take up our proper duties at Your Electoral Serenity's court city.

Inasmuch as I was also commissioned to make inquiries at Florence regarding the violinist, Grünschneider,[21] and being somewhat acquainted with his person, I have not wanted to neglect reporting to Your Electoral Serenity most humbly. I have acquired very reliable information to some extent that he, the aforementioned Grünschneider, would not be of future use except in *tantzgeigen*,[22] whereas he is quite unaccomplished [*imperfect*] and ignorant in *Music*. I truly want in no way to prescribe to Your Electoral Serenity in this matter; rather on the contrary, I will spare no effort in the acquisition of his person should further orders be given to me in this case. I should also want hereby to mention most humbly that with a person like this, if we should perhaps rival or compete with other good musicians at assemblies that occur, we would by no manner of means hold our ground and reap glory from it. Inasmuch as Your Electoral Serenity can also hear a most humble account of this at Dresden, the aforementioned Grünschneider, when he was in Germany with the Grand Duke [of Tuscany] for the space of a year, in no way held his own at the imperial court, and neither was he in any measure esteemed.

I cannot however neglect to notify Your Electoral Serenity further most humbly how in this place I came into the company of a suitable violinist, and the best here in

---

21. Tobias Grünschneider was sent in 1614 to Italy by the Elector of Saxony. He was there for a long period of time in the service of the Grand Duke of Tuscany, from whom Johann Georg I recalled him on 3 May 1618. In 1629, Grünschneider was back in Venice.

22. It is not possible to say with complete certainty what Schütz means by this. He is possibly referring to performance on what the English call the *kit* and what Praetorius describes in *Syntagma musicum II* as the *Klein Geig* or *Posche*, which term seems to derive from the French *poche* and *pochette*. The physical dimensions and construction of these instruments can vary considerably, though they are typically quite narrow in width compared to their length. They may have three strings but four is the norm, tuned in fifths, sometimes at the same pitch as violins but usually a fourth or fifth higher. With brass or steel strings, the instruments and the style would seem to be best suited to accompanying dancing and dance instruction. Based on Schütz's comments, playing the violin and the *Tanzgeige* required different skill sets of the performer, and in this respect Grünschneider was deemed deficient.

Venice [i.e., Francesco Castelli]. He had previously served thirteen or more years at the Mantuan court, where not long ago the *Music* flourished above all the other courts in all of Italy. Because of these [current] disturbances,[23] he has ended up now in Venice, where in fact he still has no steady appointment because there is not a vacant position at St. Mark's at present, and he supports himself through his occasional services at daily Feast Days. Fundamentally this person is thoroughly accomplished [*perfect*], confident, and immensely qualified, as well as being equally skilled in *tantzgeigen*, and who can direct and make good an entire company of violinists beside him. Beyond all this, he is also a very devout and modest man. I believe without a doubt that Your Electoral Serenity would be pleased and most graciously satisfied with him, perhaps more than with Carlo Farina previously, or rather in future with Grünschneider.

In the event now that Your Electoral Serenity might like perhaps to extend gracious favor to him or acquire him, I have disposed him already thus far that he will most humbly serve Your Electoral Serenity for a probationary period of one year, set off immediately with me from here, and will also be content with the same allowance that Carlo Farina had hitherto. It would also not necessarily be of great expense to carry out this enterprise, in that Your Electoral Serenity, after arriving at a most gracious resolution regarding provisions and so that the good man could leave behind a little something to his wife and several children, might most graciously remit or transfer hither 100 thalers through the exchange, or an amount at your most gracious discretion. All further expenses should be avoided with care and thus everything undertaken in such a way that Your Electoral Serenity will hopefully be satisfied with us. Should Your Electoral Serenity now have a most gracious opinion on one thing or another in this matter, I look forward most humbly to hear of it.

Finally I recommend myself most humbly and most obediently to Your Electoral Serenity's enduring and customary electoral grace, as hitherto shown to me undeservingly, as well also Caspar Kittel to further continuation of electoral and fatherly beneficence and kindness, of which he for his departure [from here] indeed is still and urgently in need and awaits most humbly. Most faithfully and with utmost zeal I commend you, together with your entire most praiseworthy Electoral House, to the gracious and powerful protection of the Almighty. Dated at Venice on 29 June *St. N.* [i.e., new style] 1629.

Your Electoral Serenity's
loyal, most humble,
ever most obedient
Heinrich Schütz, in his own hand.

---

23. In 1628, France and Spain were at war in regard to the Mantuan succession, and Venice was involved in the conflict helping to defend Mantua against the Spaniards. Venice at this time was also embroiled in internal conflict between the Houses of Zeno and the Cornaro. See Gregor-Dellin, *Heinrich Schütz: Sein Leben, Sein Werk, Seine Zeit*, 168.

51. *SYMPHONIAE SACRAE I* (VENICE, 1629): TITLE PAGE AND DEDICATION (19 AUGUST 1629) (ORIGINAL LANGUAGE: LATIN)

[Title page]

Symphoniae sacrae [Sacred Symphonies][24]
by Heinrich Schütz,
Kapellmeister to the Most Serene Elector of Saxony,
suitable for various voices and instruments
à 3, 4, 5, 6.
Recently published by permission
and privilege.
Second Sacred Opus
Bassus pro Organo
[*Signum* of Gardano]
Venice M.DC.XXIX.
In the printing house of Bartolomeo Magni.

[Dedication]

To the Firstborn Son of the Saxon Elector of the Holy Roman Empire, Most Serene Prince and Lord, Lord Johann Georg, Duke of Saxony, Jülich, Cleves, and Berg, Landgrave of Thuringia, Margrave of Meissen, Count of the Mark and Ravensberg, Lord of Ravenstein, etc.

To a young man of heroic nature, splendor of the Saxon family, the most longed-for hope of the fatherland, my own Most Clement Lord, Heinrich Schütz sends abundant greetings.

Although I am absent, Excellent Prince, I am not absent from you: indeed, to the present I seem to myself to be your companion through the pleasant fields of music at the behest of your great father. For just as with the familiar generosity of that man (by which I mean, the security of my fortunes) who gave me this power, blowing for me as I sail from my port, I may be equally secure with you and wander, since you too are like a guiding star to me, so that it is wonderful how much I rejoice going through all my travels with your image in mind, as if with a personal companion. While it floats before me, and is regarded on almost the entire journey, it is no wonder that the brilliant adornments of your spirit—an image of your very great father—sown like seeds, should grow up with you wonderfully in the flower of your youth, out of the very fertile soil that is your natural talent, and portend everything wonderful for the felicity of the

---

24. SWV 257–76; RISM A/I/8 S 2287; *SA* 5; *NSA* 13–14; *SSA* 7.

Saxon land. Wherefore I think it well done that I, on the point of returning to you, contemplate bringing something which I might offer, bound by my vow, and hang up my tablet as if to my guiding spirit.[25] But it first occurs to me that I might offer you something from my studies not of the common sort and that above all would meet with your approval, which very thing turned out nicely. Hear, by your clemency: when I made land in Venice, I cast my anchor in the place where as a youth I had served the apprenticeship of my art under the great Gabrieli. But Gabrieli, immortal gods, what a great man! If garrulous antiquity had seen him (let me say it in a word), it would have set him over the Amphions, or if the Muses were desirous of marriage, Melpomene would be rejoicing in no other husband but him, so great was he in the art of summoning the modes. His fame conveys this, but the fame is an enduring one. I myself am a most trustworthy witness, since I enjoyed the benefit of this excellent man in four full years of training under him. But this I leave aside. Having stayed at Venice amongst old friends, I learned that the method of composition, having changed considerably, had in part cast off the ancient modes,[26] in order to charm the ears of today with new enchantment; in order to bring forth some things in this style for you from the store of my industry and in accordance with my plan, I applied my mind and strength to this end. But I see that, while toiling away at whatever kind of work it might be, I undergo a perilous risk before you, a young man, a most praiseworthy prince very well educated in other noble virtues, so experienced in this art in accordance with the highest expectations. To this I add your most noble prefect Volrad von Watzdorf, a master of the same art, I would say, were it not for him a respite from more serious concerns, as it is for princely men such as yourselves; but accept this, O Prince, and you, most noble Volrad, since I offer these gifts sincerely. And what does it matter, that the highest divinities look upon pure hands that are not full, hands which sincerity of spirit, not waters from the spring, have cleansed? Why should I not believe that such men, so close to the gods, should behave thus toward me? But if these pieces of mine should provoke a certain aversion, I shall appeal to that familiar clemency, that companion of the Prefect, and I shall plead as an excuse the shortness of time, the inconvenience of travel, and a mind grasping perhaps for things beyond its reach in the hope of your favor. Farewell, adornment of your famous house, and continue as before to keep me, I fervently pray, in the bosom of your clemency.

In Venice, 19 August [1629].

---

25. Schütz alludes here to Horace Ode 1.5, lines 13–16. In this extended maritime metaphor the poet has escaped from his obsession with flirtatious Pyrrha, figured as shipwreck, and hangs up his dripping clothes to the powerful god of the sea: "me tabula sacer / votiva paries indicat uvida / suspendisse potenti / vestimenta maris deo." ("As for me, a votive tablet on his temple wall records that I have dedicated my drenched clothes to the deity who rules the sea.") See Horace, *Odes and Epodes*, 35.

26. The term in the original is *antiquos numeros*. Pfatteicher's translation (128) renders this as *the old [medieval] church modes*, though Strunk (73) translates it as *the ancient rhythms*.

52. SCHÜTZ TO JOHANN GEORG I (24 AUGUST 1629)

Letter requesting additional money to settle debts in Venice

[D-Dla: Loc. 8687/1, Kantoreiordnung so Kurfürst Moritz...1548, fol. 101r)][27]

Most Illustrious, Most Noble Elector. To Your Electoral Serenity, together with supplication to God for every welfare of the body and soul, I pledge my most humble, most obedient services to the best of my ability and means, first and foremost.

Most Gracious Lord, in consequence of carrying out the described and desired travel I undertook to Italy with Your Electoral Serenity's most gracious consent, I have fallen into considerable need, and that [money] which was transferred to me by Friedrich Lebzelter upon Your Electoral Serenity's most gracious command, as well as what I have contributed of my own up to now, will in no way suffice.

Because I did not want to importune Your Electoral Serenity beyond the previous amount, I have thus had necessarily to contrive [*ingegniren*] or struggle as best I could in order to raise enough on credit from good people in this place that, with God and honor, I might again leave the country, which then, also through God's continued help, shall now happen at the earliest possible date.

With this my most humble supplication I submit to Your Electoral Serenity my most obedient, fervent request, may it please you most graciously to consider it, that not only here abroad, for carrying out my good intention (which I do not want to cut short this time), but also to some degree at home the claims of the *Kapellknaben* have hit me somewhat hard, and one thing and another else even harder, to show to me your electoral favor and to issue a most gracious command to your chamberlain, God willing, that an installment of 300 thalers from my salary be made available to me upon my arrival in Leipzig at the coming Michaelmas fair [i.e., September 29] (as modesty forbids me to ask for more). I will thus be able to redeem my good name and to pay off the incurred debts. Without Your Electoral Serenity's aid, I would otherwise remain here in desperate straits, for I know no other recourse for my deliverance. That Your Electoral Serenity might most graciously protect me and allow your electoral most gracious affection be shown further toward me (as I too for my part gladly strive now and in the future, to the utmost of my powers, to serve you with praise and honor), I therefore ask for this with most humble, sincere, and continued diligence, and await most obediently your noble, most gracious resolution. With utmost loyalty I commend Your Electoral Serenity to divine protection. Dated at Venice, 24 August, new style, 1629.

Your Electoral Serenity's
most humble,
most obedient
Heinrich Schütz, in his own hand.

---

27. Document is in Schütz's hand. Transcribed in *Schütz-GBr*, Nr. 30; *Schütz-Dokumente*, Nr. 57.

53. EXCERPT FROM PHILIPP HAINHOFER'S TRAVELOGUE
(27 OCTOBER 1629)

Hainhofer's account of the visit to Augsburg by Schütz, Caspar Kittel, and Francesco Castelli

[D-W: Cod. Guelf. 11.22.Aug.2°, fol. 256 (also in Cod. Guelf. 37.32.Aug.2°, fol. 321; and Cod. Guelf. 38.2.Aug.2°, fol. 256f)]

When I arrived home,[28] with God's help (*frustra conatur, cui non Deus auxiliatur*[29]), I found before me musicians—namely, Heinrich Schütz, Electoral Kapellmeister; Caspar Kittel, lutenist and theorbist, whom the elector had transferred to Italy into a sixth year and to learn thanks to his noble generosity [*liberalitate*]; and Francesco Castelli, formerly the excellent violinist to the Serene Vincenzo, Duke of Mantua[30]—who had come from Italy and had already waited eight days in Augsburg for me. They thanked me for the money exchange arranged for them; resided here for an additional few days; and, as I honored them in my house, they, in honor of me and some invited friends, allowed us to listen to their praiseworthy art. Although it is usually said "Es ist kein so gut Lied, man wird seiner müd,"[31] we would have listened twice as long to them; for as "jeg Vögelchen singt, als es geschnäbelt ist,"[32] so too have these musicians sufficiently demonstrated that they have invested their time in music well.

---

28. Philipp Hainhofer (b. 21 Jul. 1578; d. 23 Jul. 1647) was an influential merchant, banker, and political agent who also possessed a great understanding and appreciation of the arts. He studied in Italy, Germany, and Holland, and traveled widely as a diplomat for the city of Augsburg. Hainhofer is perhaps best remembered today for his famed cabinets of curiosities (*Kunstschränke*), which he designed and commissioned, some of which still survive and adorn the collections of the Rijksmuseum in Amsterdam, the Art Institute of Chicago, and the Museum Gustavianum in Uppsala.
29. "Whoever does not have God's help strives in vain." This Latin adage seems to be derived from Psalm 127:1: "Except the LORD build the house, they labor in vain that build it." There are numerous German variants of this: Cornelius Becker's rhymed version (Leipzig, 1602), "Wo Gott zum Haus nicht gibt sein Gunst, So arbeitet jedermann umsonst," which was set by Schütz as SWV 232. It appears in settings by Hans Leo Hassler, Johann Pachelbel, Adam Gumpelzhaimer, and even into the eighteenth century with a setting by J. S. Bach (BWV 438). The chorale originates no later than 1533 with Joseph Klug's *Geistliche Lieder*.
30. Hainhofer is mostly likely referring not to Vincenzo Gonzaga, Duke of Mantua (b. 21 Sept. 1562; d. 9 Feb. 1612), who had also employed Claudio Monteverdi (b. 15 May 1567; d. 29 Nov. 1643), but rather to the son Vincenzo II (b. 7 Jan. 1594; d. 25 Dec. 1627), who reigned briefly from 1626 until his death and was succeeded by Charles, Duke of Nevers (Carlo I Gonzaga) (b. 6 May 1580; d. 21 Sept. 1637).
31. "There is no song so good, one will not tire of it."
32. This is given as a maxim in one of Hainhofer's *Lautenbücher*: "Each small bird sings according to its beak." The various transcriptions of Hainhofer's text show variant spellings of the title: "Elck Vogelken singht, also git gibickt," "elcke vogelken singht, alss het gebeckt ist," which suggests the books may have been copied from dictation rather than from the written word. See Lüdtke, *Die Lautenbücher Philipp Hainhofers (1578–1647)*.

54. SCHÜTZ TO GEORG PFLUGK (LATE 1629)

Memorandum addressing various music matters at the Dresden Court, including support for four Kapellknaben *and payment for newly appointed Francesco Castelli*

[D-Dla: Loc. 8687/1, Kantoreiordnung so Kurfürst Moritz…1548, fol. 61r][33]

Memorandum to the Electoral Saxon Marshal of the Palace in regard to matters pertaining to the musicians.

1.

The specification of the items that I brought with me from Italy and the appropriate receipts should follow in future, God willing.

2.

Regarding the four *Tafelknaben*: To negotiate with the Lord Chamber Councillor in what manner, partly in provisions and partly in money, they might be lodged with Caspar Kittel.

3.

Instructions to issue regarding the Italian violinist, Francesco Castelli:[34]

1. To *Signor* Lebzelter: that, commencing 1 November, he would have 10 Venetian ducats paid out each month to his [Castelli's] wife.
   Each calculated at 6 *scudi*, 4 *soldi*.
2. To the Lord Chamberlain [i.e., Johann Sautor]: that he would moreover pay 11 *Reichsthaler* per month, as stipend and tuition for the boy who has already commenced study with Carlo Farina.
3. One pitcher of wine every day in the cellar.
4. Wood—[this] will likely be solicited at another time.
5. NB. I forgot to mention to our Most Gracious Lord the livery needed, as before by Farina. This good man [Castelli] will probably be happy to have it, even if nothing fine is available.

4.

Regarding modifications to the choir-desk, etc.: bringing His Right Honorable Worship into the church and, in the presence of a joiner, communicating my opinion to him, and likewise our Most Gracious Lord's resolution.

---

33. The document is in Schütz's hand. Transcribed in *Schütz-GBr*, Nr. 32; *Schütz-Dokumente*, Nr. 59.
34. By 1629, Francesco Castelli (d. 1631) had already lived thirteen years in Mantua as violinist at the ducal court, ruled at the time by Ferdinand (reg. 1612–26), succeeded by Vincenzo II (reg. 1626–27) and Charles I (Carlo) (reg. 1627–37). In 1630, the violinist traveled with Schütz to Dresden. See Hainhofer's account of Castelli's visit, 27 October 1629.

5.

Beyond this, what His Electoral Serenity would most graciously command me to draw up in writing.

6.

Regarding the most necessary new positif: To solicit most earnestly whether the organ builder could obtain 30 thalers.

55. SCHÜTZ TO THE DRESDEN COURT (LATE 1629 OR EARLY 1630)

Memorandum regarding musical purchases in Italy, boarding of Kapellknaben, support for Francesco Castelli, and modifications to the choir-desk in the palace chapel

[D-Dla: Loc. 8687/3, Memorial, die Verbesserung der Musik betr. um 1650, fol. 3r–v]³⁵

Register of those items which our Most Gracious Elector and Lord could have assigned to and commanded of the Lord Marshal of the Palace.

1.

That he would see what instruments and other musical items [i.e., compositions] Heinrich Schütz brought with him from Italy; and prepare a report of it and most humbly present the detailed account upon His Electoral Serenity's safe return home.

2.

Because His Electoral Serenity most graciously decided that all *Tafelknaben*, or discantists who attend at table, should henceforth be sent to Caspar Kittel for instruction—and, indeed, as soon as possible—the aforementioned Lord Marshal of the Palace should consider how they might be housed with him, discuss it with the Lord Chamber Councillor, and report back to His Electoral Serenity in this matter.

3.

Because His Electoral Serenity has also most graciously consented to support, for a probationary period of one year, the Italian violinist, Francesco Castelli, who has most humbly offered his services, His Worship, the Lord Marshal of the Palace, in the meantime and until the safe return of our Most Gracious Lord, in the name of His Electoral Serenity, might enjoin upon:

1. Friedrich Lebzelter, that he shall cause to have paid each month to the said violinist's wife in Venice, and beginning 1 November, 10 Venetian *ducati correnti*, each calculated at 6 *scudi*, 4 *soldi*. This will amount to 8 to 9 thalers.

---

35. The unsigned document is in Schütz's hand. Despite the date given in the shelf number for this item, it cannot possibly be from 1650, but rather shortly after Schütz's return from Italy at the end of 1629. Transcribed in *Schütz-GBr*, Nr. 33; *Schütz-Dokumente*, Nr. 58.

2. The Lord Chamberlain, that he, at the pleasure of our Most Gracious Lord, shall cause to have paid and remitted to him monthly 10 or 12 *Reichsthaler* as well for the subsistence of the Italian. The boy, who has begun training under the said violinist, must also be included here [in the expenses].
3. That each day a jug of wine and some wood, as previously for Carlo Farina, also be provided for him.

4.

Because the Kapellmeister requests some modification to the choir-desk in the chancel of the church, for the better promotion and disposition of the *Music*, the Lord Marshal of the Palace (possibly as well in consultation with Dr. Hoë [von Hoënegg],[36] if it pleases) should also listen to his opinion, and either initiate work on it or, if they should find this modification of consequence, to report back to our Most Gracious Lord about it.

56. SCHÜTZ TO JOHANN GEORG I (22 APRIL 1630)

Letter regarding payments and advances following his trip to Italy

[D-Dla: Loc. 8687/1, Kantoreiordnung so Kurfürst Moritz…1548, fol. 130r][37]

Most Serene, Most Noble Elector, Most Gracious Lord.

I report most humbly to Your Electoral Serenity that the 300 thalers, on which I heretofore relied in Italy, were paid out and settled by the Lord Chamberlain at the last fair in Leipzig. However, *Signor* Lebzelter took it and kept a considerable portion of the aforesaid amount, and reimbursed himself for payments made for transporting several cases. Otherwise I would not have owed so much still on the letter of exchange.

If I should yet invest something among the merchants in addition to this, I would thus further solicit Your Electoral Serenity most humbly in connection to this fair that you would have another couple of hundred *gulden* paid out to me in advance of my salary and issue a most gracious command to the chamberlain in regard of this.

And, should it please you, Your Electoral Serenity can see most graciously from the account, which was handed over to the Lord Marshal of the Palace, where that 600 thalers received by Friedrich Lebzelter was spent. I commend myself most humbly to Your Electoral Serenity's enduring favor. Dresden, 22 April 1630.

---

36. Matthias Hoë von Hoënegg (b. 24 Feb. 1580; d. 4 Mar. 1645) was born of noble stock in Vienna and received his theological training in Wittenberg. He first came as the Third Court Chaplain to Dresden in 1602/03, became Superintendent in Plauen in 1604, went to Prague in 1611, and from 1613 until his death in 1645 was the Principal Court Chaplain in Dresden. He was the first to receive the title of *Oberhofprediger* (Senior Court Chaplain) and enjoyed considerable influence at court during the Thirty Years' War.
37. The document is in Schütz's hand. Transcribed in *Schütz-GBr*, Nr. 35; *Schütz-Dokumente*, Nr. 61.

Your Electoral Serenity's
most humble,
most obedient
Heinrich Schütz,
Kapellmeister, in his own hand.

57. SCHÜTZ DIRECTED TO JOHANN GEORG I (MID 1630?)

Memorandum regarding a belated account following his return from Italy, planned changes to the Kapelle, and the recruitment of a new tenor for the Dresden Court

[D-Dla: Loc. 8687/3 Memorial, die Verbesserung der Musik betra. um 1650, fol. 1r–v][38]

Memorandum of what I have to advance most humbly to our Most Gracious Elector and Lord, in regard to improvement of the *Music*:

1.

Why have I not as yet composed and before now submitted my written opinion, which His Electoral Serenity previously ordered me to draw up upon my return to Sachsenburg from Italy?[39] Namely, for the [following] reasons: first, because I find myself too inadequate to propose and to carry out such reform or revision on my own; and secondly, on account of his constant, arduous duties of all kinds, I did not want to importune His Electoral Serenity herein, but to defer this enterprise until some future, perhaps better time.

2.

However, in the event that it might most graciously please His Electoral Serenity to undertake a little preparation for such improvement by degrees, it would be my most humble recommendation that, via a written or spoken command (but not beyond what is in this notice), the Chief Treasurer would be adjoined to the Lord Marshal of the Palace, that they together would hear from the Kapellmeister and some of the senior and best instrumentalists what kind of deficiencies might exist in the *Music*, and then most humbly apprise His Electoral Serenity of it. Such examinations could be arranged according to the following four headings:

1. Among the instrumentalists
2. Among the singers
3. Among the instrumentalist *Knaben*
4. Among the singer *Knaben*

---

38. Written in Schütz's hand but unsigned. Transcribed in *Schütz-GBr*, Nr. 34; *Schütz-Dokumente*, Nr. 64.
39. Sachsenburg is a castle near Frankenberg, Saxony, approximately 24 km due east of Freiberg.

His Electoral Serenity should also be informed most humbly that this revision, and hence improvement, does not incur greater expense, and would therefore not be disadvantageous or harmful to any of the musicians, insofar as several of the same [*Knaben*] could remain nonetheless in the chapel at the choir-desk, several others could be promoted to service where they would perhaps be just as competent, and some could be taken on in their place (especially singers, of which there is the greatest shortage).

Memorandum regarding the tenor from Eilenburg.[40]

A half year ago and again now in my travel down to Leipzig, I heard in Eilenburg a tenor sing—a good, poor fellow, a *Baccalaureus*[41] in the school there, by the name of Georg Hempel—whose voice so exquisitely pleased me, possibly as much as any I can recall having heard in Germany. I would propose for the consideration of our Most Gracious Elector and Lord whether, for the sake of closer examination, His Electoral Serenity might have orders sent to his Superintendent there, Dr. Polycarpus,[42] that he send the said person up here to Dresden for this coming Easter, keep his position vacant in the interim, and await further instruction.

58. SCHÜTZ'S ELEGY ON THE DEATH OF JOHANN HERMANN SCHEIN († 19 NOVEMBER 1630) (ORIGINAL LANGUAGE: LATIN)

To the Blessed Deceased.

Beloved Schein,[43] accept this final funerary tribute which you sought for yourself while still alive. I have already performed this service enough—for many friends, whose own death removed them from this world before their time. What remains, but for me

---

40. Eilenburg—Schütz writes *Eulenburgk* —is ca. 25 km northeast of Leipzig, and lies midway on a major route between Torgau and Leipzig.
41. A *Baccalaureus* is a minor position in a school.
42. Polycarpus Leyserus (Polykarp Leyser) (b. 20 Dec. 1586; d. 15 Jan. 1633) was a Protestant theologian, Professor of Theology and Superintendent in Leipzig.
43. Johann Hermann Schein, though he never traveled abroad, was tremendously important among German composers as one of the first to adapt the modern Italian styles of the madrigal, monody, and the concerto to the traditional features of Lutheran Church music. His earliest studies in music were under the Hofkapellmeister Rogier Michael in Dresden, followed by studies in the *Fürstenschule* in Pforta and at Leipzig University. After a period as Kapellmeister in Weimar, he succeeded Sethus Calvisius (b. 21 Mar. 1556; d. 24 Nov. 1615) as Thomaskantor in Leipzig in 1615, which position he held until his death. Of the so-called "Three Famous S's" (*Drei Berühmte S.*)—Schütz, Schein, and Scheidt—the closest friendship existed between Schütz and Schein. In 1630, Schütz visited Schein on his deathbed, and at the Thomaskantor's request composed a six-voice parentation motet (SSATTB, bc) on the text of 1 Timothy 1:15 ("Das is je gewisslich wahr"), published in January the following year (SWV 277) and dedicated by the printer to Schein's widow and sons. A slightly revised version of the motet (SWV 388) was incorporated seventeen years later in the *Geistliche Chor-Music* of 1648.

finally to render the same service to myself, and for me myself to be the singer at my own funeral.

[November 1630]

[Original]

Ad B. Defunctum.
QVod tibi, vivus adhuc, Scheini dilecte, petebas;
Hoc cape supremum Funeris officium.
Hactenus exsolvi sat—multis istud Amicis,
Qvos sua Mors terris abstulit, ante diem.
Qvid restat, nisi munus idem ut mihi denique solvam,
El sim Cantator Funeris Ipse mei.

59. SCHÜTZ TO THE DRESDEN COURT (PRESUMABLY JANUARY 1631)

Recommendation for the transportation of musicians and instruments from Dresden to Leipzig for the Assembly of Princes, February—April 1631[44]

[D-Dla: Oberhofmarschallamt, I, Nr. 7, Reise Churfürstens zu Sachssen…nach Leipzig auf den Evangel. Convent-Tag 1631, unnumbered notice between fols. 95 and 96][45]

Musicians.

Two coach-wagons, for twelve persons comprising singers and instrumentalists.
   A baggage-wagon for the cases of instruments.
   A small double-harnessed wagon for the *Knaben*.

Or perhaps the instruments together with the *Knaben* could be transported by water to Torgau, and from there by public conveyance to Leipzig.

NB: If the two Englishmen are to go along,[46] they shall be brought down in addition to this.

---

44. The occasion for this item was the Assembly of the Princes at Leipzig, February—April 1631, referred to variously as the *Konvent protestantischer Stände*, the Leipzig Assembly, or the Leipzig Colloquy. It was the intention of the Protestant Electors to call an assembly of the various Protestant estates in an attempt to form a unified, neutral party. The assembly was attended by the two Protestant electors, Johann Georg I of Saxony and Georg Wilhelm of Brandenburg, together with lesser potentates, and administrators of the Protestant dioceses and the Imperial Free Cities. Together they formed the so-called *Leipziger Bund*, a Protestant alliance that hoped to protect its constituent members both from the Imperial forces and from the invading Swedes.
45. The document is in Schütz's hand. Transcribed in *Schütz-Dokumente*, Nr. 67.
46. Two English musicians employed by the court around this time were John Price and John Dixon.

60. SCHÜTZ TO THE DRESDEN COURT (PRESUMABLY JANUARY 1631)

Memorandum detailing which musicians were to travel to Leipzig

[D-Dla: Loc. 8687/1, Kantoreiordnung so Kurfürst Moritz…1548, fols. 103r; 102 (missing)][47]

[In Schütz's hand]

In addition to the *Sänger-Knaben*, which Caspar Kittel shall take with him to Leipzig, the following instrumentalist *Knaben* will be used at the same service, who by the looks of it are in great need of vestments, as follows:

1. Daniel Hemmerlein,   who studied with the Italian.[48]
2. Gabriel Günther   plays the small English cittern.
3. Michael Grundt[49] ⎱ play trombones and
4. Christian Krüger[50] ⎰ violins as well.

Heinrich Schütz, in his own hand.

[Written in a second hand]

Those with Caspar Kittel

1. Matthias Weckmann[51]
2. Philipp Stolle[52]

---

47. As with the preceding item, this undated document could have been written in 1631, possibly January, since the assembly of the Protestant electors, princes, and nobles took place in Leipzig from 10 February until 2 April, and on which occasion the Saxon Elector was present with the Kapelle. Transcribed in *Schütz-GBr*, Nr. 38; *Schütz-Dokumente*, Nr. 66.
48. Daniel Hemmerlein was housed or in the care of Heinrich Schütz prior to 1633 (*Schütz-GBr*, 320).
49. According to *Schütz-GBr* (320), Grundt is mentioned in the Dresden *Kapellverzeichnis* as being absent by 1632.
50. According to *Schütz-GBr* (330), Krüger was a *Kapellknabe* in Dresden in 1631, boarded with Wilhelm Günther, then with a *Herr* von Hartenstein, and was back in Dresden around 1642.
51. The organist and composer Matthias Weckmann (b. ca. 1616; d. 24 Feb. 1674) was born in the Thuringian village of Niederdorla near Mühlhausen, and owing to his innate musical talent was sent to the Electoral Court in Dresden as a *Kapellknabe* and became a student of Schütz. At the elector's expense, Weckmann went to Hamburg in 1637 where he studied the Netherland style of Sweelinck's school under Jacob Praetorius (b. 8 Feb. 1586; d. 21/22 Oct. 1651) and Heinrich Scheidemann (b. ca. 1596; d. 26 Sept. 1663). After his return to Dresden, he became court organist to the Electoral Prince in 1641, and of the Danish Prince-Elect in 1642. In 1647, Weckmann was in Dresden again. With permission of the elector, he went as organist to the Jakobikirche in Hamburg in 1655. There he founded the city's famous *collegium musicum* in 1665, which, however, collapsed following his death in 1674. Weckmann was also a composer of considerable distinction.
52. Philipp Stolle (b. 1614; d. 4 Oct. 1675) originally came from Bohemia, entered the Dresden *Kurprinzliche Capella* as *Instrumentist* in 1641, prior to which time he was already a discantist around 1631 and housed with Caspar Kittel and Augustus Tax. In 1634, he was in Copenhagen at the Kapelle of Prince-Elect Christian (b. 10 Apr. 1603; d. 2 Jun. 1647), the second son of Christian IV. In 1642, together with Matthias Weckmann, he presumably traveled again with Schütz to Copenhagen for another period of service. By 1647, he was back in Dresden. In 1653, the Elector of Saxony recommended him for a position in Altenburg, but Stolle was instead appointed to the Kapelle in Halle by the Administrator there, succeeding Samuel Scheidt as Kapellmeister in 1654. In later life he turned to opera composition.

3. Andreas Krause[53]
4. Martin Köckeritz[54]

[on a separate leaf]

    Discantists
Matthias Weckmann
Philipp Stolle } with Caspar Kittel
Rohtkopf [i.e., redhead] from Radeburg[55]
a small *Schwartzkopf* [i.e., dark-haired boy]
    Kapellknaben
Friederich Grohmann[56]
Abraham Friderich[58] } with the Vice-Kapellmeister[57]

Simon Michael[59]
Augustin Michael[61] } with their father [i.e., Simon Michael][60]

Christian Pitzsch[62] with Thomas Tax[63]
    Older *Knaben*
Daniel Hemmerlein, who studied with the Italian
    With *Herr* Schütz:
Christian Krüger with *Herr* Schütz
Michael Grundt, who plays trombone under Augustus Tax
Gabriel Günther, the lackey's son, with no one

---

53. *Schütz-GBr* offers no information on this musician.
54. Nothing is known about him, though possibly he was a relative of Johann Köckeritz.
55. It seems most likely that *Rohtkopf* (*red haired*) and *Schwartzkopf* (*black haired*) are just physical descriptions of the two *Knaben* previously mentioned by Schütz—i.e., Andreas Krause and Martin Köckeritz. Radeburg is a town some 19 km northeast of Meissen and 20 km north of Dresden.
56. Nothing more is known about Grohmann.
57. Zacharias Hestius (b. 8 Oct. 1590; d. 1 Jun. 1669) was born in Ullersdorf bei Dresden, was first *Kapellknabe* in Dresden, in October 1608 went to Schulpforta; and in 1611, at the expense of the Elector of Saxony, to Wittenberg to study at the university. In 1615, he became Cantor in Luckau (Lower Lusatia), and a year later was at the *Fürstenschule* in Meissen. On 26 July 1624, Hestius was appointed Vice-Kapellmeister in Dresden, where he stayed until his move to become Pastor in Königstein on 1 January 1642, where he remained until his death.
58. Nothing more is known about Abraham Friderich.
59. Son of Simon (Sr.), perhaps the grandson of Rogier Michael and nephew of Tobias Michael.
60. Father of the other Simon (Jr.) and Augustin. He was a tenor in the Dresden Kapelle and died before 1633.
61. Augustin Michael was the brother of Simon (Jr.), and died before 1633.
62. Nothing more is known about this person.
63. Thomas Tax was appointed instrumentalist to the Dresden Kapelle in 1586. In 1599, he was made custodian of the instruments, in 1612, entrusted with the training of two *Kapellknaben*, and is still mentioned in the Kapelle register in 1632.

Fifer Georg's son with Köckeritz[64]
Martin [Knabe],[65] the bass who copies for me

61. SCHÜTZ TO GEORG PFLUGK (28 FEBRUARY 1631)

Letter concerning the re-acquisition of the bassist, Hans Hasselt, for the Dresden Court

[D-Dla: Loc. 8687/1, Kantoreiordnung so Kurfürst Moritz…1548, fols. 145r–v, 146v][66]

[Address]

To the Noble-Born, Worshipful and Honorable Lord Georg Pflugk of Posterstein and Vollmershain, Highly Ordained Electoral Saxon Marshal of the Palace, my Most Benevolent Lord and Affectionate Patron, Dresden

[Text]

Most Noble, Worshipful, Honorable, Most Benevolent, Lord Marshal of the Palace, affectionate Lord and Patron, together with wishes to you for every welfare from God, I pledge my most willing services, first and foremost.

I give Your Noble Worship to understand herewith, confidentially as it were, that I felt the loss of Hans Hasselt from the company considerably at my recent service, not only for my part, but rather our Most Gracious Lord himself these days was inclined to agree in this instance also, and I sensed from it that His Electoral Serenity himself regretted losing him. If he were then to be resident once more in Dresden, and indeed I would not consider it easy to acquire him again, I therefore wanted to write to Your Noble Worship hereby with this question, [to consider] at your discretion, whether you think it might be worth the effort to acquire his person again, for the contentment of our Most Gracious Lord (as I generally remarked) and then as well for the success of the *Music* (since he does, after all, have an excellent voice)?

---

64. Johann Köckeritz was born in Dresden and probably served as choirboy in the electoral chapel. A preserved travel pass of 14 June 1596 suggests that he was sent for training in Italy, which he probably undertook at the expense of the elector. In 1606, he was employed as instrumentalist in the Dresden *Hofkapelle*, with an annual salary of 228 *gulden*, 12 *groschen*. On 1 August 1612, Köckeritz was reappointed at a reduced salary of 200 *gulden*. He was still shown to be in office in 1632, though there is no further reference to him after that.
65. Martin Knabe (d. 1652) identifies himself in 1635 as *Musicus et poët. Studiosus*. When he applied in 1636 for the organ position in Weissenfels, which position he also won, he seems to have had Schütz (for whom he had worked as a copyist) and Samuel Scheidt as referees. On the occasion of an audition for the succession of Johan Pretzel of Groitzsch, who died in 1636, the Weissenfels Councillors promised to establish a proper organist's salary for him. They seem not to have kept their word, for Knabe felt neglected, in a notice of 20 November 1636. In 1647, he received a church salary of 10 *gulden*. On 7 September 1647, the Council gave him a wedding present of 2 *gulden*, 6 *groschen*. Knabe also served as *Baccalaureus* in the school. See Werner, *Städtische und fürstliche Musikpflege in Weissenfels bis zum Ende des 18. Jahrhunderts*, 32–33.
66. The document is in Schütz's hand. Transcribed in *Schütz-GBr*, Nr. 37; *Schütz-Dokumente*, Nr. 68.

Provided that Your Noble Worship might approve my course of action, I am in no doubt that, for the attainment of this end, you yourself would implement convenient means through Hasselt's friendship. I for my part make this modest suggestion to you, that you, without mentioning my person, summon the brother of Hasselt's wife, by the name of Gottfried Hanitzsch and who sits in the revenue-department together with Wildvogel,[67] and propose to him that, for the honor of honorable friendship, Your Noble Worship would make amends for Hasselt's person before our Most Gracious Lord and to that end would arrange it that his salary shall remain unaffected. I am in no doubt that this friendship will go toward keeping him in Dresden, as then Your Noble Worship could also possibly advise him in this case that, for the sake of his wife and children, you would feel obliged not to let him leave. As regards his fool-headedness, he could be straightened up and set to rights perhaps in Dresden as well as elsewhere, for an obedience befitting friendship.

I assure Your Noble Worship that it would please our Most Gracious Lord if we could keep him, and would also hope it would not be difficult to obtain the command that his salary should continue unaffected. For my part, I myself must confess that we would not be badly served by his beautiful voice; what he lacks in style and pronunciation could also then be enjoined upon him, and this minor irritation completely remedied.

I dutifully commend Your Noble Worship herewith to the powerful protection of the Almighty, and me to your steadfast favor, awaiting your brief reply. Signed at Leipzig, 28 February 1631.

Your Most Noble Worship's
ever most dutiful
Heinrich Schütz, in his own hand.

62. SCHÜTZ TO PHILIPP HAINHOFER (23 APRIL 1632)

Letter re-ordering various musical works from Naples and observations on the strained political and confessional situation in Germany

[D-Hs: Sup. ep. 48. fols. 457r–458v][68]

[Address]

To the Noble, Most Honorable, and Highly Respected *Herr* Philipp Hainhofer, Princely Pomeranian Council there, my Most Benevolent Lord and highly esteemed friend, to his benevolent hands
Augsburg

---

67. Georg Wildvogel later became Privy Chamber Secretary to Duke August (*Schütz-GBr*, 330).
68. The document is in Schütz's hand. Transcribed in La Mara, 70–72; *Schütz-GBr*, Nr. 39; *Spagn.*, Nr. 45; *Schütz-Dokumente*, Nr. 72.

[Text]

Noble, most honorable, highly respected, Most Benevolent Lord and highly esteemed friend, may the Lord's blessing be with you for all salutary welfare of the soul and the body, together with my most diligent service, to the best of my ability and means, first and foremost.

I write to my Most Benevolent Lord to inform you that, already more than a half year ago, I asked *Herr* Friedrich Lebzelter to order various musical compositions from Naples, and hence gave him a list. Consequently I am apprehensive, having also understood as much from the aforementioned *Herr* Lebzelter, that this inventory might also be taken from the messengers in a robbery on the way. As I could forbear no longer setting quill to paper to my Most Benevolent Lord, I kindly request that you do me the favor, through your people, of ordering various printed musical compositions according to the enclosed specification, and have me informed of the cost in due course. The payment for them shall be conveyed by *Herr* Lebzelter, and your efforts gratefully recompensed furthermore when occasion allows.

As regards our situation here, my Most Gracious Lord is informed daily by *Herr* Lebzelter. Our Most Gracious Lord, as far as I have heard, assembles a select army of several thousand men on horseback and on foot, which may the dear Lord [God], along with His Electoral Serenity, keep, protect, and bestow fortune and blessing upon his proposed plan. Francesco Castelli,[69] the treble violinist I brought with me from Italy, died already more than a year ago. *Signore* Caspar Kittel, my other traveling companion, also recently lay ill with a dangerously high fever, but from which God rescued him, and offers my Most Benevolent Lord hereby his fervent greetings and service. I was especially loath to hear how my Most Benevolent Lord earlier nearly ran into trouble with the Imperial [authorities][70] on account of an intercepted letter; but praise, glory, honor, and thanks be to Almighty God, Who in turn graciously delivered my Most Benevolent Lord and many thousand devout Christians worried by their conscience, possessions, and goods, and created space [for them].[71]

In yesterday's sermon for Jubilate Sunday, our Senior Court Chaplain, *Herr* Dr. Hoë [von Hoënegg] stated how the Protestant Church up to the present, because of the great oppression at the hands of the Catholics, also suffered much misery, but how the Lord Christ now has begun anew to gladden the hearts of many thousands, even a hundred thousand, in Upper Germany,[72] and Augsburg in particular, and moreover beautifully applied the current situation to the Gospel. Inasmuch as I have also been personally

---

69. See also the documents from 29 June and 27 October 1629.
70. This is at variance with the translation in *Spagn.* (352–53) in which Hainhofer is suggested to be in the company of the imperial troops, and that they all nearly were led into trouble.
71. The space created was not in heaven, as *Spagn.* suggests and editorially inserts (353), but rather in Augsburg.
72. *Spagn.* wrongly translates *oberteutschlandt* as *Northern Germany* (353). *Oberdeutschland* refers to Germany's south, just as *Niedersachsen* refers to lower Saxony and the northern part of the country.

moved by this, I offer heartfelt congratulations to my Most Benevolent Lord and our fellow Christians in Augsburg on the occasion of this restored liberty of worship,[73] and wish for them what was in the conclusion of yesterday's Gospel: namely, that the joy with which the Lord Christ has begun to gladden the many thousands of hearts in Augsburg can never again be taken from them by any one. Amen. Would that my Most Benevolent Lord kindly greet *Herr* Dr. Nathan and all his family on my behalf, and continue toward me with steadfast favor and friendship. I, in turn, remain obliged and most willingly at your service to the best of my ability and means, and herewith commend us all most diligently to divine protection. Signed at Dresden, 23 April 1632.

My Most Benevolent *Herr's*
ever most loyal and willing
Heinrich Schütz,
Electoral Saxon Kapellmeister, in his own hand.

Music from Naples.

Ascanio Majone. Canzonettas *à* 3.
Scipione Stella. First, second, third, and fourth books of madrigals *à* 5.
Scipione Dentice. First, second, third, fourth, and fifth books of madrigals *à* 5
Scipione Lacorcia. First, second, and third books of madrigals *à* 5
Camillo Lombardi. Canzonettas for several voices.
Cico Lombardi. First, second, third, fourth, and fifth [books of] canzonettas *à* 3.
[Carlo Gesualdo di] Venosa. Eighth [book of madrigals] *à* 6.
D. Giovanni Maria Sabino. First, second, third, and fourth books of motets.
D. Carlo Pedata. Canzonettas *à* 3 books one, two, etc.
Frottolas by Father [Giuseppe Veggiano dello] Grillo for several voices.
Francesco Grandesa. Canzonettas *à* 3.
D. Alfonso Verde. Motets for several voices.
D. Alfonso Montesana [da Maida]. First, second, and third books of madrigals *à* 5.
Canzonettas by [Pietro Antonio] Giramo. The third, fourth and fifth books *à* 3.
Lamentation *à* 6 by [Carlo Gesualdo], Prince of Venosa.
Jean de Macque. Sacred compositions for several voices as available.
Giovanni Maria Trabaci. Motets and other sacred works.
Also the Masses of the same [composer].
Abbate Matthias. Canzonettas *à* 3.
Teseo. Canzonettas and motets for several voices.

It is requested that he be commanded to find, with the advice of some musician, these and other good composers as well that are found in the bookshops of Naples.

---

73. The literal translation of *gewissens freÿheit* is *freedom of conscience*, adopted from the French and Latin expressions.

63. SCHÜTZ TO FRIEDRICH LEBZELTER (6/16 FEBRUARY 1633)

Letter requesting assistance in obtaining a leave of absence to travel to Denmark

[DK-RA: Kongehuset Arkiv, A1, Christian 4. Prins Christian (5.), indkomne Breve fra ikke-fyrstelige personer, kronologisk ordnede 1631–47, nr. 31 (2 fols.)][74]

[Address]

To the noble, worthy and most distinguished *Herr* Friedrich Lebzelter, [His] Electoral Serenity's well-appointed Privy Gentleman of the Chamber, to my especially benevolent *Herr* and much-valued stalwart friend, to his own hands
 Hamburg.

[Text]

My most willing services always, in addition to wishes for a blissful, joyous new year, together with every welfare of body and soul, I pledge once more, first and foremost.

Noble, worthy, and especially benevolent *Herr* and stalwart valued friend. Your letter dated at Friedrichsburg the 8/18[75] January arrived safely today, the reply to which I shall not and will not neglect, and kindly report to you herewith that, in respect to the current adverse circumstances to my profession here, I have occupied myself with it now for nearly three quarters of a year and have endeavored most humbly to obtain from my Most Gracious Lord a most gracious discharge for perhaps one year, that I might sojourn in Lower Saxony (which place I have never seen) or where it might please me. But no matter how I have asked, I have had no success up to the present. The continuing oppressive conditions for us (of which you are aware, and the continuation of the wearisome war might not yet abate in the near future) strongly impels, indeed forces, me to persevere in my calm resolution, as I was indeed resolved to put my intention to our Most Gracious Elector and Lord with due, most humble discretion, before your most recent letter to me arrived.

I take as a good omen for my proposition and as a special ordinance from God that now such a noble sun yet rising in the world immediately regards this my plan (according to your favorable writing) with gracious eyes and, as it were, in bloom. Hence I for my part remain steadfast so much the more in my plans, barring an act of God. You know well enough, however, how very difficult it is to obtain a leave of absence from our Most Gracious Lord, and I must go about it gently, to be sure, so that I not offend our Most Gracious Lord; and in all modesty I should also not want to jeopardize or foolishly

---

74. The document is in Schütz's hand. Penned on the same side as the address is an indication of the letter's arrival in Hamburg: "- 1633–6 February from Dresden, 14 [February] in Hamburg. Heinrich Schütz." Transcribed in *Schütz-GBr*, Nr. 41; *Schütz-Dokumente*, Nr. 73.
75. Schütz provides both the Julian and Gregorian calendar dates.

forfeit other favors which I have earned at this court over the past several years or the arrears still owed to me. If it would please His Most Royal Serenity most graciously to entreat our Most Gracious Elector and Lord with a few lines concerning this, that His Electoral Serenity in the meantime would most graciously permit me to serve him most humbly for one year (as I could likely get away under these current circumstances), it to my mind would be in the best advancement of this undertaking. In the event that His Royal Serenity has any hesitations in this matter, he could perhaps, through you, urge upon the Lord High Chamberlain to put forward this enterprise in person, and with due discretion. If I had him on my side, I would hope to put the matter through all the sooner. Apart from that, moreover, I also intend to speak to him [i.e., the Chamberlain] on my behalf at the first opportunity, though I rather doubt that he would deal with me, and leave it instead to a mediator. But the majority of those, who are about our Most Gracious Lord on a daily basis, would prefer to occupy themselves with keeping His Electoral Serenity in good humor than to put forward matters which might be annoying to him (among which I take to be included this request for a leave of absence), but I would have no doubts [about it] were His Electoral Serenity's aforesaid Lord High Chamberlain to make a gracious entreaty about this. As if upon a good foundation, he would the more willingly rise up and, God willing, receive the matter. All of which I hereby submit to you to consider and furthermore to mediate with His Royal Serenity as soon as possible, and especially request most ardently that you recommend me most humbly before the aforementioned Royal Serenity should the opportunity present itself, and convey my most humble desire to serve him with due reverence. I myself noticed sufficiently His Royal Serenity's singular inclination toward, and even love for, the profession of music in connection to his presence here at the performance of my, in truth, simple music, and have definite accounts of this apart from your report. My qualities are inferior, and I can pride myself on nothing other than that I have been among the foremost musicians in Europe and have acquired but a shadow of their art. Nevertheless, I would hope with God's help to serve His Royal Serenity in such manner (provided that my work would otherwise please him), to provide his *Music* or Kapelle with a considerable quantity of appropriate pieces or compositions, not only of my own invention (as the least worthy) but of the very foremost composers in Europe as well, which works I have collected with considerable effort. I should also hope to bring [the *Hofkapelle*] into good order.

Would that you also, when there is occasion someday, inform His Royal Serenity most humbly in conversation [*per discursum*] that during my recent travels to Italy I engaged myself in an unusual manner of composition: namely, how a comedy with diverse voices can be composed in recitative style and brought to the stage and enacted in song, which things to my knowledge (in this manner as I am thinking) are completely unknown in Germany up to now, and owing to the difficult circumstances here at home, have been neither practiced nor promoted. And because I think it is a pity that such truly majestic and princely inventions remain neglected (among which, it is true, my music would not rank, and on account of some additional items I have listed), and by other and better talents neither acknowledged nor practiced, I would then upon my arrival not neglect to propose works of this kind to His Royal Serenity, for attendance upon him at current and future solemnities, at his most gracious pleasure. It remains, finally, for the advancement of this my proposition that I might perhaps receive most gracious leave for myself, at the earliest opportunity, provided that I catch His Electoral Serenity at a good time; for in truth, I am now of less than no use here and am only losing ground. In any case, if you can arrange that, I would be most obliged, as I have already prepared some barrels and small cases for the way;[76] thus is my request directed to you that you might kindly suggest to me how I might send these things down, together with a letter of shipment—as making a fuss here would be of no use—or if I should perhaps register them to be sent to you in Hamburg (as though they belonged to the aforementioned Royal Serenity), I also look to your advice and opinion. I remain obliged to you once more for your kind affection toward me; in return I pledge my honorable service and friendship to the best of my ability and means, commending us on all sides most faithfully to divine protection. Signed in Dresden, 6/16 February 1633.

My benevolent *Herr*'s
most dutiful, loyal friend always,
Heinrich Schütz, in his own hand.

The news, and today's beheading of Captain Vopelius carried out here in Dresden, you shall hear about from others.[77]

64. SCHÜTZ DIRECTED TO JOHANN GEORG I (9 FEBRUARY 1633)

Memorandum petitioning for leave to travel to Denmark

[D-Dla: Loc. 8687/1, Kantoreiordnung so Kurfürst Moritz... 1548, fols. 181r–182v][78]

Most Humble Memorandum to the Electoral Serenity of Saxony and my Most Gracious Lord.

---

76. *Schütz-GBr* (126) transcribes the original text as *Schlahfassen*, read *Schlagfassen*. A *Schlagfass* is a large cask, barrel, or hogshead used for transporting goods. Notably, several of the examples in the authoritative *DWB* refer to its use in transporting books and reading material, most likely because they are easier to roll than to lift.
77. Captain Johann Vopelius, in charge of Saxon defenses, quickly surrendered to the imperial troops of Heinrich Graf von Holk (b. 18 Apr. 1599; d. 9 Sept. 1633) following Holk's military successes. All of this followed shortly after major battles between Protestant and Imperial troops, including the Battle of Lützen, 16 November 1632, in which some 9,000 soldiers died, including the Swedish King, Gustavus Adolphus (b. 9 Dec. 1594; d. 16 Nov. 1632). Holk had marched on Leipzig, took the surrounding towns, and bombarded Leipzig on 21 October 1632. On 2 November, Pleissenburg surrendered after a brief defense. That sealed Vopelius's fate, and for this reason he was publicly executed in the Neumarkt in Dresden.
78. The document is in Schütz's hand. Transcribed in *Schütz-GBr*, Nr. 40; *Schütz-Dokumente*, Nr. 74.

From the outset I beg in most humble devotion for my sake that His Electoral Serenity (amid his other pressing duties at the present time) might not take amiss the present repeated and following memorandum of mine, but rather, at his most gracious pleasure, consider in electoral grace, most graciously grant and allow me, with springtime fast approaching, to undertake the travel to Lower Saxony most humbly and repeatedly requested by me.[79] To this end I would once more most obediently remind His Electoral Serenity [of the following]:

1.

In these current unsettled times of war, I could quite easily take leave of my service since there would be no great demand in the present circumstances to produce any elaborate music; and apart from that, the company of instrumentalists and singers has become considerably weak and diminished, since several [of them] would no longer be able to travel, owing to old age and physical infirmity, and have otherwise left to seek opportunities elsewhere, also in part because of the war. Consequently, it would not be possible to perform music with large forces or for multiple choirs. Furthermore, if God should improve the times, as hoped, and would His Electoral Serenity be honorably served according to the plan I have in mind, a considerable readjustment and improvement to our collegium would certainly and necessarily have to occur.

2.

The *Music*, as it is now still appointed in my presence (and, according to the circumstances of our time, might perhaps still be tolerable and serviceable), shall nevertheless remain in good health and not be diminished through my absence. Also prior to my departure, with foreknowledge of our inspector, it shall be put into and left in good order.

3.

Indeed my absence for a period of time would provide a convenient opportunity and suitable preparation for future, beneficial reform and improvement to our collegium (should the times someday allow this once again).

4.

The purpose of this journey of mine, once more, would be solely directed toward escaping for a time the prevailing hardships and hindrances of the current war and others in our beloved fatherland, affecting me too in my studies, and [escaping] to those places in Lower Saxony, if possible, in order to advance my profession with all diligence, without disturbance to my spirit.

In loyal, most humble sincerity, I also could not withhold from His Electoral Serenity that a short time ago, without any prompting or effort on my part, the young royal Danish Prince-Elect caused me to be called upon by Friedrich Lebzelter as to whether I could obtain most gracious leave to go to him down there [i.e., Lower Saxony] for the sake

---

79. Lower Saxony in these documents refers to Denmark or Northern Germany in general.

of improving and organizing his *Music*, [and who] would graciously acknowledge this with regard to me, and would again dismiss me at any time at pleasure [of His Electoral Serenity].

Insofar as it would perhaps occur as a favor to the aforementioned Royal Prince, our Most Gracious Lord's beloved, future son-in-law (especially in view of the impending solemnities), this service would also be in some ways beneficial and useful to me for my part, but especially to the Electoral Kapelle here; and this absence of mine for such a short time would be quite harmless.[80] I thus would request and hope so much the more that His Electoral Serenity would, in electoral grace, give thought and consideration to this most humble and perhaps not immoderate request of mine.

5.

Given the circumstances of the present time I would want in no way to importune His Electoral Serenity with demands for money, but rather just this, asking most obediently for forbearance: I would carry this out no less at my expense as well, with God's help. I live in the most humble hope, however, that, if perhaps a payment should be made to the *collegium musicum* in the meantime, I would hereby most humbly request that my share shall likewise be remitted to me and not withheld.

6.

Apart from an act of God, it would reside with His Electoral Serenity to determine the time of my return. I for my part would desire most humbly one year, or that His Electoral Serenity would recall me in writing sometime after that, should he most graciously deign to allow this.

7.

As guarantee of my continuing service to this Electoral House and beloved fatherland (so long as I in my lowly profession might be of value to them), all my household goods and possessions that God has bestowed upon me would stay here and in the land. Just as it has been up to now, and thus in the future, God willing, His Electoral Serenity shall find in me no traces of dishonesty.

8.

Finally, were I found to be suitable and ordered to do so, I would again be willing most humbly to carry out a commission outside my profession in those places. In addition to the salvation of my soul, I should want for nothing greater than the reputation and welfare of His Electoral Serenity and his praiseworthy house.

Signed at Dresden, 9 February 1633.
Heinrich Schütz, in his own hand,
Kapellmeister.

---

80. For a detailed study of "The Great Wedding" in which Schütz played such an important role, see Wade, *Triumphus nuptialis danicus: German Court Culture and Denmark. The "Great Wedding" of 1634*.

65. FRIEDRICH LEBZELTER TO CHRISTIAN (V), PRINCE-ELECT OF DENMARK (15 FEBRUARY 1633)

Letter regarding the acquisition of Schütz for the Royal Danish Court in Copenhagen

[DK-RA: Kongehuset Arkiv, A1, Christian 4. Prins Christian (5.), indkomne Breve fra ikke-fyrstelige personer, kronologisk ordnede 1631–47, nr. 31 (1 fol.)]

[Address]

To the Most Serene, Most Powerful Prince and Lord, Lord Christian V of Denmark, Norway, Prince-Elect to the Wends and Goths, Duke of Schleswig, Holstein, Stormarn, and Dithmarschen, Count of Oldenburg and Delmenhorst, my Most Gracious Lord

[Text]

Most Serene, Most Powerful Prince.

   To Your Illustrious Royal Serenity I pledge my most humble, most obedient services to the best of my ability and means always, first and foremost. Most Gracious Lord, Your Royal Serenity undoubtedly still recalls most graciously that you most graciously commissioned me this 7 January at Friederichsburg with finding out whether Heinrich Schütz, appointed Kapellmeister to His Electoral Serenity of Saxony, my Most Gracious Lord, might enter into your active service or at least obtain most gracious dismissal to reside most humbly with Your Royal Serenity for a period of one year. Accordingly I wrote most obediently to the aforesaid Kapellmeister the very next day. What he declares on this matter and how extremely eager he is to serve Your Royal Serenity most humbly can be most graciously understood from the enclosed original correspondence, among other things. In order that he might now be most graciously dismissed in a proper way before His Most Gracious Electoral Serenity, and as he might not receive consideration if he himself offered to undertake this, thus is it left to Your Illustrious Royal Serenity's most gracious pleasure whether you yourself might kindly write as indicated to His aforementioned Electoral Serenity, or in such a fashion, to have a most gracious command dispatched to me that I could submit to him, that for this purpose he [Schütz] might obtain dismissal for one year. It is to be hoped the means will then emerge for Your Illustrious Royal Serenity to keep him longer in service.

   Should it also most graciously please Your Royal Serenity to forward your most gracious passport for him, the Kapellmeister, for his accompanying servant and baggage at the same time, I hope to arrange it so that he might come down as soon as possible and yet before Easter. Your Illustrious Royal Serenity can most graciously rest assured that you shall have in this Kapellmeister such a well-qualified person, the likes of which in his profession are seldom to be found in the empire at present. He is ardently coveted by many, and even by distinguished Catholic potentates who would give him assurances on account of his religion. Thus I await Your Royal Serenity's further most gracious command on this subject, shall accede to it then most obediently, and also commend myself most humbly thereby to your steadfast favor.

Dated at Hamburg, 15 February 1633.

Your Royal Serenity's

most humble, obedient, and faithful servant,

Lebzelter, in his own hand.

66. FRIEDRICH LEBZELTER TO CHRISTIAN (V), PRINCE-ELECT OF DENMARK (13 NOVEMBER 1633)

Letter documenting Schütz's arrival in Hamburg

[DK-RA: Kongehuset Arkiv, A1, Christian 4. Prins Christian (5.), indkomne Breve fra ikke-fyrstelige personer, kronologisk ordnede 1631–47, nr. 31 (2 fols.)][81]

[Address]

To the Most Serene, Most Powerful Prince and Lord, Lord Christian V of Denmark, Norway, Prince Elect to the Wends and Goths, Duke of Schleswig, Holstein, Stormarn and Dithmarschen, Count of Oldenburg and Delmenhorst, my Most Gracious Prince and Lord

[Text]

Most Serene, Most Mighty Prince.

To Your Illustrious Royal Serenity I pledge my most humble service to the best of my ability and means always, first and foremost. Most Gracious Prince and Lord, Your Illustrious Royal Serenity shall remember most graciously that you previously ordered me to strive as much as possible to determine whether the Most Serene Elector of Saxony and Burgrave of Magdeburg, my Most Gracious Lord, might most graciously allow his appointed Kapellmeister, Heinrich Schütz, to serve most humbly before Your Illustrious Royal Serenity for a period of time. Now I in truth would have preferred to have been able to set about this work sooner, since his service at court is not needed in the prevailing troubled period of great suffering and war, but all manner of impediments presented themselves, such that it could not happen conveniently. He came here to Hamburg already two months ago, and at his own expense stayed during that time with his people here until he might learn that Your Illustrious Royal Serenity arrives in your customary Residence at Hadersleben.[82] When he then received news of it from the Lord Governor of Glückstadt,[83] and furthermore that Your Illustrious

---

81. This material in the original location is not paginated or otherwise numbered.
82. Haderslev, Denmark.
83. Lykstad, Denmark.

Royal Serenity will be there shortly, he set out on his way and would most humbly enter into your service. I consider it unnecessary to describe his impeccable qualifications and to recommend them most humbly, since it is expected that in everything which Your Illustrious Royal Serenity shall most graciously command of him, he shall give most undoubtedly such obedient satisfaction that you shall derive from it singular, most gracious pleasure. I wanted to notify Your Illustrious Royal Serenity of this most obediently, to whom I commend myself most humbly thereby to your steadfast benevolent favor.

Dated at Hamburg, 13 November 1633.
Your Illustrious Royal Serenity's
most humble, obedient servant,
Lebzelter, in his own hand.

67. MEMORANDUM REGARDING PREPARATIONS FOR SCHÜTZ'S APPOINTMENT TO THE DANISH COURT (LATE 1633)

[DK-RA: Tyske Kancelli, indenrigske afdeling, Indkomne breve, kronologisk ordnede, A93, 1515–1670 (1 fol.)]

Memorandum.

At the pleasure of His Royal Majesty, our Most Gracious Lord, His Princely Serenity requests most graciously that the following items might be drawn up in the Royal Chancellery in regard of His Royal Majesty's most highly esteemed Kapellmeister, Heinrich Schütz. To wit:

1. By virtue of his appointment he shall have an annual salary of 800 *Reichsthaler*, which then as with other court servants shall be paid monthly in equal amounts. It and other items too shall be expressly entered into the terms of the appointment—that he shall supervise the musical company, such that they might attend to their bounden service and, in default of which, he shall be obliged to indicate the disobedient and insubordinate ones to the Court and also to His Royal Majesty.

2. Two passports—one for his servant, Moses Eichler, who should travel in advance with the Kapellmeister's baggage, and then one for the Kapellmeister himself, and both must indicate to Glückstadt by water and land.[84]

3. A notice to Dresden to have this communicated privately to His Royal Majesty, at his most gracious pleasure, that 100 *Reichsthaler* might be transferred with the first post to the aforesaid Kapellmeister for his expenses.

---

84. Glückstadt, located on the River Elbe approximately 50 km downriver from Hamburg, was founded by Christian IV in 1617 and fortified in 1620. It was established both to extend his influence and to compete against Hamburg for trade. Christian IV was King of Denmark, as well as Duke of Schleswig and Holstein.

68. SCHÜTZ'S ENTRY IN JOACHIM MORSIUS'S *STAMMBUCH* (21 JANUARY 1634) (ORIGINAL LANGUAGE: LATIN)

[D-LÜh: *Album Morsianum*, Ms.hist.4° 25.4, fol. 775r][85]

Blessed Jerome: The whole world is full of riches for the one who believes: but the faithless lacks even a penny.[86]
[Inserted in a second hand] Ambrose, vol. 3, bk 10, no. 82. Within the church, the faithful man is rich, for the faithful man has an entire world of riches.[87]
I shall sing to the Lord in my life, I shall sing psalms to my God as long as I live.[88]
Heinrich Schütz, the Kapellmeister, for the time being, of the Most Serene King of Denmark and Norway, otherwise of the Most Serene Elector of Saxony, was gladly placing his respect and love by the very famous and excellent man, *Herr* Joachim Morsius.[89] In Copenhagen, 21 January, in the year 1634.

[Original]

B. Hyeronimus
Credenti totus mundus divitarium est: infidelis autem etiam obolo indiget.

---

85. Originally a *Stammbuch* was a volume for the detailed recording of one's family and genealogy. Over time a *Stammbuch* became a more generalized place for friends, acquaintances, and visitors to enter signatures, maxims, poetry, crests and drawings, and even musical notation. The German custom of keeping a *Stammbuch* as an *album amicorum* was transplanted to England in the middle of the seventeenth century, where it became an *Album of Friends*. The document is in Schütz's hand with insertions in a second hand. Transcribed in *Schütz-GBr*, Nr. 42; *Schütz-Dokumente*, Nr. 75.
86. The text is taken from St. Jerome's *Epistola ad Paulinum presbyterum, de omnibus divinae historiae libris* (Nr. 53), written in 395, and drawn from Proverbs 17:6 (Septuagint). See Jerome, *Sancti Evsebii Hieronymi Epistvlae, Pars I*, vol. 54, 464.
87. The maxim derives from St. Ambrose's letter to the Church at Vercellae, likewise echoing the second part of Proverbs 17:6 (Septuagint). Both the quotation and citation are consistent with the mid-sixteenth-century edition of writings by St. Ambrose, *Omnia quotquot extant D. Ambrosii Episcopii Mediolanensis Opera* (Basel, 1555), comprising three volumes in one. The inserted text is not included in *Schütz-GBr*.
88. Psalm 103:33. Schütz's setting of this psalm (SWV 260) had been recently published in the *Symphoniae sacrae* (Venice, 1629).
89. Joachim Morsius (b. 3 Jan. 1593; d. 1643/44) was the son of a wealthy Hamburg goldsmith. Described (*ADB* 22, 327–29) as having "a richly gifted but completely intractable nature" ("eine reich begabte, aber völlig zuchtlose Natur"), Morsius was a consummately restless figure, spending most of his time and all of his fortune traveling. He was well educated, served briefly as chief administrator of the University Library in Rostock from 1615, married a wealthy woman whom he abandoned before 1617, obtained an M.A. from Cambridge University in 1619, became involved in mysticism and the Rosicrucians, was brought by his family before the Council in Hamburg for prodigality, later incarcerated in consequence of his own brother's grievances, freed in 1640 through the intervention of Christian IV, King of Denmark, and died suddenly in Gottorp (Schleswig-Holstein) in late 1643 or early 1644. Morsius's expansive library, collection of letters, writings on arcane subjects, *Stammbücher*, engravings, and such were purchased by the Lübeck Council in 1648 and currently reside in the Stadtbibliothek Lübeck.

[Inserted in a second hand] Ambros. Tom. 3, Lib. 10, ep. num. 82. In Eccl[e]sia quidem fidelis dives est, fideli enim totus mundus divitiarum est.

Cantabo DOMINO in vita mea, psallam DEO mea *Quam diu fuero.*

Clarissimo ac praestantissimo viro Dño Joachimo Morsio, observantiae et Amoris ergo lubens apponebat. Haffniae die 21 Januarii Ao. 163[4][90] Henricus Sagittarius[91] pro tempore Ser^{mi} Daniae et Norwegiae Regis, alias Ser^{mi} El^{ris} Sax^{ij} Capellae Magister.

69. ZACHARIAS HESTIUS DIRECTED TO JOHANN GEORG I (23 APRIL 1634)

Communication concerning Schütz's repeated absence and shortages at the Dresden Court

[D-Dla: Loc. 8687/1, Kantoreiordnung so Kurfürst Moritz…1548, fol. 186r]

With the most submissive request, the undersigned entreats His Most Serene Elector of Saxony (etc.), and Burgrave of Magdeburg (etc.), His Most Gracious Lord, in most humble obedience that: because the charge of the *Music* in the Divine Service has for the most part always devolved upon him [i.e., Hestius] *ex officio*, especially during the past and repeated absence of Kapellmeister Heinrich Schütz, enduring this becomes all the more burdensome and difficult at present, when following deaths, in addition to departures and retirements, of most of the vocalists and instrumentalists attached to the Electoral Kapelle, with so few persons continuing to perform [music] without alternation. And particularly in German *Lieder*, the voice will seize up, not without sensitivity and more frequent natural shortness of breath and physical stamina. For that reason, may His Electoral Serenity be graciously pleased to order and decree that, for his recovery and better development by means of God-given restoratives and of sustaining the natural life forces, a certain draught of wine from the Electoral Court wine cellar and a bite of bread might be dispensed to him, according to your most gracious apportioning, if not daily, then weekly, perhaps on each of the appointed sermon days. His Electoral Serenity shall be requited with daily, faithful service, in most humble obedience. Dated at Dresden, Saint George's Day [i.e., 23 April 1634].

Electoral Serenity's
most humble, most dutiful,
obedient servant,
Zacharias Hestius,
Vice-Kapellmeister, in his own hand.

---

90. The last digit of the date is lost owing to damage to the paper. *Schütz-Dokumente* (186) proposes a dating of 1635 for the *Stammbuch* entry.
91. *Schütz-GBr* (127) fails to include Schütz's name in his transcription.

70. CHRISTIAN IV, KING OF DENMARK, TO JOHANN GEORG I (25 MAY 1635)

Draft of a letter expressing thanks and requesting leniency toward Schütz for his extended absence from the Dresden Court

[DK-RA, Kongehuset Arkiv, Christian 4., Prins Christian (5.), Koncepter til åbne og lukkede breve af Christian (5.) (til fyrstelige personer og andre) 1631–1647]

[Address]

To the Elector of Saxony
Nykøbing,[92] 25 May 1635

[Text]

Worshipful Prince, Much Beloved Lord Cousin and Father. The exhibitor [of the document], your Saxon Kapellmeister and much beloved *Herr* Heinrich Schütz, hastens to return to Your Dilection. As we have pondered over our indebtedness on this occasion, and wish to thank Your Dilection most graciously and reverentially for letting us have the aforesaid Kapellmeister for so long at our earlier wedding and other services, with an additional request that Your Dilection might not take offence at your aforesaid Kapellmeister's lengthy absence, but rather instead continue with utmost clemency toward him for our sake, owing to his most praiseworthy, diligent services executed in this place, assuring Your Dilection at the same time that, if we on our part can display in similar ways and more our filial affection through corresponding favor and service, we shall be ready to do so at all times. Faithfully commending you herewith to God's merciful protection. Date.

71. DANISH TRAVEL PASS ISSUED TO SCHÜTZ (25 MAY 1635)

Travel and security pass issued to Schütz for his travel from and back to Denmark

[DK-RA: Kongehuset Christian 4., Prins Christian (5.), Koncepter til åbne og lukkede breve af Christian (5.) (til fyrstelige personer og andre) 1631–1647, nr. 24 (1 fol., r-v)]

Security pass [*Passus securitatis*] for Heinrich Schütz
Nykøbing, 25 May 1635

We, Christian V, do give notice herewith in that the presenter [of this document], the accomplished Kapellmeister of our Most Gracious *Herr* Father and Electoral Saxon Dilection, our dear distinguished Heinrich Schütz, for his return travel from here once

---

92. Nykøbing (now Nykøbing Falster), Denmark, is approximately 120 km southwest of Copenhagen.

again to Dresden, and then, in accordance with his circumstances, from there back here again to these domains, might be free generally to pass through securely and ably without suspicion at all times. Thus in the absence of His Most Honorable Royal Majesty we deemed it highly necessary to provide him with our present, open passport. Accordingly in regard to all the admirals, vice-admirals, as well as ships at sea and on the rivers, as also to all senior and junior military officers on horseback and on foot, cavalry and infantry in general, who are herewith requested according to one's rank,[93] that they might allow the aforesaid Kapellmeister, together with his accompanying man-servant and belongings, to pass and as well as to return [*repassirn*] freely, safely, and unimpeded, neither to offend his person nor his man-servant and belongings, nor to have them offended by others, but together instead to guard and protect against all unlawful force; and, upon his request to continue his journey, to bestow all proper assistance, aid, and advancement; and he shall be allowed to pass. This do we certify for all to know. Date.

72. *MUSICALISCHE EXEQUIEN* (DRESDEN, 1636): TITLE PAGE AND DEDICATION

[*Title page*]

Musicalische Exequien [Musical Obsequies] [94]
as were celebrated at the stately and venerable funeral
of His late Most Noble Lord,
Lord Heinrich
the Younger and Eldest Reuss, Lord of Plauen, former Counsel to
His Imperial Roman Majesty;
Lord of Greiz, Kranichfeld,
Gera, Schleiz, and Lobenstein, etc.,
now of blessed Christian memory,
recently on the fourth day of February at Gera, before and
after the funeral sermon,
as repeatedly requested during the lifetime of His late Grace, arranged and sung to a
quiet, *verdackte* organ,[95]
for performance with 6, 8, and more voices.
Also including duplicate basso continuo parts—the one for the
organ, the other for the conductor or for the *Violone*—in which is to be found a
separate index of the musical compositions included in this slight work,

---

93. This phrase is followed by the letters: v f. l. g. g. u. g. b. It is unknown what this signifies.
94. SWV 279–81; RISM A/I/8 S 2289; *SA* 12; *NSA* 4; *SSA* 8.
95. In the introduction to the *SSA* edition of the *Musicalische Exequien*, *verdackte* is translated as *discreet* (xxxviii). It is possible that it refers to a covered stop on the organ (*gedackt*), which produces a soft, subdued sound. It was also the practice in seventeenth-century funerals for the nobility to drape or blanket (i.e., *verdecken*) the church interior in black cloth. Not only did this evoke a particular atmosphere visually, it muted the sound of the instrument.

together with the ordinances
or preparations for the benevolent reader.
As a final, humble memorial of honor, and upon request,
set to music and prepared for publication by
Heinrich Schütz, Electoral Saxon Kapellmeister.
Printed in Dresden by Wolff Seyffert in the year 1636.

[Dedication]

To
Her Most Noble Ladyship, Lady
Magdalena Reuss of Plauen,[96]
born Countess of Schwarzburg and Hohenstein,
Lady of Greiz, Kranichfeld, Gera, Schleiz,
and Lobenstein, etc.,
and also to the
Most Noble Lords,
Lord
Heinrich the Second,[97]
the Younger Reuss,
and Lord
Heinrich the Third,
the Younger Reuss, brothers, Lords of Plauen,
Lords of Greiz, Kranichfeld, Gera, Schleiz,
and Lobenstein etc.

To His late Most Noble Grace's
Widow and Sons,
To his [Schütz's] gracious Lady and Lords,
humbly dedicated
by
the Author.

---

96. Magdalena, Countess of Schwarzburg-Rudolstadt (b. 12 Apr. 1580; d. 22 Apr. 1652) was Heinrich Posthumus's second wife. Posthumus married the seventeen-year-old countess on 21 May 1597 following the death of his first wife, Magdalena, Countess of Hohenlohe-Langenburg (b. 27 Dec. 1572; d. 2 Apr. 1596), who died prematurely of tuberculosis.

97. According to a family tradition dating back centuries, all males born into the House of Reuss were named Heinrich. Of the four sons still alive at the time of Posthumus's death, Heinrich II (b. 14 Aug. 1602; d. 28 May 1670) was eldest and thus succeeded his father. As did his father before him, Heinrich II maintained ties to Schütz, consulting him on musical matters. Heinrich III (b. 31 Oct. 1603; d. 12 Jul. 1640) is also named in the dedication because he had reached the age of majority, whereas Heinrich IX (b. 22 May 1616; d. 9 Jan. 1666) and Heinrich X (b. 9 Sept. 1621; d. 25 Jan. 1671) were still minors.

73. *MUSICALISCHE EXEQUIEN* (DRESDEN, 1636): ELEGY ON THE DEATH OF HEINRICH POSTHUMUS REUSS

To the blessed deceased in Christ, the Most Noble Lord,
Lord Heinrich, the Younger and Eldest Reuss,
Lord of Plauen, etc.

Was it then not enough of this punishment and rod,
with which the Almighty God out of righteous spirit
scourged us for our grievous sins and great misdeeds
now through the fierceness of war;
for what good things previously existed
now lie wholly and utterly trampled underfoot and destroyed
all order is torn asunder, laws are perverted,
the schools are laid waste, the churches are demolished?
That this misfortune had to befall us as well,
that you, oh worthy champion, should be taken from us
through death's fury in these, such dismal times,
and increase for us so much thereby our sorrow and grief?
You, who were for the muses their shelter, protection, joy, and bliss,
You, who were a bright sun of piety,
You, who newly founded our schools and built up our churches,
furnished them well and intently looked on,
so that the worship service be conducted free from falsehood,
and adorned most sweetly with singing and playing.
You, who like David himself
lifted Your voice and turned Your hand to the art of music
to God's glory and praise, with other musicians
whom You so greatly loved, that of such fellow artists,
You too would have engaged four thousand [1. Chron. 24:5]
if You had had David's wealth and riches.
What can I say here, how my inadequate song
and rustic sound, you used to hold in equal esteem
with the most beautiful things; and what favor and benevolence
and what acts of kindness you bestowed upon me again and again
on account of this art; above all because I had my origins and came into
this world within your dominion,*   *Köstritz, a mile
which you considered an honor to yourself   away from Gera
and therefore loved me all the more.
But now you have been torn away from us:
You, however, are there in the Master Order
of the heavenly choir, where Asaph everlasting,

together with Heman, Jeduthun and others of the host of singers[98]
sing songs of praise, exalt, glorify the Triune Holy God
through wonderfully sweet sounds, and the most beautiful melodies
with whom together You also raise up your voice
and let resound a new song in praise of Him.
Now then, rejoice in such delight and joy;
if God will rescue me, too, from this fear and misery,
to that place, there to dwell amid
the company of the elect and the heavenly cantorate;
so let us together, with angelic melodies,
joined together with the cherubim and seraphim, extol
the Almighty forever and ever, singing: Holy, God,[99]
Yea, Holy, Holy is the great Lord of Hosts.[100]
May we likewise join in with the choir and the twenty-four elders
assembled in the most lovely forms around the throne of the Lamb,
and sing: You, O Lord, are worthy of the power and glory.[101]
Yea, with the great multitude of thousand upon thousand hosts
to let us continue singing for all eternity:
the Lamb is most worthy to receive, ever more,[102]
Power, Wisdom, Riches, Strength, and Blessing, Glory and Honor.
For now, may you look favorably upon what my muses offer
to you here at last, in honor of your memory,
and remember, inasmuch as it is poorly crafted,
that it was prepared still in this mortal world.
Heinrich Schütz

[Original]

War es denn nicht genug an dieser Straff vnd Ruhte /

---

98. The reference to the biblical figures is from 1 Chronicles 25:1: "Moreover David and the captains of the host separated to the service of the sons of Asaph, and of Heman, and of Jeduthun, who should prophesy with harps, with psalteries, and with cymbals." There are also references in 1 Chronicles 25:6: "All these *were* under the hands of their father for song *in* the house of the LORD, with cymbals, psalteries, and harps, for the service of the house of God, according to the king's order to Asaph, Jeduthun, and Heman": and 2 Chronicles 35:15: "And the singers the sons of Asaph *were* in their place, according to the commandment of David, and Asaph, and Heman, and Jeduthun the King's seer; and the porters *waited* at every gate; they might not depart from their service; for their brethren the Levites prepared for them." There are additional references in 1 Chronicles to Heman as a singer (1 Chron 6:33), to Asaph as a singer who with Heman played cymbals (1 Chron 15:19): "So the singers, Heman, Asaph, and Ethan, were appointed to sound with cymbals of brass."
99. Isaiah 4:4.
100. Revelation 4:8.
101. Revelation 4:11.
102. Revelation 5:12.

Mit der / der höchste GOtt / vns / aus gerechtem Muhte /
    Umb vnsre schwere Sünd / vnd grosse Missethat /
    Durch der Bellonen Grimm biß her gesteupet hat;
Indem was gutes nur war vormals angerichtet /
Nun lieget gantz vnd gar zertreten vnd zernichtet /
    All' Ordnung ist zertrennt / Gesetze sind verkehrt /
    Die Schulen sind verwüst / die Kirchen sind zerstört?
Daß eben auch darzu diß Vnglück muste kommen /
Daß Ihr / O wehrter Held / vns würdet hingenommen
    Durchs Todes Wüterey / in der so trüben Zeit /
    Vnd mehren vns dadurch so sehr die Noht vnd Leid?
Der Ihr den Musen wart ihr Schirm / Schutz / Freud vnd Wonne /
Der Ihr der Gottesfurcht wart eine helle Sonne /
    Der Ihr habt Schulen neu= vnd Kirchen aufferbaut /
    Vnd sie bestellet wol / vnd embsig zugeschaut /
Damit der Gottesdienst werd ohne falsch geführet /
Vnd mit Gesang vnd Klang auffs lieblichste gezieret /
    Der Ihr / wie David selbst auch eure Zung vnd Hand /
    Durch gantz kunstreichen Schall / erhoben vnd gewandt
Zu GOttes Ehr vnd Preiß / mit andern Musicanten /
Die Ihr geliebt so sehr / daß solcher Kunst Verwanten
    Vier tausent gleichfals Ihr euch hättet auch bestellt /   1. Chron. 24.5
    Wann Ihr gewesen wärt ihm gleich am Gutt vnd Gelt.
Was soll ich melden hier, wie mein geringes Singen
Vnd Bäuerischen Thon / Ihr auch den schönsten Dingen
    Zuachten pflaget gleich / vnd welche Huld vnd Gunst /
    Vnd was für Woltaht Ihr mir wegen solcher Kunst /
Erwiesen offtermals: bevorauß weil genommen
Ich meinen Vrsprung hat / vnd auff die Welt war kommen
    In euer Herrschafft* Grund / in dem Ihrs selbst für Ehr   **Kösteritz/ eine Meil*
    Euch hieltet / vnd darümb mich liebtet desto mehr.   *weges von Gera*
Nun aber seyd Ihr hin von vns gerissen worden:
Jedoch Ihr euch befindt dor in dem Meister Orden
    Deß himmelischen Chors / wo Asaph immerdar /
    Sampt Heman / Jedithun vnd andrer Sänger Schaar /
Den dreymal Heilgen GOTT lobsingen / rühmen / preisen
Durch wundersüssen Thon / vnd allerschönste weisen /
    Mit welchen Ihr zugleich auch eure Stimm erschwingt /
    Vnd zu desselben Lob ein neues Lied erklingt.
Wolan / ergetzet Euch in solcher Lust vnd Freuden;

Wenn mir verhelffen wird auß dieser Angst vnd Leiden
Auch Gott an solchen Ort / daselbst zuwohnen bey
Der Ausserwehlten Schaar / vnd Himmels=Cantorey;
So wollen wir zugleich auff Engelische Weisen /
Mit sampt den Cherubin vnd Seraphin hoch=preisen
Den Höchsten für vnd für / vnd singen: Heilg GOtt /   Es. 4.4
Ja Heilig / Heilig sey der grosse Zebaoht.   Apoc. 4.8
Wir wollen mit dem Chor der vier vnd zwantzig Alten /
Die ümb deß Lammes Stuhl / in lieblichsten gestalten
Dort haben ihre Sitz / einstimmen gleicher weis /
Vnd singen: Dir O HErr gebühret Krafft vnd Preiß.   Apoc. 4.11
Ja mit dem grossen Heer von viel=viel tausend Scharen /
Zusingen wollen wir in Ewigkeit fortfahren:
Das Lamb höchstwürdig ist zunemen / mehr vnd mehr /   Apoc. 5.12
Krafft / Weißheit / Reichthumb / Stärck / vnd Lob / vnd Preiß und Ehr.
Indeß seht günstig an / was meine Musen schenken
Euch wollen hier zu letzt / zum Ehren angedencken /
Vnd achtet / weil es ist gar schlechtlich zubereitt /
Daß es geschehen sey noch in der sterblichkeit.

74. *MUSICALISCHE EXEQUIEN* (DRESDEN, 1636): MEMORANDA AND INSTRUCTIONS FOR PERFORMANCE

Separate Index of the Musical Items found in this work, together with the Ordinances for the Benevolent Reader.

There are only three pieces or *concertos* to be found in this slight musical work. 1. All those passages from Holy Scriptures and verses of Christian hymns which His late Grace had recorded and written on the outside of the lid and on both sides, as well as at the head and foot, of his coffin made in secret during his lifetime, are gathered together and set in a *concerto*, in the form of a German *Missa*, after the manner of the Latin *Kyrie, Christe, Kyrie Eleison; Gloria in excelsis; Et in terra pax, etc.* 2. The passage or text which His late Grace selected and ordered for his funeral: "Herr, wenn ich nur dich habe, etc." 3. The Canticle of Simeon [*Canticum Simeonis*] "Herr, nun lässest du deinen Diener in Friede fahren, etc."[103] ordered by His late Grace for his stately interment, during which a separate choir with another text is introduced, which begins: "Selig sind die Toten, etc."[104] Following now are the Ordinances and Preparations for each *concerto*.

---

103. "Lord, now lettest thou thy servant depart in peace."
104. "Blessed are the dead which die in the Lord."

I.
Ordinance of the Concerto or the German burial Missa: Nacket bin ich vom Mutterleibe kommen

1. This *concerto* composed after the manner of a Latin or German *Missa* is concerted to the organ *6. Vocum* or by six singers strictly speaking, and has two discantists, one alto, two tenors, and a bass. 2. In the alto part, however, there are also two passages for a bass voice (when the alto drops out or is silent), which is intended to lend greater variety to the *concerto,* and hence must also be assigned and sung. 3. From these six *concertato* voices six other voice parts can be additionally copied out (where the word *Capella* is indicated and up to the next vertical line[105]), and thus a separate choir or *Capella* can be set up and introduced. 4. For the benefit of the singers, I have transposed the basso continuo a fourth lower, with the appropriate chords for accompanying these works on the organ, knowing that a fifth lower would have been more natural to the organ and perhaps would have better served inexperienced organists. 5. Because I had to bring together verses of German hymns in several modes into one composition [*corpus*], I hope prudent musicians shall forgive me where occasionally I have had to stray outside the bounds of the *Ninth Mode* to follow the chorale tunes. 6. Whoever might like this work of mine could make good use of it now and then in place of a German *Missa,* and perhaps at the Feast of the Purification [of the Virgin Mary][106] or on the sixteenth Sunday after Trinity.[107]

II.
Ordinance for the Motet: Herr, wenn ich nur dich habe.

It is in *Octo Vocum* for two equal choirs, and can also be arranged and performed without the organ, according to preference.

III.
Ordinance for the Canticle of Simeon: Herr, nun lässest du deinen Diener in Friede fahren

1. It is to be noted that this *concerto* is for two choirs, and each choir has its own text. *Chorus primus* is in five parts and recites the words of Simeon: "Herr, nun lässest du deinen Diener." *Chorus secundus* is in three parts, for two discantists and one baritone or high *bass,* and sings the following passage, among others: "Selig sind die Toten, die in dem Herrn sterben." With this *invention* or *Chorus Secundus,* the author wishes in some measure to introduce and intimate the joy of the disembodied blessed soul in

---

105. A *Strichlein* is a small vertical line that goes through the staff, like a barline.
106. *Festo Purificationis.*
107. *Dominica XVI post Trinitatis.* Bieritz, *Das Kirchenjahr. Feste, Gedenk- und Feiertage in Geschichte und Gegenwart,* 172. The thematic accent for the Sixteenth Sunday after Trinity is Christ's power over death, shown through his raising Lazarus from the dead as recounted in the Bible (John 11).

heaven, in the company of heavenly spirits and holy angels. 2. *Primus chorus* is placed close to the organ, *secundus chorus* however in the distance, and as it is considered by each to be most desirable. 3. Whoever might wish to have this *chorus secundus* copied out once or twice, and to assign these parts to different locations depending on the circumstances of the church, the author hopes the effect of the work might be greatly augmented.

A few reminders for the *violone* or the great bass viol, included here in place of an appendix, since there was still room.

That the *violone* or the great bass viol, when properly played, is the most convenient, most agreeable instrument for the *concertato* voices when they *concert* and sing alone to a quiet organ, and a singular adornment to the *Music*, is evinced not only by the effect itself but confirmed moreover by the example of the most famous musicians in Europe, who these days make use of this instrument all the time in their performances, as mentioned above. Consequently it was not inadvisable, in connection to publishing the concerted musical compositions, to have yet another copy made of the basso continuo [part] for the *violone*, and to add it to this work along with the one for the organ. As also occurs with the present slight work of mine, I am resolved to do this in such a manner, and in future with other of my editions soon to follow, God willing. Although a separate and properly arranged *bass* for the aforementioned *violone* could be prepared and published, and not just the print of the *bass* for the organ, we will just keep to this print for the sake of sparing expenses. It is assumed that everyone who has learned to play this foundational [*fundamental*] instrument will know how to proceed using a keen ear and good judgment. For the sake of those with less experience, however, I have included three brief memoranda about how the *violone* can be discreetly played from this print of the organ bass part:

1. Wherever alto or tenor clefs are indicated, the *violone* can likewise play along, but always an octave lower. For example, in a vocal trio, as for two discantists and an alto, the *violone* can play the alto an octave lower with good effect. It is, however, important to take note of the following:

2. When these upper parts, such as discant, alto or tenor, enter fugally one after the other, then the *violone* remains silent and first joins in with the bass.

3. One should observe in particular as well that, when two or more bass voices alone *concert* [to the organ], then the *violone* remains silent, because the bass voice provides the *Fundament* without it, and the *violone* playing the same strings [*Chorden*] or unisons produces an unpleasant harmony.

Should one thing and another more be called to mind, the ear and practice shall develop and instruct.

75. SCHÜTZ TO JOHANN GEORG I (9 AUGUST 1636)

Petition for the third of three electoral printing patents

[D-Dla: Loc. 10 757, Privilegia, Bd. 3, 1628–1640, fol. 406r–v][108]

[Address]

To the Most Serene, Noble-Born Prince and Lord, Lord Johann Georg, Duke of Saxony, Jülich, Cleves and Berg, Grand Marshal and Elector of the Holy Roman Empire, Landgrave in Thuringia, Margrave of Meissen, of Upper and Lower Lusatia, and Burgrave of Magdeburg, Count of the Mark and Ravensberg, Lord of Ravenstein, my Most Gracious Elector and Lord

[Text]

Most Serene, Most Noble Elector. To Your Electoral Serenity I pledge my most dutiful services in most humble obedience, to the best of my ability and means, first and foremost.

Most Gracious Lord, I write most humbly to inform Your Electoral Serenity of my resolve to assemble henceforth and then further to have published, with God's help, one part after the other, those musical works which I composed and set down in my twenty-year service to Your Electoral Serenity, partly on behalf of the Christian evangelical church music, and partly, in addition to this, for honorable enjoyment and recreation. However, because of the present conditions and that, in addition to the other fine arts, music in particular now flourishes but little, it will be scarcely possible to bring these works of mine to press. Those booksellers too, to whom I previously offered them, amid other difficulties, protest and excuse themselves primarily on account of disturbing and ruinous reprinting [i.e., pirating].

Thus I am occasioned with this my most humble letter to solicit Your Electoral Serenity most obediently and most diligently. May it please you in electoral grace, and for the sake of my faithful, most humble service previously rendered, to do me the extraordinary electoral favor and, for the promotion of this undertaking of mine, most graciously grant me a general patent for all those musical works that I might prepare for publication with God's help, so that not only for my sake, but rather and as fully for the sake of my publishers too, I and thus we together might have recourse to this in order to prevent the aforesaid ruinous reprinting.

And again to earn this great favor from Your Electoral Serenity, I remain most willingly in dutiful, most humble devotion, to the utmost of my ability and means.

Dated at Dresden, 9 August 1636.

Your Electoral Serenity's

---

108. The petition, written in a copyist's hand and signed by Schütz, was submitted just prior to the publication of the first part of the *Kleine geistliche Concerte* in 1636. Transcribed in *Schütz-Dokumente*, Nr. 78.

most humble and obedient
Heinrich Schütz, Kapellmeister, in his own hand.

76. SCHÜTZ TO THE DRESDEN COURT (AFTER 9 AUGUST 1636)

Remarks on the publishing and presentation copies of Kleine geistliche Concerte I & II

[D-Dla: Loc. 10 757, Privilegia, Bd. 3, 1628–1640, unnumbered folio precedes fol. 406][109]

Part One of the Small Church Concertos
with 1, 2, 3, 4, and 5 voices,
to be followed as soon as possible by Part Two, God willing.

It is my humble request, that it might be to communicated to the Electoral Saxon High Consistory—and the second part might here be added to part one of the small concertos *à* 1, 2, 3, 4, and 5—that in regard of the delivery of the exemplars, I would be inclined to submit six copies to the High Consistory should I publish my works myself; but should I have a bookdealer to publish them, as many again, and thus twelve copies, would be submitted.

77. *KLEINE GEISTLICHE CONCERTE I* (LEIPZIG, 1636): TITLE PAGE AND DEDICATION (29 SEPTEMBER 1636)

[Title page]

Part One
of the *Kleine geistliche Concerte* [Small Sacred Concertos][110]
with 1, 2, 3, 4, and 5 voices, together with
added basso continuo for the organ.
Set to music
by
Heinrich Schütz,
Kapellmeister to the
Electoral Serenity of Saxony.
ORGAN
By privilege of the Electoral Serenity of Saxony.
Leipzig
Published by Gottfried Gross, Bookseller
M DC XXXVI [1636].

---

109. The document is in Schütz's hand. Transcribed in *Schütz-Dokumente*, Nr. 79.
110. SWV 282–305; RISM A/I/8 S 2290; *SA* 6; *NSA* 10–12.

[Dedication]

To the Most Noble, Worshipful, and Worthy
Lord Heinrich of Friesen at Rötha,[111]
the Electoral Serenity of Saxony's and Highly Ordained President
of the Appellate Court at Dresden, Head
of the Offices Colditz, Rochlitz, Leisnig, and Bornum, also
Director of Land-tax and Beverage-
tax, etc.
My Most Benevolent and Most Venerable
Patron.

All can see how the praiseworthy [art of] music, among the other liberal arts, has not only been thrown into great decline and in some places utterly devastated through the continual, dangerous events of war in the dear fatherland of our German Nation, standing alongside other general ruin and widespread disorder which this unholy war brings with it. I myself also suffer this with regard to some of my musical compositions which I have had to set aside owing to a lack of publishers up to now, as at present, and until the Almighty might perhaps most quickly and graciously grant better times. In the meantime, however, and so that my God-given talent in so noble an art does not fall completely into disuse, but rather might create and offer something, if only slight, I decided to compose and now publish sundry small concertos, as harbingers, so to speak, of my musical works to the glory of God, but especially to have them issue forth under Your Most Noble Worship's name, not only because you have always shown yourself to me to be my most benevolent, well-disposed patron, but that you are gifted as well with great skill and extraordinary qualities, more so than many other noble persons, and no less highly skilled in the noble art of music (to which I might sincerely attest) and a great admirer of the same. It is my steadfast hope that Your Most Noble Worship will accept in the best spirit this well-intentioned dedication from me, and might appreciate these small concertos such that they might be used occasionally alongside other recreations and delectations. In return I remain obliged always to Your Most Noble Worship for all possible services, most faithfully commending myself and this small work of mine to your continuing favor and most benevolent protection. Dated at Dresden, 29 September 1636.

To serve Your Most Noble Worship,
[Your] ever most willing
Heinrich Schütz,
Electoral Saxon Kapellmeister.

---

111. Heinrich the Elder, Baron of Friesen (b. 24 Apr. 1578; d. 30 Jun. 1659), was married in Schweinsburg 3 September 1601 to Katharina of Einsiedel (b. 10 Aug. 1585; d. 9 Feb. 1668).

78. SCHÜTZ DIRECTED TO GEORG PFLUGK (1 FEBRUARY 1637)

Memorandum requesting leave to travel to Denmark to retrieve compositions and an outstanding honorarium from the Royal Court

[D-Dla: Loc 8687/1, Kantoreiordnung so Kurfürst Moritz...1548, fol. 193r–v][112]

> To be given to the Lord Marshal of the Palace: Memorial of what to present most humbly to His Electoral Serenity on my account.

In consequence of the present time and continuing state of war, neither His Electoral Highness nor his Kapelle could be particularly served by my person, and hence, in a word, I would be of nearly no use either to God or to man, or to myself least of all. In consideration of these conditions so adverse to my profession, not only would the talent God granted me decline and perish, but I would in time be thrown into all manner of unbearable distress on account of my circumstances. Moreover, my best musical compositions are still in Denmark, and I have my honorarium from the Prince as well as other claims there, which without my personal attendance, as I understand it, would not likely be remitted to me.

Thus with unceasing loyal and most humble devotion, I would most obediently learn from His Electoral Serenity whether under these circumstances His Electoral Highness might not allow to occur that, with his most gracious permission, I journey again to that place, and either return again immediately after claiming my things or, during this military unrest, perhaps stay for a period with His Majesty and his *Music* in the interim (but with the retention of my current appointment and title of office, which I will use ever and always both privately and in the publications of my musical works, so long as it pleases God and His Electoral Serenity).

With regard to my most obedient and most willing return, should God spare my life, and should Your Electoral Serenity once again be attended by my person, this would be sufficiently assured, since I would be leaving my children, house, and home, and all kinds of important obligations here in the land. For that reason I would have cause to travel frequently back here again, especially since the way is not so far, and such a journey, with God and good fortune, can likely be completed within fourteen days' time.

I live finally in the most humble hope that His Electoral Serenity would, after most gracious consideration of the above-mentioned reasons, not only not take umbrage against me on account of this my testimony, but rather much more in these troubled times, out of electoral special grace, most graciously allow me to pursue this my plan.

Signed at Dresden, 1 February 1637.
Heinrich Schütz,
Kapellmeister, in his own hand.

---

112. The document is in Schütz's hand. Transcribed in *Schütz-GBr*, Nr. 46; *Schütz-Dokumente*, Nr 81.

79. PRINTING PATENT GRANTED SCHÜTZ BY EMPEROR FERDINAND III (3 APRIL 1637)

[A-Whh, Impressorialakten "Sagittarius," fols. 5r-6v and 7r-8r][113]

We, Ferdinand III, by Grace of God, Elected Roman Emperor, Ever Expander of the Empire, King of Germania, Hungary, Bohemia, Dalmatia, Croatia, and Slavonia, etc., Archduke of Austria, Duke of Burgundy, Styria, Carinthia, Carniola, and Württemberg, Count of Tyrol, etc., acknowledge publically with this letter, and make known to all by these presents, that Our and the Empire's beloved, faithful *Henricus Sagittarius* most humbly gives us to understand how he planned to have printed those *Opera Musicalia* which he composed partly in Latin, partly in German, sacred as well as secular, partly as well without text, so that this might not be reprinted by others to their advantage but to his great loss and disadvantage. He thus solicited and petititoned Us for Our Imperial *Privilegium Impressorium*.

We have graciously examined this most humble, reasonable petition, and morever with mature consideration, good counsel, and rightful understanding, and have granted the aforementioned *Sagittarius* this special favor and liberty.

We also make known herewith by virtue of this letter that he may have the aforesaid *Opera Musicalia* publically issued in print, reissue these from time to time, sell them or have them for sale, which is permitted him or his direct heirs within five years, effective as of this date; by anyone else, whoever he may be, in no place, neither in larger nor smaller format, neither reprinted [in whole], nor reprinted in part [*distrahiret*], have for sale or distribution, unless he has previously come to fair terms with the aforesaid *Henricus Sagittarius*, and received from him licence and permission. We hereby expressly command all Our subjects and lieges, for their sake, in particular however book-printers, bookdealers, and booksellers, of the Empire, as well as of our hereditary kingdom, principality, and land, that you, or any one of you, by yourself or someone on your behalf within the fixed period of five years, may neither have cause to have reprinted [in whole] nor reprinted in part the aforementioned *Opera Musicalia*, to sell, distribute, or have for sale, nor permit others to do such, under penalty of five Marks in *Löthiges* gold,[114] half of which is payable into our Imperial Treasury, and the other half to the aforesaid *Sagittarius*, without exception. To avoid Our and the Empire's severe displeasure and punishment, also the aforesaid penalty [*Poen*] and seizure of your prints, the aforesaid *Supplicant* wherever he or his

---

113. For a transcription of the German document, see Wessely, "Zwei unveröffentlichte Heinrich Schütz-Dokumente," 7–10. A preliminary draft of the privilege can be found on fols. 9r–10r. In one of the court copies (fol. 6r), the original date and witnesses have been crossed out, and the date for the renewed privilege "8. Augusti 1642" is inserted in the margin, corresponding to Schütz's petition of 25 April of that year.
114. Löthiges Gold is full-weight, unalloyed gold (*DWB*).

descendants might find the same [prints] with you, are authorized without impediment to confiscate each and every one, and to trade and do with as they please, whereby they shall have committed no crime. The aforesaid *Henricus Sagittarius* shall be obliged and duty bound to forward at his own expense four *Exemplaria* of each piece of the above-referenced musical items without charge to our Imperial Court Office, as this occurs and before which no *Exemplar* may be sold or given away. This letter, in witness thereof, is secured with Our Imperial seal, given in Our City of Vienna, the third day of April, sixteen hundred and thirty-seven, in the first year of the Roman Empire, the twelfth year of the Hungarian, and the tenth year of the Bohemian.[115]

Ferdinand.
witnessed
Ferdinand Graf Kurtz.
By command
Johann Söldner, Doctor

L.S. [i.e., *locus siglii,* place of the seal]
witnessed
Ph. Strahlendorff.
By command of the Holy Imperial and Royal Majesty
Johann Söldner, Doctor

80. DANISH TRAVEL PASS INTENDED FOR SCHÜTZ (16–31 MARCH 1639)

Travel and security pass drafted by Prince-Elect Christian for Schütz's safe return to Denmark but apparently never used

[DK-RA, Kongehuset Arkiv, Christian 4., Prins Christian (5.), Koncepter til åbene og lukkede Breve af Christian (5.), 1634–36 (til fyrstelige Personer og andre) 1635, Nr 1–100; the pass for Schütz is Nr. 81 (fol. 1r–v), 25 May 1635]

We, Christian V, do give notice herewith that we most graciously requested for our services here and sent for the presenter [of this document], the distinguished and much beloved Heinrich Schütz, that now amid these current perilous times he might everywhere pass through and arrive all the more securely. Thus for greater insurance we wish to have him provided most graciously with this open pass and covering letter, accordingly addressed principally to each and every senior and junior military officer, as well as cavalry and infantry in general. It is our most gracious wish that they, to whom this passport is presented, would allow the aforesaid Heinrich Schütz, together with his possessions, not only to pass freely securely and unimpeded on water and land, neither to offend and encumber his person and possessions, nor to have or allow them to be offended and encumbered [by others], rather on the contrary to demonstrate and have him provided

---

115. Ferdinand III (b. 13 Jul. 1608; d. 02 Apr. 1657), the son of Ferdinand II, became King of Hungary in 1625, King of Bohemia in 1627, and Holy Roman Emperor on the death of his father, 15 February 1637.

for, as one of our own on this his journey, with every appropriate advancement, escort, and protection. This we do certify for all to know. Date.

81. *KLEINE GEISTLICHE CONCERTE II* (DRESDEN, 1639): TITLE PAGE AND DEDICATION TO FRIEDRICH III, DUKE OF SCHLESWIG-HOLSTEIN-GOTTORP (2 JUNE 1639)

[Title page]

Second Part
of the *Kleine
geistliche
Concerte* [Small Sacred Concertos][116]
with 1, 2, 3, 4, and 5 Voices
together with the added basso continuo
for the organ.
Set to music
by
Heinrich Schütz,
Kapellmeister to the
Electoral Serenity of Saxony
*Quintus et Ultimus
Bassus ad Organum*
with permission of the Roman Imperial Majesty.
M. DC. XXXIX
Printed in Dresden in the Electoral Saxon Publishing House
by the Heirs of the late Gimel Berg.

[On the verso of the title page of the Basso Continuo partbook]

To the benevolent reader, who might wish to buy this or other of the author's available musical works, it is hereby announced that these are available in Dresden from Johann Klemm, Court Organist, as well as in Leipzig from Daniel Weixer, Organist at St. Nicolai, and can be purchased for a reasonable price.

[Dedication]

To the Most Reverend, Most Serene,
Illustrious Prince and Lord,
Lord
Friedrich,

---

116. SWV 306–37; RISM A/I/8 S 2291; *NSA* 10–12.

Elected Archbishop and Bishop of the
Diocese Bremen and Verden, Coadjutor of Halberstadt,
Heir to Norway, Duke of Schleswig, Holstein,
Stormarn, and
the Dithmarschen, Count of Oldenburg and Delmenhorst,
My Most Gracious Prince and Lord.[117]

Most Reverend, Most Serene, Illustrious Prince, Most Gracious Lord, among other fine virtues which merciful Heaven instilled in Your Royal Serenity, not least of all is the singular love and inclination which you bring to the free and praiseworthy arts, in particular as well to worthy music, following the example of the greatest champions of the world. As I studiously observed this, and can be a truthful witness to it, at the Royal Wedding of the Crown Prince of Denmark and Norway (Your Serene Highness's most venerable brother, also my Gracious Lord) held a few years ago in Copenhagen. Through my admittedly minor official duty and service at the Royal Kapelle at that time, Your Serene Highness was most graciously moved to acknowledge me with such favor. For that reason I cannot feel myself unhappy, and have abundant reasons to acknowledge this with most humble praise and thanksgiving for the rest of my life.

Most Gracious Lord, with no other purpose in mind, I have placed Your Serene Serenity's most reverend name at the front of the present musical work of mine (as it is published by me for every sort of use).

I am ashamed, it is true, to appear before you with such a small and insignificant little work. But since the wickedness of the current times, hostile to the free arts, will not allow my (without wishing to boast) better works that I have at hand to come to light, it must remain this humble [work] for the present. But should the arts, now as if suffocated under military arms and trampled in the mud, be raised again through God's mercy to their former dignity and worth, and should the Almighty spare my life until such time, I will not forget then to make a more ample pledge to Your Serene Highness in accordance with my debt. In the meantime I do wish greatly that you deign to take from me with most gracious hands this insignificant and slight work, and be well disposed toward me with your royal favor always, as well as permit me all my life to remain in the course of time,

Your Serene Highness's
most humble servant,
Heinrich Schütz.
Dresden, on Holy Whitsuntide [Feast of Pentecost],
2 June 1639.

---

117. Frederik III, Duke of Schleswig-Holstein (b. 18 Mar. 1609; d. 9 Feb. 1670) was the second-eldest son of King Christian IV of Denmark (b. 12 Apr. 1577; d. 28 Feb. 1648). Frederik had known Schütz personally at least since the "Great Wedding" of 1634, and in 1639 was Archbishop of Bremen in addition to holding other administrative posts. With the death of Frederik's eldest brother, Christian, in June 1647, he became the likely heir to the throne and indeed succeeded his father as King of Denmark in 1648.

82. DRESDEN COURT MUSICIANS TO THE COURT PRIVY COUNCILLOR (21 OCTOBER 1640)

Petition from all the Dresden court musicians for intercession regarding unpaid salaries

[D-Dla: Loc. 7287/3, Einzelne Schriften, Kammersachen, insonderheit Besoldungsrückstände der Civil-, Militair- und Hofdiener v. Bitten um deren Verabfolgung [new title page has "Verabschiedung"] 1592–1677, fol. 190r–v)]

To the Electoral Serenity of Saxony's Highly Esteemed Lord Privy Councillor, Great and Most Noble Worship, Our Highly Respected, Most Learned, Most Venerable *Herr*, Your Right and Most Noble, Most Gracious, Highly Respected Lordship, we offer our most obedient services first and foremost.

Your Highly and Most Noble Worship, Highly Respected Lordship shall still recall most benevolently what we the undersigned supplicants addressed to you a short time ago, in addition to the delivery of a most humble petition to His Electoral Serenity. Insofar as we have been provided with no resolution since then, cold winter's arrival, for which we shall be in need of wood, bread, salt, butter, clothing, and other things one needs inevitably for subsistence, compels us to trouble Your Highly and Most Noble Worshipful, Most Venerable Lordship once again with this memorial, which we would rather be excused from doing, in the most subservient hope Your Most Noble Worshipful, Most Venerable Lordship might dispose His Electoral Serenity to that end, should it please him (since we cannot imagine that our previous, repeated, affecting, most humble supplications have been duly brought forward to His Electoral Serenity), so that on account of the salary withheld from us now into the tenth year (without which we have no other means to comfort us) we lose everything hereby, let alone have saved anything, but also in this case risk honor and our good names, in that, instead of due recompense for our continuous service, which in some instances spans more than thirty-six years, we must innocently suffer abuse inside and outside the law-courts, to relieve us in some measure at this time through his highly respected intercession and patronage, and so that we might be paid with gracious means and not have cause in future to perform our most humble services, especially in the church, with sighs and moans as we have until now, on account of our livelihood, which runs quarterly to a little over 600 *Reichsthaler*. Thus this, our most humble endeavor and petition, forced out of utmost need, concerns the Glory of God first and foremost, then His Electoral Serenity's reputation.

We take comfort in Your High and Most Noble Worshipful, Most Venerable Lordship's most highly esteemed unfailing patronage, which we will always take pains to earn with most willingly obedient service and the fervent prayers of ourselves and our families. Dated at Dresden, 21 October 1640.

Your High and Most Noble Worshipful,
Highly Respected Lordship's

most willingly obedient
Electoral Saxon
Vocal and Instrumental Musicians
collectively.

83. SCHÜTZ TO JOHANN GEORG I (7 MARCH 1641)

Memorandum regarding imminent demise of the Kapelle and request for permission to fill positions

[D-Dla: Loc. 8687/1, Kantoreiordnung so Kurfürst Moritz…1548, fols. 209r–210v, 211r][118]

[Address]

To the Most Serene, Noble-Born Prince and Lord, Lord Johann Georg, Duke of Saxony, Jülich, Cleves and Berg, Grand Marshal and Elector of the Holy Roman Empire, Landgrave in Thuringia, Margrave of Meissen, of Upper and Lower Lusatia, and Burgrave of Magdeburg, Count of the Mark and Ravensberg, Lord of Ravenstein, our Most Gracious Elector and Lord

[Text]

Most Serene, Illustrious Elector,
Most Gracious Lord.

Although the present most humble memorandum of mine (in regard to our already almost completely defunct *Music*) might be deemed ill-timed by Your Electoral Serenity in view of the miserable conditions that still prevail in our beloved fatherland, it could also in the same way perhaps be given consideration by you. I thus hope to absolve myself from this breach of propriety and to obtain a most gracious pardon; for no less than when a physician [treats] a dangerous illness before it becomes fatal, I out of my incumbent duty should not neglect herewith to intervene on behalf of our *corpus musicus* as though it were drawing its last breath.

Should our aforesaid collegium be left helpless in this way yet longer; or in accordance with God's will, should any of the very few persons still remaining die or otherwise become physically unable (which is inevitable with the passing years); the restitution of the failed *Hofkapelle* (and especially in the way it was in former times, in praise of God and of Your Electoral Serenity's desired good reputation) would either be impossible or indeed certainly very difficult. Together with the losses over time, and without doubled or tripled expenditures, it might never again attain to that level.

---

118. The address is the hand of a copyist; the rest of the letter is in Schütz's hand. Transcribed in La Mara, 73–76; *Schütz-GBr*, Nr. 48; *Schütz-Dokumente*, Nr. 90.

Your Electoral Serenity will judge and decide for yourself, according to your superior mind, when and to what extent (in view of the times) you most graciously intend again to restore this establishment. This most humble memorandum of mine in no way aims now at the immediate complete recovery of our Kapelle, but rather, as mentioned, at forestalling the impending self-evident ruin, and only that a seed of the *Music*, as it were, might be preserved at Your Electoral Serenity's court. In my modest opinion and estimation, this could most expediently occur: namely, if the following *Knaben*, as quickly as possible, were selected, appointed, provided for, and educated in music:

First.
Four *Kapell-* or *Sänger-Knaben*

These, and indeed those with the best voices, could be selected here and there from within the land, and subsequently entrusted to someone, at Your Electoral Serenity's pleasure, for their instruction and supervision.

One of these positions could be filled by the organist Johann Klemm's son,[119] who is already accomplished [*Perfect*] in music, and moreover is still young and available.

Second.
Four Instrumental *Knaben*,

which, as with the previous ones, can likewise be selected from within the land and, in particular, drawn from amongst the municipal musicians [*Stadtpfeifer*] (so that they already have a start in it), and then entrusted to Augustus Tax for instruction on all the instruments.

The yearly disbursements and expenses for the aforementioned eight *Knaben* are duly submitted for Your Electoral Serenity's most gracious pleasure and further consideration. In addition to that, however, this is most humbly mentioned and left to your discretion: that you might most graciously consent and decree that the annual maintenance allowance for every *Knabe* be left most graciously at the previous, old levels:

1) 75 *gulden* for the cost of room and board, linens, shoes, laundry, and mending allowance, etc., whereby one should consider in particular that this is inclusive of the quite arduous work of training a *Knabe*.
2) One or two liveries for the year, at Your Electoral Serenity's discretion.

This, Most Gracious Elector, in my modest opinion, is the one, most expedient means by which Your Electoral Serenity can not only preserve in some measure your *Hofkapelle*, and maintain a small *Music* at your electoral table, but also readily complete and supplement the *collegium musicum* in better times soon to arrive, God willing, with

---

119. Johann Heinrich Klemm, the son of Johann Klemm, was still in the Dresden *Hofkapelle* around 1666 (*Schütz-GBr*, 335).

the acquisition of a pair of good Italian or other instrumentalists,[120] and as many good singers, at your most gracious pleasure. But this can hardly be expected without these preliminary arrangements now most humbly set down and expressed by me.

Now should this most humble proposal of mine most graciously please Your Electoral Serenity and [should you] have this put into effect, there is no doubt that you affirm herewith a piece of the stately regalia pertaining to you, considering that it is not fitting for every potentate as it is for the electoral and royal highness to form and to maintain *Kapellen* in their court cities. You render moreover unto our dear God that duty and honor which He Himself in His Word ordained and commanded in praise of Him, just as all devout potentates, before and after the birth of our Lord and Redeemer Jesus Christ, have offered Him in their religious assemblies. You also preserve at your Electoral Court hereby that profession which in the midst of the seven liberal arts gleams brightly and shines far, no less than does the sun amongst the seven planets. Who knows, too, whether amid the present heavy burden of government, Your Electoral Serenity might not more than once be refreshed in spirit thereby, and in return be blessed all the more richly by dear God with sound, lasting good health and other electoral well-being? I fervently implore Almighty God that it might come to pass, recommend and commend myself most obediently to Your Electoral Serenity for continuing electoral favor, as well as for a most gracious resolution, and finally to remain as well loyally and most diligently in my position for the rest of my life, which has been again granted me and prolonged by dear God after my recent serious illness, perhaps for the sake of this work and other eventual, most humble, and indeed modest services from me.

Your Electoral Serenity's
most obedient
Heinrich Schütz, Kapellmeister,
in most humble devotion always.
Written and submitted in Dresden, the seventh day of March 1641.

84. SCHÜTZ TO JOHANN GEORG II, ELECTORAL PRINCE OF SAXONY (14 SEPTEMBER 1641)

Memorandum regarding the appointments of Matthias Weckmann, Philipp Stolle, Friedrich Werner, and Augustus Tax

[D-Dla: Loc. 4520, Bestallungen, Expectanz-Schein, Besoldungen und Reverse 1601–1650, Vol. II, fols. 191r–v, 197r–v][121]

---

120. Schütz writes *Instrumenten* in the manuscript, but it seems most likely in the context of this writing that he is referring to the acquisition of musicians and not instruments.
121. The document is in Schütz's hand. *Schütz-GBr*, Nr. 49 reproduces the transcription from *Sachs-Chronik*, 548–49, footnote 31, believing that the location of the original in the Hauptstaatsarchiv in Dresden was unknown. The original was located for transcription in *Schütz-Dokumente*, Nr. 92.

In the name of the Lord, the fourteenth day of September, the Feast of the Elevation of the Cross,[122] 1641, His Serene Lord Johann Georg, Duke and eldest Electoral Prince of Saxony etc., has taken into his service and employ the following persons for his musicians.

Matthias Weckmann,
as his Court Organist.

1) He shall diligently serve both in the church and at table, or anywhere else His Serenity shall decree.
2) And although His Princely Serenity prepared a separate ordinance for him regarding the sustenance and instruction of his discantists and *Sängerknaben*, so indeed shall Weckmann have the aforementioned boys frequently sing individually to a harpsichord, regal or positif, and in this way assist in practice so that they might be trained to sing correctly and to accomplish themselves in *Music* all the more quickly.
3) He shall also be obliged to attend the weekly general rehearsal, as shall be arranged.

In return, an annual salary of 200 *gulden* in currency has been allotted to him by His Princely Serenity, and beyond this a livery. The salary shall be remitted to him in quarterly payments of 50 *gulden*.

The [starting] date must be 14 September, as above. Attention shall be given to the requisites which otherwise belong to an appointment. In my opinion [*meo judicio*] it would be enough if these clauses were to be brought here, so that they be solemnly pledged with a handshake, which would also have to occur upon the delivery of the appointment.

Philipp Stolle, as theorbist and singer.

1) His Princely Serenity ordains that he shall diligently serve where commanded of him, not only with the theorbo and in singing or vocally [*vocaliter*], but rather also on the discant violin and other viols.
2) Moreover, he shall be obliged in particular to give instruction at specific times each day to His Princely Serenity's *Singknaben*, to direct and to supervise them, and to train them to the best of his abilities in an appropriate, Italian style of singing.
3) He shall likewise be obliged as well to attend the weekly general rehearsal, as it shall be arranged, and not to absent himself from it.
4) And at His Princely Serenity's most gracious request, he has also accordingly promised most humbly to take on one of these well-qualified *Knaben* and to instruct him to the best of his ability on the theorbo and in singing. Hereafter, in the event this boy has been sufficiently developed by him and has advanced to a respectable degree, he shall be able to assist and rehearse alongside on theorbo and on his own later on,

---

122. *Festo Exaltationis Sanctae Crucis.*

may it please His Princely Serenity. His Princely Serenity pledges to him in return that, on account of his applied diligence, he [Stolle] shall be recompensed separately. With regard to salary: in addition to a livery, His Princely Serenity has allotted 170 *gulden* and an additional 10 *gulden* for strings, which altogether makes 180 *gulden*.

This likewise shall be paid to him quarterly at 45 *gulden*.

Friedrich Werner, as instrumentalist.

1) He shall with humble diligence serve His Princely Serenity on various wind as well as stringed instruments appropriate to an instrumentalist, both in the church and at table, or wherever else that might be commanded of him.

2) He shall diligently attend the rehearsal, however His Serenity shall arrange it.

In return His Princely Serenity has allotted him, in addition to a livery, an annual salary of 150 *gulden*, which shall be paid to him quarterly at 37 *gulden*, 10 *groschen*, 6 *pfennige*.

3) And beyond this, His Princely Serenity also offers to him the most gracious hope: he shall be rewarded with an additional, most gracious increase [to his salary], provided that the additional diligence and the consequent improvement in his art, as he has promised, is perceived.

Augustus Tax.

His Princely Serenity has conferred upon him the directorship of his *Instrumental Music* such that he shall devotedly spend time with the instrumentalists to rehearse with them frequently, and even daily if necessity requires, the better to instruct and to qualify them, which he also pledged and agreed to do. In return His Princely Serenity has allotted to him an annual recompense of 50 thalers, which likewise shall be paid to him quarterly at 12 thalers, 12 *groschen*. But should it please His Princely Serenity subsequently to commit to him, Tax, one or more boys for instruction, a separate arrangement and adjustment shall be made with him in that case.

85. SCHÜTZ TO FERDINAND III, HOLY ROMAN EMPEROR (25 APRIL 1642)

Petition seeking an extension to the Imperial patent of 1637

[A-Whh: Impressorialakten "Sagittarius," fols. 1r–v, 2v; court copy, fols. 3r–v, 4v][123]

[Address]

To the Roman Imperial Majesty, and to the Royal Majesty of Hungary and Bohemia, the most humble *Memorial* of the Electoral Saxon appointed Kapellmeister in Dresden: Regarding the extension of an Imperial Privilege obtained in 1637 for his musical compositions.

---

123. Transcribed in *Schütz-Dokumente*, Nr. 94.

[Text]

Most Serene, High and Mighty, and Most Invincible Roman Emperor, and King of Hungary and Bohemia.

Most Gracious Lord, to Your Imperial Majesty is due my most humble and everlasting gratitude that, upon my most obedient petition, you granted me great Imperial favor in 1637, and for those musical works [*Opera Musicalia*] that I composed partly in Latin and partly in German, both sacred as well as secular, also in part without text, and at that time had planned to have published, most graciously accorded your Imperial patent [*Privilegium*] (as per the enclosed genuine copy) for five years. I have in truth had some of these musical compositions published, but still have many originals and am inclined to publish the remainder together with what I additionally assembled during this time. Whereas the five-year period has now expired, however, I fear that there may be someone who might reprint it for his own gain but at a great loss and disadvantage to me.

For that reason I direct to Your Imperial Majesty my most humble petition, may it please you most graciously, to grant me this Imperial favor still, and to extend most graciously to me and my heirs the aforementioned Imperial patent [*Privilegium*] for a further ten years, and to have it drawn up like the previous one. This Imperial favor I shall never forget to extol all my life, and to petition before Almighty God for the constant, felicitous welfare of Your Imperial Majesty and your most praiseworthy House, and the vanquishing of all your enemies and those of the empire. Dated at Dresden, 25 April 1642.

Your Imperial Majesty's
most humble,
most obedient
Henricus Sagittarius, in his own hand.
Johann Leue, in his own hand.

86. SCHÜTZ'S SECOND APPOINTMENT TO THE ROYAL DANISH COURT (3 MAY 1642)

[DK-RA: Tyske Kancelli, indenrigske afdeling, Uregistrerede koncepter til patenter, A13, 1533–1669 (2 fols.)]

Conferral of [the Office of] Kapellmeister
on
Heinrich Schütz, Copenhagen
3 May 1642

We, Christian [IV], do hereby attest before one and all that We most graciously have reappointed and taken into service Our beloved, loyal Heinrich Schütz, the erstwhile

Electoral Saxon Kapellmeister, upon the Saxon Elector's obliging release for Ours in Our royal Kapelle here.

[We] also make known herewith and by these presents, that he shall and will be principally faithful, devoted, and ready to serve Us, Our domains, princedom, and lands at all times, and to support Us and the same for their benefit and promotion, and to aid to the utmost, and conversely to prevent, avert, and repel harm, as much as possible according to his abilities.

In particular he shall have full charge over the direction of Our Kapelle and cantorate as most graciously commanded of him herewith, together with the persons belonging to them, including the instrumentalists, singers, and *Knaben*, and earnestly to dispose them toward an elegant *harmonie* and each person to the carrying out of his bounden duties; to inform [*informieren*] to the best of his abilities, and moreover to apply himself earnestly with utmost diligence to all that which is otherwise consistent and beneficial to the appointment of a laudable Kapelle and cantorate. In sum, with constant attendance both in the church and wherever it is commanded, he is to be mindful of what is incumbent upon a faithful and diligent Kapellmeister; moreover of what is becoming and proper in all humility before Us in grace; before all, however, to obtain and to achieve glory, to present himself, perform, and prove himself at any time. And should ever one or another of the musical company in his charge show himself to be obstinate [*refractari*] and disobedient, he shall immediately notify Us or Our Lord Marshal of the Court of the same in order that appropriate and mutually agreeable action shall be taken.

In return and for his faithful service, We wish to have paid to him annually 800 *Reichsthaler* in total, in such a way that he shall be paid monthly, and thus in each month 66 thalers, in the last of the year, however, 74 *Reichsthaler*, either from Our Royal Revenue Officer or through Our Court Clerk of the Muster-Roll [*Hofmusterschreiber*], as long as this Our appointment lasts, and without fail. Our people shall execute this in good faith in accordance with the aforesaid document.

87. SCHÜTZ TO THE DRESDEN COURT
(15 JULY 1642)

Memorandum regarding arrangements for assigning Knaben *to court musicians for board and training*

[D-Dla: Loc. 4520, Bestallungen, Expectanz-Schein, Besoldungen und Reverse 1601–1650, Vol. II, fol. 198r and an unpaginated leaf before fol. 205r (address)][124]

---

124. The document is in Schütz's hand. *Schütz-GBr*, Nr. 52, relies on the earlier transcription from *Sachs-Chronik*, 549, footnote 32, unable to locate the original in the Hauptstaatsarchiv in Dresden. The original was located for the transcription in *Schütz-Dokumente*, Nr. 95.

[Address]

To *Herr* Matthias Weckman and *Herr* Philipp Stolle, both well-appointed musicians to His Most Princely Serene Lord, Lord Duke Johann Georg, Eldest Electoral Prince of Saxony, to their benevolent hands

[Text]

Herr Matthias Weckmann and *Herr* Philipp Stolle as well, both well-appointed musicians to His Princely Serenity, Lord Johann Georg, Duke and eldest Electoral Prince of Saxony, together with kind greetings, are hereby given notice in what manner His aforementioned Princely Serenity today, after careful consideration, has most graciously concluded that each of them shall take on a discant *Knabe* and train him in singing and on his instrument, in return for which His Princely Serenity will give them 50 thalers in cash for a whole year for each *Knabe*, and, in addition to this, provide them with the livery of his pages as well, and to have his secretary draw up this consent in writing, authorized in His Princely Serenity's hand, and delivered to them. I did not want to neglect informing them of this news and admonishing them to solicit discussion of this matter with the Lord Secretary. Commending all of us all to divine protection, together with wishes for a blessed day,

Dresden, 15 July 1642.
H. Schütz,
Kapellmeister.

His aforementioned Princely Serenity has also granted that the two notes for 50 thalers might be calculated as of the past quarter at Trinity, of which he could likewise notify the aforesaid Lord Secretary (in order to avoid delays in this enterprise).

88. SCHÜTZ TO SOPHIE ELISABETH, DUCHESS OF BRUNSWICK-LÜNEBURG (22 OCTOBER 1644)

Letter concerning the purchase of an organ, his intentions to spend time in Hildesheim, and the Duchess's progress in composition

[US-NYpm: Mary Flagler Cary Music Collection, S396.S692, fol. 27r–v][125]

---

125. The document is in Schütz's hand. Transcribed in *Spagn.*, Nr. 19; *Schütz-Dokumente*, Nr. 97.

[Address]

[in a second hand]

To the Serene, Noble Princess and Lady, Sophia Elisabeth, Duchess of Brunswick and Lüneburg, born Princess of Mecklenburg, my Gracious Princess and Lady[126]

[Text]

Serene, Most Noble Princess,
Gracious Lady.

With humble and profound thanks I have modestly taken note of that which you had conveyed to me just now through your lackey: that Your Royal Grace, at her most gracious pleasure, shall undertake a certain expedition to Her Royal Ladyship, the widow, in Schöningen.[127]

In regard of that I consider this small reminder still worth mentioning: since a certain positif currently in Hamburg, and in fact in St. Peter's Church beside the great organ gallery, under the care and supervision of Jacob Praetorius,[128] is subject to public sale and consequently will certainly not remain unsold for long, it might therefore please Her aforesaid Royal Ladyship, the widow, to come to a resolution. In the event it should not be possible for the payment to be made both presently and in full, I would have to make accommodations herein, though would nevertheless be better served by payment in cash. Finally, should Your Royal Serenity make known her intentions in this matter, I shall humbly and obediently make payment in the meantime, without any benefit to myself.

---

126. Sophie Elisabeth, Duchess of Brunswick-Lüneburg (b. 20 Aug. 1613; d. 12 Jul. 1676), daughter of Johann Albrecht II, Duke of Mecklenburg-Güstrow (b. 5 May 1590; d. 23 Apr. 1636), was a poet, composer, and able administrator. In 1635, she was married to August the Younger, Duke of Brunswick-Lüneburg (b. 10 Apr. 1579; d. 17 Sept. 1666), the founder of the famed Herzog August Bibliothek in Wolfenbüttel. See Geck, *Sophie Elisabeth, Herzogin zu Braunschweig und Lüneburg (1613–1676) als Musikerin*.
127. Anna Sophia, Duchess of Brunswick-Wolfenbüttel (b. 18 Mar. 1598; d. 19 Dec. 1659), born Margravine of Brandenburg, was the daughter of Johann Sigismund, Elector of Brandenburg (b. 8 Nov. 1572; d. 23 Dec. 1619), sister of his successor Georg Wilhelm (b. 13 Dec. 1595; d. 1 Dec. 1640), and sister of Maria Eleonora (b. 11 Nov. 1599; 28 Mar. 1655) who was consort to Gustavus Adolphus, King of Sweden (b. 9 Dec. 1594; d. 6 Nov. 1632). Anna Sophia was married in 1614 to Friedrich Ulrich, Duke of Brunswick-Lüneburg (b. 5 Apr. 1591; d. 11 Aug. 1634), for which occasion Michael Praetorius composed the wedding music. When her husband discovered her love affair with Franz Albrecht, Duke of Saxe-Lauenburg (b. 31 Nov. 1598; d. 10 Jun. 1646), Anna Sophia fled to Schöningen and the protection of her powerful family, and from there supported the university in nearby Helmstedt and founded Schöningen's Latin school, the Anna-Sophianeum. She devoted her energies and resources to rebuilding the town following the destruction by fire in 1644, and sponsored the construction of a new and still-extant organ in the Vincenzkirche by Jonas Weigel, a student of Gottfried Fritzsche (b. 1578; d. 1638).
128. The composer and organist, Jacob Praetorius, was the second son of Hieronymus Praetorius (b. 10 Aug. 1560; d. 27 Jan. 1629), and was organist at the Petrikirche from 1603. He was particularly influential as a teacher as well, counting Matthias Weckmann among his best-known students.

Insofar as I propose to travel on business to Hildesheim still this week (should [prevailing] uncertainties allow it), and shall likely remain still for a period of time here in Brunswick as well (though contrary to my wishes and with little [personal] advantage), I trust Your Royal Grace shall graciously allow, and be content, that I postpone my travel there [i.e., Wolfenbüttel] until the following week. In case I hear that it shall be convenient for you then as well, I will then present myself obediently and unfailingly, and discuss and consider with Your Royal Grace productively and with utmost diligence the composition of our musical work at hand. In the meantime commending you most faithfully herewith to divine protection for all favorable royal welfare, I remain

Your Royal Grace's
most humble, faithful servant,
as long as I shall live,
Heinrich Schütz, in his own hand.
Brunswick, 22 October 1644.

[PS] We safely received from the lackey the arias that were recently forwarded, and I see from this that Your Royal Grace has improved appreciably from my modest instruction. We would thus hope this small work, in addition to the praise of God, shall serve as a lasting and suitable memorial to you.

FIGURE 1 Heinrich Schütz. Engraving by Augustus John, 1627–28.
Source: Ratsschulbibliothek Zwickau, Sign. 46.2.4, fol. 79. (Document Nr. 1)

FIGURE 2 Moritz, Landgrave of Hesse-Kassel. Engraving by unknown artist.
Source: Herzog Anton Ulrich-Museum, EKieser Verlag AB 3.2. (Document Nr. 1)

FIGURE 3 Johann Georg I, Elector of Saxony. Painting by Frans Luycx (b. 1604; d. after 1656).
Source: Sächsische Landesbibliothek—Staats- und Universitätsbibliothek Dresden, Deutsche Fotothek, photo by Hans Loos, before 1945. (Document Nr. 2)

FIGURE 4 The Electoral Palace in Dresden. Engraving by Anton Weck, ca. 1680, from *Der Chur-Fürstlichen Sächsischen weitberuffenen Residentz- und Haupt-Vestung Dresden Beschreib: und Vorstellung: Auf der Churfürstlichen Herrschafft gnädigstes Belieben in Vier Abtheilungen verfaßet/ mit Grund: und anderen Abrißen/ auch bewehrten Documenten/ erläutert/ Durch...Antonium Wecken* (Nuremberg: Froberger, 1680).

Source: Herzog August Bibliothek Wolfenbüttel: Gm 4° 270, Taf. 12. (Document Nr. 2)

FIGURE 5 Michael Praetorius. Woodcut by unknown artist, from *Musae Sioniae* (Regensburg, 1605).

Source: Sächsische Landesbibliothek—Staats- und Universitätsbibliothek Dresden, Deutsche Fotothek, photo by Regine Richter, 2007. (Document Nr. 7)

Figure 6 Samuel Scheidt. Engraving by unknown artist, from *Tabulatura nova* (Hamburg, 1624).

Source: Sächsische Landesbibliothek— Staats- und Universitätsbibliothek Dresden, Deutsche Fotothek, photo by Walter Möbius, 1939. (Document Nr. 25)

FIGURE 7 Johann Georg II, Electoral Prince of Saxony. Engraving by unknown artist before 1656.

Source: Sächsische Landesbibliothek— Staats- und Universitätsbibliothek Dresden, Deutsche Fotothek, photo by Hans Loos, before 1945. (Document Nr. 51)

FIGURE 8 Johann Hermann Schein. Painting by unknown artist, 1620.

Source: Museum für Musikinstrumente der Universität Leipzig (Photo by Gregory S. Johnston). (Document Nr. 58)

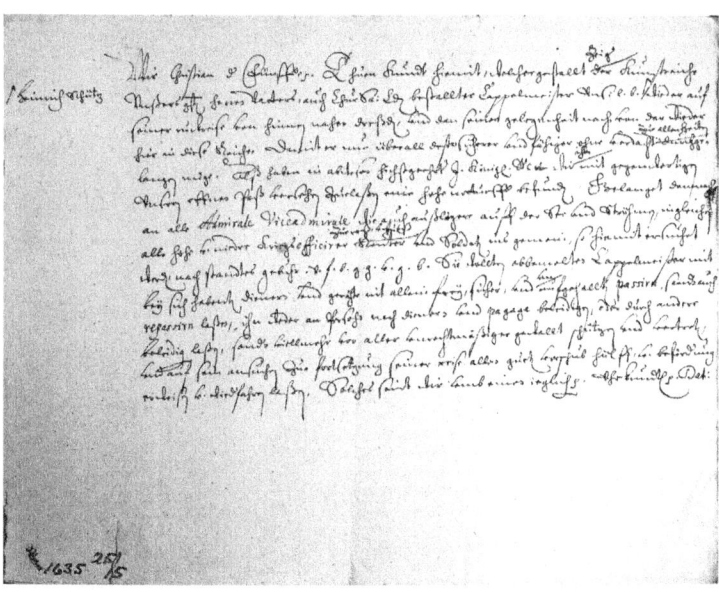

FIGURE 9 Draft of a travel and security pass issued to Schütz by the Danish Court, 25 May 1635.
Source: DK-RA: Kongehuset Christian 4., Prins Christian (5.), Koncepter til åbne og lukkede breve af Christian (5.) (til fyrstelige personer og andre) 1631–1647, nr. 24 (Photo by Bjarke Moe). (Document Nr. 71)

FIGURE 10 Sophie Elisabeth, Duchess of Brunswick-Lüneburg. Engraving by unknown artist.
Source: Herzog Anton Ulrich-Museum, Brunsvic.2.II. 3.64. (Document Nr. 88)

FIGURE 11 August the Younger, Duke of Brunswick-Lüneburg. Engraving by Konrad Buno, 10 April 1662.
Source: Herzog Anton Ulrich-Museum, KBuno AB 3.24. (Document Nr. 152)

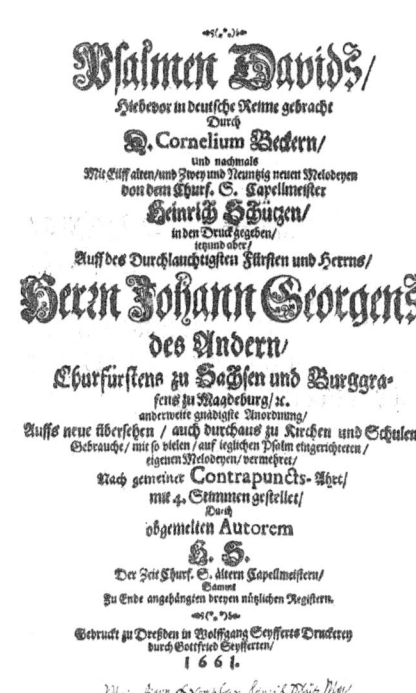

FIGURE 12 Title page from the second edition of the *Becker Psalter* (Dresden, 1661), with Schütz's autograph.
Source: Herzog August Bibliothek Wolfenbüttel: 1.2.3 Musica 2°, Titelbl. (Document Nr. 153)

FIGURE 13 Organ galleries in the Dom St. Peter and Paul, the palace church in Zeitz. (Photo by Gregory S. Johnston) (Document Nr. 158)

A

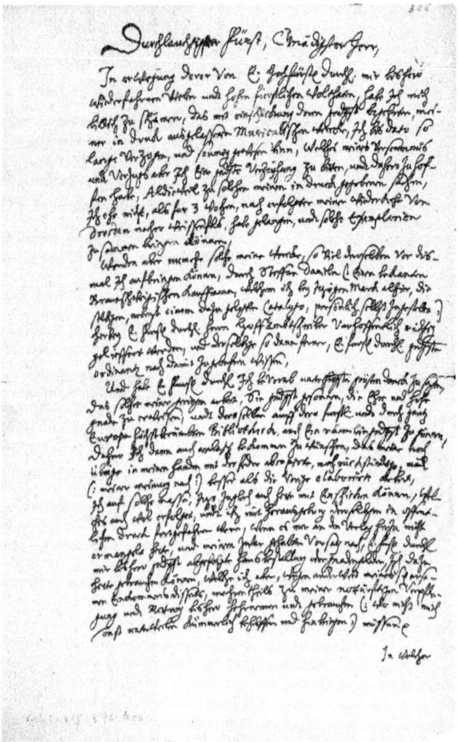

B

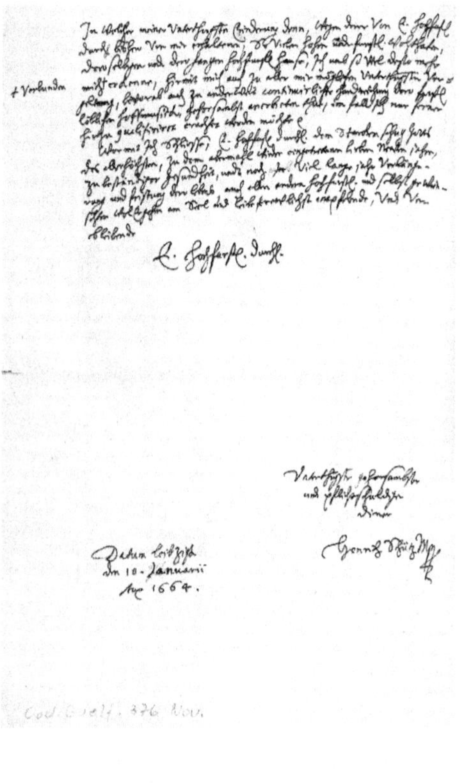

FIGURE 14 A AND B Schütz's handwritten letter to August the Younger, Duke of Brunswick-Lüneburg, 10 January 1664.
Source: Herzog August Bibliothek Wolfenbüttel: Cod. Guelf. 376 Novi, fol. 322r/v. (Document Nr. 160)

FIGURE 15 Heinrich Schütz. Engraving by Christian Romstet, from the printed funeral sermon, 1672. *Source:* Sächsische Landesbibliothek—Staats- und Universitätsbibliothek Dresden, Deutsche Fotothek, photo by Regine Richter, 1998. (Document Nr. 167)

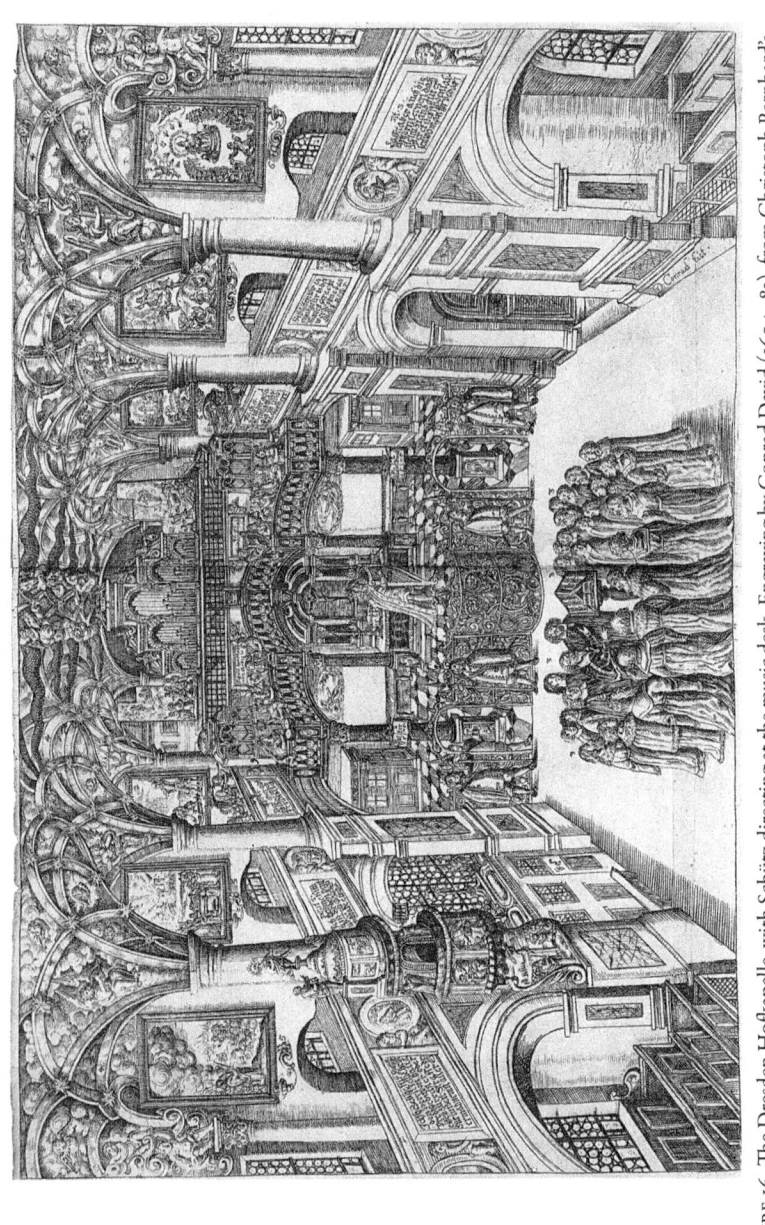

FIGURE 16 The Dresden Hofkapelle, with Schütz directing at the music desk. Engraving by Conrad David (1604–81), from Christoph Bernhard's *Geistreiches Gesangbuch* of 1676.

Source: Herzog August Bibliothek Wolfenbüttel: S 379.4° Helmst., Frontisp. (Document Nr. 168)

3
Old Age (1645–56)

---

89. SCHÜTZ TO THE WOLFENBÜTTEL COURT (EARLY 1645)

Memorandum requesting details about the court's musical establishment

[D-Wa: 1 Alt. 25 No. 294, fol. 5r]¹

In the name of the Lord [*In noie Dni*]
    Points in regard of which I humbly request somewhat more precise information:²

1.

Regarding the company of instrumentalists

1. How large the same should be
2. What instruments they should use
3. From which it shall then be concluded what senior instrumentalist is required

---

1. The document is in Schütz's hand. Transcribed in *Schütz-GBr*, Nr. 55; *Spagn.*, Nr. 21; *Schütz-Dokumente*, Nr. 102. The dating of April 1645 is suggested by *Schütz-GBr* (306). An earlier date, however, is more likely—perhaps late 1644 or early 1645—since it is clear from Schütz's letter of 17 March 1645 that he is already aware of the specific needs of the Kapelle and that he has in fact already discussed details with his Wolfenbüttel patrons.
2. *Spagn.* (249) has Schütz being asked (rather than asking) for more precise information.

2.

Regarding the company of singers

1. Of how many persons
2. Of the discantists, *Knaben*, falsettists, and eunuchs
3. What language the vocal music shall employ

3.

On the employment of the sacred music

1. At table
2. For the church services with sermons
3. For a main special musical worship service in the church

4.

Regarding the secular music at table

5.

Regarding the secular[3] academic and theatrical *Music*

6.

On the location for performing in the church

1. The chancel in the castle church
2. The chancel in the city church

7.

On the present administration of the various necessary instruments

1. To that end, a room where the daily rehearsal can take place
2. Inspection of and responsibility for the same [instruments]

Schütz.

---

3. *Spagn.* (250) has "secular music" as separate category from "academic" and "theatrical" music. There is no comma between "*Weltlichen*" and "*Academischen*" in the original, meaning that *weltlich* (secular) is a modifier, just as it was in the preceding line.

90. SCHÜTZ TO SOPHIE ELISABETH OF BRUNSWICK-LÜNEBURG (17 MARCH 1645)

Letter concerning an unnamed musician of interest to the Wolfenbüttel Court

[D-Wa: 1 Alt 25 no. 294, fol. 4r–v][4]

[*Address*]

To the Serene, Most Noble Princess and Lady, Lady Sophie Elisabeth, Duchess of Brunswick and Lüneburg, born Princess of Mecklenburg, my Gracious Princess and Lady

[*Text*]

Serene, Most Noble Princess,
Gracious Lady.

Upon my arrival here in Brunswick, I also found among others the enclosed missive, from which our Gracious Prince and Lord, together with Your Princessly Grace, at your most gracious pleasure, can graciously see for yourselves that that musically serviceable bird, which up to the present I deemed worthy of recommending to both Your Princely Graces, shall now, for our part, fly past and subsequently quit this land. Since I cannot know what now is to be done in regard of this point, I did not want to neglect notifying Your Royal [Grace] of this humbly, and moreover to submit it for your gracious consideration,[5] to enquire into our Gracious Lord's judgment and thought,[6] and to let me know in return how you shall view the exigencies [of the situation].

I commend most loyally Your Princessly Grace herewith to divine protection for all princely welfare, and remain

Your Princessly Grace's
ever humble, obedient
Heinrich Schütz, in his own hand.
Brunswick, 17 March 1645.

---

4. Transcribed in *Schütz-GBr*, Nr. 54; *Spagn.*, Nr. 20; *Schütz-Dokumente*, Nr. 98.
5. *Schütz-GBr* (155) and *Spagn.* (243) transcribe the original text as *Berufung*, read *Bereifung*.
6. *Schütz-GBr* (155) transcribes the original text as *Erinnerung*, read *Meinung*.

91. SCHÜTZ DIRECTED TO JOHANN GEORG I (21 MAY 1645)

Memorandum regarding the state of the Dresden musical establishment, his desire for retirement, and an honorary appointment to the Royal Court in Denmark

[D-Dla: Loc. 8687/1, Kantoreiordnung so Kurfürst Moritz...1548, fol. 218r–v][7]

Memorial.

What I propose to request most humbly before our Most Gracious Elector and Lord on my account, upon my imminent arrival in Dresden, God willing, namely:

1

Inasmuch as the Electoral *Hofmusic* in these adverse times has fallen into utter decay, I have become old as well; and since soon hereafter a restoration of the same shall be undertaken, it would indeed be impossible for me for my part again to direct young people in continuous daily rehearsal as is necessary, to set the operation in motion, and to direct the same properly in future.

Thus would it now be my one wish, that I live free from all ordinary service henceforth, and the office I have had up to now be converted into a pension (equal only to a couple of hundred *Reichsthaler* annually, subject to correction), that the payment however be included with that of the Court Chaplains; and when they would receive theirs, my quota might be remitted simultaneously to me each time as well.

2.

Nonetheless I would be inclined, as long as God might grant me health and strength, to retain for myself the office of Kapellmeister and directorship of the Electoral *Music* in future; also in every way to advise dutifully what is best and beneficial for the same, and to assist to the very best of my ability; and not only to rehearse frequently with them in private, but rather to direct personally at occasional solemnities and feast days in the church whenever possible, as well as to attend obediently at table or wherever else His Electoral Serenity would have me especially commanded, and in accordance with my ability and means to provide and have the music performed, above all in the presence of visiting rulers or envoys.

3.

Prior to my departure from Copenhagen, the Royal Majesty in Denmark also most graciously requested of me and negotiated to some extent that, at future solemnities in those places as well, I should return on call and at such time also preside over the directorship

---

7. The document is in Schütz's hand. Transcribed in *Schütz-GBr*, Nr. 56; *Schütz-Dokumente*, Nr. 99.

of the Royal *Music* there. To that end he then had a house-appointment of 200 thalers established for me (according to which I have taken on and accepted this situation, conditional to ratification by our Most Gracious Elector and Lord), in addition to the promise that, when I would be there in person and to serve, I should be recompensed separately on that account. Thus I live most humbly in the hope (insofar as I, at the same time, most obediently request this) that Your Electoral Serenity would also most graciously grant and permit this honor and advantage, in consideration that this shall not be disreputable to him, nor will it ever do harm to his Electoral *Music*, since I would not remain in Denmark permanently, but rather would hasten home again at any time.

Signed at Leipzig, 21 May 1645.

Heinrich Schütz, in his own hand.

92. SCHÜTZ DIRECTED TO JOHANN GEORG I (28 SEPTEMBER 1645)

Memorandum regarding his desire for retirement in Weissenfels, and postscript on the restoration of the Kapelle

[D-Dla: Loc. 8687/1, Kantoreiordnung so Kurfürst Moritz…1548, fols. 219r–221r, 289r–v (Postscript)][8]

[Address]

To the Most Serene, Noble-Born Prince and Lord, Lord Johann Georg, Duke of Saxony, Jülich, Cleves and Berg, Grand Marshal and Elector of the Holy Roman Empire, Landgrave in Thuringia, Margrave of Meissen, of Upper and Lower Lusatia, and Burgrave of Magdeburg, Count of the Mark and Ravensberg, Lord of Ravenstein, my Most Gracious Lord

[Text]

Memorial.

What is requested before our Most Gracious Elector and Lord to seek most humbly for my sake:

1.

In my preparations for this Leipzig fair, I must to that end make a necessary journey once again to Weissenfels. Even if winter should arrive unexpectedly in the meantime and catch me inopportunely, I am of no use here given the current state of the *Hofkapelle*,

---

8. The document is in Schütz's hand. Transcribed in *Schütz-GBr*, Nr. 57; *Schütz-Dokumente*, Nr. 100.

and in particular it would be impossible for me at this time to set up housekeeping once again at this end (since another good man, with whom my child also resides, still occupies my house). It would therefore be my most humble request that, with His Electoral Serenity's most gracious permission, I should like to remain in Weissenfels until Easter, God willing.

2.

On account of my now advancing old age and, without wishing to boast, from youth having endured considerable work, much travel and study, I would greatly desire quieter circumstances and more liberty for myself (whereby I have in mind at the same time to complete my various musical works already started). In addition would I be occasioned to approach His Electoral Serenity most obediently, so that my current regular appointment might be converted into a pension, and subject to correction, set equal to only a couple of hundred thalers annually, but that the payment be included amongst the Court Chaplains' salary and my quota be remitted to me at the same time as to them.

3.

And inasmuch as I would also have claims in some respects in Weissenfels, not for myself alone, but for a surviving sister there as well, a widow and without children, in whose company then (on account of our modest little property there) it would be advantageous to set up household and to spend time there, I would hope that it might be allowed to me in electoral grace, according to my circumstances and inclination, to come and go there, and to reside.

4.

Nonetheless, I would be most humbly willing to retain the office of Kapellmeister in future (should His Serenity continue to consider me worthy of the same), to appear most obediently at any time upon most gracious demand,[9] barring an act of God, and in particular, may it please His Electoral Serenity, to have the defunct *Hofkapelle* established anew, to assist the same therein with most humble, most loyal diligence, to watch over its progress in my absence and presence alike, and to provide it with the necessary musical pieces and compositions so that no deficiency should appear, and to put everything in good order for services that take place, even in my absence.

5.

Moreover, insofar as the provision of 200 *Reichsthaler* previously requested by me most humbly, for covering the expenses of the travel and lodging *en route* and here in Dresden,

---

9. *Schütz-GBr* (161) transcribes the original text as *Anforderung*, read *Erforderung*.

will not go very far at all, I thus hope (in consequence of which I then most obediently request at this time) His Electoral Serenity on this point might still most graciously supplement and grant me:

1. A commission for tax-free beer.
2. Another commission to the attendant at Weissenfels for free oats for a pair of horses annually, so that I would be able to present myself [at court] at any time as needed and without delay.
3. When I personally should wait upon His Serenity upon demand, that 4 thalers payment be granted[10] weekly to me and a copyist (which in my occupation I can in no way do without), that a note might be signed by the Lord Marshal of the Palace, and that I likewise be referred to the attendant at Weissenfels on account of the payment.

Finally I would live in the most humble, great hope that His Electoral Serenity, after most gracious consideration of this my most humble petition, might not deem it inappropriate, and that he would therefore allow me to be met on this matter with a most gracious, desired resolution, as my life comes to an end. His Serenity could in turn rest assured that, as long as God might still grant me the strength, in weal and woe (as I hope I have not shown to the contrary up to now), for the glory of God and in service and for the reputation of His Electoral Serenity, I shall henceforth pursue my profession with unremitting diligence in future and for the rest of my life; and what I in my hitherto long-standing service may not yet have done to be deserving, I shall apply myself to the best of my abilities.

Signed at Dresden

on the Vigil of St. Michael the Archangel [*vigilia Michaelis archangeli*] [28 September] 1645.

Heinrich Schütz, in his own hand.

Postscript,

concerning the restoration or re-establishment of the Electoral *Hofkapelle*

Subject to correction, of course, it would be my most humble well-intentioned suggestion that His Electoral Serenity might not want to have the entire musical body [*corpus musicum*] newly founded and appointed all at once, but rather in stages, one after the other, and indeed the three companies or collegia in order, namely:

1. the *Kapellknaben* or discantists
2. the instrumentalists
3. the vocalists or singers

---

10. *Schütz-GBr* (161) transcribes the original text as *guetwilligst*, read *gewilliget*.

And indeed as for the first two, it is expected that this would not be difficult to achieve, and likewise at reasonable expense, only that it might require some time, and would hence be necessary to have that done as early as possible in order that these two companies might be set up once again.

With the third company, however—namely, the vocalists or singers—it would be somewhat more expensive and more difficult to enter into because one would have to seek them from abroad, perhaps also in part even amongst the Italians (in order that the Electoral Highness might be worthily served), which would also be sound advice over time, and it would be good to obtain [those] with proper style, with which I am somewhat familiar. But even if only the first two of the aforementioned companies might be restored, His Electoral Serenity would immediately notice and hear a commendable beginning of a new *corpus musicum*.

And if my proposal should most graciously please His Electoral Serenity, and it is commanded that one should start work on it, I would request that His Electoral Serenity might have a person designated with whom I could discuss this further and who could most humbly and properly report and subsequently present everything for His Serenity's most gracious consideration and ratification.

Signed as above

on the Vigil of St. Michael Archangel [*vigilia Michaelis archangeli*] [28 September] 1645.
Heinrich Schütz, in his own hand.

93. JOHANN KLEMM TO JOHANN SAMUEL SCHEIN
(9 MARCH 1646)

Letter written on behalf of Schütz regarding an employment opportunity for Schein in Leipzig

[D-BAUs: Neues Archiv Rep. VIII.VII.A.h.2/1b, fol. 4r–v][11]

[Address]

Delivered to *Herr* Johann Samuel Schein,[12] well-appointed organist in Bautzen

[Text]

My willing service together with wishes for every salutary welfare of the body and of the soul, first and foremost.

---

11. Scribal copy of Klemm's original.
12. Little is known about Johann Samuel Schein, son of the Thomaskantor and composer, Johann Hermann Schein.

Most honorable and erudite, and especially benevolent *Herr* Schein, the *Herr* Kapellmeister, Heinrich Schütz, sends you his kind regards, and at the same time reports that he promoted you before many distinguished people when he was in Leipzig recently (though he is again resident in Weissenfels), such that you shall soon be invited to Leipzig. When your post [at St. Petri] is to be filled again, the *Herr* Kapellmeister [has in mind] a fine fellow who was with him in Denmark and still resides with him, is said to play quite well (though I have neither seen nor heard him), and accordingly he [Schütz] would be glad to see him promoted.

Thus he also requests that in the event you would call upon him, and for his sake propose this person before the Council and Lord *Primarius*[13] Martin Gumprecht there and help to promote him to that end; and should it come to an audition, the *Herr* Kapellmeister himself should want to introduce him. I am to have reported to you on behalf of the *Herr* Kapellmeister that he is still unmarried, and around twenty-three or twenty-four years old; he [Schütz] also expects you shall do your duty by your people thereby; but if you wish to come to Leipzig and view him more closely, he is willing in turn to assist you with the means; and for that reason you should reply to me as soon as possible and make known your intentions in this regard.

Herewith commending all to God's protection, Dresden, 9 March 1646,
Your willing,
good friend,
Johann Klemm,[14]
Court Organist, resident at Schaller's brewing-house in the Nassengasse.

94. SCHÜTZ TO THE DRESDEN COURT (24 MAY 1646)

Partial memorandum regarding the boarding and expenses for twelve Knaben *at the Dresden Court*

[D-Dla: Loc. 8687/1, Kantoreiordnung so Kurfürst Moritz...1548, fols. 224r, 230r][15]

---

13. A *Primarius* is an *alderman* or *senator*, according to *DWB*.
14. Johann Klemm (b. ca. 1593; d. ca. 1657), from Oederan about 15 km southwest of Freiberg, entered the Saxon Court as a *Kapellknabe* in 1605, was sent to Augsburg at the elector's expense to study organ under Christian Erbach (b. ca. 1570; d. 1635) from 1613 to 1615, and was appointed Court Organist in Dresden in 1625. In addition to playing, composing, and teaching, he also became involved in music publishing, working first with the Leipzig organist Daniel Weixer, and later with another Schütz protégé, Alexander Hering. He published the second set of Schütz's *Symphoniae sacrae* (Dresden, 1647) and the *Geistliche Chor-Music* (Dresden, 1648).
15. Transcribed in *Schütz-GBr*, Nr. 51; *Schütz-Dokumente*, Nr. 103.

[Copyist's hand]

Register of the Electoral Saxon Instrumentalists
and Musicians [*Musikanten*], as are available on Trinity Sunday, 1646.
To wit:

Annual salaries:

400 *gulden*	Heinrich Schütz, Kapellmeister and Inspector of the *Musica*
228 *gulden*, 12 *groschen*	Sebastian Hirnschrötl
228 *gulden*, 12 *groschen*	Augustus Tax
150 *gulden* …	Jonas Kittel
200 *gulden* …	Zacharias Hertel
150 *gulden* …	John Dixon, the Englishman
180 *gulden* …	Johann Klemm
185 *gulden*, 15 *groschen*	Christoph Kittel
	Johann Georg Hofkontz, NB one still does not know how much he should be paid annually
40 *gulden*	Jonas Jägerdörfer, timpanist
50 *gulden*	Tobias Weller, organ builder
29 *gulden*, 11 *groschen*	Johann Huber, bellows treader

[Schütz's hand]

NB

Nr. 2. Regarding sustenance of
Six *Kapellknaben*:
[one wishes] most humbly to
learn,

Whether His Electoral Serenity might grant most graciously to each one annually: 60 *gulden* in cash. For board and everything, as well as laundry and shoe money

Item one livery from the Court
Item 7 *gulden* tuition[16]
Which for all six annually amounts to

360 *gulden* in cash
Six liveries
42 *gulden* tuition

---

16. *Schütz-GBr* (152) wrongly transcribes the number as "1."

Nr. 3.
Regarding sustenance of six instrumentalist *Knaben*:
It is hoped that these can be sustained at the same cost.
Grand total for the sustenance
of these twelve persons amounts to 804 *gulden* in cash
Item twelve liveries.

Nr. 4.

If His Electoral Serenity should be satisfied, the aforementioned *Knaben* should be boarded out accordingly:

Six instrumentalist *Knaben* to Augustus Tax
Three *Kapellknaben* to [Christoph] Kittel, Organist
Three *Kapellknaben* to Johann Klemm, Organist

95. SCHÜTZ DIRECTED TO JACOB WELLER, SENIOR COURT CHAPLAIN (30 JULY 1646)

Memorandum regarding the appointments of Johann Georg Hofkontz and Christoph Kittel, and his request for retirement, forwarded with a note by Weller to Johann Georg I

[D-Dla: Loc. 8560/8, Schreiben von und an den Oberhofprediger Dr. Jacob Weller 1646–51, fols. 3r–6v][17]

In the name of the Lord [*In noie Dni*]

In general:

A.

1. That all my most humble memoranda were intended such that nothing obstructive or unfit slips into His Electoral Serenity's *Hofkapelle*, but rather to provide it with none but qualified and useful people, and thus (with God's and His Electoral Serenity's help) that it might once again be transformed into a glorious state so that it might shine forth as a light and be celebrated amongst other evangelical *Kapellen*.

2. That in the engagement of musicians, and in setting up of their appointments, a general parity and fairness might be preserved according to each person's qualifications and duties, since the inequality otherwise would always give rise to spite, resentment, and negligence in service. In this respect, those who have the lowest salaries gladly shift the duties onto the others.

But since His Electoral Serenity might perhaps most graciously grant an advantage to one [musician] over another, it would be better advised were the same [advantage] shown

---

17. The document is in Schütz's hand. Transcribed in *Schütz-GBr*, Nr. 58; *Schütz-Dokumente*, Nr. 104.

and conferred upon them through a separate gratuity rather than with a disproportionate increase in salary.

Beyond this is also to be considered: if perchance an extravagant appointment should be made to an unqualified [musician], what then would a properly qualified fellow command for a salary (should such a person also perhaps be engaged in future)?

B.

Concerning Johann Georg Hofkontz's appointment.[18]

To inform His Electoral Serenity most humbly that the previous tutor [*Praeceptor*] of the *Kapellknaben* by the name of Andreas Petermann,[19] [the one] with the big nose which His Serenity also mentioned recently, went under the title of Court Cantor [*Hofkantor*]. Thus the aforementioned Hofkontz should not be ashamed to have the same [title]. The office of Vice-Kapellmeister and the appointment, however, I mention once again, for the reasons cited, is to be left vacant at present.

Concerning the amount of the aforementioned Johann Georg Hofkontz's salary:

The same [amount] is duly submitted to His Electoral Serenity for his determination. But should one want to keep his qualities and fairness in sight, and maintain parity as well, it could perhaps be disposed in the following way:

> 150 *gulden* as a tenor and Kapelle singer
> 50 *gulden* on account of being tutor
> 50 *gulden* on account of the office of Cantor

Total: 250 *gulden*

Beyond this perhaps an additional 50 *gulden* on account of lodging and wood that he must get back for the *Kapellknaben* expenses, which in total would thus amount to 300 *gulden* annually at most. But as mentioned previously, everything is for His Electoral Serenity's consideration and resolution.

The *Kapellknaben*, in my opinion, should be assigned to the Court Organist [Christoph] Kittel (perhaps also a few to Johann Klemm) with whom they can best and most quickly become accomplished and trained to sing correctly, which would by no means happen otherwise were they to be sent elsewhere. And because it is His Electoral Serenity's most gracious will that, as in former times, they should always proceed in good order with their tutor into the church, they can thus always assemble at his place both for church as well as for school lessons.

---

18. Johann Georg Hofkontz (b. 17 Aug. 1615; d, 19 Jul. 1655) was born in Trautenau in Bohemia. He studied at the University of Königsberg and Frankfurt an der Oder, became Cantor in Guben (1638–41) and on 2 January 1642 was appointed tenor at the *Hofkapelle* in Dresden. In 1651 he referred to himself as *Vizekapellmeister* (Vice-Kapellmeister) and spent the remainder of his career in Dresden.

19. It is very doubtful that in 1646 Schütz could be referring to the same Andreas Petermann identified in *Schütz-GBr* (338). The Andreas Petermann named in *Schütz-GBr* was born ca. 1532 in Dresden, served as Cantor of the Dresden Kreuzschule between 1561 and 1585, was *Knabenpraeceptor* (tutor) from 1586 until his retirement, and died in 1611 while Schütz was still studying under Gabrieli in Venice. Supplementary biographical information for this musician can be found in Vollhardt, *Geschichte der Cantoren und Organisten von den Städten im Königreich Sachsen*, 411.

C.
Concerning the appointment of Christoph Kittel, Court Organist.

For this diligent man, and useful to the *Hofkapelle*, it is my humble opinion that the current yearly salary granted him (namely, 250 thalers) be left as is; but because the appointment was drafted somewhat questionably, it could be calculated in the following manner, namely, that he should have:

1. 200 thalers, as a Court Organist and on account of his diligent attention to the organ, etc.

2. 50 thalers, on account of his assembly of varied, suitable musical works. He has also promised to assemble yet more and, when urgently needed, to have them further splendidly presented and used in the Electoral Kapelle.

Likewise, that he is also willing to hold a fixed rehearsal each day with the *Kapellknaben* and to apply particular diligence to them.

NB. His Electoral Serenity is hereby reminded confidentially that in this way, as long as his Kapellmeister Heinrich Schütz is alive, it should not be necessary to engage a Vice-Kapellmeister.

3. The Lord Marshal of the Palace might on a future occasion be reminded most humbly how His Electoral Serenity, perhaps in time, can graciously benefit this good man on account of the lodging sought by him.

4. With respect to those *Kapellknaben* who may be committed to his care, however, it would not be inappropriate to draw up and to deliver to him a separate note in regard to lodging and board.

D.
Most humble memoranda concerning my own person.

That the function of my office, first and foremost, consists not in personal attendance and service at all times but rather much more in the composition and arrangement of appropriate musical pieces of all kinds, the close supervision of the entire operation, and seeing that the companies [*collegia*] of vocalists, instrumentalists, and *Kapellknaben* might be kept in good order and practice.

Consequently I would once again most humbly request that His Electoral Serenity not take it amiss but instead might graciously permit me to reside in future at my home in Weissenfels, for reasons enough stated previously in a separate memorandum in that regard. I would be most humbly willing in return:

1. To travel back and forth several times voluntarily.

2. To appear at all times, barring an act of God, upon written communication from the *Herr* Senior Court Chaplain.[20]

---

20. Jacob Weller (Jacob Weller von Molssdorf) (b. 5 Dec. 1602; d. 6 Jul. 1664) was born in Neukirch (Vogtland), was already teaching in Wittenberg in 1631, became Superintendent in Brunswick in 1640, and in 1646

3. Should His Electoral Serenity in future see that the *Hofkapelle* suffer harm, not pertaining to or because of my absence, I would be ready to arrange my affairs to that end and apply myself completely to it anew. At present, however, it would be impossible, because I rented out my house and consequently could not so soon set up a household here [in Dresden] again.

Finally, and so help me God, this all was done in order the better to advance my profession without impediment, as it is hoped His Electoral Serenity shall then hear, would that God prolong my life somewhat. One could indeed reach me at any time, and I would surely set things here in such order that no deficiencies appear in my absence, and a fitting service would ensue upon his most gracious command.

NB. Hofkontz can however do little in this enterprise in my absence except perhaps that he, in my stead, provide the beat [in performances], which for him will still be a privilege.

E.

Sundry ancillary memoranda.

1. That, following my completed travel to Denmark, I still have arrears to my accounts in Lower Saxony.
2. Suggestion regarding our hitherto accrued salaries of several years.[21]

Most Illustrious Elector, Most Gracious Lord.

Your Electoral Serenity. Pardon me most graciously that I, for my part, must also trouble you amid such arduous official businesses. The Kapellmeister Schütz had the accompanying memorandum delivered to me in the past hour, so that I, most humbly, could report in person from it. I wanted however most humbly to send this to Your Electoral Serenity to let you first acquaint yourself perchance from it. I leave it to Your Electoral Serenity's most gracious pleasure, when or if you should want to hear me on this matter, and would then present myself most obediently if commanded of me. May Jesus Christ be, dwell, and live in grace with Your Electoral Serenity. Dresden, 30 July 1646.

Your Electoral Serenity's
most humble *Vorbeter*[22]
with God, and servant
of the Word,
Dr. Jacob Weller, in his own hand.

---

succeeded Matthias Hoë von Hoënegg as Senior Court Chaplain in Dresden, where he spent the remainder of his life. A staunch and vociferous supporter of Lutheran Orthodoxy, Weller was highly influential in the courts of Johann Georg I and II.

21. No signature or date is given, but the date would be the same as in Weller's accompanying letter, 30 July 1646.
22. *Vorbeter* is a person who leads in prayer or in worship, taken from the verb *vorbeten* (to say, pronounce, or recite a prayer).

96. SCHÜTZ TO CHRISTIAN SCHIRMER (7 SEPTEMBER 1646) (ORIGINAL LANGUAGE: LATIN)

Initial response to Marco Scacchi's Cribrum musicum ad triticum Syferticum *(Venice, 1643) (Original language: Latin)*

[I-Bc: G. B. Martini, E50/4, fol. 158r–v][23]

Latin copy of the letter of the highly celebrated and excellent man *Herr* Heinrich Schütz, most worthy Kapellmeister of the Elector of Saxony, to *Herr* Christian Schirmer, translated from the German.

The very pleasant letter of your lordship, and also that of *Herr* [Christian] Werner your Cantor, but especially the published disputes between *Herr* Marco Scacchi and *Herr* [Paul] Siefert,[24] together with adjoining appendices reached me, indeed properly, but at an inconvenient time, by roundabout ways, as I was occupied by annoyances, partly in Weissenfels, and partly in Dresden, and on that account it has been impossible for me thus far to go through them with due care, and much less does it recommend itself to bring my untimely judgment to bear on this matter. Indeed, I for my part would wish that *Herr* Siefert had not begun this business, since insofar as my judgment has weight and insofar as I was able to gather from a cursory and random reading, *Herr* Scacchi, whose compositions I have not yet seen, is a well-grounded musician of distinction, and therefore I shall not be able to pass by in silence that it seems to me that I should agree with him in many respects: especially when I shall have inspected those writings more carefully (once I have returned, after these three months of traveling, to Weissenfels and my current house and home). And if God grants me health, I shall reply properly to *Herr* Siefert in the next eleven days; I would wish that your lordship would convey it to *Herr* Siefert from me, prefaced by my cordial greeting, and apologize as well as you can for my delay in replying. I for my part shall not make myself judge and arbiter of this dispute, and much less will I enter into quarrels of this kind with anyone. I shall open my mind and my sincere feelings only according to the wishes of *Herr* Siefert, and I hope that he will receive this in good faith. I also ask that he greet *Herr* Kapellmeister [Kaspar] Förster for me most warmly, and that

---

23. The Latin translation of Schütz's letter originally written in German is found in *Judicium Cribri musici, idest litterae quaedam certo tempore a praestantissimis artis musicae in germania professoribus et peritis transmissae, mihique M. Scacchi* ... (Judgment of the Musical Sieve, that is, a letter transmitted at a certain time by the most outstanding professors and experts of the musical art in Germany, to me M. Scacchi.) Published ca. 1649 in Warsaw, the document exists today in a handwritten copy made by Giovanni Battista Marini. See *Schütz-Dokumente*, 244–46; and Werbeck, "Heinrich Schütz und der Streit zwischen Marco Scacchi und Paul Siefert," 63–79.

24. Paul Siefert (b. 23 May 1586; d. 6 May 1666) was a German composer and organist from Danzig (now Gdańsk, Poland) who spent most of his career in Poland. After a brief spell at the Warsaw court, Siefert returned in 1623 to Danzig as organist at the Marienkirche. In 1627, after an unsuccessful bid for the position of Kapellmeister of the Marienkirche, Siefert entered a bitter twenty-five-year feud with the successful candidate, Kaspar Förster (bap. 28 Feb. 1616; d. 2 Feb. 1673) and, consequently, with Marco Scacchi (b. ca. 1600; d. between 1681 and 1687), Kapellmeister at the royal court in Warsaw.

he thank him most humbly for sending the *Cribrum* [*musicum ad triticum Syferticum*]²⁵ of *Herr* Scacchi, which (controversy aside) I admire and find to be like a miracle for good composers (as much, admittedly, as I was able to see cursorily, and as if through a lattice²⁶). And seeing that he indicated to me that the aforesaid *Herr* Scacchi had published some Masses, I beseech the same *Herr* Förster most warmly to procure these for me at a good price, likewise (since thus far I have seen little or nothing of his concerted music and madrigals) to share with me at least something from his written compositions, which would be of the utmost pleasure to me. With these words I commend His Lordship to his Lord Majesty. Dated at Calbe,²⁷ in the city of the archdiocese, 7 September 1646.

97. HEINRICH II REUSS TO SCHÜTZ (22 OCTOBER 1646)

Draft of a letter requesting Schütz's recommendation to fill the position of Music Director at the Gera Gymnasium left vacant on the death of Peter Neander

[D-GZsa: Landesarchiv Greiz, Reuss jüngerer Linie Konsistorium Gera, Fach 49, Nr. 1, fol. 18r–v]

[Address]

To Heinrich Schütz, well-appointed Kapellmeister to the Royal Majesty in Denmark and Electoral Serenity of Saxony

[Text]

Heinrich II.²⁸

We offer our kind greetings and affectionate good intentions foremost, most honorable, highly esteemed, erudite, most graciously beloved [friend]. We could not forbear asking after your circumstances, and are gladdened to learn that you still enjoy good health and salutary welfare.

We write further to inform you how the post of the *cantor figuralis* [figural Cantor] as *quarta collega*²⁹ in our *Gymnasium*³⁰ is vacant, which we would gladly fill again (the

---

25. *Musical Sieve to the Wheat of Siefert*.
26. This is an allusion to Cicero's *De Oratore* 1, 35, 162.
27. Calbe is located on the River Saale in modern-day Saxony-Anhalt, approximately 29 km southeast of Magdeburg. Until 1680, Calbe belonged to the Archdiocese of Magdeburg and served as a summer and secondary see for the Administrator of the Archdiocese, August, Duke of Saxe-Weissenfels, for whose baptism Schütz was first called to Dresden in 1614.
28. The Reuss family was partitioned into Elder, Middle, and Younger lines in 1564. Heinrich II (b. 14 Aug. 1602; d. 28 May 1670), like his father, Heinrich Posthumus, was head simultaneously of the Elder and Younger lines. The Middle line of the family died out in 1616.
29. Heinrich II was looking for a replacement for Peter Neander (1575–1645), who had been the key musical figure at the Gera Rutheneum since it was founded by his father, Heinrich Posthumus, in 1608.
30. Classical college or grammar school.

sooner the better) with a qualified person who might direct the musical choir [*chorus musicus*] as well as faithfully and diligently teach the cherished youths in the class connected to this official duty.

We do not doubt that you know of suchlike candidates who can be usefully employed for this purpose and seek advancement. It is thus our modest request to you that you would suggest at will to us down here [i.e., Gera] one or two persons you consider sufficiently qualified for this [position], according to your innate discretion, and have your sincere and faithful appraisal sent to us here, in order that we shall be prepared to express our gratitude for it. We remain then, with affectionate good intentions always. Dated at Gera castle, 22 October 1646.

98. SCHÜTZ TO MARTIN KNABE (30 OCTOBER 1646)

Letter regarding Heinrich Reuss II's letter and the vacant position in Gera

[D-GZsa: Landesarchiv Greiz, Reuss jüngerer Linie, Konsistorium Gera, Fach 49, Nr. 1, fols. 19r–20v][31]

[Address]

To *Herr* Martin Knabe, highly learned musician and distinguished organist, to his most benevolent hands in Weissenfels

[Text]

Most honorable and especially highly favored *Herr* Martin, distinguished dear friend.

I write herewith kindly to inform you that His Most Noble Grace, Lord Heinrich II, the Younger and at this time Eldest Reuss, Lord of Plauen, etc., also my Gracious Lord, on the twenty-third of this month,[32] wrote to me from Gera and commissioned me with a certain matter. Because one must not act precipitately or in haste in such an undertaking, I do in truth have suggestions in mind already but nevertheless should like to examine and compare more closely the qualifications of the people in some measure; but this cannot be done conveniently or properly before my return to Weissenfels (which, with God's help, might first happen perhaps in three weeks' time). It is thus my most diligent request to you that you would show me the singular favor, and as soon as possible have a short letter sent off to *Herr* Michael Kühnel, His Grace's Court Organist, and through him extend to His Most Noble Grace my humble and most obedient greetings, in addition to this give notice of the state of affairs, and solicit something of a postponement in this matter (until my return home, as mentioned above).

---

31. The document is in Schütz's hand. Transcribed in *Schütz-GBr*, Nr. 60; *Schütz-Dokumente*, Nr. 106.
32. The letter from Heinrich II is actually dated 22 October, not 23 October as Schütz has written.

Inasmuch as I would most obediently assist His Most Noble Grace as much as possible in this matter, I in return am ready to compensate you for your efforts and, in addition to commending [you] to divine protection, always to remain,

Your obliging and most dutiful friend,
Heinrich Schütz, in his own hand.
Leipzig, 30 October 1646. In haste.

99. BAUTZEN TOWN COUNCIL TO SCHÜTZ (5 MARCH 1647)

Letter requesting Schütz's recommendation to fill the organ post at St. Petri made vacant by Johann Samuel Schein's departure[33]

[D-BAUs: Neues Archiv Rep. VIII.VII.A.h.2/1b, fols. 5r–v, 6r–v][34]

Our kind greetings and service foremost, Most Honorable and Esteemed, especially benevolent Lord and Friend. Our organist until now, Johann Samuel Schein, has resigned his office, hopefully for an improved situation. Thus it will be incumbent upon us to consider, prior to his departure, how this post might again be filled, moreover, with a suitable subject [*Subjecto*].

Insofar as we have received reports from other places that a young man resides with you, who is sufficiently qualified to occupy this organist's post, it would also be mentioned that he shall have received good reports of the circumstances of this office here and be well disposed toward accepting it. He should also be aware already that the likely salary level for the post remains the same and, on account of excessive damages greatly suffered here, not to be increased or revised.

Thus we should like to ask you and request herewith, whether you think him to be sufficiently qualified for this office,[35] to report to us candidly with a reply of a few words about him. In this case and since the aforementioned young man should be inclined to accept this vacant organist's post, we could have it happen that you might like perhaps to offer others additionally, and as soon as possible might have himself heard by playing the audition [*Proba*] before us here. According to circumstances or quality we might then be able to comment in respect to his acceptance, and be willing to express to you once more our friendship and service.

Signed Bautzen, 5 March 1647.

Bürgermeister and Councillors of the same place.

---

33. The correspondence between Schütz and Bautzen is reproduced in *Schütz-GBr* as Nrs 61 and 62. Unfortunately, *Schütz-GBr* simply copies the transcription from Biehle, *Musikgeschichte von Bautzen bis zum Anfang des 19. Jahrhunderts*, which itself contains scribal errors, omissions of letters, words, and passages of text. See Biehle, 20–22. The town of Bautzen is located some 60 km west of Dresden; as the center of Upper Lusatia (Oberlausitz), it was adjoined to electoral Saxony as a consequence of the Peace of Prague in 1635.
34. Fol. 5r–v is the final, clean copy of the letter; fol. 6r–v is a draft of the letter bearing the same date.
35. *Kirchen Music Dienst* (church music service) is crossed out in the original, but included in *Schütz-GBr* (308).

100. SCHÜTZ TO THE BAUTZEN TOWN COUNCIL (14 MARCH 1647)

Letter recommending Alexander Hering for the position of organist in Bautzen

[D-BAUs: Neues Archiv Rep. VIII.VII.A.h.2/1b, fol. 8r (in Schütz's hand), 11v (address), and fol. 9r–v (fine copy made by civic authorities)][36]

[Address]

To the Right Honorable, Right Worshipful, Most Learned and Most Wise *Bürgermeister* and Council, my especially Most Benevolent Lords, Most Esteemed Friends, in Bautzen

[Text]

Most Honorable, Highly and Well-Respected, Most Learned, Most Wise, Especially Most Benevolent Lords, Most Highly Esteemed Friends.

That you not only kindly notify me of the imminent vacancy of your organist's post, but rather, in addition, benevolently wish to offer this position to a young man (who has entered into his fourth year assisting me up to now with writing, but in addition to that has also devoted himself to the organist's art), I have understood, among other things, from your most recent, pleasant letter forwarded to me from Bautzen the fifth of this [month], which I accordingly acknowledge with all due gratitude, since I would gladly like to see the young fellow mentioned here (who for all that is now something over twenty years old) at an organ, in order to put better into practice that which until now he understood intellectually. After due discussion with me, he is dutifully inclined to this vocation in particular.

We both would therefore obligingly request the Lordships to remain steadfastly by your benevolent offer and inclination toward us, and furthermore to appoint no one else to this position until my aforesaid former copyist by the name of Alexander Hering, barring an act of God, shall personally present himself for audition no later than fourteen days before Easter. I do not doubt that you on all sides, and the Director of your musical choir above all, shall be most favorably satisfied with his qualities. Thus will I also live obligingly in the hope that you shall have him favorably met with this position, as I intend to send him off in such a way that he might succeed *Herr* Schein as soon as possible upon his [Schein's] departure, and that the Divine Service be thus continuously provided for, of which I should not refrain to give notice in dutiful response to the same news. Commending you to the favor of God's care, I remain my Benevolent Highly Esteemed Lords'

most dutiful
Heinrich Schütz, Kapellmeister, in his own hand.
Weissenfels, 14 March 1647.

---

36. Transcribed in *Schütz-GBr*, Nr. 61; *Schütz-Dokumente*, Nr. 108.

[PS] A short time ago I also sent off a brief letter to your *Herr Primarius* in this matter, which letter I suspect also will have arrived in the interim, and thus he shall have communicated my greetings to my Most Highly Esteemed Lords, as is my hope.

101. BAUTZEN TOWN COUNCIL TO SCHÜTZ (11 APRIL 1647)

Letter outlining the Council's rejection of Alexander Hering to the position of organist in Bautzen

[D-BAUs: Neues Archiv Rep. VIII.VII.A.h.2/1b, fol. 10r, early rough draft on 12r]

Our kind Greetings and Service foremost, Right Honorable and Highly Esteemed, and especially favorable *Herr* and Friend. What you sent most recently, dated 5 March, regarding the young man who until now resided in your employ—namely, whether he would be able to warrant the office and manage the organ service *at the principal and parish churches here*[37]—was duly delivered to us.

From what we understand from it, the aforesaid fellow is rather and principally a scribe and copyist, and only secondarily practiced in organ playing, and who would now first bring into practice [*ad praxin*] what he may have understood intellectually therein. All the same, it is incumbent on us, however, as public authorities, that for such an organ in such a fine church congregation in this cherished city, an expressly and already aptly well-practiced and polished organist should be appointed. Several persons of this kind have also already declared themselves, from which we hope to be able to provide this service laudably, to our good satisfaction, and for the continuation of the cherished Divine Service. As we are unanimously of this opinion, we thus want to notify you of this news herewith so that the aforementioned youth might not take the trouble of coming here in vain. We the undersigned wish to thank you kindly, and readily reciprocate your friendship and service at any time.

Signed at Bautzen, 11 April 1647.

Bürgermeister and Council.

102. SCHÜTZ TO THE BAUTZEN TOWN COUNCIL (28 APRIL 1647)

Letter guaranteeing Hering's qualifications and suitability for the organist's post in Bautzen

[D-BAUs: Neues Archiv Rep. VIII.VII.A.h.2/1b, fols. 13r–v, 18v (address)][38]

---

37. *Hiesiger Haubt Vndt PfarrKirchen* (the main and parish churches in this place) is crossed out in one copy but not in the other.
38. Because of the way this document has been sewn into the file, Schütz's letter enfolds other documents, making it look like the address is on a later folio when in fact it is the same sheet of paper. Transcribed in *Schütz-GBr*, Nr. 62; *Schütz-Dokumente*, Nr. 109.

Old Age (1645–56)

[Address]

To the Right Honorable, Most Worshipful, Highly and Most Learned, Greatly and Most Wise Lord *Bürgermeister* and Council of the Town of Bautzen, my especially Most Benevolent, Highly Esteemed Lords. Bautzen

[Text]

Right Honorable, Most Worshipful, Wise, Especially Most Benevolent, Highly Esteemed Lords and Friends.

I should not withhold from you how your second letter, dated at Bautzen 11 April (New Style), was also safely delivered to me in Weissenfels on Palm Sunday of the Old Calendar. However, since my former assistant and copyist until now, Alexander Hering, had already been gone four days by that time, and on his way to Bautzen, I was obliged to postpone my reply until now and to see how this matter would play out.

Now initially and upon reading this second letter of yours, I was little short of dismayed that on account of my previous letter sent to you, you took such offence from it and were occasioned to reject the aforesaid former copyist of mine (whom you had summoned a short while ago to fill your vacant organist's position). Thus was I comforted upon my arrival in Dresden two days ago to learn that you indeed finally elected and confirmed this young man anew after the completed audition as your organist. I am hereby most grateful to my Highly Esteemed Lords all and sundry on account of that, and would assure you once more that I hope, God willing, you shall not have erred in the least in making this choice.

Even if indeed I am not yet prepared to praise, and cannot yet praise, the aforementioned young fellow at present for an absolute mastery in this difficult profession (if it is to be learned upon a proper foundation [*Fundament*]), he is nonetheless for all that on the right track with his studies, according to the proper instruction he has received [from me], without boasting, so that with the grace of divine help, it is to be expected that he shall still achieve mastery over many a thing hereafter (which shall be regarded as excellent through the cry of the common people), and thus surely prove himself to my Most Benevolent Lords better qualified in his position from day to day, as generally occurs in all other professions as well when it is dealt with in proper order and tended to with continual diligence. Although it is beyond my expectation, if now or in future a single deficiency appears in the aforesaid and now currently appointed organist or, on the other hand, might you be able otherwise to come upon a subject [*subjecto*] better suited to you, I herewith offer once again most obligingly (upon prior notification from you of, say, a quarter year) to relieve you ungrudgingly of the same at any time again and, with divine help, to procure a situation for him elsewhere. And my Most Benevolent Lords ought by no means give offence to me, as I will devote myself in no way to impede the Divine Service with my people but, on the contrary, preserve and to enrich it honorably. I herewith obligingly and faithfully commend you all into His divine protection to show mercy, and myself to His constant favor. I, for my small part, remain my Most Esteemed Lords', all and sundry, always ready and most willing

Heinrich Schütz, Kapellmeister, in his own hand.

Signed Dresden, 28 April (Old Style) 1647.

103. *SYMPHONIAE SACRAE II* (DRESDEN, 1647): TITLE PAGE AND DEDICATION (1 MAY 1647)

[Title page]

Symphoniarum sacrarum
Secunda Pars,[39] [Sacred Symphonies, Part II]
in which are to be found
German
concertos
with 3, 4, 5, that is, one, two, three
vocal and two instrumental voices
[such] as violins or suchlike
together with added, doubled basso continuo,
the one for the organist, the other
for the Violone,
set to music
by
Heinrich Schütz,
Electoral Saxon Kapellmeister
[*Prima Vox*]
By Privilege of the Royal Imperial Majesty
M. DC. XLVII.
Op. 10 [*Opus Decimum*]
Printed in Dresden by the Blessed Heirs of Gimel Berg, Electoral Saxon
Court Book-Printer. Published by Johann Klemm,
Court Organist there, and Alexander Hering,
Organist at Bautzen.

---

39. SWV 341–67; RISM A/I/8 S 2292; G 7; *NSA* 15–17.

[Dedication][40]

To the Most Serene, Mighty,
Noble Prince and Lord,
Lord Christian V,[41]
Prince of Denmark, Norway, of the Wends
and Goths; Duke of Schleswig, Holstein,
Stormarn, and of the Dithmarschen; Count of Oldenburg
and Delmenhorst, etc.,
My Most Gracious Prince and Lord.

Most Serene, Mighty Prince, Most Gracious Lord, two years ago, and in connection to my personal most humbly rendered service in Copenhagen at that time, Your Royal Highness accepted and received with particular grace the present and slight musical work composed by me, at that time written out only by hand. Out of innate princely inclination toward all the praiseworthy arts, and above all toward noble music, you used and performed the same work several times; and you assured me genuinely and nobly as well that you took most gracious pleasure in this my most humble dedication—all of which I remember with constant, most humble recollection, and find myself thus bound in return, out of my indebted gratitude, to extol evermore, as much as possible, your heroic spirit and admirable princely virtues; and, as with the undeserved great favor shown to me, to endeavor at each and every opportunity to requite with most indebted service, if only to some degree.

Accordingly, since for various reasons, and in part stated here in the memorandum to the reader, this slight work should appear now in print (after diligent revision carried out by me, and in some respects expanded and improved), I have thus thought it in every way proper to my indebtedness not to pass by Your Royal Serenity in silence this time either, but rather now with this new and public edition wanted to renew my previous and first most humble dedication, above all, however, to demonstrate and assert anew at the same time hereby my unceasing most-indebted devotion.

May it thus please Your Royal Serenity now to accept anew, with your gracious eyes and hands, as you did in former times, my aforementioned unworthy slight work (which in deep humility I herewith present to you once more), and with royal favor and grace to remain steadfast and continue to show affection toward my humble person and to the laudable profession of music (which up to now, in these chaotic martial times, has otherwise suffered great diminution in its patrons).

---

40. The dedication is included only in the vocal and violin partbooks.
41. The dedicatee of this work is Prince-Elect Christian, who was referred to as Christian V during his lifetime in the reasonable expectation that he would succeed his father, Christian IV, as King of Denmark. He died before his father, however, and Christian IV's second son, Frederik III, was crowned king in 1648. Thus it was Frederik III's son, Christian, who eventually became Christian V, King of Denmark in 1670.

May the Almighty, Whose honor, glory, and praise the heavenly hosts sing without end, again grant harmoniousness and concord everywhere and in all life's stations; and also, to the glory of His holy name, long keep Your Royal Serenity, together with Your Royal Consort[42] and all the most praiseworthy Crown of Denmark, in health and happiness, and in all prosperity pleasing to Him; to the elevation in particular of the liberal arts and of beloved music, hitherto greatly diminished, as well as the welfare of my unworthy person. To His fatherly care I most faithfully and most humbly commend Your Electoral Highness, and myself then to your steadfast most gracious affection. Dresden, the first day of the month of May, 1647.

Your Royal Serenity's
most humble and most dutiful servant,
Heinrich Schütz.

104. *SYMPHONIAE SACRAE II* (DRESDEN, 1647): PREFACE TO THE READER

[On the verso of the title page of the basso continuo partbook]

This small work is available not only from the publishers, but also in Leipzig from Johann Rosenmüller,[43] distinguished musician in the same place, and likewise from Delphin Strungk,[44] celebrated organist at Saint Martin's Church in Brunswick.

To the Benevolent Reader.

Benevolent dear reader, it should be mentioned to you here that, in the year 1629, when I had traveled to Italy for the second time and sojourned there for a spell, I also composed in a short period of time, in accordance with the small talent God bestowed on me, which I mention without boasting, a small Latin work for one, two, and three vocal parts, together with two added violins, or similar instruments, in the prevailing musical

---

42. Magdalena Sybille of Saxony (b. 23 Dec. 1617; d. 6 Jan. 1668) was the daughter of the Saxon Elector, Johann Georg I. She became Princess-Elect of Denmark upon her marriage in 1634 to Prince-Elect Christian. After Prince-Elect Christian died in 1647, she married Friedrich Wilhelm II, Duke of Saxe-Altenburg (b. 12 Mar. 1603; d. 22 Apr. 1669).
43. Johann Rosenmüller (b. 1619; d. 10 Sept. 1684) studied in Leipzig and is listed as an assistant at the Thomasschule in 1642 under Tobias Michael (b. 13 Jun. 1595; d. 26 Jun. 1657). He had become the first assistant by 1650, was appointed organist at the Nicolaikirche in 1651, and in 1653 the city council of Leipzig promised him he would one day succeed Michael as Thomaskantor. Rosenmüller and several choirboys were charged with homosexuality, leading to imprisonment, but Rosenmüller was able to flee Leipzig, found employment as a trombonist at San Marco in Venice, and eventually returned to Germany where he spent the remainder of his life in Wolfenbüttel.
44. Delphin Strungk (b. 1600/1601; d. ca. 10 Oct. 1694) was organist at the Marienkirche in Wolfenbüttel from 1630, then at the court in Celle from 1632 to 1637, and finally in 1637 as organist at the Martinikirche in Brunswick where he remained until his death.

style I encountered there at that time, and had published and printed in Venice under the title *Symphoniae sacrae*.

Because copies of some of it found their way to Germany and into the hands of musicians there, and it was brought to my attention how it was valued by them, and that in some distinguished places had been repeatedly performed completely underlaid throughout with German texts instead of the Latin, I let this serve as a special inducement for me to attempt a small work of the same kind in our German mother tongue. After having thus undertaken it, I completed the same, alongside other of my work, with God's help, as it is presented here.

It is true that, after that and up to the present, I have been not a little hindered in bringing it out in public print, not only by the miserable hostile times which continue unremitting in our beloved fatherland—and for music no less than otherwise for the other free arts—but as well, and indeed chiefly, by the current Italian style which still remains unknown to most, both with respect to the composition and to the correct performance of it (whereby indeed, in the opinion of the astute Claudio Monteverdi, as stated in the foreword to the eighth book of his madrigals, music shall now have attained its ultimate perfection).

And experience (to admit the truth here reluctantly) up to now has repeatedly proven how this modern Italian composition and works written in that style, together with its proper measure [*Mensur*], a good many of us Germans, for our part, and so many of whom hereby not uneducated, neither rightly know about the black notes applied therein nor play them properly, in that (even those places where one believes there to be a good *Music*) pieces composed in this way are oftentimes so badly played, mishandled and, as it were, downtrodden that they arouse nothing but disgust and vexation to a discerning ear, so too to the author himself, and a wholly unjustified denigration to the laudable German Nation, as though it were unfit in the noble art of music (for, indeed, there is certainly no lack of such accusations from some foreigners).

But since this slight work, already completed by me some years ago, was most humbly presented by me at that time in handwritten copy to the Most Serene, Mighty Prince and Lord, Lord Christian the Fifth,[45] Prince of Denmark, Norway, of the Goths and Wends etc., as can be seen, among other things, from the preceding most humble dedication, I heard subsequently how many pieces from this composition of mine (as then is customary) were carelessly and defectively copied out, circulated here and there, and also came into the hands of distinguished musicians, I was thus induced to take the same pieces in hand myself once more and after thorough revision hereby convey them through publication to those who might seek pleasure in them.

My concern is for prudent musicians, educated in good schools (for whose pleasure, next to the glory of God, these few humble copies are now being published), and they will note the effort I have taken and not be at all displeased by the style I have introduced here.

---

45. Schütz is referring to Prince-Elect Christian (b. 10 Apr. 1603; d. 2 Jun. 1647) who died in Werbitz just a few weeks after the composer had dedicated the work to him.

Thus to the others, chiefly however those to whom the proper beat [*Tact*] in the aforementioned modern music, and the black notes, as well as the constant drawn-out musical stroke on the violin, are not known, let alone practiced, among us Germans (but nonetheless might take pleasure in hearing something from it), it is my kind request that, before they venture to perform publicly one or the other of these pieces, they should not be ashamed therefore to obtain instruction in advance from those knowledgeable in this manner and not be vexed through private practice, so that neither they nor the author himself, through no fault of his own, might receive unexpected derision instead of the proper gratitude.

Inasmuch as I have in a few respects also followed Claudio Monteverdi's madrigal "Armato il cor" in the concerto "Es steh Gott auf,"[46] as well as one of his *ciaccona* with two tenor voices, I leave it for those who are familiar with the aforementioned composition to judge the extent to which this occurs.[47] I would that no one on that account draw my remaining work into undeserved suspicion, for I am not in the habit of adorning my work with foreign plumage.

Finally, should God spare my life yet longer, I make this further offer to publish in the near future, with His gracious help, more of my (in truth) unworthy works, and chief among them such that might be used even by those who are not and neither plan to be professional musicians, but with good effect nevertheless.

Farewell.

105. *SYMPHONIAE SACRAE II* (DRESDEN, 1647): APPENDED LIST OF PUBLISHED WORKS

Detailed account, for the information of the benevolent reader, of the various musical works issued in print by the author up to the present.[48]

Madrigals for five voices. Printed in Venice, 1611.

Opus 1.

German Psalms together with sundry motets and concertos, with eight and more voices. Part One in folio. Printed in Dresden, 1619.

Opus 2.

---

46. SWV 356.
47. Monteverdi's "Zefiro torna" and "Armato il cor d'adamantina fede" were published in the *Scherzi musicali cioè arie, & madrigali in stil recitativo, con una ciaccona* (Venice, 1632). *Ciaccona*, better known by the French term *chaconne*, was originally a brisk dance based on variation technique, often in the form of ground basses or ostinato variations built on a number of short, recurring harmonic or melodic units, or both, sometimes exploiting shifts between simple and compound meters.
48. The index of works is found on the last page of the *Bassus pro Violone* of the *Symphoniae sacrae*, Part Two, 1647.

Historia of the Resurrection of the Lord.
Printed in Dresden, 1623.
Opus 3.

Cantiones sacrae [for] four voices. Printed in Freiberg, 1625.
Opus 4.

Dr. Becker's [Small] Book of Psalms with One Hundred and Three Melodies, of which Ninety-Two are new ones by the Author. One book in octavo printed in Freiberg, 1628.
Opus 5.

Symphoniae sacrae, Part One, for 3, 4, 5, 6 voices.
Printed in Venice, 1629.
Opus 6.

Musicalische Exequien.
Printed in Dresden, 1636.
Opus 7.

Sacred Concertos, Part One, for 1, 2, 3, 4, 5 voices.
Printed in Leipzig, 1636.
Opus 8.

Sacred Concertos, Part Two, for 1, 2, 3, 4, 5 voices.
Printed in Dresden, 1639.
Opus 9.

Symphoniae sacrae, Part Two, with 3, 4, and 5 voices.
Printed in Dresden, 1647.
Opus 10.

106. SCHÜTZ DIRECTED TO JOHANN GEORG I (BETWEEN 20 JUNE AND 22 JULY 1647)

Memorandum regarding musical preparations for a princely baptism in Dresden

[D-Dla: Loc. 8687/1, Kantoreiordnung so Kurfürst Moritz...1548, fols. 288r–v, 290r][49]

---

49. *Schütz-GBr* (201) suggests that this undated document may have originated in 1642 in connection to the baptism of the eldest daughter of Johann Georg II, Sibylla Maria (b. 16 Sept. 1642; d. 17 Feb. 1643). *Schütz-Dokumente* (262) offers a compelling argument suggesting that the baptism must have been for

Memorandum
Regarding the *Music's* attendance at the impending
(may God grant good fortune) princely baptism.

First.
Vocalists or Singers which are already on hand

1. Sebastian Hirnschrötl
2. Joseph Nusser[50]
3. Jonas Kittel[51]
4. The new one who currently sings in the church before the choir-desk.[52]
5. Philipp Stolle, Duke Johann Georg's theorbist.
6. Johann Klemm's son. The only discantist.

[My] humble suggestion, for consideration, how the aforementioned company of singers for this service could be further strengthened somewhat:

1. If His Electoral Serenity, may it graciously please him, to urge upon Kleinhempel[53] in Leipzig that he might acquire from the Cantor there [i.e., Tobias Michael[54]], two or even one of his best discantists, and to send them to us here as early as possible (in order to rehearse the necessary pieces). Inasmuch as the best boys will probably be found at this place at present, I have heard a few recently that I rather liked and wanted to write to the aforementioned Cantor myself.

2. In regard to other singers, we would also still be in urgent need of a few more, and I hope these summoned persons would arrive together around the same time, and who would serve alongside for a small honorarium. And I will certainly see to it how we might

---

Johann Georg III (b. 20 Jun. 1647; d. 12 Sept. 1691), the future Saxon Elector (1680–91). Transcribed in *Schütz-GBr*, Nr. 50; *Schütz-Dokumente*, Nr. 111.

50. Joseph Nusser (or Nosser) was appointed to the Dresden *Hofkapelle* in 1606, and was installed as Vice-Kapellmeister in 1614. After twenty years of service to the court, he petitioned to retire but was still on the court roster in 1632, identified as one of the basses in 1637, but had been removed from the roster by 1651. *Schütz-GBr*, 336.

51. Jonas Kittel is already mentioned in 1631 as a bass in the Dresden *Hofkapelle*, and is still mentioned in the Dresden Kapelle roster in 1651. *Schütz-GBr*, 336.

52. *Schütz-GBr* (346) proposes that Schütz was perhaps referring to Christoph Bernhard (b. 1 Jan. 1628; d. 14 Nov. 1692). If the dating of the document is close to being accurate, however, then the singer in question could hardly be Bernhard; according to Kerala J. Snyder (*Grove-Mus*), Bernhard did not join the Electoral Kapelle until ca. 1648 when he was approximately twenty years old, receiving a formal appointment to the *Hofkapelle* on 1 August the following year.

53. Conrad Kleinhempel was *Accisrat* (Excise Councillor) and *Flossinspector* in Leipzig from 1637, and became *Flossverwalter* (Raft Inspector and Raft Administrator, respectively) in 1659. He apparently functioned as an agent in Leipzig for the Duke of Saxony. *Schütz-GBr*, 336.

54. Tobias Michael (b. 13 Jun. 1595; d. 26 Jun. 1657) succeeded Johann Hermann Schein as Leipzig's Thomaskantor, chosen in late 1630 and confirmed in the position in April 1631. Michael also adopted the Italian style in his best-known work, *Musicalische Seelenlust* (1634–37).

make do with this company and get through it in some measure, but we are in most urgent need of the discantists, as is easy to imagine.

Secondly.
The available instrumentalists are:

1. Augustus Tax
2. Zacharias Hertel[55]
3. The Englishman[56]
4. Friedrich Werner,[57] Duke Johann Georg's instrumentalist, who in fact is still currently living in Vienna with the imperial cornettist Sansoni, but he will hopefully arrive here by then as well.
5. Perhaps still in addition to these is also a pair of novices from the *Knaben*, which one might be able to employ in something from time to time.

Most humble suggestion, for consideration, how
this assembly of instrumentalists could be further fortified in some respects for this
occasion.

This assembly has this central deficiency: the fundamental part is lacking in it, namely, the bass [instrumental] voice, such as the great bass viol, the great trombone, great bassoon. A person of this kind must be acquired of necessity, because not a single service can be properly given without him. In addition to this, however, for better strengthening in other parts of such company, it is recommended:

1. Herman from Halle,[58] who also served that time at the wedding. Perhaps Duke August could have him summoned here for the baptism.[59] He was instrumentalist [*Instrumentist*] to the former Archbishop.[60]

---

55. Zacharias Hertel was a cornetto player of sufficient renown that Samuel Scheidt named him as the dedicatee of his *Padouanen* of 1621.
56. According to *Schütz-GBr*, it is not clear to whom Schütz was referring in this entry. It is quite possibly "Johann Dixon, Englender [*sic*]"—i.e., John Dixon—who is identified on the roster of electoral musicians from 1637. The index of musicians is reproduced in Frandsen, "Music in a Time of War," 35. According to *Schütz-GBr* (352), Dixon is still at court as late as 1663.
57. Friedrich Werner (b. 3 Oct. 1621; d. 4 Apr. 1667), a native Saxon and brother to Christoph Werner (*Schütz-GBr*, 338), apprenticed under one of the municipal musicians and entered the Electoral Prince's Kapelle in 1641. Around 1645, Werner was sent at the Electoral Prince's expense to study under the famed Giovanni Sansoni in Vienna. He was also at the Danish Court around 1634 and 1647. He became Senior Instrumentalist (*Oberinstrumentist*) in 1663.
58. The full identity of this musician is not known.
59. August, Duke of Saxony (b. 13 Aug. 1614; d. 4 Jun. 1680), the second son of Johann Georg I to reach adulthood, was named Administrator of Magdeburg, and became founder of the Saxe-Weissenfels line. On 23 November 1647, he was married to Anna Maria (b. 1 Jul. 1627; d. 11 Dec. 1669), daughter of Adolph Friedrich I, Duke of Mecklenburg (b. 15 Dec. 1588; d. 27 Feb. 1658).
60. Since the sixteenth century, the Archdiocese of Magdeburg had been governed by Protestant administrators. In 1631, following the siege and sack of Magdeburg at the hands of Imperial troops under the command of

2. Likewise, a young fellow by the name of Christian Krüger is in the employ of Hartenstein these days, into the services of which lord he entered (before this, however, he had also been our *Kapellknabe* and was trained here), who can also be used well on various instruments. In the event that His Electoral Serenity should care to allow 2 thalers weekly for board and lodging, I should think to get him here for that, and he could thus rehearse with us in good time and better fit in with us.

3. In case His Electoral Serenity would also want to order a few additional instrumentalists for the impending baptism (for the sake of varying the instruments, and so that one could also employ perchance a trombone choir in the church, just as the dance music could be all the more fully voiced), suchlike, also from Halle or Leipzig, would also be most humbly recommended by us.

For the third.

Regarding the organists, there are enough of them at hand, namely:

1. Johann Klemm
2. Matthias Weckmann, Duke Johann Georg's [organist]

For the fourth.
Inasmuch as His Electoral Serenity cannot be unaware that we will be in urgent need of money, owing to repairs of various instruments, as well as for the purchase of strings, I would most humbly urge His Electoral Serenity to have 50 *gulden* paid out to me for this, for which I will faithfully keep accounts, spend nothing except out of utmost necessity, pay from it the expenses (to the extent it will suffice) for the aforementioned Hartenstein instrumentalist, as well also for the Leipzig discantists, when they arrive, and after that most humbly submit the bill.

For the fifth.
Because it is also highly necessary that the currently discordant company should be well rehearsed ahead of time, and hereto a location in the palace would be very convenient for us where we would have all the instruments close at hand, it is also my most humble, tentative query whether perhaps Duke Moritz's small chamber could be given to us for such rehearsal, since our positif is already in there.[61]

Tilly, governing authority was given to the Catholic Administrator, Leopold Wilhelm of Austria, until 1638. While Leopold Wilhelm enjoyed the benefits of an Archbishop, he lacked the canonical qualifications to bear the title. He was expelled in 1638 by the Swedish army and the archdiocese was turned over to August, Duke of Saxony.

61. Moritz, Duke of Saxony (b. 28 Mar. 1619; d. 4 Dec. 1681), the youngest son of Johann Georg I, became Duke of Saxe-Zeitz in 1652. It was with Duke Moritz that Schütz later had significant contact in regard to building up the musical establishment at the newly established court in Zeitz.

107. SCHÜTZ TO CHRISTIAN REICHBRODT, PRIVY CHAMBER SECRETARY (21 SEPTEMBER 1647)

Memorandum regarding the appointment of the Italian musician, Agostino Fontana

[D-Dla: Loc. 8687/1, Kantoreiordnung so Kurfürst Moritz…1548, fols. 244r, 245v][62]

[Address]

To *Herr* Christian Reichbrodt, Lord Privy Chamber Secretary to His Electoral Serenity of Saxony, to his benevolent hands

[Text]

Dresden, on the twenty-first day of the month, September 1647

Most humble memorandum: What may be necessary to mention before our Most Gracious Elector and Lord in regard to the Italian musician, Agostino Fontana.[63]

1.

To give His Electoral Serenity a most humble report, that the aforementioned Italian (even though he now has a fixed salary of 500 *Reichsthaler* from the King of Denmark, and has also been offered by the Duke of Gottorp, in addition to the position of Kapellmeister, the same yearly support and beyond that the construction of a new residence) is still quite eager to enter most humbly into his service and office, according to his written acceptance, and shall spend the rest of his life in this Electoral House.

2.

With regard to his annual salary, before his departure and after my discussion with him, he declared himself to be satisfied with 400 thalers, which then (subject to correction) could be most graciously granted to him by our Most Gracious Lord, and his written appointment calculated in such a way that he should receive annually 300 thalers as a Vice-Kapellmeister (*nota bene*: to which office he aspires in particular) and beyond this another 100 thalers for teaching and rehearsing not only the discantists but rather

---

62. The document is in Schütz's hand. Transcribed in *Schütz-GBr*, Nr. 66; *Spagn.*, Nr. 1; *Schütz-Dokumente*, Nr. 112.
63. Little is known about Agostino Fontana. Schütz became acquainted with him in Copenhagen where Fontana served as an Alto in the Danish Court of King Christian IV (b. 12 Apr. 1577; d. 28 Feb. 1648). In May of 1647, Fontana traveled from Copenhagen to Dresden as part of the expansive retinue of the Prince-Elect Christian V (b.10 Apr. 1603; d. 2 Jun. 1647), the Saxon Elector's son-in-law. Fontana's appointment to the Saxon Court seems not to have materialized, for on 15 December 1647 he was appointed Kapellmeister to the Danish Court, where he died in 1650. See Frandsen, "Allies in the Cause of Italian Music," 1–40.

the second group of all the singers or vocalists, and should thus increase to 100 thalers quarterly.

3.

Beyond this he has asked me repeatedly, both verbally while he was here and now in writing, to recommend him most humbly to our Most Gracious Elector and Lord (because he would be little able to save or to prosper from such a regular appointment as his) that he should like to receive His Highly Esteemed Electoral Serenity's most gracious pledge in regard to an endowment for the purchase of a house. Since this is what is absolutely necessary to accommodate this foreigner, I thus hope too that His Electoral Highness does not lack the means and hence, with regard to this matter, shall also permit me to convey to him most gracious and appropriate assurance.

4.

Indeed he also requested, when he was here, that his salary here might begin as soon as his appointment in Denmark might end. If His Electoral Serenity prefers, I shall write to him in such a way that instead of the travel expenses and without decrease in his salary, he shall have 100 thalers upon his arrival, and then shall his appointment begin. All is submitted however for His Electoral Serenity's most gracious consideration and pronouncement.

Heinrich Schütz, in his own hand.

108. JOHANN GEORG II TO JOHANN GEORG I (29 SEPTEMBER 1647)

Memorandum in support of Schütz's promotion of Agostino Fontana at the Dresden Court

[D-Dla: Loc. 8563/2, Des Kurprinzen z. S. Johann Georg II. Handschreiben an seinen Vater, den Kurfürsten, 1634–1656, Vol. 1, fol. 136r–v][64]

29 September 1647
Most Serene, Noble-Born Elector, Most Gracious Lord and Father.

1. I report to Your Grace most obediently herewith that I discussed further with your appointed Kapellmeister how, in his opinion, it perhaps might be arranged with the

---

64. The document is in the hand of Johann Georg II. For a transcription, alternate translation, and discussion of this document, see Frandsen, "Allies in the Cause of Italian Music," 19–20. Johann Georg II (b. 31 May 1613; d. 22 Aug. 1680), the eldest surviving son of Johann Georg I and Magdalene Sibylle of Prussia (d. 31 Dec. 1586; d. 12 Feb. 1659), became Elector of Saxony upon the death of his father, 8 October 1656. Saxony began its economic recovery from the Thirty Years' War during his reign, and the arts in particular benefitted from his patronage. See Frandsen, *Crossing Confessional Boundaries*; and Watanabe-O'Kelly, *Court Culture in Dresden*.

Italian, Agostino Fontana, of course at your most gracious pleasure. With regard to the first point in the Kapellmeister's memorandum, it contained in itself certain ways, as I can hereby assure Your Grace most obediently that the aforesaid [Fontana] himself promised me that, as soon as he is released from his current service, he shall seek no other lord than Your Grace, and will end his life in your service.

2. With regard to the Kapellmeister's appointment, he [Schütz] said not only that he had always been and always will be most humbly content with it, but also that Your Grace had bestowed other favor upon him besides, which he once again acknowledges with most humble gratitude. With regard, however, to this point on behalf of the Italian, he is yet of the opinion that for everything which he charged to him [Fontana], he might receive an annual salary of 300 thalers and the title of Vice-Kapellmeister, considering that the previous Vice-Kapellmeister [pl.] had received salaries of 300 *gulden*. Whereas this amount would scarcely suffice, for the extra 100 thalers he shall be obliged to instruct not only all the *Knaben*, but rather all the vocalists as well, insofar as it would be much more expensive otherwise to issue money for individual instruction. Thus the total annual amount would be 400 thalers. With this he shall and will direct the Latin Masses and Vespers in the church at any time, both at the choir-desk as well as in other locations. With respect to the other sermon and feast days, equally on Sundays and holidays, also in the prayer-meetings, the current tenor, Hofkontz, could prepare the German hymns, as he has done up to the present; and he could, at Your Grace's most gracious discretion, have the title Court Cantor. Similarly the Italian shall be obliged to serve at table and anywhere else the *Musica* is needed or required, not only in the Court City but also when traveling abroad.

3. In regard to this [third] point, Your Grace, at your pleasure, shall in future take into gracious consideration.

4. This [fourth] point in like manner, about which I wanted to notify you most obediently, is also subject to your most gracious consideration.

Your Grace's
must humble, obedient son,
Johann Georg, Duke of Saxony.

109. SCHÜTZ TO AUGUST, DUKE OF SAXE-WEISSENFELS (28 DECEMBER 1647)

Letter of invitation to the wedding of Euphrosyne Schütz and Christoph Pincker

[D-Dla: Loc. 11978. Gesandtschaftsschreiben d. Anno 1646/66 Vol. 1, fols. 109r–110v][65]

---

65. The document is in a copyist's hand, signed by Schütz. Transcribed in *Schütz-GBr*, Nr. 68; *Schütz-Dokumente*, Nr. 115.

[Address]

To the Most Reverend, Most Serene, Noble Prince and Lord, Lord August, Postulated Administrator of the Archdiocese of Magdeburg, Primate [i.e., Archbishop] of Germania, Duke of Saxony, Jülich, Cleves and Berg, Landgrave of Thuringia, Margrave of Meissen, of Upper and Lower Lusatia, Count of the Mark and Ravensberg, Lord of Ravenstein, my Most Gracious Prince and Lord[66]

[Text]

Most Reverend, Most Serene, Noble Prince and Lord, I pledge to Your Princely Serenity my most humble and most obedient service always, first and foremost.

Most Gracious Prince and Lord.

May it please Your Princely Serenity most graciously to hear from your most obedient servant, that the Most Serene Elector of Saxony and Burgrave of Magdeburg, Your Princely Serenity's Most Honorable Lord Father, my Most Gracious Lord, most graciously conferred upon my unworthy self the *Direction* of his Electoral Kapelle in 1614 and at the same time of the appointed princely solemnities on which occasion Your Princely Serenity received holy baptism. Since that time I have executed my office with most dutiful diligence, and to the full extent of the qualities bestowed upon me by the Almighty. I perceived thereby that Your Princely Serenity yourself not only takes particular pleasure in the liberal art of music, but has abundantly shown as well your most gracious affection in regard to my unworthy self, in which I then humbly rejoiced greatly each time. I feel most humbly confident as yet in Your Princely Serenity that you shall in future continue in this most gracious kindness with regard to me still, and not take it amiss if I should presume humbly to ask Your Princely Serenity, should it most graciously please you, to have your most gracious affection reveal itself on a point of honor near to my heart, that is, of my own dearest *Jungfrau* daughter, Euphrosyne,[67] whom I recently betrothed in marriage to the Most Learned *Herr* Christoph Pincker the Younger,[68] Doctor of Laws, planned wedding ceremony, on 25 January 1648, may God grant good fortune and peace. At this occasion it would be a particularly great honor, should it please you, if Your Princely Serenity most graciously would distinguish and illuminate the wedding day of my aforementioned dear daughter and her beloved groom by most graciously consenting to send a delegate in Your Princely Serenity's stead, for which I most meekly petition. Should I be

---

66. August (b. 13 Aug. 1614; d. 4 Jun. 1680), the second son of Elector Johann Georg I, was the Administrator of the Diocese of Magdeburg. He was appointed to the position at the age of thirteen in 1628, and spent his time in Halle, which flourished culturally during his time there. He married 23 November 1647 to Anna Maria (b. 1 Jul. 1627; d. 11 Dec. 1669), daughter of Adolph Friedrich, Duke of Mecklenburg. Their marriage produced eight children.
67. Euphrosyne Schütz (b. 28 Nov. 1623; d. 11 Jan. 1655) was the youngest daughter of Heinrich Schütz and Magdalena Wildeck (b. 20 Feb. 1601; d. 6 Sept. 1625).
68. Christoph Pincker (b. 16 Aug. 1619; d. 24 May 1678).

graciously granted this my most humble petition in accordance with my cherished hope, my dear daughter and future son-in-law, in addition to myself, would greatly rejoice, and acknowledge and extol with most indebted gratitude for the rest of their life, and I would devote myself to the utmost with most humble, unremitting service for Your Princely Dilection's most gracious expression, to which I deeply desire to be called upon in grace by Your Princely Serenity.

Dresden, 28 December 1647.
Your Princely Serenity's
most humble, most obedient
Heinrich Schütz,
Kapellmeister, in his own hand.

110. SCHÜTZ TO WILHELM IV, DUKE OF SAXE-WEIMAR (6 JANUARY 1648)

Letter seeking a written introduction to the court of Ernst "The Pious," Duke of Saxe-Gotha-Altenburg

[D-WRl: Bestand Fürstenhaus, Einladungen zu Hochzeiten von Verschiedenen an den Herzog Wilhelm 1625–1662, A 294, fols. 74r–75v][69]

[Address]

To the Serene, Noble-Born Prince and Lord, Lord Wilhelm, Duke of Saxony, Jülich, Cleves and Berg, Landgrave of Thuringia, Margrave of Meissen, Count of the Mark and Ravensberg, Lord of Ravenstein, etc. My Most gracious Prince and Lord[70]

[Text]

With due reverence I herewith give Your Princely Grace most humbly to understand that, though I in truth up to the present tried with all diligence to be in Weissenfels prior to this Christmas now past, and in that case to offer from there most obediently my personal presence at the pleasure of Your Princely Grace, I was in fact completely kept from these my plans because of all manner of responsibilities that suddenly arose—in consequence of which, necessity (and in particular to make various arrangements for my daughter's wedding) occasioned me despite all to make a trip to Leipzig, where I arrived safely yesterday evening.

---

69. The document is in Schütz's hand. Reproductions and transcriptions of this document can be found in Thiele, "Heinrich Schütz und Weimar," 62–82. Also transcribed in *Schütz-Dokumente*, Nr. 117.
70. Wilhelm IV, Duke of Saxe-Weimar (b. 11 Apr. 1598; d. 17 May 1662).

Thus I also did not want to forbear asking Your Princely Grace with a humble missive from here, primarily entreating you with utmost humility to accept in Princely Grace my enclosed humble letter of invitation to the now impending honorable wedding of my own child, [which letter is] intended in no way to solicit a stately present (which I have not yet merited from Your Princely Grace up to now, and which I do not seek here, least of all) but rather that Your Princely Grace's gracious affection toward my, in truth, unworthy person, might appear in some measure and be honorably mentioned at these proceedings, a great honor to me and my dear child, which, it is to be hoped, could then perhaps occur as well with a small token agreeable to yourself.

Moreover, insofar I have taken the liberty likewise of offering to Your Princely Grace's most venerable *Herr* brother, Lord Duke Ernst,[71] Princely Grace [etc]., an exemplar of my most recently issued musical work in humble invitation to the aforesaid impending wedding, and hereby to introduce to you my unworthy person in some measure as well, *for which reason I also approached Your Princely Grace and*[72] wanted to submit to you, whether you might forward to your highly esteemed princely *Herr* brother my aforesaid humble letter of invitation (which the messenger has with him in addition to the musical work) and at the same time add a few lines underneath to recommend and to bring my person into gracious commerce, should it please His Princely Grace.

As I now live in the most humble and great confidence that, with your renowned great discretion and the hitherto perceived gracious affection toward me, Your Princely Grace shall overlook all my preceding coarseness and discourtesy, and moreover beyond the noble clemency previously shown to me, and grant me every gracious good will in response to this present honor requested by me. Your Princely Grace can *thus certainly rest assured*,[73] from my, in truth, insignificant person, that at every possible occasion and in accordance with my modest qualities wherein you in future might detect something suitable, I in return, with most faithfully humble and willing spirit, will assist you to the best of my ability, and where my powers do not suffice, it shall not be for want of will.

The day after tomorrow I intend to return to Dresden, and to supply my two young people there at this difficult time with the provisions available to me, after which task

---

71. Ernst I, Duke of Saxe-Gotha-Altenburg (b. 25 Dec. 1601; d. 26 Mar. 1675), known as "der Fromme" (the Pious), was a skilled ruler who importantly elevated his lands from the ruins of the Thirty Years' War through prudent fiscal management, reducing taxes, and supporting education for all his subjects. In 1650, he appointed Wolfgang Carl Briegel (b. May 1626; d. 19 Nov. 1712) to the position of cantor and tutor to the ducal family at Schloss Friedenstein, eventually naming him Kapellmeister. A prolific composer, Briegel wrote mainly sacred music at the court, though he did compose various instrumental works and some ballet during his tenure in Gotha.
72. Thiele (75) omits the following text from his transcription: "deswegen E.F.Gn. in Unterthänigkeit ich anlangen, Vndt."
73. Thiele (75) also omits the following text from his transcription: "sich anderes theils gewislich versichert halten."

then I shall not tarry but rather as soon as possible after obtaining my Most Gracious Lord's permission, find myself once again in Weissenfels, and shall strive to the best of my ability there to make accessible and revive anew my musical vein which previously, more than ever, had dried up. May dear God bestow His grace upon me in one thing and another, and to Whose divine gracious protection I herewith commend Your Princely Grace, together with your sublime princely house, with most humble, most faithful diligence—above all, however, with zealous heart wishing you yourself as well as your dearly beloved consort, young princes and princesses, as my Gracious Prince and Lord, Gracious Princess and Lady, and Gracious Princes and Princesses all a healthy, peaceful and joyous princely blessing abundantly filled with your every desire for soul and body, and remaining in closing,

>Your Princely Grace's
>most humble, most ready,
>and most willing servant, always,
>Heinrich Schütz, in his own hand.
>Leipzig, 6 January 1648.

111. AUGUST OF SAXE-WEISSENFELS TO SCHÜTZ (18 JANUARY 1648)

Draft of the response to Schütz's invitation to the wedding of his daughter

[D-Dla: Loc. 11978. Gesandtschaftsschreiben d. Anno 1646/66 Vol. 1, fol. 111]

To the Electoral Saxon Kapellmeister at Dresden, Heinrich Schütz.

To begin, [our] gracious greetings first and foremost, honorable, dear, special friend. We have safely received your missive from the twenty-eighth of last month and year, in which you gave us to know of the coming marriage of your daughter, *Jungfrau* Euphrosyne, to *Herr* Christoph Pincker, the Younger, Doctor of Laws, and, in addition to this, requested a deputation of a delegate at the arranged consummation of marriage on the twenty-fifth of this month in Dresden. Now, in the first instance, we should willingly assign this official duty to a specific person. Because you made no suggestion hereto, and as we do not know who might be at this festivity, we thus made arrangements with Jeremias Gumprecht, merchant in Dresden, that he shall bring along and deliver to you a present on [our] behalf, which, at your discretion, you shall give charge to someone from the invited [guests] who shall offer it in our place to the bride and groom in addition to the customary congratulations, if it is not too inconvenient, and to whom we remain with gracious affection and well disposed.

Dated at Halle, 18 January 1648.

112. SCHÜTZ TO AN UNNAMED PERSON (EARLY 1648) (ORIGINAL LANGUAGE: LATIN)

Assessment of the Scacchi-Siefert Dispute, specifically of Scacchi's Cribrum musicum *and Siefert's* Anticribratio musica

[I-Bc: G. B. Martini, E50/4, fols. 158v–159r][74]

Second Latin letter of the most excellent *Herr* Heinrich Schütz to his friend, translated from the German.

A few days ago I received from *Herr* Förster a certain letter amongst others addressed to me, to which indeed I would have replied in turn, but in the interim, having learned of the ill health of that man who is most dear to me, decided that it would be better to direct my reply to your lordship than to the Kapellmeister himself, as he ought to receive that reply spoken by someone outside the dispute. Hence, when a good opportunity has presented itself, I most warmly beg that your lordship apologize to him for me in this matter, that you offer to him my most cordial greetings, that you convey as soon as possible my friendship toward him, and at the same time thank him profusely for sending the *Cribrum musicum* of the most excellent *Herr* Marco Scacchi. And now, since *Herr* Siefert himself has also sent me the *Anticribatio*, I have accordingly read through the works of both; and according to my judgment, for what it is worth, I have thus found, as I had greatly hoped, that *Herr* Siefert (who indeed is unknown to me by sight) never initiated or entered into anything with such a musician so solidly trained and well grounded (who will certainly yield, as I predict, to scarcely any composer, whether of our German nation or even of his own). Since indeed the writings of this kind demonstrate—more precisely, it is apparent enough and beyond from them—that the most excellent *Herr* Scacchi is not only highly learned in theory, but also a man well versed in practice, who therefore not undeservedly is in charge of the most celebrated and famous Kapelle on account of his excellent qualities. All of these things, and especially the highest praise and his celebrated name, which is conceded by all expert musicians to *Herr* Marco Scacchi in this profession, ought to have deterred and restrained *Herr* Siefert; but one must be silent in these matters, and I find myself inadequate and incapable in this, that I should dare to act as an arbiter and judge—rather, I wish that I never got involved in this business (which was begun without me). However, I confess and affirm this one thing, that in a manner similar to this (in which *Herr* Marco Scacchi in his *Cribrum* treats of *Herr* Siefert) I myself in my youth was also instructed and molded by my teacher, Giovanni Gabrieli of blessed memory: may it please his lordship also to report this, prefaced by a greeting, and with a good and suitable opportunity presenting itself for letting him know of my sincere

---

74. The Latin text and German translation are reproduced in *Schütz-Dokumente*, Nr. 123.

friendship, and may he say to him that my intention in contending with him is that this matter be quietly put to rest and set aside, and finally buried in oblivion because, indeed when things have been brought to such a head, moderation would be best. I ask again and again, however, that his lordship, out of his relationship of trust with *Herr* Siefert, fulfill this commission with respect to *Herr* Siefert (whose qualities I for my part esteem and hold to be of great worth, and I personally do not countenance any part of his reputation and fame to be lost) as excellently and honorably as possible. Further, you have my utmost thanks for the very kind promise made by *Herr* Förster, who agreed to procure for me some of the compositions of *Herr* Marco Scacchi, in particular the Masses in royal folio which are to be sung at the choir-desk, concerning which matter I dealt and came to an agreement with a certain Danish [*sic*] musician (who has been staying with me for some time lately in Dresden, Agostino Fontana by name), that if he himself does not come in person to Danzig, he shall at least communicate by letter with *Herr* Antonio Gratta, and explain my wish that he buy some music. And in this business at the same time I wish to ask the aforesaid *Herr* Kapellmeister most courteously to grant me one or the other work for a fair price, and unhesitatingly to indicate to *Herr* Fontana (who is in Copenhagen) whatever is agreed upon, and to assure him by his bond. I appreciated the very warm greeting of *Herr* Marco Scacchi from the letter of *Herr* Förster, to whom I indeed owe, and shall owe as long as I live, my deepest gratitude: asking again and again, that when the opportunity arises, he greet him in return in my name with redoubled care, and now include me most courteously among his servants and better friends, and at the same time apply his diligence and urge him to complete and to publish the treatise on the art of counterpoint which *Herr* Marco Scacchi promised in his book, which certainly will be of great use especially to our German nation, and bring to him immortal fame and glory to his name.[75] In the year 1648.

Heinrich Schütz.

113. JOHANN GEORG II TO GIOVANNI SANSONI (29 MARCH 1648) (ORIGINAL LANGUAGE: ITALIAN)

Letter of recognition and gratitude drafted in Italian by Schütz on behalf of the Electoral Prince

[D-Dla: Loc. 8553/6, Verschiedene Handschreiben an Kurfürst Johann Georg I., 1611–1655, fol. 3r][76]

---

75. There is no evidence that this proposed work was ever written. Schütz seems to refer to it again in his preface to the *Geistliche Chor-Music*.
76. The document is in Schütz's hand. This letter is reproduced in Kobuch, "Neue Sagittariana im Staatsarchiv Dresden," 109–10. Kobuch assumes that Johann Georg I is responsible for the letter, a view shared in *Schütz-Dokumente*, Nr. 119. Mary Frandsen, however, makes a strong case for Johann Georg II as the impetus for the

To our very dear learned master, Giovanni Sansoni, master of chamber music in the musical establishment of the Holy Imperial Majesty.

By the Grace of God, Johann Georg, Duke of Saxony, Jülich, Cleves and Berg, etc.

Along with our gratitude and every good affection that we always bear toward your virtuous qualities, we shall not fail to preserve always in good memory those favors already received from you through our musician, Friedrich Werner, completely in accordance with our wishes.

We know well that your labors and merits call for richer compensation, which for the present does not appear with this [letter] of ours. We hope, nevertheless, that you will receive this small gift as testimony of the favor and the thanks we bear you, reassuring yourself that you have found and will always find with us favor and good affection.

Dresden, 29 March [1648].

114. *GEISTLICHE CHOR-MUSIC* (DRESDEN, 1648): TITLE PAGE AND DEDICATION (21 APRIL 1648)

[D-W, 12.1–7 Musica fol.]

[Title page]

Musicalia ad Chorum Sacrum[77]
That is:
Geistliche Chor-Music [Sacred Choral Music]
with 5, 6, and 7 voices, to be performed both
vocally and instrumentally,
composed
by
Heinrich Schütz,
Kapellmeister to the Electoral Highness of Saxony,
whereby the basso continuo, on the advice and wishes [of the publisher],
not, however, out of necessity,
is also to be found.
Part One.
CANTUS
M.DC.XVLIII
Opus 11
Dresden
Published by Johann Klemm, Electoral Saxon Court Organist.

---

letter. See Frandsen, "Music in a Time of War," 53, fn. 104. Among other things, the electoral title is never used, neither in the letter nor in Sansoni's reply. Transcribed in *Schütz-Dokumente*, 273–74.

77. SWV 369–97; RISM A/I/8 S 2295; *SA* 8; *NSA* 5.

Printed by the Heirs of Gimel Berg, Electoral
Saxon Court Book-printer.

[Verso of the title page of the basso continuo part]

This and other works by the author are available in Leipzig from Samuel Scheibe, Bookseller, and in Brunswick from Delphin Strungk, Organist at St. Martin's Church.

[Dedication]

My Highly Ordained Lords *Bürgermeister* and Councillors, Most Worthy, Great and Right Honorable, Highly and Most Learned, Highly and Most Wise, especially Most Benevolent Lords, as well as Highly and Greatly Esteemed High-Born and Dear Friends of the Electoral City of Leipzig.

After the completion of the present, modest, though hopefully useful, slight work of mine, as I thought for a while and considered to whom I should like to dedicate and present this work composed for choir, I found indeed in the end, after deliberating in my mind, that it would be fitting for me to offer it to none lesser than to my Highly and Most Benevolent Lords. For, since assuming the Office of Kapellmeister here [in Dresden], I have observed sufficiently and seen in point of fact how your Musical Choir [*Musikalischer Chor*] in Leipzig has always ranked above all others in this Most Laudable Electorate, and (not to deprive other cities their due) was ever nigh on being well appointed;[78] and, moreover, previously established for itself a laudable reputation and acclaim in that its choir directors trained themselves well in a good and well-qualified *Musaeo* (so to speak),[79] since the time the late Johann Hermann Schein[80] was educated in his youth among good *Musici* (indeed, before my time here) in and at the highly esteemed Electoral Court Chapel. In like fashion, its current Director [Tobias Michael], the son of my predecessor, the former Electoral Kapellmeister, Rogier Michael,[81] thus received his start accordingly and obtained a solid foundation in music, and in practice has proven himself admirably up to the present time.

I am thus moved by virtue of this to dedicate formally *Part One* of the aforementioned *Chor-Music* of mine to my Highly and Most Benevolent Lords, and to their distinguished choir (which in truth would be worthy of a more distinguished and better present) to offer up a modest gift with the devoted request that you might benevolently consider

---

78. *Wohlbestallt* or *wohlbestellt* used by Schütz to describe the music in Leipzig is a term more likely to be applied to a well-appointed *Hofkapelle*.
79. "Academy of the arts."
80. See earlier reference to Schein from 19 November 1630.
81. Rogier Michael (b. ca. 1553; d. after 25 Jan. 1619) was of Dutch origin, trained in Austria, and served as a tenor in the *Hofkapelle* of Georg Friedrich, Margrave of Brandenburg-Ansbach (b. 5 Apr. 1539; d. 25 Apr. 1603) at Ansbach from 1572 to 1574 when he moved to Dresden. From 12 December 1587 on, he served as Hofkapellmeister, later assisted by Michael Praetorius and Heinrich Schütz as his health failed, and was succeeded ultimately by Schütz in 1619.

and accept the same, and use it in accordance with the occasion of the time, above all else in honor of Almighty God, and to think kindly of my humble person, to maintain and to strengthen this choir in your churches and schools as up to the present time, and also in future (especially in more peaceful times, which may Almighty God soon graciously grant this Most Praiseworthy Electorate, and indeed the entire Holy Roman Empire) to take the matter diligently in hand, as you are quite favorably disposed to do without my caution.

With that, I commend my Highly and Most Benevolent Lords to the Almighty's gracious protection for your desired and peaceful well-being, and remain also ready and devoted always to accede to you, to the best of my abilities. Dresden, 21 April 1648.

My Highly and Most Benevolent Lords'
willing servant always,
Heinrich Schütz.

115. *GEISTLICHE CHOR-MUSIC* (DRESDEN, 1648): PREFACE

My Benevolent Reader:

It is well known and evident today that, since the concerted style of composition with basso continuo came our way from Italy and into use in Germany, it has become extremely popular with us, and hence may also have won more adherents than perhaps any other ever before, of which the various musical works issued periodically in Germany and found in the bookshops offer ample testimony. Now I am in no way objecting to this enterprise but rather to the contrary note here in our German Nation all manner of talents highly skilled and favorably disposed to the profession of music, to whom I also happily grant their due praise and myself willingly concede. But since, for all that, there is no doubt, even amongst all musicians educated in good schools, that in the most demanding study of counterpoint, no one can rightly set out on other types of composition and properly deal with or manage them, unless he has already be sufficiently schooled in the style [of composition] without basso continuo and, at the same time, has acquired the necessary requisites of a regulated composition: namely (among others), *dispositiones modorum; fugae simplices, mixtae, inversae; contrapunctum duplex; differentia styli in arte musica diversi; modulatio vocum; connexio subjectorum*, etc.,[82] and other such things; about which the learned theorists write at length, and students of counterpoint are instructed orally in the school of practice [*Scholâ Practicâ*]; and without which, according to learned composers, not a single composition can succeed (even if this may sound as though it were a celestial harmony to those ears not properly trained in music) or indeed be valued much more highly than a hollow nut, etc.

---

82. "Orderly arrangement of the modes; simple, mixed and inverted imitation; double counterpoint, different styles of composition according to genre; modulation of the voices; connecting of themes."

I was thus occasioned to undertake once again a slight work of this kind without basso continuo, and perhaps in this way to encourage a few—especially, however, some of the novice German composers—that, before they proceed to the concerted style, they might first crack this hard nut (wherein is to be found the true kernel and the very foundation of good counterpoint) and therein pass their first test: just as in Italy, the true university of music (when I in my youth first began to lay my foundations in this profession), it was invariably the practice then that the novices always had to begin by properly composing and issuing a small sacred or secular work of this kind without basso continuo, just as this good system is presumably still observed there. May each consider in the best spirit my well-intended exhortation for the advancement of music, as well as the enhancement of our nation's reputation, and which is meant to demean no one.

One cannot however proceed without saying that this style of church music without basso continuo (which pleased me thus to entitle *Geistliche Chor-Music*) is not always all the same, but rather that some of these compositions are intended actually [to be sung] at the choir-desk,[83] or for a full choir comprised of both vocal and instrumental voices. Others, however, are written in such a manner that, for better effect, the parts should not be duplicated, triplicated, and so forth, but rather can be distributed singly in vocal and instrumental parts, and in this way can be performed to good effect with organ accompaniment as well as entirely antiphonally [*per Choros*] (when it is a composition for eight, twelve or more voices). Both types are to be found then in the present slight work of mine, published here with few voices (and principally among those at the end, and for which I therefore did not have the text underlaid), as the prudent musician [*Musicus*] will himself likely recognize in several previous [works] of that kind, and thus will know how to proceed properly with the arrangement. I wish to declare and beg publicly at the same time herewith that no one might read from this, what was just raised, that I wanted to promote or recommend this or any one of my published musical works as instruction or as definite models (the meagerness of which I myself readily confess) but rather I want much more to direct each and all herewith to the Italian and other classical authorities [*Classicos Autores*], old and new, canonized (as it were) by all the most distinguished composers, who will copy these out [in score] and diligently examine their splendid and incomparable works. They are a shining example of this and the other style, and can guide one on the right path to the study of counterpoint. In addition to this I am hopeful, and already have some information, that a musician well known to me and highly knowledgeable in theory as well as practice will have a treatise come out presently, which moreover shall be very beneficial and useful, especially to us Germans, and which I did not want to fail to solicit diligently that it might come to be for the sake of the general study of music [*Studio Musico*].

---

83. George J. Buelow translates the original *zum Pulpet* as *in front of the pulpit*. The word *Pulpet* in the original is a variant of *Pult*, which normally is understood as the reading-desk or choir-desk. The usual German word for *pulpit* was *Kanzel* or *Predigtstuhl*. Buelow, "A Schütz Reader: Documents of Performance Practice," 29.

Finally, since some organists might perhaps wish to play along properly and accurately with this work of mine, composed without basso continuo, and will not be annoyed transcribing this into tablature or score,[84] I live in the hope that not only will he not regret the diligence and effort applied to it, but rather that this kind of music will achieve all the more its desired effect.

God be with us, all and sundry, in Grace!

Author.

116. SCHÜTZ TO THE DRESDEN COURT (7 JULY 1648)

Memorandum regarding compensation for Christoph Kittel and Augustus Tax, and for the maintenance of the Dresden Court's musical instruments

[D-Dla: Loc. 8687/1, Kantoreiordnung so Kurfürst Moritz...1548, fols. 249r–258v][85]

[Schütz's hand]

Most humble memorandum in matters pertaining to the musicians.

Four points which are most necessary to mention and consider immediately for the confirmation and maintenance of the Electoral Court *Music* now re-established to some extent.

1.

That a small bonus still be negotiated with Kittel, the Court Organist, and given to him for the support of two discantists. A.

2.

Since both instrumental *Knaben*, who now study with Augustus Tax, have as yet absolutely nothing except for the bare expenses, utmost need requires that something additionally be directed to them for clothing, shoes, laundry allowance, etc. B

3.

That Augustus Tax, on our Most Gracious Lord's command, be given command over the instrument room and the diligent rehearsal [*Exercitium*] with the instrumentalists. C

---

84. Buelow (30) does not translate *Partitur* (score), or perhaps subsumes it under tablature.
85. Transcribed in *Schütz-Dokumente*, Nr. 122.

4.

That His Electoral Serenity might also have something established for the stringing and repair of various instruments, which are employed in connection to the *Music*, and also to repay that which Augustus Tax advanced up to now (according to his note). D

Heinrich Schütz, in his own hand.

Dresden, 7 July 1648.

[in the hand of Christoph Kittel]

Item this to be given to the Electoral Saxon Kapellmeister, *Herr* Heinrich Schütz, my most benevolent friend [*Herr Schwager*], whether the following might be most graciously granted annually for the two *Kapellknaben*:

1) A free beer,[86] either to brew at my house or, insofar as it is possible, to obtain beer from the citizenry instead,
2) Ten bushels of grain, or for each instead a small Court Bread daily,[87]
3) Two stacks of wood—namely, one stack of hard, and one stack of soft,
4) Each day two portions of raw meat, or just three times a week,
5) A half bushel of salt, or even just a quarter,
6) Clothing for the two *Knaben*.

NB. For the instruction of these two *Knaben* I would require nothing, if only the favor could be granted me that my salary for the most urgent support of me and mine might most graciously be arranged, and thus it would seem to me that this request is a modest one.

[Schütz's hand]

Pertains to
Letter [*Litera*] A.
Request of Court Organist Kittel
regarding the boarding of two discantists

[copyist's hand]

B. In regard to the previously most humbly requested 12 *gulden* annually for each of our two instrumentalist fellows assigned to Augustus Tax, I have provisionally drafted the enclosed, as is set out in a certificate for each one, to submit now to our Most Gracious Lord to execute the same, or to have it better arranged. If this draft of mine shall serve sufficiently as a report, and should it please our aforementioned Most Gracious Lord to

---

86. *Freibier*, according to *DWB*, can be either a beer dispensed free of charge or one brewed free of taxes.
87. Court Bread (*Hofbrot*) is bread of a specific shape and size, and of a quality suited to princely household (*DWB*).

execute or to sign these two certificates, 3 *gulden* would have to be written in after the word *Quartaliter*, for which an empty space was left, in order to petition humbly for vestments for each, but we hold that still in reserve in the event that it might not be appropriate to address that at present.

Letter B.
Official report to the Electoral Saxon Lord Marshal of the Court;
Regarding 12 *gulden* yearly for each of the two instrumentalist *Knaben*.

C. It is also a noteworthy point that Augustus Tax, in the name of our Most Gracious Lord, was commanded and commissioned [as follows]:

1. The supervision of the *instrument* room, such that, in the presence of the Kapellmeister, perhaps also of Duke Christian (who currently has the key for it), he shall receive the key and, with Johann Klemm (who has a fine hand for writing), have a proper inventory drawn up of the existing instruments [*instrumenta*], which thereafter our Most Gracious Lord can see on request, and thus this enterprise can be preserved in an accurate state.

2. The weekly rehearsal [*exercitium*] with the assembled instrumentalists. If indeed they are able to practice efficiently amongst themselves apart from that, which sometimes does not happen, he shall urge them on to to better diligence in this case if orders in the name of Our Most Gracious Lord were also issued by the Lord Marshal of the Court.

NB. Our Most Gracious Lord is to be reminded most humbly for just this reason, and so that Tax should take on the administration of the instrument room, that His Electoral Serenity shall degree for him free board and a pitcher of wine each day with the Electoral Prince's musicians, in such way that he has no claim for further recompense.

Letter C.
For the information of the Lord Marshal of the Court,
how Augustus Tax might be commanded
regarding the instrument room, the supervision of the same,
Item the rehearsal with the instrumentalists:

D. Regarding Augustus Tax's notice, what he for the necessary reparations of various instruments hitherto paid out, and connected to it, in the event we otherwise have to play, and should the enterprise as it currently exists be somewhat restored, we must not shirk but rather are required to pay these minor expenses, as they occurred with my foreknowledge. Thus it is likewise my most humble petition, in addition to Tax's, His Electoral Serenity might command and most graciously grant us the repayment of this 14 *gulden* 16 *groschen* in accordance to the enclosed certificate.

Letter D.
For the Information of the Electoral Saxon Lord Marshal of the Court, regarding 14 *gulden* 16 *groschen* which were advanced previously by Augustus Tax according to the enclosed *Specification*:

[copyist's hand]

Most Honorable Lord Marshal of the Court.

You see from the accompanying enclosure *sub litera* **A.** what Kittel requests annually for the boarding of [the] two discantists. Though it is true that I would heartily promote his welfare, a good fellow, thus I do worry, as Your Noble Worship yourself believes, that our Most Gracious Lord is unlikely to concede to him all these points. We shall instead help to fulfill this entire undertaking if we approach His Electoral Serenity with the same requests at this time. And thus would it be my humble opinion to attempt to have the following conceded to him by our aforementioned Most Gracious Lord at this time:

1) A tax-free beer, which (subject to correction) could happen through a command to the bookkeeper (with whom I have already spoken in this regard) that, for the two discantists, he give Kittel a certificate each year allowing one tax-free brewing of beer, or instead to pay the money for it, and to settle accounts with the Treasury.

2) Some wood—he requests a stack of hardwood, and one stack of softwood, which in my opinion might be accorded to him. In case our Most Gracious Lord does not wish concede to that, however, it would be worth asking whether the half of it might be obtained, insofar as something is still better than nothing at all.

3) For grain, or instead four loaves of Court Bread daily, he desires ten bushels, which, if those are not to be had, could perhaps be moderated to a half *Malter* [i.e., four bushels].

4) We reserve, for the time being, our most humble request in regard to vestments for each of the *Knaben*.

Please keep private my humbly drawn up, confidential thoughts, [written] upon request, and dispose of them after reading.

[second copyist's hand]

Inasmuch as the Elector of Saxony, Burgrave of Magdeburg, etc., our Most Gracious Lord, for the arrangement of his Court *Music* and palace Kapelle, takes on Clemens Thieme as an instrumentalist *Knabe* and has him committed to Augustus Tax for education and instruction, thus should His Electoral Serenity's appointed chamberlain from this time forth, and beginning from the date below, let him have *Quartaliter* _____ *gulden* for linens, shoes, laundry allowance, etc., which shall be placed in account. Signed at Dresden, *Reminiscere* Sunday, 27 February 1648.

[In the hand of Augustus Tax]

What had to be paid out necessarily and financed up to the present by the undersigned for the sake of the Electoral Saxon Court *Music*:

For the reparation of the largest bass viol or *Violon* in the instrument room:	5 *gulden*, 15 *groschen*
Item for 3 brass mouthpieces for the trombones, at 8 *groschen* each:	1 *gulden*, 3 *groschen*
Item for a mouthpiece for the large *quartposaune*:	12 *groschen*
Item for three bundles of strings:	3 *gulden*, 9 *groschen*
Item for the repairs to the two tenor violins, at 12 *groschen* each:	1 *gulden*, 3 *groschen*
Item for reeds for the bassoon, bombard,[88] and shawms:	2 *gulden*, 6 *groschen*
Item a small bench for the great viol upon which one is able to stand:	4 *groschen*
Item for repairs to the great *Quartposaune*:	6 *groschen*
Total:	14 *gulden*, 16 *groschen*.

Augustus Tax,
Instrumentalist, in his own hand.

[Copyist's hand]

Letter A.
For the information of the Electoral Saxon Marshal of the Court regarding the boarding of two discantists with the organist, Christoph Kittel.

117. ALEXANDER HERING TO THE BAUTZEN TOWN COUNCIL (30 AUGUST 1648)

Letter requesting dismissal from his organist's position at St. Petri

[D-BAUs: Neues Archiv Rep. VIII.VII.A.h.2/1b, fols. 15r–16v]

Noble, Most Honorable, Right Worshipful, Highly and Most Learned, Highly and Most Wise, especially Most Esteemed Lords and Patrons.

Your Most Honorable, Right Worshipful, Most Wise Council will be aware that you accepted me as appointed organist almost a year and a half ago on the recommendation of Heinrich Schütz, the well-appointed Kapellmeister to His Electoral Serenity,

---

88. Called *Pommer* and *Bombart* by Praetorius, the bombard is a tenor or bass member of the shawm family. See Praetorius, *Syntagma Musicum II: De Organographia*, 36–37.

for which I am most grateful to Your Right Worshipful, Most Wise Council, and would hope for my small part that this office, in which I truly applied myself and endeavored, may have been administered such that Your Right Worshipful, Most Wise Council might have had adequate satisfaction therein. Yesterday the enclosed letter from the *Herr* Kapellmeister, Heinrich Schütz, was forwarded to me in which the Lord God places another situation before my eyes and as good as offers it to me, which among other things can be seen in the aforementioned letter. I did not want to forbear revealing this to Your Right Worshipful, Most Wise Council, and in addition to this am quite inclined not to let slip away from me this good fortune and employment presented to me by God and distinguished people as an advancement, but rather to accept and acknowledge this with gratitude.

As it behooves me to petition for a dismissal before Your Most Honorable, Right Worshipful, Most Wise Council, I direct to Your Most Honorable, Right Worshipful, Most Wise Council my diligent petition to dismiss me most benevolently and to accept that the services performed by me in the church hitherto were carried out to the best of my abilities. I am entirely hopeful that Your Most Honorable, Right Worshipful, Most Wise Council will not think worse of me as a poor fellow seeking for myself a change for the better.

Of course I would not undertake to move away all at once from here, and am prepared in fairness not to leave from here but to remain in my office until another organist takes my place, to which end I myself am prepared to assist, and after the dismissal shall have cause to be personally grateful to Your Most Honorable, Right Worshipful, Most Wise Council that you took me into your service and supported me up to now. I await Your Most Honorable, Right Worshipful, Most Wise Council's favorable reply and dismissal, and commend most faithfully Your Most Honorable, Right Worshipful, Most Wise Council into God's protection, and remain,

Your Most Honorable, Right Worshipful Council's
dutiful servant,
Alexander Hering.
Bautzen, 30 August 1648.

118. JOHANN GEORG HOFKONTZ TO JOHANN GEORG I (16 MAY 1649)

Letter of complaint about Schütz's absences from the Dresden Court

[D-Dla: Loc. 8687/1, Kantoreiordnung so Kurfürst Moritz…1548, fols. 271r–273r]

Most Illustrious, Most Noble Elector: to profess my indebtedness to Your Electoral Serenity with my most humble, most faithful services to the extent of my ability and means, I remain eternally obliged and ready.

Most Gracious Lord, Your Electoral Serenity will most graciously recall that already in January 1642 you had me installed as Vice-Kapellmeister in place of *M.* Zacharius Hestius,[89] insofar as Your Electoral Serenity yourself ordered this appointment to be drawn up; which you also undoubtedly would have carried out several years ago had not your Kapellmeister Heinrich Schütz (whom, with God as my witness, I have always accorded due respect, and in all my life approached not a step too closely) presumed to belittle and disparage me before Your Electoral Serenity; to recruit another, who is of the Catholic religion, in my place; or, because he cannot well abide hearing the title Vice-Kapellmeister, rebuffs me with a rather inferior title and office; etc. However, should Your Electoral Serenity rebuff the aforesaid Kapellmeister Schütz and from your own Electoral lips, and deliver me, your poor, innocent, slandered servant, God shall reward Your Electoral Serenity most abundantly with thousandfold blessings and most highly desired welfare for a peaceful, healthy life.

Most Gracious Elector and Lord, although it would be very befitting and commendable of Kapellmeister Schütz if he as the principal member [*membrum principale*] and head of the Kapelle remained steadfastly with the Kapelle entrusted to him, provided it with musical works, consistently attended the same in word and deed, and thus performed the duties of his office [*quod sui oset Officÿ*], it is indeed known to Your Electoral Serenity and almost everyone else, that he, as otherwise befits a shepherd, for many years has tended little to his sheep but rather abandoned them, traveled from one province to another, [regardless of whether] Your Electoral Serenity's Kapelle might have been provided for or left forsaken.

On the other hand, Your Electoral Serenity shall most graciously remember that not only in the three years that *Herr* Schütz resided in Denmark, Brunswick, and Weissenfels did I serve your Electoral Kapelle with utmost diligence to the best of my ability and means, did my part at princely baptisms, noble weddings, and other services at table (regardless that he was here for a few weeks, put in an appearance, and performed his bounden duty on a few Sundays), but for the last four years I have had to organize the performances belonging to the feast-day, Sunday and holiday services, as well as the orderly singing at the weekly sermon and daily prayer sessions, and thus at the same time earn for Kapellmeister Schütz his appointment and bread, from which I however obtain no thanks other than the extreme belittling and contempt expressed before Your Electoral Serenity and other distinguished persons, all of which I leave and commit to God's disposal. For particular consideration is the fact that this is nothing new to our profession and has very often occurred before this, that one person cannot well suffer another who has worked with utmost and perhaps better diligence, and instead conspires against, belittles and only looks for ways to get rid of him.

---

89. *Magister* Zacharias Hestius (1590–1669) was Vice-Kapellmeister of the Dresden *Hofkapelle*. *Magister (M.)* is the second highest academic grade.

I comfort myself however in this matter that Your Electoral Serenity has never taken an ungracious displeasure at these church duties and others of mine, but rather has been most graciously satisfied in every respect. Moreover, the Senior Court Chaplains as inspectors [*Inspectores*] of the Kapelle, namely, the late *Herr* Dr. Hoë, and now *Herr* Dr. [Jacob] Weller, also have not required a single complaint to be registered in regard to me, praise God.

Most Gracious Elector and Lord, as the matter thus stands, truly and evidently, that the aforesaid Kapellmeister Schütz belittles me out of sheer envy before Your Electoral Serenity, has spitefully impeded me so long in conferring my appointment, once again has sat now for a year in Weissenfels, and concerns himself little or not at all with the Kapelle, whereas I on the other hand, with the help of Your Electoral Serenity's Court Organist, Christoph Kittel, who has quite splendid musical compositions, must diligently look after the Kapelle one way and the other; perform the daily and most of the other tasks [*labores*], without relief since others attend only certain days or hours in the week. Even Agostino the Italian,[90] whom the Kapellmeister wants to promote in my place, is not required to come in.

Since for all that I have looked after your Electoral Kapelle for seven and a half years, constantly, steadfastly, most faithfully, and diligently, I therefore petition Your Electoral Serenity herewith most humbly, may it please you now, to have carried out and to the appropriate degree conferred upon me the aforesaid appointment (decreed and readied long ago by Your Electoral Serenity himself) in accordance with your most gracious wishes. And because I am not by nature so much interested for the sake of a title, I leave it to Your Electoral Serenity's most gracious pleasure, since the title or name of Vice-Kapellmeister will be vexatious beyond measure to *Herr* Kapellmeister Schütz, whether you would allow me to be named Director, Court Cantor (even though Your Electoral Serenity maintains an Electoral Kapelle and not a cantorate) or Vice-Kapellmeister, in keeping with the title and office of my predecessor.

Your Electoral Serenity promotes hereby the proper management of the Kapelle and Divine Service, and do me, your poor but most faithful servant, the great kindness, in that I am hopeful to be lifted out of uncertainty and in future to attain welfare and a happy marriage. And for this great kindness shown to me, because it relates to the Glory of His Holy Name, the Most Clement God shall suitably reward Your Electoral Serenity with long and healthy life, as well as most prosperous and blessed reign. Dresden, 16 May 1649.

Your Electoral Serenity's
most humble,
most faithful servant,
Johann Georg Hofkontz.

---

90. Hofkontz writes "Augustino" but is referring to Agostino Fontana.

119. SCHÜTZ TO BURKARD BERLICH (3 JULY 1649)

Letter regarding the conditions and costs of placing Kapellknaben *in the care of Christoph Kittel*

[D-Dla: Loc. 8687/1, Kantoreiordnung so Kurfürst Moritz...1548, fol. 283r–v][91]

[Address]

To *Herr* Burkard Berlich,[92] Highly Ordained Council and Chamber Secretary to the Electoral Serenity of Saxony, to his most benevolent hands in Dresden

[Text]

Most Highly Esteemed Lord Chamber Secretary.

Inasmuch as I was informed yesterday that our Most Gracious Elector and Lord shall not be disinclined in regard to lodging for a number of *Kapellknaben* with the Court Organist, Kittel, I would not want to forbear mentioning further hereby with good intentions and for consideration only (since I have not been able to go out for several days owing to a minor infirmity or to attend to this negotiation personally, should it go ahead in the meantime) where, for the sake of this enterprise, my most benevolent friend [*Herr Schwager*] would have to be casually vigilant, namely:

1. The support most humbly proposed by me for four *Kapellknaben*, of which we cannot have fewer in number, was intended since it shall be difficult enough as it is, among these four, to maintain two able, accomplished discantists at all times, insofar as several mutate in the following years, and the young *Knaben* cannot be so quickly trained as to join in with the mature, accomplished musicians without mistakes. In this way, it would thus be convenient also to have together a couple of sets of bedding,[93] and similar support in the house.

2. The 2 thalers in cash per week were also intended by me for four *Kapellknaben*, so that there would be a half thaler for each, beyond beer, bread, and what else is to be found in my memorandum.

3. It is not proper for me to give the metes and bounds from where His Electoral Serenity shall have these 2 thalers per week paid. In the interim, however, I would think that, only through a verbal and not through a written command, His Electoral [Serenity] could have the bookkeeper notified that he should pay these 2 thalers per

---

91. The document is in Schütz's hand. Transcribed in *Schütz-GBr*, Nr. 73; *Schütz-Dokumente*, Nr. 129.
92. Burkard Berlich (Burkhardt Berlichio) (b. 23 Apr. 1603; d. 1 Aug. 1670) studied law in Jena and Leipzig, and entered the service of Johann Georg I in 1637. He was appointed to council in 1651, entered the lower ranks of nobility as a *Pfalzgraf* (Count Palatine) in 1652, and ultimately fell into disfavor under Johann Georg II. *ADB*, 2, 405.
93. *Schütz-GBr* (199) transcribes the original text as *Bretwercken*, read *Bettwercken*.

week and, at his discretion, deduct and account for it in future, should our dear God hereafter graciously again grant us perhaps a change for the better in the land. Thus must the mode of payment for the entire *collegium musicum* be changed, so that afterwards changes could also be made again to the payment of these *Kapellknaben*. In the meantime, however, this piece of the chief appurtenance of the *Music* would be preserved, and good discantists trained in the meantime, of which one in better times hereafter would have available [to serve],[94] God willing.

4. My most benevolent friend should feel at liberty to see to it that our Most Gracious Lord's consent for it might first occur, but you should reserve the formal drawing up of it in writing until you have had further verbal discussion with me, since I am mindful that this consent be directed to the benefit of the people and of the Kapelle[95] and not for the private advantage of any one individual.[96] I beg dutifully for forgiveness if I am perhaps bothersome herewith, remaining together with most diligent salutation,
My Highly Esteemed Lord's
most dutiful [servant] always,
Heinrich Schütz.
Dresden, 3 July 1649.

Postscript.

5. Insofar as I also suppose that our Most Gracious Elector and Lord might be of the opinion that the annual salary of 250 thalers assessed to the Court Organist Kittel runs somewhat high, thus can it be reported to His Electoral Serenity that the previous organist, named "Tall Hans,"[97] indeed had only 200 thalers initially, but then an annual bonus of 50 thalers was given to him by General Taube,[98] Marshal of the Court at that time. And after that, in my absence, these 250 thalers were also directed toward and paid to the aforesaid Kittel by *Herr* Dr. Hoym.[99] As he has received nothing separately up to the present in regards to the *Knaben*, however, he is also willing now, for fair support, to take care of and to train them diligently, which in truth is an arduous task. I am thus of the opinion that our Most Highly Esteemed, Most Gracious Lord can well acquiesce to him and, in consideration of the *Knaben*, let him have this full appointment of 250 thalers in future, everything subject to correction.

---

94. Only the "*zu*" of the verb exists on the damaged leaf. *Schütz-GBr* (199) and *Schütz-Dokumente* (301) reasonably proposed the verb *bedienen* as a possibility.
95. "*Ad utilitetem publicae et Capellae.*" *Schütz-GBr* (199) transcribes the original text as *publicam*, read *publicae*.
96. "*Ad privatum alicujus commodum.*"
97. It is not known who is meant by "der lange Hans."
98. Heinrich von Taube (b. 1592; d. 1666).
99. Christoph von Hoym was appointed in 1647 as Chief Overseer (*Oberaufseher*) to the *Grafschaft* (Earldom, County) Mannsfeld.

120. SCHÜTZ TO HEINRICH VON TAUBE, MARSHAL OF THE COURT (BETWEEN DECEMBER 1649 AND FEBRUARY 1650)

Memorandum regarding the introduction of four Kapellknaben *at the Dresden Court*

[D-Dla: Loc. 4520, Bestallungen, Expectanz-Scheine, Besoldungen und Reverse, Bd. 2, 1601–1650, fol. 347r–v][100]

[Address]

To Lord Heinrich von Taube, the Highly Ordained Lord Marshal of the Court to the Electoral Serenity of Saxony

[Text]

I am writing to inquire most humbly of our Most Gracious Elector and Lord whether it might please His Electoral Serenity to have maintenance set up for the following four discantists (which Duke Christian together with the Kapellmeister have selected as Electoral *Kapellknaben*),[101] namely:

1. Adam Merkel.
2. Christoph Richter
3. David Silberling, who previously at one time went over to the Swede.
4. Christoph Kreichel, who not long ago also left the service of Colonel Bose.

They shall be presented at the first service, one after the other, to His Electoral Serenity.

121. SCHÜTZ TO THE DRESDEN COURT (11 FEBRUARY 1650)

Memorandum regarding Christoph Kittel's compensation for the four Kapellknaben *placed in his care*

[D-Dla Loc. 4520, Bestallungen, Expectanz-Scheine, Besoldungen und Reverse, Bd. 2, 1601–1650, fol. 349r][102]

---

100. The document is in Schütz's hand. Transcribed in *Schütz-Dokumente*, Nr. 132.
101. Christian I, Duke of Saxony (b. 27 Oct. 1615; d. 18 Oct. 1691) was the third surviving son of Johann Georg I and the Elector's second wife, Magdalene Sibylle of Prussia. He was appointed Administrator of the former Diocese of Merseburg in 1650. In 1657, following the death of his father in 1656 and in keeping with the late elector's will, Christian became ruler of the newly established Duchy of Saxe-Merseburg.
102. The document is in Schütz's hand. Transcribed in *Schütz-Dokumente*, Nr. 133.

What Christoph Kittel, Electoral Court Organist, requests for the maintenance of the four *Kapellknaben*:

1.

For each, a half thaler in cash per week. This makes a weekly total of 2 thalers.

2.

Beer and bread from the court, for each one every day.

3.

One stack of hardwood and one stack of softwood annually for the four.

4.

One tax-free beer for the four.

5.

For each one a livery from the court tailor, once yearly.

Signed at Dresden, 11 February 1650.
Heinrich Schütz, Kapellmeister, in his own hand.

122. *SYMPHONIAE SACRAE III* (DRESDEN, 1650): TITLE PAGE AND DEDICATION (29 SEPTEMBER 1650)

[Title page]

Symphoniarum sacrarum
Tertia Pars [Sacred Symphonies, Part III],[103]
wherein are to be found
German
concertos,
for 5, 6, 7, 8, that is, three, four,
five, six vocal and two instrumental voices
such as violins, or suchlike, together with several complementary parts [*Complementa*],
which can be also understood from
the index of the appended doubled basso continuo

---

103. SWV 398–418; RISM A/I/8 S 2295; *SA* 10–11; *NSA* 18–21.

and used at one's pleasure,
set to music
by
Heinrich Schütz,
Kapellmeister to the Electoral Serenity of Saxony.
PRIMA VOX.
With permission of His Roman Imperial Majesty.
M.D.C.L.
Opus 12 [*Duodecimum*]
Printed in the Electoral Saxon Resident City of Dresden.

[Dedication]

To the Most Serene, Illustrious Prince and Lord, Lord Johann Georg, Duke of Saxony, Jülich, Cleves and Berg, Grand Marshal of the Holy Roman Empire and Elector, Landgrave in Thuringia, Margrave of Meissen, of Upper and Lower Lusatia, Burgrave of Magdeburg, Count of the Mark and Ravensberg, Lord of Ravenstein.

Most Gracious Elector and Lord. As Your Electoral Serenity, I hope, graciously remembers and recalls for how long, and now in the thirty-fifth year, I have been your steadfast servant in most humble duty and with all due loyalty. It will be recalled by you no less that, each time according to my modest ability, I have offered with most humble diligence the modest talent bestowed upon me by God and have served you with it, both in Your Electoral Serenity's *Hofkapelle* and otherwise at other events that have occurred up to now, and at various past solemnities.

Thus it remains likewise fresh in my mind always in what manner, during those wearisome thirty years of war, Your Electoral Serenity never completely withdrew your favor and helping hand, neither from the other free arts nor from the noble art of music, but rather have always hastened to assist the same as much as possible. In particular, however (during the continuing unrest in our universally beloved fatherland, the German Nation), you have demonstrated toward my unworthy person testimonies of favor of every kind: when, for the advancement of my profession, you most graciously permitted me not only to complete anew a journey to Italy in the years 1628 and 1629 (and there to acquire information about the new and now customary manner of music introduced since the time of my first return from there) and provided great support in the matter, but rather, after the completion of my journey, upon the issued request elsewhere from His Royal Majesty of Denmark, Christian IV, now at rest with God, you most graciously allowed that I reside for a time at his royal Kapelle to administer the directorship [*Directorium*] (which, without wishing to boast, was conferred upon me at that time), and in this way was able to keep my modest knowledge in the art of music in constant practice and to acquire further experience.

Neither is it to be passed over in silence hereby the most gracious means granted me some time ago by Your Electoral Serenity through which the publishing or issue of my musical work can also be further promoted in future and its publication facilitated.

To express my most humble gratitude to Your Electoral Serenity for this noble and great kindness, I remain duly bound and, moreover, shall further do my utmost, through additional, most humble service (as long as my now diminished strength can permit), that I might earn anew the abundant favor shown me and derive for it further comfort for myself in future.

And toward this end is also directed the most humble dedication of the present, twelfth slight work of mine, which with Your Electoral Serenity's noble name set at the head, I sent forth herewith to traverse the world, not only as a public testimony to my ever-indebted gratitude, but rather also to declare to each and everyone (above all, however, those who are pleased by my compositions) through what opportunity, favor, and assistance these now come to light and (should God grant me life) may still continue to appear in future; and that the thanks and the glory for it (in case there is anything of worth to be found in them) are due to Your Electoral Serenity alone.

Hence then to yourself my most humble, most diligent request: may it please you most graciously to receive and to accept from me in electoral grace my well-meant dedication and presentation of this my work (without boasting), in loyal devotion, completed not without effort, and also to continue to remain with your customary benevolence and grace hitherto shown toward me, your faithful, old servant.

Whereupon, together with many thousands, I wish with all my heart that the Almighty God may preserve Your Electoral Serenity in good and continuing health for many years to come, for the good of Your Electoral Great House and as comfort for your loyal subjects. And may He grant that you enjoy to the fullest, in all favorable prosperity, the return of peace to your praiseworthy land through His grace (for which we give everlasting thanks to our Merciful God) after enduring so long the heavy burden of war, and to rejoice in it, and fruitfully apply and use the same for the advancement of the glory of God and the preservation of the good free arts.

Dated at Dresden, on the Feast of St. Michael the Archangel [29 September] 1650.
Your Electoral Serenity's
most humble and ever-willing
Heinrich Schütz.

123. *SYMPHONIAE SACRAE III* (DRESDEN, 1650): PREFACE FROM THE *BASSUS AD ORGANUM* PARTBOOK

Benevolent Dear Reader.

There is no doubt that well-informed and experienced musicians will know already and for themselves how to arrange and perform quite properly this present work, as well as other printed musical works, of mine. But because this page would otherwise have to remain *vacirend* or blank, I considered it worthwhile to have a few reminders noted here, hoping that no one will be opposed to hearing as well my opinion on this subject in some measure, as that of the author.

1. Thus the complementary parts [*Complementa*] appended to this work, according to one's good pleasure [*ad beneplacitum*], are to be found in four separate books, and it is to be seen from the index of the basso continuo to which concertos they belong, and how many voices belong to each one. It still bears mentioning in general thereby that although most of the complementary parts [*Complementa*] in the aforesaid index, each scored only *à* 4, and only four parts are present here in print, which can be duplicated (when they are copied out one more time), and distributed as it were between two choirs, such as vocal and instrumental, and arranged with the others. The rest is left to the judgment of the prudent conductor.

2. I have had the figures [*Signaturen*] indicated with all possible care above the bass [part] for the organ. A good many Italians are accustomed today to employ no numbers, professing that experienced organists would have no need of them and without them would know well to play in accordance with the counterpoint, whereas the inexperienced [organist] would not find the musical concordance [*Concordantz*] or harmony, even if one did put the figures right above it [i.e., the bass] for them. This in itself is indeed doubtless true: it is not such a simple thing to play properly from the basso continuo and to satisfy a musical ear with it, despite what many a man might suppose. That I, however, make use of the aforementioned figures [*Signaturen*] in my published compositions up to now follows the precept: *Abundans cautela non nocet.*[104]

3. The organ must be stopped with discretion (depending on whether the complementary parts [*Complementa*] are added or left out).

4. Finally, I also wish here to draw attention to all that which was already mentioned to the reader [*ad Lectorem*] in the published Part II of my *Symphoniae sacrae* concerning modern music [*musica moderna*] or "on the current manner of composition" and, furthermore, regarding the appropriate, rightful beat [*Tact*]. Faithfully commending us all to God's gracious care,

Author.

124. *SYMPHONIAE SACRAE III* (DRESDEN, 1650): APPENDIX TO THE *BASSUS AD ORGANUM* PARTBOOK

Appendix.

It is not to be withheld from the gentle reader that, after applying considerable effort, the typographical errors [*Errata Typographica*] that slipped into the present slight work

---

104. "Abundant caution does not harm."

are now hopefully corrected here for the most part. And though a few may still occur, they will also be easy to correct. Nevertheless, one should still take note, and change at will, what was perhaps forgotten or overlooked in the following concertos:

1. In the Concerto Nr. 8, "O süsser Jesu Christ,"[105] in the introductory *Symphoni* [*sic*], two *Instrumental* middle parts are to be found with the *Alto* and *Basso Complementi*. The *Bassus Instrumentalis* is omitted. But because the same perhaps would also be necessary, should one want to set up a separate instrumental choir [*Chorus Instrumentalis*], the prudent conductor will indeed know to extract from the *Continuo* such a *Bass* for a bassoon, trombone or another [bass instrument] and to add to the other instruments.

2. In the Concerto Nr. 9, "O Jesu süss, wer dein gedenkt,"[106] at the beginning it should further read: *Super Lilia Convallium*, by Alessandro Grandi,[107] upon which [melody] it was also set by the author, and who in no way wants to have it [i.e., Grandi's original melody] issued as his own invention.

3. In the Concerto Nr. 19, "Herr, wie lang willt du mein so gar vergessen,"[108] the same sort of error is repeated as was committed in the aforementioned Concerto Nr. 8, and the *Bassus Instrumentalis* to the three middle parts in the *Complement*-books was left out of the print, which deficiency then (and thus more of the kind that may occur in this slight work) can be easily rectified by extracting a separate instrumental bass part [*Bassi Instrumentalis*] from the *Continuo*, just as was previously noted in the Concerto Nr. 8.

125. SCHÜTZ TO JOHANN GEORG I (14 JANUARY 1651)

Memorandum detailing Schütz's life, his request for retirement and pension, and the proposed appointment of Giovanni Andrea Bontempi

[D-Dla: Loc. 8687/1, Kantoreiordnung so Kurfürst Moritz...1555, fols. 291r–294v][109]

---

105. SWV 427.
106. SWV 406: "O Jesu süss wer dein gedenckt."
107. Alessandro Grandi (b. 1586; d. after Jun. 1630) was an important Italian church composer of the Venetian school, who is counted among the first major contributors and cultivators of the cantata. Since he probably was a personal student of Giovanni Gabrieli, one can reasonably assume that he was personally acquainted with Schütz. Grandi was already *maestro di cappella* at the Holy Ghost Church in Ferrara in 1610, in 1617 was a singer in the *cappella* at San Marco in Venice, and in 1620 was made deputy to Claudio Monteverdi. In 1627, he was *maestro di cappella* at Santa Maria in Bergamo, where he died of the plague in 1630. *Lilia convallium*, from 1625, was scored for four voices and two violins. See Roche, "What Schütz Learnt from Grandi in 1629," 1074–75.
108. SWV 416: "Herr wie lang wiltu [*sic*] mein so gar vergessen."
109. Transcribed in La Mara, 77–85; *Schütz-GBr*, Nr. 77; *Spagn.*, Nr. 2; *Schütz-Dokumente*, Nr. 141.

[Address]

Most humble memorandum: To the Most Serene Elector of Saxony, Burgrave of Magdeburg, my Most Gracious Lord, Most Serene, Noble Elector, Most Gracious Lord

[Text]

With the present most humble submission of my slight work which now appears under Your Electoral Serenity's exalted name, I am at the same time occasioned to touch in some respects upon my rather difficult life from my youth up to the present. In deep devotion I ask Your Electoral Serenity to receive this from me in grace and, if not adverse to it, to consider it at your leisure. That is to say: not very long after I came into this world, in the year 1585, on St. Burckhard's Day, rather already in my thirteenth year, I left my late parents' house at Weissenfels, and from that time on have always lived abroad. Initially I served for several years as a *Kapellknabe* in the *Hofkapelle* of Landgrave Moritz in Kassel, in addition to the *Music* was at the same supported and educated in the school and in learning Latin and other languages.

And as it was never the wish of my late parents that I should ever make a profession of music, then or in future, I set out on their advice for the University of Marburg (in the company of one of my two brothers,[110] who subsequently became a Doctor of Laws and who died a few years ago in Leipzig a member of the Supreme Court of the Judicature, and in Your Electoral Serenity's employ) after I lost my treble voice. It was my intention to pursue the studies, apart from music, in which I had made a considerable start elsewhere, to choose for myself a secure profession and one day therein to obtain an honorable station. This plan of mine was soon changed for me, however (undoubtedly through the will of God), in that, namely, Lord Landgrave Moritz came to Marburg one day (who perhaps may have noticed during the time when I served as a *Kapellknabe* at his court that I was to some degree naturally skilled in music) and made me the following proposition: Because a highly celebrated but quite old musician and composer [Giovanni Gabrieli] in Italy was still alive at that time, I should not miss the opportunity to hear him and to learn something from him, and the aforementioned Princely Grace offered me at the same time a yearly stipend of 200 thalers to undertake such a journey, which proposition (as a young man eager to see the world) I most willingly accepted with humble thanks, and thereupon in 1609, in some respects against my parents' wishes, departed for Venice. Indeed, upon my arrival (after I had spent a short time with my master) I soon realized the gravity and depth of the study I had undertaken in composition, and that I had only an unfounded and rudimentary[111] beginning in it, and consequently very much regretted

---

110. Georg Schütz.
111. In other translations of this passage, *schlecht* is rendered as *poor*. But as often as not at this time, *schlecht* (i.e., *schlicht*) means *simple*, and *plain*, not just *poor*. The present translation prefers "rudimentary," mainly

that I had turned away from those customary studies at German universities, and in which I had already made considerable progress. I nonetheless had to resign myself to be patient and to devote myself to that study for which I had come. Therefore, and from that time on, I set aside all of my previous studies and began to deal with the study of music exclusively, with the greatest of all possible diligence, and to see how I might succeed at it. With God's help, without wishing to boast, I then progressed in my studies to such a degree that after three years[112] (and one year before I returned from Italy) I had printed there my first slight musical work in the Italian language, to the enthusiastic approval of the most celebrated musicians in Venice at that time, and sent it from there to Lord Landgrave Moritz (to whom I also dedicated it as a most humble expression of gratitude). After the publication of the aforementioned first slight work of mine, I was exhorted and encouraged not only by my teacher, Giovanni Gabrieli, but also by the Kapellmeister and other distinguished musicians there,[113] that I should persevere in the study of music and could confidently hope for every felicitous success in it. And as I remained another year after this (though at my parents' expense) to learn even more in these studies, it so happened that my aforesaid teacher died in Venice, and whom I also accompanied to his final resting place. On his deathbed, he bequeathed to me out of singular affection, in memory of him, one of his rings left behind, which after his death was presented and delivered to me by his father confessor, an Augustinian monk (from the cloister where Dr. Luther had also once lived). Thus the aforementioned premonition of Lord Landgrave Moritz in Marburg was true: that whoever wanted to learn something from this certainly very highly gifted man could not have delayed any longer than had I.

When I returned to Germany from Italy for the first time in 1613, I resolved in truth to keep my, now, well-laid foundations in music to myself for a few years, and to keep them and myself out of sight, as it were, until I had refined the same somewhat more, and could then make my mark with the publication of a worthy work. And also at that time I was not lacking counsel and urging from my parents and relatives, whose opinion, in brief, was that I should make use of my in truth modest qualifications and strive to obtain advancement, but should treat music as an avocation. In compliance with their repeated and unrelenting exhortations, I was finally persuaded and was just about to seek out again the books I had previously set aside, when Almighty God, who undoubtedly had singled me out from the womb for the profession of music, thus ordained that in 1614 (I do not know whether it was mentioned perhaps by *Herr* Christoph von Loss, then Privy Councillor, or by the

---

because it would be unlike Schütz to use a letter such as this to show disrespect and ingratitude for the training he received and appreciated in Kassel under Georg Otto. Likewise, it is more likely that Schütz's choice of *Wichtigkeit* and *schwere* pertains more to the gravitas of the study of music than to its *importance* or *difficulty*, which is the usual translation.

112. Actually it would be two years and not three, since Schütz arrived in Venice in 1609 and his book of madrigals was published in 1611.

113. The *Maestro di Cappella* at the time was Giulio Cesare Martinengo (b. 1564 or ca. 1568; d. 10 Oct. 1613), who succeeded Giovanni Croce (b. ca. 1557; d. 15 May 1609) and who in turn was succeeded on his death by Claudio Monteverdi in 1613.

Councillor of the Treasury [Gottfried von] Wolffersdorff,[114] also Captain at Weissenfels) I should be called to Dresden for service at the impending princely baptism of Duke August, the current administrator of the archdiocese of Magdeburg. And after my arrival and upon passing the audition, the directorship of your *Music* was at once most graciously offered to me in the name of Your Electoral Serenity, from which then my parents and relatives, as well as I myself, palpably felt the immutable will of God in connection to my person, and my uncertain thoughts hereby were given purpose, and I was induced not to decline the honorable employment offered to me but rather to accept it with most humble thanks, and to pledge to administer the office to the best of my abilities.

Your Electoral Serenity will, I hope, in some measure still recall my, in truth, meager though painstaking duties performed since 1615 (in which year I assumed the present appointment and, as long as it shall please God and Your Electoral Serenity, shall continue to hold) and hence, to the present, more than thirty-five years.

And might I extol the kindness and favor bestowed upon me by God over such a long time that, together with my private studies and publication of various musical works, I have served Your Electoral Serenity most humbly at all manner of past solemnities during this time, such as imperial, royal, electoral and princely assemblies, at home and abroad, but in particular your own dear children's weddings too, each and every one, no less than at their Christian baptisms (without exception but for the now Lady Landgravine at Darmstadt,[115] and Lord Duke Johann Georg, the Electoral Prince). From the beginning of my directorship of Your Electoral Serenity's *Hofkapelle*, I have always tried to the very best of my abilities to establish its fame above all others in Germany, and have helped, I hope, to preserve its reputation and fame to a considerable degree, up to this very moment. Now I would sincerely and very much hope that Your Electoral Serenity's *Hofkapelle* could continue to be directed by me in the manner in which it has been administered by me up to now. Consequently, however, without wishing to boast, not only on account of my constant study, travel, writing, and other continuous work pursued since my youth (which my arduous profession and office made unavoidably necessary, the smallest difficulty and responsibilities of which then, in my opinion, even a good many of our own scholars might not be able to judge properly, because such study is not pursued at our German universities), but rather also on account of my now advancing old age, failing eyesight and stamina, I can no longer trust myself nor dare to serve the same properly, nor at my present age to uphold the good name that to some degree I had made for myself in my younger days. On the physician's advice, unless I also want to put my health at risk or even collapse forthwith,

---

114. Gottfried von Wolffersdorff had studied at the electoral school in Pforta near Naumburg and there befriended Johann Hermann Schein. Schein subsequently became house music director and tutor to the children of von Wolffersdorff in Weissenfels (1613–15), and it was on the nobleman's recommendation that Schein was appointed Kapellmeister to the court of Johann Ernst the Younger, Duke of Saxe Weimar in 1615.

115. Sophie Eleonore of Saxony (b. 23 Nov. 1609; d. 2 Jun. 1671) was married 1 April 1627 to Georg II, Landgrave of Hesse-Darmstadt (b. 17 Mar. 1605; d. 11 Jun. 1661).

I must now avoid and abstain as much as possible from the constant study, writing, and application of mind. Thus I am necessarily compelled to present this with due modesty to Your Electoral Serenity hereby for your most gracious consideration, and moreover to request in most humble devotion, may it please Your Grace (not only for the reasons I have drawn upon, but also in consideration of the fact that all Your Electoral Serenity's dearest noble children are now married), to remove me in future to somewhat quieter circumstances, and (so that I might be able as well to assemble my musical works started in my youth, complete them, and submit them for publication in my memory) to release me from regular service, and to the extent that it should please Your Electoral Serenity, to have me considered and declared, as it were, a pensioner. I would be prepared in which case to accept something of a possible adjustment to my current salary, should it please Your Grace. At the same time, I am as willing as obliged (in the event that Your Electoral Serenity wishes not to allow me to step down from your Kapelle, and neither to appoint another Kapellmeister at this time, but rather to be content with the slight service that I shall be able to provide with my daily ever-diminishing powers) to persevere in future to assist in every possible way and to strive further to deserve the title of Kapellmeister to Your Electoral Serenity and your noble house, and hope to take [that title] with me ultimately to the grave, if only in future (especially since all those old musicians with whom I first started my directorship thirty-five years ago are now dead; the remaining very few however, on account of infirmity and age, are no longer particularly fit for further service) another qualified person might be adjoined to me to ease my work, who would deal daily with the young people now progressing in the Electoral Kapelle, keep up the necessary rehearsal, also occasionally organize the *Music*, and give the beat [i.e., conduct].

Inasmuch as my powers diminish still further (should God allow me to live yet longer), it might perhaps occur and befall me (Your Electoral Serenity will most graciously forgive me that I mention this), as with one not badly qualified old cantor living in a renowned place and whom I know well, who wrote to me some time ago and complained bitterly to me that his young town councillors were very dissatisfied with his old style of music and would thus quite happily be rid of him, hence said straight to his face in the town hall: a tailor of thirty years and a cantor of thirty years are of no use in the world. There is also some truth to it, that the young world has a tendency both to become bored of and to change the old customs and styles. And although I would never expect this from Your Electoral Serenity's *Herren* Sons (for my Gracious Lords, in venerable grace, have treated me kindly), something similar could happen to me at the hands of others, even from some of the up-and-coming young musicians who for the most part promote their new styles and cast off the old, though without good reason. And inasmuch as [Giovanni] Andrea Bontempi,[116] Italian eunuch of Duke Johann Georg, the Electoral Prince, has spoken of

---

116. Giovanni Andrea Bontempi (b. 21 Feb. 1625; d. 1 Jul. 1705) was an Italian composer, singer, librettist, historian, and architect who came from Perugia. From 1643 to 1650 he was a singer at San Marco in Venice. He entered the Electoral Court of Johann Georg I at Dresden in 1651. Following the death of elector's death in 1656, his successor Johann Georg II amalgamated the electoral and his princely *Kapellen* to form a

it many times that especially since his youth he has been more given to composition than to singing, and also of his own accord offered to me that, at my request, he would gladly serve in my place and direct the *Music* any time, I should like at the conclusion of this communication of mine to Your Electoral Serenity to find out, and to ask your most gracious opinion on this subject: namely, whether, with your most gracious consent, I might accept the aforementioned [Giovanni] Andrea Bontempi's proposition and allow him recurrently to direct the *Music* in my place? This then, in my modest judgment (of course, subject to correction), Your Electoral Serenity could have happen all the sooner, and observe and listen for a time as though it were a trial period, since he does not request for his service any increase to his salary or change of his title, but rather is willing to be content either way with the support provided for him by his Most Gracious Lord Electoral Prince. This young man is quite highly qualified for such an occupation. I have obtained sufficient reports from Venice (where he resided for eight years) that at some celebrated feast-days there, he often publicly directed the *Music* in their churches in place of the Kapellmeister. Thus there is all the less to question with regard to his qualifications. Moreover, in his other activities up to the present, he appears to be a discreet, polite, and accommodating fine young man. Whatever Your Electoral Serenity's most gracious wish shall be now in this matter, I beg a most gracious communication, since without Your Electoral Serenity's knowledge it would be unbecoming of me to make use continuously of this person's services. I commend most humbly and obediently hereby: you, to the powerful protection of the Almighty, lasting and excellent health, long life, blessed reign, and every other welfare you yourself might wish for soul and body; myself, however, to steadfast electoral grace. Dated at Dresden, on the fourteenth day of January, in the year of Christ our true Savior and Redeemer, 1651.

Your Electoral Serenity's
most humble, duty-bound old servant,
Heinrich Schütz, Kapellmeister, in his own hand.

126. SCHÜTZ DIRECTED TO THE DRESDEN COURT (21 FEBRUARY 1651)

Memorandum proposing the court appointments of the instrumentalist Friedrich Sultz and his two sons

[D-Dla: Loc. 33 344, Nr. 1949, Registratur über das 10. Bestallungsbuch, 1646–1651, Nr. 99, [no folio numbers given in the original] r–v][117]

---

single company in which Bontempi shared the musical direction of the Kapelle with Heinrich Schütz and Vincenzo Albrici (b. 26 Jun. 1631; d. 8 Aug. 1690 or 1696). In 1664, Bontempi turned away from music to his other interests in stage design and machinery for the court theatre. When Johann Georg II died in 1680, Bontempi moved back to Italy and retired to his villa near Perugia.

117. The document is in Schütz's hand though unsigned by him and instead bears the signature of Christian, Duke of Saxony, perhaps as authorization. Transcribed in *Schütz-Dokumente*, Nr. 142.

Dresden, 21 February 1651.

What is to be humbly sought, and to be diligently requested for the execution of which, before the Electoral Highly Ordained Chamber Councillors, pursuant to the most gracious consent of the Elector of Saxony, Burgrave of Magdeburg, our Most Gracious Lord:

1. That Friedrich Sultz be appointed anew as an instrumentalist and to be sworn in, from Michaelmas [29 September] 1650 onward.[118] He in fact held an appointment here with us previously, but during the past times of war had to seek his livelihood elsewhere for a number of years. He came back again, however, prior to the recently consummated princely nuptials here and has served alongside from that time forth.[119] Into this written appointment, however, in particular beyond the regular formula, the following points might be inserted:

   1. That for the administration, custody, and maintenance of all His Electoral Serenity's brass, woodwind, bowed and other instruments, in addition to the room in the palace designated for this, he shall be commanded to guard against all damages and loss (the likes of which have occurred in previous times therein) with all possible diligence. Moreover, should any instruments go missing, he shall be duly bound to replace them.
   2. Those instruments, which would be needed for services that take place, no matter whether in the church or elsewhere, he shall always keep in ready and, with the help of the *Kalkant*[120] or the *Knaben*, transport them to the location where they are needed.
   3. Twice or at least once each week he shall arrange a private rehearsal with all the instrumentalists in the instrument room or elsewhere (especially since it might occur inopportunely there in winter), have all manner of instruments employed and brought into practice.
   4. His Electoral Serenity has granted him an annual salary of 200 *gulden* for everything, beginning at [*sub dato*] Michaelmas 1650.

On this point it should also be known that the aforesaid Friedrich Sultz has most humbly recommended and presented two of his sons, the one Ludwig, the other Jacob Sultz, both of whom have made a good start on all kinds of wind and other instruments, as young instrumentalists to our most gracious Elector and Lord for His Electoral Serenity's

---

118. This name, as is often the case, exists with variant spellings in the seventeenth century (Sulz, Sultze, Sulze, etc.). The one used here, Sultz, is a modernized spelling, also used in *Schütz-Dokumente*. The spelling "Sulz" is preferred by Kobuch and *Spagn.*, whereas Siegfried Köhler, in his *Heinrich Schütz: Anmerkungen zu Leben und Werk*, prefers "Sulze."
119. Schütz is certainly referring to the double marriage of Johann Georg's sons on 19 November 1650 to two daughters of Philipp, Duke of Schleswig-Holstein-Sonderburg-Glücksburg: Christian I (b. 27 Oct. 1615; d. 18 Oct. 1691), who became Duke of Saxe-Merseburg, married Christiane (b. 22 Sept. 1634; d. 20 May 1701); and the youngest son, Moritz (b. 28 Mar. 1619; d. 4 Dec. 1681), who became Duke of Saxe-Zeitz, married Sophie Hedwig (b. 7 Oct. 1630; d. 27 Sept. 1652).
120. The *Kalkant* is the bellows blower or bellows treader.

service and attendance. His Electoral Serenity has noticed that there has been hitherto a want of instrumentalists in the Electoral Kapelle, and these two young fellows are already sufficiently qualified on various instruments that they would be suited for employment in his *Music* to quite a considerable degree. To that end Your Electoral Serenity has also most graciously declared in regard to these two sons of Friedrich Sultz that they (because they are still young people) should not yet be taken into regular service at this time, but rather that 100 *gulden* annually, and hence quarterly 25 *gulden*, be bestowed upon each for their provisioning until they, God willing, might hereafter through their improved qualifications be appointed as regular instrumentalists, whereupon they should at the same time be most graciously assured.

[*signed by*] Christian, Duke of Saxony, in his own hand.

The appointment or subsistence allowance of Friedrich Sultz's sons must also begin from Michaelmas; from that same time on, especially at the princely nuptials, they have always been employed.

127. SCHÜTZ TO CHRISTIAN REICHBRODT (11 APRIL 1651)

Memorandum containing several points to be conveyed to the Elector, including which musicians are expected to travel as part of the entourage and a repeated request for retirement with a pension

[D-Dla: Loc. 8687/1, Kantoreiordnung so Kurfürst Moritz...1548, fol. 300r–v][121]

[Address]

To *Herr* Christian Reichbrodt, Highly Ordained Privy Secretary to the Electoral Serenity of Saxony in Dresden, to his most benevolent hands

[Text]

Most Highly Esteemed beloved *Herr*:

1. I ask dutifully for information on whether our Most Gracious Lord might be taking along on the journey those musicians whose names were recorded by Lord Duke Johann Georg.
2. *Item* whether he might wish to show himself in the aforementioned matter to be the most benevolent patron of my son-in-law and also consequently [*per conseqvens*] of me and my family.

---

121. The document is in Schütz's hand. Transcribed in *Schütz-GBr*, Nr. 79; *Schütz-Dokumente*, Nr. 144.

3. With that I offer most humbly that I will conform my thoughts to live and to die here in Dresden, except that it might be permitted me in the meantime to travel to Weissenfels now and again.

4. Because of my increased disability,[122] however, and other reasons more, I wish furthermore for nothing less than to be declared a pensioner, and that His Electoral Serenity, in my now advanced age, do me the favor that he had bestowed on the previous two Kapellmeister, Michael Praetorius and Rogier Michael, both of whom I found still in electoral office when I came here to Dresden for the first time. As I was still young, however, I served here for both of them in their place and as good as earned their salaries for them. Notwithstanding that, I by no means wish to resign, but rather I am willing always to assist the Electoral Kapelle according to my ability and means for so long as I shall live and thereby to remain, only that I might be taken from the trouble of dealing alone[123] with those currently upcoming young people,[124] *Item* the constant annoyance, and daily commotion and impediments, which are impossible to endure any longer, the extent of which I could demonstrate sufficiently at another time. I beg dutifully for forgiveness, most faithfully commending us all and sundry to divine protection in grace herewith,

My Most Highly Esteemed [*Herr's*]
most loyal servant always,
Heinrich Schütz, in his own hand.
Dresden, 11 April 1651.

128. SCHÜTZ AND JOHANN GEORG HOFKONTZ TO CHRISTIAN, DUKE OF SAXONY (14 AUGUST 1651)

Letter petitioning the Duke to intervene with the Elector on behalf of the suffering members of the Hofkapelle

[D-Dla: Loc. 8687/1, Kantoreiordnung so Kurfürst Moritz…1548, fols. 311r–312r][125]

[Address]

To the Serene, Noble-Born Prince and Lord, Lord Christian, Duke of Saxony, Jülich, Cleves and Berg, Landgrave in Thuringia, Margrave of Meissen, of Upper and Lower Lusatia, Count of the Mark and Ravensberg, Lord of Ravenstein, my Most Gracious Prince and Lord

---

122. *Schütz-GBr* (219) transcribes the original text as *Herrn gekommenen*, read *heran gekommenen*.
123. *Schütz-GBr* (220) transcribes the original text as *alhier*, read *alleine*.
124. *Schütz-GBr* omits the line of the original: "zu bleiben, nur das ich der Mühe, mit denen Itzo aufkommenden."
125. The document is in the hand of a copyist, signed by Schütz and Hofkontz. Transcribed in *Schütz-GBr*, Nr. 80; *Schütz-Dokumente*, Nr. 145.

[Text]

To my Most Gracious Prince and Lord, Serene, Noble-Born Prince. To Your Princely Serenity, I remain all my life obliged to attend most humbly with my services, day and night, to the best of ability.

Most Gracious Lord, however tiresome I am with my repeated writing and reluctantly reminding Your Princely Serenity, thus I am driven to it by the constant, repeated runaround, the enormous lamenting, misery, and wailing of the entire company of poor, abandoned members of the Kapelle who live in such misery that it could move even a stone in the earth to have pity. Now with God as my witness, their misery and piteous lament go so near to my heart that I do not know how I can offer them adequate comfort or hope of a single change for the better.

The majority of the company, whom one should never have thought otherwise capable of it, are completely resolved and say: rather than having to bring their Most Gracious Lord further into disrepute should they beg someone for a piece of bread, they are compelled out of inevitable want to take to the road. It is impossible for them to stay and to bear any longer what they have now borne for a long time. They would be forced to leave, leaving their debts to be paid by whoever wishes to. It is abuse enough that no one would even lend them a *groschen* anymore.

On their behalf, I thought it proper out of bounden duty in connection to my Most Gracious Elector and Lord to notify Your Princely Serenity as our Most Gracious Inspector and Lord of this pressing need and my obligation, and to bring it into most gracious consideration that, for all that, it is to be pitied that the company which was assembled with great effort and labor should again be taken asunder.

For their sake, my most humble, most ardent petition is addressed to Your Princely Serenity, may it indeed please you, to solicit compassionately yet on our behalf sometime before His Electoral Serenity as your dearly beloved Lord Father, that he would have a single quarterly installment paid out to the company in order that one might only be able to retain them. And apprise me most graciously on account of this, whether a single comfort or hope might be given to them; that one would not have them thus suffer want and seek their bread in other places. Should Your Princely Serenity's efforts fail to bear fruit, which I certainly hope does not happen, it would be impossible for me to hold them any longer; in which case I shall have done my best herewith and be absolved. I commend Your Princely Serenity to divine rule and favor.

Dresden, 14 August 1651.
Your Princely Serenity's
most humble, most loyal servant,
Heinrich Schütz,
Electoral Kapellmeister, in his own hand.
Johann Georg Hofkontz.

129. SCHÜTZ TO CHRISTIAN REICHBRODT (19 AUGUST 1651)

Letter regarding the ongoing suffering amongst musicians at court, his need for assistance, and the roles of Christoph Bernhard and Johann Georg Hofkontz

[D-Dla: Loc. 8687/1, Kantoreiordnung so Kurfürst Moritz…1548, fols. 316r–317v][126]

[Address]

To *Herr* Christian Reichbrodt, Highly Ordained Privy Secretary to the Electoral Serenity of Saxony, Our Most Gracious Lord, at present in the Electoral Residence in Marienberg,[127] to his most benevolent hands

[Text]

Especially Most Benevolent *Herr*, Highly Esteemed Dearest Friend.

Inasmuch as Duke Christian's Princely Grace, during his current brief visit here, and still in some small measure patiently disposed toward our indigent musicians, a good number of which intend to leave, has ventured with a gracious offer of hope not only to intercede presently in their distress with His Most Gracious Lord Father, the Elector of Saxony, but rather that [you] my Highly Esteemed *Herr* for your part too would help unfailingly once again to cooperate with utmost diligence, willingly make yourself available in future, and also commanded of me that I should now send a brief letter back to him, His Princely Grace.

1. In due compliance with which command, I report to you briefly without any equivocation and in sum, though unhappily, that there has long been unbearable, tremendous privation and lamenting amongst the entire electoral musical assembly. As for me, regardless of my now advancing old age, I could still perhaps choose for myself a distant Imperial or Hanseatic city as my final refuge in this world; God knows, I would rather with all my heart be a cantor or organist in a small town than to remain longer in these conditions, where my dear profession disgusts me, my possessions and courage are stripped from me. But it must be borne with patience in order not to vex others with my impatience or to set them a bad example.

I have helped out a large number of decent people every day and up to this very moment, not only by holding out hopes for an imminent change for the better but rather also with the advancement [of money] from the remaining very little that I possess (as

---

126. The document is in Schütz's hand. This is arguably the most problematic transcription in *Schütz-GBr*, Nr. 81—missing lines, missing words, wrong words, missing parts of words, etc. Transcribed in *Schütz-Dokumente*, Nr. 146.
127. Marienberg is situated approximately 30 km southeast of Chemnitz. A wealthy mining town in the sixteenth century, most of Marienberg burned to the ground in 1610, was plundered by Holk in the Thirty Years' War, and lost around 2,000 inhabitants to plague or some other epidemic in 1632/33.

you can imagine). But this can no longer continue henceforth in future, in view of the fact that I have nothing left, and I can attest in good conscience that the cash *item* from repayable securities, a portrait and small cup,[128] in the amount of 300 thalers which I still had left, I have already disbursed amongst them. I never would have thought that their salaries would have been cut off in such a way.

A large number of them have detailed to me that in four years, as of next October, they have not received more than three quarterly payments, less half a month. Thus it is then easy to imagine into what circumstances many a good fellow has fallen. I do not wish to importune my Highly Esteemed *Herr* with the particulars of every need and shameful condition, but just for those concerning our Bassist. I hear that he subsists like a sow in a pig-sty, has no bedding,[129] sleeps on straw, and has already pawned his coat and doublet. His wife came to me yesterday, and begged me for God's sake that I would show them fatherly charity and help them get away. To this end she also delivered to me a petition in which he sued for most gracious dismissal, which I humbly give in addition to His Most Praiseworthy, Gracious Lord, Duke Christian for his information. With regard to the rest, although they do not live a sow's life as does the aforementioned, this does not lessen the suffering. They are indebted beyond what each person possesses. How long it shall now continue in such a way is easy to imagine, and it is my thousandfold request to you my Highly Esteemed *Herr* in this case that, in the event this collegium of ours might soon collapse altogether, that you would help attest to my innocence in its downfall and consequently protect me before our Most Gracious Lord, as I never neglected with appropriate humble reminders of it from me, both in person as well as written, of which importuning you in particular received your share sufficiently each time, and to which you yourself can attest.

2. Moreover, I would have yet another point to bear in mind in the event it should otherwise most graciously please our Most Gracious Lord to restore this failing collegium of ours. And in truth, my Most Benevolent *Herr* can well judge for himself why our Most Gracious Elector should by no means allow the same to dissolve; it is through it that German dignity has still been preserved in some measure up to now, and insofar as it has come ever closer to perfection, it would thus be a shame indeed were one to allow it to perish at the moment it blossoms. The costs, too, in comparison to what is laid out in other places for similar collegia, would come to a tolerable amount, as you yourself know. Finally, I find it neither laudable nor Christian that in such a praiseworthy, great land, in which previously it was possible to support the bleating of so many monks and priests,[130] one now cannot or does not want to sustain even twenty musicians. Yet I live in the most

---

128. *Schütz-GBr* (345) proposes that the picture is the one that Landgrave Moritz had given him in 1617, and that the *Becher* was the one given to Schütz by Johann Georg II for his wedding in 1625 (320).
129. Joshua Rifkin and Eva Linfield in *Grove-Mus* translate *Bettwerck* as *bedstead*. The German for *bedstead* is Bettstelle (Bettgestell, *sponsa*), whereas Bettwerk or Bettwerck (Bettzeug, *lintea*), according to *DWB*, is bedding (*sheets, blankets*).
130. This line is omitted in *Schütz-GBr*: "worinnen hiebevor so vieler Regimenter Munche v. pfaffen geblecke haben können unterhalten werden, itzo." The derogatory word Schütz uses is *Geblecke* (modern *Geblöke*),

humble hope that His Electoral Serenity will reconsider, and shall realize his gracious promise made repeatedly to us in past (namely, that our salaries should again be made available to us). Above all, if in addition to Lord Duke Christian, as our Chief Inspector of our collegium and my Most Benevolent Lord, also [our] Lord Senior Court Chaplain, *Herr* Dr. Weller, and you altogether would humbly advise our most benevolent Lord in this matter, in regard of which then I and the forsaken company entrusted to me most humbly petition.[131]

As mentioned above, I hope in this way moreover to promote and to help set the aforesaid collegium on good, solid footing once and for all—however, subject to correction—and with our Most Gracious Lord's previously customary consideration and most gracious consent offer a discussion of the following few points:

1. Although in consideration of my advanced age and disability, and on account of my lengthy service hitherto rendered to the Electoral House, I would have sufficient reason to request most humbly for release from my toilsome office and at the same time for a small pension for life [*ad vitam*], that I indeed in such a way would be ready to remain in it [i.e., his office] longer, and as long as God might grant me strength, if His Electoral Serenity would only favor me by assigning to me a young, qualified substitute. For this then I would gladly have our young Alto [i.e., Christoph Bernhard],[132] already present, whom our Most Gracious Lord previously supported for a year in Denmark with the Italian [i.e., Agostino Fontana], and hereby also propose, with my full consent, I would be willing also to cede to him 100 *gulden* annually from my ordinary salary into the treasury. This matter would also entail no major designation of offices, and he would retain his Alto position for a little while before [taking up] the second—just that 100 *gulden* would be given to him separately to act subsequently as my substitute. What kind of well-qualified young man he is, and what kind of service he could provide in future, time would tell, and our Most Gracious Electoral Princes also have good reports of his qualities already.

2. Johann Georg Hofkontz's designs might also be accommodated in such a way, and the office of Vice-Kapellmeister be conferred upon him in God's name, inasmuch as it does not matter to me, and I will be quite content just to have someone to assist me in my daily, ever-increasing inability, under whatever title that might be.

3. We still need to have a tenor in our company, the likes of which we also would have proposed already, if only there had first been an agreement with regard to our provisioning. It is my hope, with divine help, before my end, to create a fine, not over-expansive

---

which is the lowing, bellowing, bleating, or baaing of cattle and sheep. Similarly, he uses the word *Pfaffen*, which especially since Luther's time became a derogatory label for priests or the priesthood.

131. This entire sentence was omitted in *Schütz-GBr*.
132. Christoph Bernhard (b. 1 Jan. 1628; d. 14 Nov. 1692) was a singer, composer, and music theorist. He was probably in the Electoral *Hofkapelle* in 1648, and the following year received a contract to teach singing to

German musical body to represent our Most Gracious Lord in such a way that it shall achieve nothing less than glory among the discerning.

My Highly Esteemed *Herr*, may you kindly forgive my importunate writing which far exceeds the bounds of courtesy, consider one and another point at your good leisure, and proceed with it according to your well-known refined discretion and as much as possible. I do not doubt at all—the extent of your continuing affection toward me and the collegium entrusted to me is sufficiently known to me—that your virtuous spirit itself shall move you to promote us to the best of your ability and means, and to bear off the *palmam gloriae hujus et futurae vitae*.[133] To this I sincerely wish for you God's grace and blessing, most faithfully commend your family to His divine power, and remain your obliged faithful servant always.

While it is given, life to the living.[134]
Heinrich Schütz, in his own hand.
Dresden, 19 August 1651.

If this second point transmitted herewith to my Most Benevolent *Herr* should possibly be discussed before our Most Gracious Lord, it will subsequently require three further alterations to my most humble memorial previously submitted with my musical compositions.

130. SCHÜTZ TO CHRISTIAN REICHBRODT (4 FEBRUARY 1652)

Memorandum on the decline of the Hofkapelle *and the departure of musicians from the Dresden Court*

[D-Dla: Loc. 8687/1, Kantoreiordnung so Kurfürst Moritz…1548, fol. 318r][135]

Most Esteemed *Herr* Reichbrodt.

I shall not conceal from you in what manner I have been given to understand that four of the electoral musicians—namely, Friedrich Sultz[136] with his two sons, as well as Clemens Thieme[137]—are earnestly resolved to petition before our Most

---

the *Kapellknaben*. He subsequently studied under Agostino Fontana in Denmark for approximately a year, was elevated to the position of Vice-Kapellmeister at the Saxon Electoral Court in 1655, but left Dresden for Hamburg in 1663 where he succeeded Thomas Selle as Cantor of the Johanneum. As a theorist Bernhard is best known for his discussion of music and rhetoric in the *Tractatus compositionis augmentatus*.

133. "The palm of glory of this and future life."
134. *Dum datur vivis vitam.*
135. Transcribed in *Schütz-GBr*, Nr. 82; *Schütz-Dokumente*, Nr. 149.
136. *Schütz-GBr* (228) transcribes the original text as *Selig*, read *Sulz*.
137. Clemens Thieme (b. 7 Sept. 1631; d. 27 Mar. 1668), a German composer and instrumentalist, was initially trained under Philipp Stolle in Dresden, and then in 1642 was taken by Schütz to Copenhagen as a *Kapellknabe*

Gracious Elector and Lord for most gracious dismissal. Now if such a thing were to happen I must of utmost necessity ask most dutifully that you might favorably and as well as possible defend most humbly my innocence[138] of this tumult and alarming decline of our electoral company. From the remaining little that I possess and beyond my means, I myself have aided and provided for[139] it [i.e., the company] in sustaining these and other musicians, one here, another there, as their testimony will bear out.

And inasmuch as the preservation of our electoral *collegium musicum*, in my modest opinion, can be hoped for in no other way than through a certain directive and payment of their salary, I therefore submit it to my most benevolent *Herr* herewith whether he might also have mention made of this point and deliberate on it before His Electoral Serenity himself or his Chamber Councillors, who (you will forgive me) in these recent times more than before have treated me unkindly. I believe that it makes it difficult at court that no means and counsel may be found for the preservation of the church service.

As regards my person, having thus reached my present advanced age, and over thirty-seven years of services performed here at the Electoral Court, rendered as well as possible, has earned for me, I hope, the privilege of spending my remaining brief life entirely as a pensioner, inasmuch as I already made a request for it before our Most Gracious Lord one and a half years[140] ago in connection to a most humble offering of one of my newly published musical works made at the time.

In case His Electoral Serenity might once more be of a mind to keep his own *corpus musicum* [musical body] about him, and most graciously have issued specific instruction in support of the same, so that one, or perhaps two or three good singers, which are still required in our collegia, could be summoned from elsewhere, I would be ready for my part, once more, not to hinder this most gracious aim, and (in case one would not willingly let me leave) to persevere thereby in future and to preside over this enterprise to the utmost of my remaining powers. In sum, it is time to consider whether one wants to allow our collegium to dissolve or to preserve it, inasmuch as the extreme privation drives each of them to alternate resolutions. May God be with us in grace.

My Most Highly Esteemed [*Herr's*] ever-willing
Heinrich Schütz, in his own hand.
Dresden, 4 February 1652.

---

in the Royal Danish Court. He joined the Electoral Saxon Kapelle in 1651 and, on Schütz's recommendation, was appointed to the Kapelle of Moritz, Duke of Saxe-Zeitz in 1663, where he rose to the station of *Konzertmeister*.

138. *Schütz-GBr* (229) transcribes the original text as *verschuldig*, read *vnschuldig*.
139. *Schütz-GBr* (229) transcribes the original text as *fürgesorget*, read *vorgesetzet*.
140. *Schütz-GBr* (229) transcribes the original text as *ihme*, read *jahren*.

131. SCHÜTZ TO CHRISTIAN REICHBRODT (28 MAY 1652)

Communication regarding Georg Kaiser's and Friedrich Sultz's intentions to leave Dresden owing to non-payment of salaries

[D-Dla: Loc. 8687/1, Kantoreiordnung so Kurfürst Moritz...1548, fol. 321r [the stamped number is 320][141]

[Address]

To the Electoral Serenity of Saxony's Highly Ordained Lord Privy Secretary, *Herr* Christian Reichbrodt,[142] to his most benevolent gracious hands in Dresden

[Text]

Most Honorable *Herr*.

It is now three weeks that I have not been able to go out (owing to the catarrh which gave me headache and, finally taking leave from there, struck me in both legs; and out of that it turned into *erysipelas* or St. Anthony's fire[143]), would already have spoken to you a long time ago, and this time cannot conceal from you that the Bass [Georg Kaiser[144]], out of penury, pawned his clothing again some time ago, and since then has been reduced to live in his house like a beast in the forest. He now stirs himself once more, and had his wife tell me that he must and will leave. Although I by no means presume now to trouble my benevolent *Herr* on his account or to dispose you against your will toward him, or that you might procure something for him from our Most Gracious Lord, which indeed I leave to your discretion, I did not want to neglect notifying you accordingly of this and, should he perhaps actually wander off *insalutato hospite*,[145] as I believe he shall, nothing is blamed on me as a result. This is mentioned to my benevolent *Herr* and Lord Marshal in advance in order that I might have a witness.

It is however a pity, a thousand pities, that such an exquisite voice should be lost to the Kapelle. It is true that nothing in his disposition makes him particularly useful for

---

141. The document is in Schütz's hand. Transcribed in La Mara, 86–87; *Schütz-GBr*, Nr. 83; *Schütz-Dokumente*, Nr. 151.
142. Christian Reichbrodt von Schrenckendorf was installed as *Hauptmann der Ämter* (Senior Minister) in Dippoldiswalde and Altenburg, and was Councillor and Privy Secretary to Johann Georg I.
143. Schütz calls it *Resipilla* or *Rose*, also known in German as *Rotlauf*. Erysipelas is an acute streptococcal infectious disease of the skin, characterized by fever, headache, vomiting, and purplish raised lesions, especially on the face. The affliction was called St. Anthony's fire because it was believed in the sixteenth century that praying to Saint Anthony would effect a cure.
144. Georg Kaiser worked in Austria for fourteen years before his appointment in Dresden. According to the Kapelle register of 1651, he had an annual income of 150 *gulden*.
145. *Insalutato hospite*, "without obtaining prior permission."

anything else,[146] and that his tongue wants to be rinsed daily in the wine-jug, but such a wide throat also requires more moisture than many a narrow one. Were the good fellow to receive his modest salary promptly and properly, it would still not be enough for grand banquets; and were one to acknowledge duly this fellow's guardianship and household, one should, as I believe, give him his modest pittance in due time. But as long as nothing happens, neither can one proclaim him to be a great spendthrift. As for my part, however, I leave it at that.

Friedrich Sultz[147] and his sons, as I hear, are also leaving. I should wish to speak personally with my benevolent *Herr*, and to make known my modest thoughts about our electoral *collegium musicum* for which, by the looks of it, the funeral bells are already ringing. I remain always my highly esteemed *Herr*'s

indebted servant,
Heinrich Schütz.
Dresden, 28 May 1652.

[PS] Most Honorable *Herr*, should you consider it appropriate, I would also ask that you might have this letter of mine forwarded as well to the Lord Marshal of the Court after reading it.

132. SCHÜTZ TO HEINRICH VON TAUBE (26 JUNE 1652)

Communication asking the Marshal of the Court for intervention in various matters pertaining to Schütz and the musicians of the Hofkapelle

[D-Dla: Loc. 8687/1, Kantoreiordnung so Kurfürst Moritz...1548, fols. 319r–v, 322v][148]

[Address]

To the Electoral Serenity of Saxony's Highly Ordained Lord Marshal of the Court, Lord Heinrich von Taube etc., to his most benevolent hands in Dresden

[Text]

Electoral Serenity of Saxony's, Highly Ordained, Most Highly Esteemed Lord Marshal of the Court.[149]

That I hereby report dutifully and, as much as possible, briefly to Your Most Noble Worship is required out of unavoidable necessity: namely, one and a half years ago now, in connection to the offering at that time of one of my published new works to our Most

---

146. *Schütz-GBr* (231) and Moser (176) transcribe the original text as *was ists*, read *war ists*. Carl Pfatteicher bases his translation on the erroneous transcription in his translation of Moser, *Heinrich Schütz: His Life and Works*, 197.
147. *Schütz-GBr* (231) transcribes the original text as *Selge*, read *Sulze*.
148. The document is in Schütz's hand. Transcribed in *Schütz-GBr*, Nr. 84; *Schütz-Dokumente*, Nr. 152.
149. Heinrich von Taube.

Gracious Elector and Lord, I delivered with it at the same time a most humble memorandum, and after detailed testimony on my rather difficult life, from youth onward as well as of my now advancing old age and hence diminished strength (all the old musicians are dead now; I alone[150] of them yet remain[151] and am unable to adapt myself to the youthful world and new[152] style of music) and, I most humbly made a most diligent request for a most gracious delivery from the actual and constant personal attendance, and for a change of my appointment to a pension, however with certain limits. Your Most Noble Worship can also learn of all this at your pleasure from *Herr* Reichbrodt, Privy Secretary, or see for yourself from the perhaps still extant memorandum, amongst other things. Although the esteemed *Herr* Reichbrodt indeed brought back to me no definite resolution at that time, he did nevertheless impart to me this news that he had thought our Most Gracious Elector and Lord was not disinclined toward [granting] it.[153] In the interim, however, the discussion of this my earlier entreaty is at a standstill, and I am meanwhile required and occasioned nonetheless to work continuously at home, as at all manner of public services,[154] which indeed I have also done most willingly to the best of my abilities.

Now, however, those reasons which prompt me to strive for quietude do not abate as yet, but rather increase daily and markedly for me, to such an extent that also on account of my failed eyesight and the continuous and large amount of writing which my profession demands, I by no means presume to preside competently over the Electoral Kapelle, and in future to protect, I hope, my good reputation in the world achieved while in my youth. On the other hand, owing to the notoriously wretched conditions of the electoral musicians at present, the burden[155] of associating with them is made completely and utterly unbearable for me, considering that it is not difficult to reckon what unpleasantness hence falls to me (as their unworthy leader). On the extreme distress that has come to pass I also want to establish clearly how I have sufficient reason in these circumstances to let myself regret that I ever invested so much industry, work, risk, and expense in the little-known and little-valued *Studium Musicum* in Germany and taken upon myself the directorship [*Directorium*] of it in this Electoral Court.

Hence, then, my utmost dutiful and most earnest petition is hereby addressed to Your Most Noble Worship, that you not only show yourself to be my lofty patron in this matter which weighs heavily on me, but rather speak as well with the esteemed Lord Privy Secretary hereby, to dispose him toward joining freely with Your Most Noble Worship, and that you both might wish to seek a way by which, with most gracious consent, I might now realize the intention purposefully initiated by me a year and a half ago.

---

150. *Schütz-GBr* (232) transcribes the original text as *alhier*, read *alleine*.
151. *Schütz-GBr* (232) transcribes the original text as *werde*, read *were* (i.e., *ware*).
152. *Schütz-GBr* (233) transcribes the original text as *neueste*, read *newe*.
153. *Schütz-GBr* (233) transcribes the original text as *hirin*, read *hirzu*.
154. *Schütz-GBr* (233) transcribes the original text as *Auffwartung*, read *Auffwartungen*.
155. *Schütz-GBr* (233) transcribes the original text as *Lust*, read *Last*.

And how through this quietening of my life (should it be granted to me) my spirits, which at present have sunk to a considerable degree, would be appreciably revived and most definitely enlivened to carry on with my profession, I would thus not wish at all to withdraw completely from the Electoral Kapelle, but rather (in the event I should otherwise have something to do with a contented company) to offer assistance to it always with further arrangements and compositions, as well as to attend it in person on occasion.

And though indeed for the sake of my various enterprises and demands of the still remaining little that I possess,[156] I now have to set out on a most necessary journey to Halle and Weissenfels (for which I also petition most humbly for most gracious permission herewith), I am indeed willing upon discussion of the same [i.e., the journey], should God keep me in good health, to present myself here again most obediently. I hope our Most Gracious Elector and Lord, in accordance with his gracious compassion shown to us repeatedly, shall meanwhile graciously intercede sometime in the extreme privation of his musicians, and also willingly offer his powerful most benevolent hand to Your Most Noble Worship and shake on it for your part in advancing this matter, as it is well known in itself that you show Christian love hereupon, and promote the reputation of the Electoral Court and the praise of God, to Whose divine protection in grace I finally commend Your Most Noble Worship herewith and remain most loyally disposed to the best of my ability and means always.

The Lord Marshal of the Court's
obliged and bounden servant,
Heinrich Schütz, in his own hand.
Dresden, 26 June 1652.

133. SCHÜTZ TO HEINRICH II REUSS (16 JUNE 1653)

Letter regarding the sale of property in Weissenfels and the presence of Italian musicians at the Dresden Court

[D-GZsa: Hausarchiv Schleiz, Nr. 116 H[errn] Heinrich Schütz Churf[ürstlich] Sächss.[ischer] Capellmeister wegen 300 fl. Bünauischer Gelder, fol. 12r–v][157]

Noble-Born, Gracious Lord.

Your Illustrious Grace, in addition to this humble salutation, I did not want to leave unreported hereby in what manner, in accordance also with my now advancing old age, and the end of my life approaching with every day,[158] I am in the process now of putting my modest worldly possessions in all possible order, and especially [those]

---

156. This appears to be a reference to Schütz's property in Weissenfels.
157. The letter is transcribed in Jung, "Zwei unbekannte Briefe von Heinrich Schütz aus den Jahren 1653–54," 231–36. Also transcribed in *Schütz-Dokumente*, Nr. 155.
158. Jung (232) transcribes the original text as *annehmenden*, read *annahenden*.

outside of Dresden, and shall then spend my remaining days in all possible peace and quiet in Dresden (to live away from which place, as I note, shall not be allowed me without diminution of the former electoral favor). Around Weissenfels here, I also have a little land property, for which the bearer [of this brief], a nobleman by the name of Alexander von Schenk, has made me an offer. As payment, however, he has offered me an outstanding debt owed by the young *Herr* Reuss of Saalburg, etc. (Your Grace's foster son, as I understand it) to his [von Schenk's] wife, the actual nature of which debt von Schenck, as he now himself is now present, will be able to certify and report.

In accord with the conditions of the calamitous times of today, of my rather wretched treatment at court as well (truth be told), I am not being unreasonably cautious that, with the negotiations of my property here, I with this morsel of bread might not fall into uncertainty and difficulty,

As I, in humble and great confidence, could not forbear disclosing to Your Grace this pending transaction, and to ask with submissive diligence for the following modest report (which Your Grace can command from amongst your people, subject to correction), namely:

1. Whether this capital of 1500 *gulden* might with certainty be available, and the tendered payment to the same by me be acceptable
2. In what manner a certain payment of the aforesaid capital (for I wish to have nothing to do with the hitherto accumulated interest) might be graciously permitted and be expected by me.

From this obtained report then, I shall see what in this case is for me to do or have done, and should it please Your Grace to pursue this negotiation with my insignificant person, should it please you, I shall accommodate myself to your gracious will hopefully so far as you shall be able to be satisfied with me, and await in humble anticipation to learn Your Grace's gracious judgment on the matter.

I humbly report moreover that, toward the Nativity of St. John the Baptist [24 June], I shall again set out from here for Dresden, to which place I was summoned a few short days ago by the Electoral Prince to listen to his new musicians recently arrived from Italy, as well as several others hired for the aforesaid solemnities. Accordingly I hereby wish to commend faithfully Your Grace, together with your dearest family, to the powerful protection of God for every desired welfare of soul and body, and to recommend myself with utmost diligence further to your long-standing well-known favor.

Weissenfels, 16 June 1653.
Your Illustrious Grace's
humble, dutiful servant,
Heinrich Schütz, Electoral Saxon
Kapellmeister, in his own hand.

134. SCHÜTZ'S ENDORSEMENT OF CASPAR ZIEGLER'S *VON DEN MADRIGALEN* (LEIPZIG, 1653/1685) (11 AUGUST 1653)

[D-W: H: QuH 118.1 (3), fols. 1r, 3r–v][159]

[Title page]

Caspar Ziegler[160]
Von den
Madrigalen [On Madrigals],
an elegant and most suitable
style of verse for music,
how they are composed in our German tongue,
in accordance with the Italian manner,
in addition to several examples
now augmented and upon repeated request
brought out in print,
with appended index.
Wittenberg
Published by the late Andreas Hartmann's Widow.
Printed in *Brüning* type.
ANNO M.DC.LXXXV.

Excerpt from the letter to me, Caspar Ziegler, from the Electoral Serenity of Saxony's Highly Ordained Kapellmeister and World-Renowned Musician, etc., Heinrich Schütz.

Highly esteemed, gracious, much beloved friend,[161] I have a great desire for a copy of your German madrigals which you intend to publish, and you shall certainly be accorded a great honor in particular on account of the same, as you give herewith the first sample of this poetic genre amongst German poets. And my friend would also rightly point out in your preface with certainty that, although German composers have repeatedly made efforts to set elegant inventions of today's new poetry with good style to music, they nonetheless have always lamented at the same time that this poetic genre, which is

---

159. See Ziegler, *Von den Madrigalen*. Additional copies of the first edition exist in the collections of the D-Gs (Sig: 8 P GERM II, 1276) and the D-Dl (Sig: Ling. Germ. rec. 618, misc. 4).
160. Caspar (Kaspar) Ziegler (b. 15 Sept. 1621; d. 17 Apr. 1690) was a German jurist, poet, and composer. Born in Leipzig, Ziegler began his university studies there, and completed them at the University of Wittenberg, where he was appointed professor in 1655. He published extensively on religious and juridical subjects but is best known today for his *Von den Madrigalen*, first printed in Leipzig in 1653 and subsequently in Wittenberg in 1685. *ADB* 45, 184–87.
161. Schütz refers to Ziegler as his *Schwager*, which literally means "brother-in-law," but it is intended here as a term of endearment and not necessarily one of kinship.

the very best suited for the creation of an artful composition, namely, the Madrigal, has not been engaged by them until now, but rather has been left aside. Indeed I previously scraped together a small work of sundry poems, and I know full well what trouble it cost me before I could fashion the music into even somewhat of an Italian style. And accordingly, etc. *[The passage is then discontinued by Ziegler.]*

Dresden, 11 August 1653.

Heinrich Schütz.

135. SCHÜTZ TO HEINRICH VON TAUBE, JACOB WELLER, AND CHRISTIAN REICHBRODT (21 AUGUST 1653)

Letter of complaint in regard to current practices and conditions in the Kapelle

[D-Dla: Loc. 8687/1, Kantoreiordnung so Kurfürst Moritz…1548, fols. 327r, 330v][162]

[Address]

To the Electoral Serenity of Saxony's Highly Ordained Lord Senior Marshal of the Court, Heinrich von Taube; as well as his Highly Appointed Father Confessor, Ecclesiastical Councillor and Court Chaplain Doctor Jacob Weller; as well as *Herr* Christian Reichbrodt, Highly Esteemed Councillor and Privy Secretary to His Electoral Serenity, my Most Benevolent, Most Venerable Patrons in Dresden

[Text]

Most Venerable Patrons.

For a necessary vindication from an undeserved accusation made against me, may it please you to consider at your leisure from the enclosed copy, benevolently and without prejudice, what I must submit most humbly before Duke Johann Georg, our Gracious Electoral Prince. And inasmuch as I suspect that this sort of baseless information about me might ultimately very well reach the ears of our Most Gracious Elector and Lord, it is thus my most humble petition to my Venerable Lords in this case that you would support me in this rightful cause and to that end help to intercede most humbly with our Most Gracious Lord, and that I might moreover be granted a verbal or written response.

Also with regard to the command issued by the aforementioned Electoral Prince for the alternation of the *Music* in the palace church on Sundays, I cannot conceal from my Venerable *Herren* how very demeaning and hurtful that will be for me, an old and yet, I hope, not undeserving man, that those Sundays (when formerly, in Doctor Hoë's day, the

---

162. The document is in Schütz's hand. Transcribed in *Schütz-GBr*, Nr. 86; *Spagn.*, Nr. 3; *Schütz-Dokumente*, Nr. 158.

directorship [*Directorium*] did not fall to me but to the Vice-Kapellmeister) I should regularly and continuously alternate with the Lord Electoral Prince's Director,[163] a person three times my junior, and castrated at that, and to vie with him for favor, as it were, on the spot amid capricious and in large part ignorant listeners and judges. For that reason I shall then have to apply—not unduly, I hope—for a most gracious privilege [*Privilegium*] so that the directorship might be conferred by me upon the Vice-Kapellmeister at that time. And indeed, with respect to the music in the electoral palace church, there would be no particular deficiency to be perceived at any time if only the musicians, and above all the elector's company whose number in any case is very small, and several of whom nearly always reside elsewhere because of inadequate sustenance here, might be obliged to uninterrupted service by paying their salaries. To conclude then, as for me, I must also protest here that now that I have given up everything but the very blood in my veins as it were, distributed in part among various needful musicians, it will be utterly impossible for me to continue any longer here in Dresden, about which I wish to report nothing specifically [*in specie*] at this time, but rather only to declare that I would rather be dead than to live longer in these oppressive conditions.

My Venerable Patrons' duty-bound
Heinrich Schütz, in his own hand.
Signed at Dresden, 21 August 1653.

136. SCHÜTZ TO JOHANN GEORG I (21 AUGUST 1653)

Letter reminding the elector and reiterating his previous request for permission to retire

[D-Dla: Loc. 8687/1, Kantoreiordnung so Kurfürst Moritz…1548, fol. 331r][164]

Most Serene, Illustrious Elector, Most Gracious Lord.

Your Electoral Serenity, I hope, shall still be able graciously to recall how I most humbly and earnestly presented to you in a detailed memorandum, now nearly into the third year (together at that time of my most humble offering of one of my slight new works that had been recently printed), my arduous life since my youth, also now advancing old age, failing eyesight, and other lost vital strengths, which are required for laudable, proficient refinement and performance of new musical inventions and compositions of all kinds, and for that reason ardently begged for most gracious retirement for my remaining brief life, and for the revision of my service and appointment into a pension or subsistence allowance, and in addition to this, however, to spend my time, as long as God might still spare my life,

---

163. Giovanni Andrea Bontempi.
164. The document is in Schütz's hand. Transcribed in *Schütz-GBr*, Nr. 87; *Schütz-Dokumente*, Nr. 157.

not in idleness but rather as much as possible with the continuation of my profession and the completion of various musical works started by me in addition to this.

Your Electoral Serenity also would have sufficiently derived from it the following: I offered most humbly and obediently to preside no less in future over the musical *corpus* [*musikalischen corpori*] (according to my ability and means, as I have done up to the present); to supply it with my own and other compositions once again, so that even in my absence no deficiencies should be perceived; and finally, too, according to the needs of the times and eventual solemnities, to attend repeatedly in person at those services, and also as much as possible to demonstrate to Your Electoral Serenity my most humble desire to serve steadfastly and to satisfy you to the best of my abilities and means for the rest of my life.

Thus, Most Gracious Lord, the considerations stated above, as well as others previously in my detailed most humbly presented memorandum, with my steadily advancing age in the meantime, oppress me yet more intensely and compel me now to take upon myself anew my previous most humble petition, to address to Your Electoral Serenity herewith once again in most humble devotion my repeated, most fervent and unremitting request, may it please you at the present time, finally to give your most gracious, and for me satisfying, resolution, so that I might be able additionally to conform my remaining brief life both to Your Electoral Serenity's most gracious desires and full satisfaction (I would never intentionally engage in anything to the contrary) and then also to my desired quietude and retirement, and under Your Electoral Serenity's protection and favor (after my services, faithfully rendered to your noble house for so long a time, for thirty-eight years, and to some extent known throughout the world through my various published works up to the present) laudably and honorably bring it to a blessed close. For this I faithfully commend Your Electoral Serenity to the powerful protection of Almighty God, to continued good health, long life, blessed reign, and every desired electoral welfare of the soul and body, and remain

Your Electoral Serenity's
most duty-bound, loyal, most humble
servant as long as I shall live,
Heinrich Schütz, in his own hand,
Kapellmeister.
Dresden, 21 August 1653.

137. SCHÜTZ TO JOHANN GEORG II (21 AUGUST 1653)

Letter complaining of the appointment of Italians and vehement defense of himself against accusations from within the community of musicians

[D-Dla: Loc. 8687/1, Kantoreiordnung so Kurfürst Moritz... 1548, fols. 328r–329v][165]

---

165. The document is the hand of a copyist. Transcribed in *Schütz-GBr*, *Spagn.*, Nr. 4; Nr. 88; *Schütz-Dokumente*, Nr. 159.

[Address]

To the Most Serene, Most Noble Prince and Lord, Lord Johann Georg, Duke and Electoral Prince of Saxony, my Most Gracious Lord

[Text]

Most Serene, Illustrious Electoral Prince, Most Gracious Lord.

I cannot avoid reporting plaintively to Your Electoral Princely Serenity, with my present most humble memorandum, the extent to which I am given to understand more and more each day how (on account of Your Serenity's musicians summoned hither from Italy and inducted into the Electoral *Hofkapelle*) not only is repeated vexatious judgment passed on me by various ecclesiastical and secular persons, but rather I must additionally hear in particular, to my greatest astonishment, that I should be considered to be and slandered as the architect and adviser of this recent change, whereby I have unfortunately noticed already malice and concealed hatred in many prominent people (by whom these foreign countries are perhaps not beloved to such a degree). Because my innocence[166] is sufficiently well-known to Your Princely Serenity, and that I never received or obtained the slightest information about the summoning of any person among the present Italians now here, the architects of this matter, who privately communicated with Your Serenity hereby and afterwards sent for the aforementioned musicians from Italy, are exposed. Thus I address to you hereby my most humble supplication, may it please you most graciously (in advance and before I might be placed by someone else, in consequence of this, under undeserved suspicion before Your Most Gracious Lord Father) to avert most graciously this suspicion from me and, above all else, free me of it most graciously within the honorable service of the Electoral *Hofkapelle*, where for this reason I find myself discredited as well. And inasmuch as I have been reproached by some, as if in proof of the accusation against me, that a document in my own hand supposedly exists in which I advised Your Electoral Serenity with regard to these Italians, I however remember nothing of the sort apart from this: that now twenty years or more ago, on his most gracious command, I had to draft a report showing in what way a Kapelle might possibly be set up and what kind of musicians belonged to its complement. I may have mentioned then the possibility of including an Italian among the vocalists, from whom the *Kapellknaben* and German singers could learn a proper style, as well as a similarly qualified Italian among the instrumentalists. One hopes that no one will still take exception to this recommendation of mine made many long years ago, and then have it attributed to the Italians now present here. If Your Serenity should wish to have the said document submitted in order to judge for yourself what is in it, I for my part also most humbly request that a copy of it be sent to me.

---

166. *Schütz-GBr* (242) transcribes the original text as *Verschuldt*, read *Vnschuldt*.

Moreover, I swear before God that I for my part was never opposed to this Italian music directorship [*Directorium Musicum*] newly established by Your Princely Serenity (even though for me and other Germans here it contributes more to the depreciation than to the elevation of our position). I am content with that and with everything else Your Serenity might further arrange with his musical body [*Corpore Musico*] in future, and shall not be reproved and disdained by me. But now I must deplore bitterly that toward the end of my life, and after so many years of my most humble, ardent and well-intentioned service rendered at this Electoral Court, it is now as though all the planets and elements rise up against me and want to wage war on me. Since that was not enough (that up to now, since my youth, I have not encountered more oppressive and miserable conditions, and someone else, perhaps of even fewer qualifications than I, perhaps will not have borne it) to have spent time in most humble and considerable forbearance, and at the same time offered up good cheer and hoped for an improvement, now, in addition to that, this tribulation befalls me, as though I were guilty of misguiding Your Serenity into irresponsible dealings and great expenses. Thus disfavor of various prominent people is heaped upon me, rather than that I should carry away the thanks I deserve.

However, I must ultimately entrust this to God and to time, and it is hoped that they shall bear witness to my innocence.

I beg Your Electoral Princely Serenity most humbly, however, not to look with disfavor upon this complaint wrested from me. I wish herewith, in utmost humility, to recommend and commit myself most humbly, once again with most faithful diligence, to your eminent protection in this my rightful cause, as well as to the continuing steadfast favor rendered up to now.

Your Serene Electoral Prince's
most humble, most obedient old servant,
Heinrich Schütz.
Dresden, 21 August 1653.[167]

138. SCHÜTZ TO JOHANN GEORG I (21 SEPTEMBER 1653)

Communication enumerating his reasons for requesting a pension and permission to retire to Weissenfels

[D-Dla: Loc. 8687/1, Kantoreiordnung so Kurfürst Moritz…1548, fols. 334r–335r, 336v][168]

---

167. *Schütz GBr* (245), *Spagn.* (139) and *Schütz-Dokumente* (367) wrongly transcribe the date at the end of the letter as 23 August.
168. The document is in the hand of a copyist, edited and signed by Schütz. Transcribed in *Schütz-GBr*, Nr. 89; *Schütz-Dokumente*, Nr. 160.

Old Age (1645–56)

[Address]

To the Most Serene, Noble-Born Prince and Lord, Lord Johann Georg, Duke of Saxony, Jülich, Cleves and Berg, Grand Marshal and Elector of the Holy Roman Empire, Landgrave in Thuringia, Margrave of Meissen, of Upper and Lower Lusatia, and Burgrave of Magdeburg, Count of the Mark and Ravensberg, Lord of Ravenstein, my Most Gracious Elector and Lord

[Letter]

The most important motives and reasons why I now strive urgently after a calming of my remaining short life, and petition most humbly for a most gracious pension or house-appointment.

1.

The first is my advancing age, failing eyesight and other physical strengths; for although I can work out my composition as soundly and as well as ever before, without boasting, with God's help, it all takes much longer and is more difficult, as one can easily imagine.

2.

Thus I believe also, on account of my many years of service discharged for this Electoral Court, that I have now finally earned peace and quiet, in view of the countless, diverse noble solemnities that have taken place during this period in the presence of imperial, royal, electoral, and princely potentates, as well as each and every princely wedding held, and christenings no less (with the exception of the Lord Electoral Prince and the Lady Landgravine of Darmstadt),[169] at all of which I attended in truth with most humble diligence, albeit according to my meager ability and means.

3.

I also have several already initiated musical works yet to complete which are very important to me, whereby I hope after my death still to serve God, the world, and my good name. To this end, however, I absolutely need a quiet and undisturbed environment, as it is my intention then, among other things, to attempt to set to music the small psalter [*Psalterbüchlein*] of the blessed Luther, translation in prose [*version in prosa*], in such a way that the common people might easily be able to learn these melodies and sing along in the churches.

4.

I have also to mention duly that those musicians (when I was first appointed here and started my directorship) are all dead now, and I alone yet remain. Beyond this too, the Electoral Kapelle is now full of nothing but young people, in amongst whom an old graybeard

---

169. Johann Georg II and Sophie Eleonore of Saxony.

does not well pride himself, considering that it is the way of the young, that they happily aspire to novelty; and antiquity is ultimately more prone to be derogated than elevated.

5.

Finally, in addition to my lost strength, I would also lack the various means to invent new compositions for the two separate *collegia musica* now present here, to commit them effectively to paper, at which I would feel anxious at having to set aside all other yet planned—good and useful, I hope—work.

6.

In conclusion, though in truth yet other reasons more could be produced, I thus hope that my intention shall be sufficiently acquitted and vindicated with the ones related here.
    Signed at Dresden, 21 September 1653.
    Heinrich Schütz,
    Electoral Saxon Kapellmeister of thirty-eight years, in his own hand.

139. SCHÜTZ TO THE DRESDEN COURT (UNDATED, PROBABLY 1653 OR 1654)

Memorandum and petition regarding his move to Weissenfels, his pension, and the role of Christoph Kittel in the Kapelle

[D-Dla: Loc. 8687/1, Kantoreiordnung so Kurfürst Moritz...1548, fol. 333r–v][170]

Memorandum with my most humble
supplication.

1.

Inasmuch as I and one of my still surviving sisters (a childless widow) still have some property together in Weissenfels, and in some measure have the means to appoint a modest household there, where I can also reside much more quietly than here in Dresden and certainly bring my musical works much further toward completion; and, truth be told, the Electoral Kapelle will be able to benefit much better and far more in my absence as well as in my presence, to which the musicians here will also be able to testify, I hope, thus is it my most humble request that it might be most graciously granted me henceforth, evermore freely and without further request for permission to move back and forth between Dresden (where I shall try to maintain my house as long as I live) and Weissenfels, and that I, after my long service, might be looked upon from now on as a

---

170. The document is in Schütz's hand. Transcribed in *Schütz-GBr*, Nr. 90; *Schütz-Dokumente*, Nr. 163.

pensioner or an appointee *in absentia*, or declared one by decree, at the pleasure of our Most Gracious Elector and Lord.

2.

Regarding the attendance, both in the church and at table in my absence as well, no deficiency would appear, for which I am no less willing to bear the responsibility, and I have therefore already come to an agreement with [Christoph] Kittel, the Court Organist (who is a diligent man and, apart from that, kept the *Kapellknaben* in constant practice), who each time would furnish for me the necessary compositions at the services, whereas the Vice-Kapellmeister would provide the beat [*Tact*] for it.

3.

For the sake of advancing my planned household in Weissenfels, I have most humbly to request:

1. As I have various claims [*Exactio*] in the Electoral Land Tax and *Tranksteuer*,[171] that the most gracious command might be sent to the Council at Naumburg or to the tax collector there and grant me to brew annually two *Bier*[172] as installment of my aforesaid tax demands.[173]
2. I wish very much (if it were possible) to have another command issued to the grain secretary at Weissenfels, that I might annually receive twenty-five Dresden bushels of grain and thirty bushels of oats at the officially set rate, and my receipt be accepted in lieu of past payments of the outstanding salary instead of cash payment, whereby His Electoral Serenity would notice a slight diminution, whereas I would be mercifully given considerable relief.

4.

If His Electoral Serenity would also resolve to have his ordinance issued with regard to my salary, at his most gracious pleasure, I am as willing as duty bound to assist in most humble obedience always.

140. SCHÜTZ TO JOHANN GEORG I (29 MAY 1655)

Letter outlining his wish to retire owing to age and failing healthy, and promises of continuing to contribute to the music at court

[D-Dla: Loc. 8687/1, Kantoreiordnung so Kurfürst Moritz…1548, fols. 339r; 347r][174]

---

171. *Tranksteuer* is the excise or duty on alcoholic or spirituous liquors.
172. *Bier* can also be a brewing of beer, so Schütz is probably referring to two brewing sessions.
173. *Schütz-GBr* (249) transcribes the original text as *abzubrauchen*, read *abzubrawen*.
174. The document is in Schütz's hand. Transcribed in *Schütz-GBr*, Nr. 93; *Schütz-Dokumente*, Nr. 167. *Schütz-Dokumente* gives the wrong shelf number for the item: [D-Dla: Loc. 33 659, Schuldforderungen an die Kammer, Bd. 39, Nr. 216°, fols. 10r–v; 47v].

[Address]

To the Most Serene, Noble-Born Prince and Lord, Lord Johann Georg, Duke of Saxony, Jülich, Cleves and Berg, Grand Marshal and Elector of the Holy Roman Empire, Landgrave in Thuringia, Margrave of Meissen, of Upper and Lower Lusatia, and Burgrave of Magdeburg, Count of the Mark and Ravensberg, Lord of Ravenstein, my Most Gracious Elector and Lord

[Text]

Most Serene, Illustrious Elector, Most Gracious Lord.

I cannot forestall writing most humbly to Your Electoral Serenity how I advanced in my toilsome life, now into its seventieth year, from my childhood and from my twelfth year on (in which year I was sent abroad at an early age by my late parents) in this world, without wishing to boast, and on account of much endured work, study, and all manner of hardship, myself now likewise weakened from fading and diminished powers, eyesight, and hearing. My musical vein or artery for painstaking compositions and for many new inventions [*Inventionen*] is also to a considerable degree dried up, leaden, and difficult. In sum I find myself in no way capable or sufficiently suited to continue presiding adequately and honorably over the current straggling musical body [*corpus musicum*] here, and to direct the same. On the contrary, it is quite impossible for me. Therefore then, and primarily in order to quieten my remaining, presumably brief life, as well as to tend better to my health, I address to Your Electoral Serenity herewith my most earnest, most humble petition (however, subject to correction), that you might deign most graciously via the Marshal of the Court, together with the Senior Court Chaplain, perhaps also in consultation with Your Electoral Serenity's dearest[175] son, the Lord Crown Prince, to have it arranged most graciously to that end, without diminution of the service, both in the church as well as at table, that I might henceforth be given the liberty I long for, to be relieved of actual, personal, regular service, and to be declared and treated as a pensioner. At the same time I nevertheless make the most humble offer that, in case my compositions or others at hand might in future be deemed worthy of performance by the Kapelle and requested of me, I shall always quite happily provide them and have them delivered, as long as I live and as much as I am able, and help here to serve the *Music*, as it were, from my home.

I have no doubt that Your Electoral Serenity shall sufficiently consider the absolute urgency of my most humble petition here. Thus I await, in the most humble hope and with great expectation, your worthy, most gracious resolution and command hereupon.

---

175. *Schütz-GBr* (252) transcribes the original text as *geliebten*, read *geliebsten*.

I commend you most faithfully to divine protection for every desired welfare of soul and body,
> Your Electoral Serenity's
> most faithful, most obliging
> servant of forty years,
> Heinrich Schütz,
> Kapellmeister, in his own hand.
> Signed at Dresden, 29 May 1655.

141. SOPHIE ELISABETH OF BRUNSWICK-LÜNEBURG TO SCHÜTZ (22 JUNE 1655)

Draft of a letter replying to Schütz's earlier communication concerning a particular falsettist and other musicians

[D-Wa: 1 Alt 25 no. 294, fol. 8r–v][176]

Sophie Elisabeth.

Our favor and gracious greeting first and foremost, honorable, artistically skilled, highly learned, specially cherished [friend].

We understood from your delivered missive of the twelfth of this month, among other things, what you pointed out to us regarding the falsettist or painter, and the Director's journey, as well as on account of the bassist, and with regard to the discantists cited in the postscript. If then it should graciously please the Illustrious Prince, Lord August, Duke of Brunswick and Lüneburg, etc., our beloved Lord and Husband, His Dilection, to consent to all the proposals made by you, then you shall carry out the same in accordance with the proposals, and that above all else see that a good bassist comes to us who, if he plays instruments besides, shall be all the more agreeable to us. Because we have as yet received no reply from the expected bassist in Kassel, this one, not unsuitable as a replacement, if the other [i.e., the one from Kassel] should come, shall urgently occupy your utmost diligence. We await your arrival and shall not neglect the necessary arrangements for your journey down here. Insofar as it still depends on the falsettist's intention to come here, Our Highly Esteemed, Beloved Princely Lord and Husband, His Dilection, still graciously desires his arrival, notwithstanding that he has postponed it for a rather long time, thus wished to reply to you without reservation,[177] and affixes our benevolent, gracious will toward you.

Written at Wolfenbüttel, 22 June 1655,
to Heinrich Schütz.

---

176. This is the draft letter, also kept as a record at court, that would be copied out in fine and then sent to Schütz.
177. *Spagn.* (257) wrongly translates this passage as "We wish you to show no restraint in your answer."

142. SCHÜTZ TO JOHANN GEORG I (21 JULY 1655)

Letter seeking assistance for himself and court musicians to access their salaries and pawned possessions

[D-Dla: Loc. 33 659, Schuldforderungen an die Kammer, Bd. 39, Nr. 216º, fols. 10r–v; 47v][178]

[Address]

To the Most Serene, Noble-Born Prince and Lord, Lord Johann Georg, Duke of Saxony, Jülich, Cleves and Berg, Grand Marshal and Elector of the Holy Roman Empire, Landgrave in Thuringia, Margrave of Meissen, of Upper and Lower Lusatia, and Burgrave of Magdeburg, Count of the Mark and Ravensberg, Lord of Ravenstein, and my Most Gracious Elector and Lord

[Text]

Most Serene, Most Noble Elector, Most Gracious Lord.

I am compelled to report to Your Electoral Serenity most humbly how I, for several years in succession now in these yet continuing difficult times, out of Christian pity have gone to the aid of various of your Electoral Kapelle attendants at their fervent entreaties in their need. And I have given assistance according to my own slender means through cash advances to several, as well as with lending to others what little remains of my household silver, preserved with difficulty, against which they have borrowed money elsewhere. As of this hour, however, I cannot again recover the money or the advanced pledges.

It is quite unbearable for me then that in addition to leaving behind the greatest share of my salary, I should be deprived moreover of my modest possessions painstakingly acquired and, as one says, be left in the lurch.

Thus I cannot forbear impressing this upon Your Electoral Serenity's mind most humbly, and at the same time most fervently implore you, may it please you, to extend to me your most gracious electoral hand in the recovery of what is mine, and to command your Lord Treasurer to make a transfer to me of 500 *gulden* by some means (as you think best), so that over time I might be able eventually to get back what is mine and not be altogether ruined as a consequence of this.

And I in return am willing to deliver to the Electoral Treasury the verified pay receipts of the aforementioned Kapelle attendants (which I meanwhile, in regard of what they owe me, received from them and have in my possession) in settlement of their claim.

---

178. *Schütz-Dokumente*, Nr. 168 (379–80), gives the wrong shelf number for this item: [D-Dla: Loc. 8687/1, Kantoreiordnung so Kurfürst Moritz…1548, fols. 339r; 347r]. The letter in a scribe's hand, with Schütz adding the concluding formula, signature, and date.

And should these their receipts not fully amount to the sum of 500 *gulden*, I shall provide the full complement for the same with my own outstanding pay receipts. And as I am truly in dire need of Your Electoral Serenity's most gracious assistance at this time, thus do I implore once more most humbly, with utmost diligence, that you in electoral grace would gladden me with a favorable resolution in this matter, and whom I herewith commend most faithfully to the protection of the Almighty for all desired welfare of soul and body.

Your Electoral Serenity's
most humble, most obliging old servant,
Heinrich Schütz,
Kapellmeister.
Dresden, 21 July 1655.

143. SCHÜTZ TO SOPHIE ELISABETH OF BRUNSWICK-LÜNEBURG (24 JULY 1655)

Letter regarding travel from Dresden, the appointment of Johann Jacob Löwe and other music matters at the Wolfenbüttel Court, the death of Schütz's daughter, and the copyist's expenses

[D-Wa: 1 Alt 25 no. 294, fols. 9r–11v][179]

[Address]

To the Serene, Noble Princess and Lady, Lady Sophie Elisabeth, Duchess of Brunswick and Lüneburg, born Duchess of Mecklenburg, Princess of Wenden, Schwerin and Ratzeburg,[180] also Countess of Schwerin, Lady of the Rostock and Stargard Domains, etc., my Gracious Princess and Lady

[Text]

Serene, Noble Princess,
Gracious Lady.
To Your Princessly Grace I humbly report herewith the manner in which the assumed Director, Johann Jacob Löwe of Vienna,[181] together with the two discantists, departed

---

179. The correct foliation for this archival document is *Schütz's* autograph letter (fols. 9r–10r), address and Sophie Elisabeth's note (fol. 10v), text of the postscript (fol. 11r) and the *Postscriptum* title (fol. 11v). Transcribed in *Schütz-GBr*, Nr. 94; *Spagn.*, Nr. 25; *Schütz-Dokumente*, Nr. 169.
180. *Spagn.* (272) transcribes the original text as *Radeburg*, read *Ratzeburg*.
181. Though of Protestant German heritage—his Thuringian father was a diplomat at the imperial court—Johann Jacob Löwe von Eisenach (bap. 31 Jul. 1629; d. early Sept.1703) was born in Vienna where direct

a few days ago, on 19 July, with several ships which set sail on the Elbe from here as far as Magdeburg. I cannot thereby conceal from Your Princessly Grace how, in the end, I practically had to drive out the said Director, who (through some unpleasant news that reached his ears—from whom I do not know) prior to his departure was made to be so reluctant that he nearly did not want to go. But he allowed himself to be calmed subsequently and is now on his way. I thus hope that (if it has not occurred already) he shall safely arrive as early as possible in your princely court [city] together with the *Knaben*, and I have sent along with the Director a humble missive to Your Princessly Grace's Lord Husband, which he shall remember to serve on His Serenity with due reverence upon his arrival.

Now how agreeable and acceptable these people shall be to your princely court, I am in truth uncertain.[182] I deem or consider it indeed advisable, for my small part (should one not be inclined to retain this director in office continuously, or should he not wish to remain director in the long run), that one should try to keep him for at least a year in the Princely *Music* for the sake of correct and proper style, to which, it is hoped, he shall initiate and train the musicians during this time. Should perhaps some modification come about subsequently, his position would be occupied at any time by another well-qualified fellow (albeit not one so learned in *Music*) but otherwise who moreover would be a good singer, who could maintain equally well the undertaken proper musical style with suitable compositions, which one could send to him. This I wanted to mention incidentally.

This Johann Jacob Löwe (as I also wrote to Your Princessly Grace's Lord Husband) is an upright, honest man in whom I perceived no notable faults at any time as long as he stayed with me; on the other hand, he is of robust Austrian humor and customs, wants to have everything according to his zealous bent, and thus I also worry that he burdens the *Knaben* perhaps somewhat too much, and they then complain about him, or might well run away altogether (as they are said to have intimated to several persons prior to their departure). To forestall such trouble, it would indeed be my wish (if it can be excused as something other than discourtesy toward you) that Your Royal Grace might draw them together to some degree under your gracious protection and to grant them an audience from time to time in order for them to present their situation themselves.

Otherwise, with respect to setting up the appointment of the aforesaid Director, there is no great hurry, just that I must humbly mention still one more time hereby that I

---

exposure to Italian compositional and performance practices played a major part in his professional development. He traveled to Dresden in 1652, where he was befriended and supported by Schütz, who subsequently recommended him to the Wolfenbüttel Court. Through Schütz's intervention he was appointed Kapellmeister to the court of Moritz, Duke of Saxe-Zeitz in 1663, which position he was forced to vacate only two years later owing to an intense and jealous rivalry with the ambitious court *Konzertmeister*, Clemens Thieme (b. 7 Sept. 1631; d. 27 Mar. 1668), another Schütz protégé. Löwe was finally appointed organist at the Nikolaikirche in Lüneburg in 1682 and spent the remainder of his life there in penury. *NDB* 15, 83–84. See also Werner, *Städtische und fürstliche Musikpflege in Zeitz bis zum Anfang des 19. Jahrhunderts*.

182. *Spagn.* (169) translates this passage as: "How one is to be fair and just to such domestic servants of your royal capital, I am indeed uncertain."

consider it reasonable on account of his great travel expenses incurred, also the food and drink for the *Knaben* on the journey down (since prior to their packing up and departure they were completely under my care), that he be compensated upon his arrival and, subject to correction, perhaps be given at once a gracious gift of 50 thalers. He is indeed far from Vienna and without money, considering he also borrowed between 30 and 40 thalers here which he still owes. In the event Your Serenity, for reasons of your own, does not want to do more, I think he shall likely be satisfied with this much at the start, considering that, upon setting up of his salary or provisioning, it is hoped he shall make the most of a modest amount.

I am anxious now to hear of their arrival, and how they take their place and appear in their obliging, humble offices. Wishing, as everything from me is well-intentioned, that it might thus moreover grow and come to good, and may it be granted success by the grace of God, into Whose divine protection for all desired welfare of the soul and body, I wish also to commend most loyally Your Princessly Grace herewith, remaining

Your Princessly Grace's
humble, obliging servant always,
Heinrich Schütz, in his own hand.
Dresden, 24 July 1655.

I have also been asked by a good friend to recommend a young person, who is an instrumentalist and who also just departed together with the Director in order to apply for a post in Lower Saxony. Whether he might now be suitable for your *Music* and necessary besides can be decided by your other musicians already appointed and by the Director arriving at the same time with him. For my part I will never advise superfluous people, but nevertheless wish humbly to have recommended him to the extent that he might first be listened to and, if there is no position vacant in the *Music*, that he might be further recommended elsewhere.

Postscript.

Dated 24 July 1655. Insofar as Your Royal Grace shall graciously recall, how you by command of your most beloved Lord Husband took me into service and commissioned me with the inspection *in absentia* of your royal *Music*, which I also hope I have quite sufficiently undertaken up to the present (not only with diligent care and trouble, but rather still with the acquisition of these two discantists and provisioning for the same, apart from the rather expensive rearing of my own from childhood), I cannot now forbear entreating Your Royal Grace most diligently too that you, according to your great discretion and at a convenient time, before the Highly Esteemed Lord, etc., will help mediate to that end, that in regard to the gracious guarantee offered me, a small written guarantee or appointment might reach my hands as well. Your Royal Grace recalls that 100 *gulden* were accorded to me, with which I am also humbly inclined to be content, also for that matter can have it happen (mindful of the old German saying, that one should in truth enjoy the favor of great lords but also let them keep their bread) that it might yet be reduced to 100 thalers, [but] just with this appended request, that it also be arranged so that the half, 50 thalers, might be paid to me at Easter, and 50 thalers again at Michaelmas, at the two Leipzig fairs during the year. The first 50 thalers might be paid at the forthcoming Michaelmas fair. In particular at present, as the Director can report on my situation, I am rather in reduced circumstances owing to the funeral expenses incurred for my last daughter who died recently in Leipzig.[183] And *Herr* Stephan Daniel, merchant in Brunswick and my good friend, who generally attends all the Leipzig fairs or markets, upon Your Serenity's gracious command, would sufficiently accede to this disbursement. I am, all told, confident of Your Royal Grace's most gracious preference in regard of this point.[184]

The copyist, who completed Your Royal Grace's small psalter for me at Weissenfels, guarantees himself of yet another recompense of 4 or 5 ducats at the next Leipzig fair.

[Sophie Elisabeth's hand, perfunctorily noted in an abbreviated fashion on the envelope]

That the Director arrived and together with the *Knaben* is still acceptable to us at the present time; that he was introduced and, indeed, as a Kapellmeister.

That regarding the *Knaben* one shall keep an eye on them, that 50 *Reichsthaler* shall be delivered to the Director. The violist [i.e., violinist], because the position here is still occupied, was not accommodated. That his [Schütz's] position could hereby be set up, it is hoped, with proper satisfaction. The copyist shall receive his due very soon.

144. SCHÜTZ'S CONTRACT AS KAPELLMEISTER IN WOLFENBÜTTEL *IN ABSENTIA* (23 AUGUST 1655)

[D-Wa: 3 Alt 461, fols. 14r–17r][185]

I, Heinrich Schütz, do hereby attest and avow, that the Serene Prince and Lord, Lord August, Duke of Brunswick and Lüneburg, my most gracious Prince and Lord, has graciously appointed and engaged me as his Senior Kapellmeister *in absentia*, also had his most gracious appointment conferred thereon, and accordingly the same follows then verbatim:

By the grace of God, we August, Duke of Brunswick and Lüneburg, before us and our Heirs one and all, attest and avow, that we have graciously appointed and engaged the highly skilled artist, our beloved loyal, Heinrich Schütz, at the present time appointed

---

183. Euphrosyne, who was married to Christoph Pincker in 1647, died in January 1655. Schütz's other daughter, Anna Justina, died in 1638.
184. In *Spagn.* (268), the full stop between "*gnädigen beförderung*" and the new sentence beginning "*Der Copist*" is omitted, which adversely affects her translation of the passage (271).
185. Transcribed in *Schütz-GBr*, Nr. 96; *Spagn.*, Nr. 26.

Kapellmeister to the Electoral Saxon Dilection in Dresden, likewise as Senior Kapellmeister *in absentia*. We also appoint, receive, and accept him in return, herewith and by virtue of this [writ], in this manner and thus: that he shall be loyal and devoted to us and our aforementioned Heirs; provide our princely Kapelle here with suitable, skilled musicians, who are well trained both in vocal as well as in instrumental music, in addition to this also and in particular with good *Kapellknaben* and basses at all times; and for this reason always correspond with our junior Kapellmeister—whom we have here at our princely court, who then next to us shall be under his senior direction and command, and whom we will not change without his prior knowledge—and when we at times on special occasions in future would require his presence and attendance, he shall thereupon arrange it to that end with His aforementioned Electoral Dilection at Dresden and disengage himself temporarily so that he shall be able to attend us here for a short time in musical matters and their senior direction; inasmuch as he shall likewise make a special solemn promise to us with a handshake thereon, instead of an oath, and bind himself by a written declaration thereupon.

For his sake and as compensation for these his efforts, we consent and promise him annually and each year separately, as long as this our appointment is not rescinded, 150 *Reichsthaler*; to have the same disbursed to him on two separate appointed dates: namely, at Michaelmas and Easter, each time in Leipzig by a bill of exchange through our current agent and merchant in our city of Brunswick, Stephan Daniel, or else through another way, in cash against a receipt; and without fail to make a start with the first semi-annual payment of 75 *Reichsthaler* this coming Michaelmas Day of this year.

We mutually reserve the right, however, if sooner or later we make a change to our appointment and no longer choose to keep him as our Senior Kapellmeister, or should he have no pleasure to serve us any longer in such a way, that thereupon one party shall intimate a firm decision to the other a quarter year beforehand. Everything without prejudice.

And in witness whereof, we have signed this letter of appointment with our own hands and had stamped with our princely seal[186] in the space below. So done in our Princely Capital and Residence Fortress, Wolfenbüttel, in the eight days of Holy Easter 1655.

I pledge accordingly herewith and by virtue of this to be loyal and devoted to His aforementioned Princely Grace; to promote His Princely Grace and his Heirs in the best possible way; to avert, prevent, and repel harm and malice to the utmost of my ability and means; above all, however, to conform obediently and dutifully to the communicated princely appointment in all words, points, and clauses, and in return shall and will be ready to attend to what incorporated therein behooves me. Without prejudice.

In verification I have signed and sealed this written declaration with my own hands. Written and delivered at Dresden, on the Vigil of St. Bartholomew, the twenty-third day of August 1655.
Heinrich Schütz,
Electoral Saxon Kapellmeister, in his own hand.

---

186. The term used in the original is *Secreti[um]*, from the medieval *sigillum secreti*.

[in a third hand]

Declaration

On His Majesty August's appointment of Heinrich Schütz, Electoral Saxon Kapellmeister in Dresden

Delivered on Holy Easter 1655

F. i.[187]

145. SOPHIE ELISABETH OF BRUNSWICK-LÜNEBURG TO SCHÜTZ (10 NOVEMBER 1655)

Draft of a letter regarding payment to Schütz and other court matters

[D-Wa: 1 Alt 25 no 294, fols. 6v–7v]

[Address]

Most Serene reply to the Electoral Saxon Kapellmeister, Heinrich Schütz

10 November 1655

J:H:H:

[Text]

Sophie Elisabeth.

Our gracious greetings first and foremost, etc.

We have learned from your recent letter of 30 October, among other things, what you should wish to address to us with regard to the continuation of your appointment, to suggest modestly in regard to the remittance of your salary, and to mention besides with regard to the Kapellmeister and the theorbist.

In gracious reply thereto, We in return give you to understand that, as far as your appointment is concerned, Our Beloved Lord and Husband, His Dilection, is graciously resolved to continue the same and to have the salary duly remitted on his behalf. However, as it will be more convenient and agreeable for His aforesaid Dilection to remit this money through his own man than in the way proposed by you, it is hoped that you shall also be in agreement with this. In the meantime you can simply deliver the items to the person who disburses the money to you and make arrangements with him to retain these items until Our Lord and Husband, His Dilection, orders him to deliver the money, and take the items from him again in exchange so they can be sent to our Kapellmeister.

---

187. *F.i.* (*fieri instituit or fieri iussit*), he had it done.

The Kapellmeister you recommended is not unbecoming to His Most Gracious Dilection and Us. Insofar as he continues in this way we are graciously satisfied with him as regards his circumstances, and do not doubt that our *Music* shall at last be brought into good order through proper diligence and supervision. You may simply send the theorbist you recommended this way, but negotiate with him beforehand regarding his maintenance as you think fit, and advise us of it as early as possible. If he wishes to pursue painting during his service, this shall not be denied him.

Wishing in grace your early reply and remaining graciously inclined toward you always.

Dated at Wolfenbüttel, 10 November 1655.

146. SCHÜTZ TO SOPHIE ELISABETH OF BRUNSWICK-LÜNEBURG (27 NOVEMBER 1655)

Letter concerning the appointment of an unidentified falsettist, theorbist, and painter, development of the musical establishment at the Wolfenbüttel Court, and outstanding payment for Schütz's service

[D-Wa: 1 Alt 25 no. 294, fols. 2r–3v][188]

[Address]

To the Serene, Noble-Born Princess and Lady, Lady Sophie Elisabeth, Duchess of Brunswick and Lüneburg, born Duchess of Mecklenburg, Princess of the Wends, Schwerin, and Ratzeburg, and Duchess of Schwerin, Lady of the Lands of Rostock and Stargard, my Gracious Princess and Lady

[Text]

Serene, Noble Princess,
Gracious Lady.

Today I safely received, with the post from eight days ago, Your Royal Grace's latest gracious missive forwarded to me, dated the twentieth of this month, and happily gathered from it that the suggestion I made in regard to the falsettist or painter was, in grace, deemed appropriate and to your liking, whereupon then I should not further conceal from Your Royal Grace how I have now engaged him with certainty in this matter, and in such a way negotiated that he pledged to me on a handshake that, if not already before Christmas, then at the future and impending New Year's fair in Leipzig at the latest, he shall set out on his way together with those merchants traveling

---

188. Fols. 2r–v are the autograph letter; fol. 3v contains Schütz's address and the brief note from Sophie Elisabeth. Transcribed in *Schütz-GBr*, Nr. 97; *Spagn.*, Nr. 28; *Schütz-Dokumente*, Nr. 172.

from there back to Brunswick and present himself most obediently at the illustrious Wolfenbüttel Court.

With regard to his pay, I indicated to him that one should expect that he would be content with the same provisioning which others receive. He has no objections to it but only this: his request would be that everything might be assessed for him in cash only, since he would very much like after all to clothe himself at his convenience and to manage his life. I do not know how high your salary might run for another now, apart from the Kapellmeister, and I imagine (indeed subject to correction) that from 150 thalers, or 3 thalers weekly, up to 200 thalers at most, will be [adequate] to negotiate and finally to settle with him. And it is to be hoped that you shall surely perceive in him a creditable person for your illustrious court, in that he shall be useful at all joyous[189] solemnities that take place. He is a rather good poet, and has exceptionally good inventions therein which he himself sets and subsequently sings to his theorbo, which then very well befits a princely table and provides a good variety amid the other music, in such a way that once more I am firmly convinced that there shall be no mistake made with the engagement and maintenance of this person, may God grant fortune upon it.

Otherwise in consideration of the second item, regarding payment of the appointment most graciously accorded to me, it has never been my intention to prescribe to Your Serenity, nor to my Most Gracious Lord, that it [i.e., the payment] might properly be made through Stephan Daniel, but rather it was only my casual suggestion in that respect, because that person, from whom this payment was commissioned by Your Serenity, has never, and as of this hour still has not, contacted me; and neither did anyone write to me [with regard to] to whom I would report on account of the receipt [of the payment] and to recommend the conveyance of my compositions to Wolfenbüttel. If I but hear of this [i.e., the court's intentions], I shall remain obediently and pleasantly content on this point, in accordance with my most humble duty.

Otherwise I was pleased to hear of the continuing good conduct of the Kapellmeister recommended by me, and I remain eager to hear further that this matter, in keeping with my good intention, of the formation of a small (in truth, not overly expansive) and rather complete Kapelle and *Music* might finally commence and that Your Princely Court [City], next to the praise of God, also obtain its glory throughout the world, inasmuch as I am then of the belief (I hope not unfounded) that the aforementioned *collegium musicum* of yours seems already to occupy an exceptional position ahead of other music establishments at other princely courts. Indeed for my part, I ascribe no particular praise to myself; since except from my advice, I have otherwise contributed little to it up to now and would like to have the Kapellmeister work with his own inventions and compositions and to have these performed. For the rest, I am as willing as obliged, not only with [the offer] of all possible sound advice from me, but rather also to assist and to submit

---

189. *Spagn.* (284) transcribes the original text as *ferneren*, read *Freuden*.

successively all musical works on hand by me and others, if only your *Music* is put on firm footing in some measure beforehand, and I shall know how I will have to adjust my aforementioned compositions.

Hereupon commending Your Royal Grace to the powerful protection of Almighty God, invoking His divine majesty graciously to grant you, together with your most highly esteemed Lord and Husband, a good close to the now waning old year, and a very happy beginning and continuation of the welcome New Year before us, and to keep and to preserve you in every princely welfare you yourself might wish for, for many long years yet to come. Amen.

Your Royal Grace's
faithful, humble old servant,
Heinrich Schütz, in his own hand.
Dresden, 27 November 1655.

I humbly beg Your Royal Grace to forgive my rudeness: namely, that on this occasion I must trouble you for this once regarding the payment to your Kapellmeister.

With the theorbist and painter I shall serve Your Royal Grace with a new humble missive again in addition to this; and should something needing attention in this area happen in advance, I shall await your gracious command.

[Sophie Elisabeth's Note]

To the falsettist, the 200 *Reichsthaler* shall be accorded once and for all as salary. Regarding the half year's money promised him, His Dilection, my Lord, proposes, that it will certainly be in Leipzig for him. It is thus much the same to him who delivers it to him, just as long as it is definitely delivered.

4

Last Years (1657–72)

147. *ZWÖLF GEISTLICHE GESÄNGE* (DRESDEN, 1657): TITLE PAGE AND CHRISTOPH KITTEL'S PREFACE

[Title page]

Zwölf
geistliche Gesänge [Twelve Sacred Songs][1]
with four voices
for small cantorates, for choir
in addition to the basso continuo to be used here at one's discretion,
which
were composed heretofore
by the Electoral Saxon Kapellmeister,
Heinrich Schütz,
in his spare time,
now brought together and with his permission
sent to press
by
Christoph Kittel,

---

1. SWV 420–31; RISM A/I/8 S 2297; *SA* 12; *NSA* 7; *SSA* 15.

appointed Organist to
the Electoral Saxon Kapelle.
Basso Continuo.
Opus 13 [*Decimum Tertium*].
Dresden, printed by Wolffgang Seyffert's Printing House,
1657.

[Preface]

Most benevolent dear Reader.

In the long time that I have spent most humbly in the service of His Electoral Serenity of Saxony etc., I have assembled various compositions by His Electoral Serenity's duly appointed Kapellmeister, Heinrich Schütz, with which I trained the Electoral *Kapellknaben* committed to my care. These twelve pieces amongst others seemed to me of such value that, with the permission of the aforementioned Author, I wanted to prepare them for publication for the glory of God and for Christian use in churches and schools, and wanted thereby to mentioned a few things:

1. This *Composition* is for full choir, and properly intended and arranged for vocal and instrumental performance without the organ.

2. Hence the basso continuo, to be used only at pleasure thereby and not out of necessity, is also attached and published together on the recommendation of the publisher; and organists, who perchance propose to join in with their organ[s], are kindly reminded to transcribe if not the entire slight work nevertheless some pieces from it (above all, however, the Mass and the Magnificat) into their customary [letter] tablature or score, and to play from it.

3. In the joyful song of St. Bernhard: *Item* in the hymn "Christe fac ut sapiam," where it is indicated first and second choir, that is not to suggest as though it were in eight parts but rather that, where adjuvants and two copies are at hand, these pieces can be heard with better effect as if *per Choros* [i.e., antiphonally]. In my opinion, the Litany is particularly well suited to this, but did I not write it out again since the distinction between the first and second choir is otherwise known well enough, and the conductor of the *Music* shall surely know, at his discretion, what to do, or for the sake of instruction, to partition one choir from the other and to indicate that underneath.[2] Farewell.

Christoph Kittel.

---

2. In the Litany, Schütz marks underneath which is Choir 1 and Choir 2.

148. ZWÖLF GEISTLICHE GESÄNGE (DRESDEN, 1657): FIRST MEMORANDUM IN THE BASSO CONTINUO PARTBOOK

Memorandum.[3]

Because the German verse of this *Jubilus* is very long and was written in fifty strophes, one should know that the author has incorporated these into ten sections, and under each section five strophes, and composed five *arias* on them. The last one of these is in *Sesquialtera*, after which then the repeat sign [*Signum Repetitionis*] has been indicated so that one might then start again from the beginning with a new section and thus continue at one's discretion. Consequently, however, and of no less importance, since performing all ten sections at once might become altogether too long, it is left to each individual to choose, at his discretion, whether to continue or to leave off, or even to extract and to perform on its own one or more sections, according to the church feasts and times.

The strophe appended at the end, "Nun sei dem Vater Dank,"[4] serves as a conclusion whenever one wishes to leave off, just as the psalms generally conclude with the Gloria.

149. ZWÖLF GEISTLICHE GESÄNGE (DRESDEN, 1657): SECOND MEMORANDUM IN THE BASSO CONTINUO PARTBOOK

Memorandum.[5]

The author in no way objects to the manner of singing the Litany practiced in our Evangelical churches up to the present, and neither does he desire to introduce change to it. Nevertheless, he has repeatedly heard with annoyance how the same [Litany] in some places, contrary to all comeliness, has been slowly and even tediously lengthened to such an extent that, in his opinion, one also loses all joy and [sense of] devotion from it. Thus has he been induced to set his hand to it and to arrange it after the manner of litanies in a fixed meter [*Mensur*], which in this belief and hope will be issued here for publication so that they can be sung now and then, if not by the congregation, then indeed by the choir and with the organ in alternation, and without great loss of time The congregation too will be able to follow, if not with its voice, nevertheless in spirit with its devotion.

---

3. This memorandum is included before Nr. 8—*Jubilus S. Bernhardi à 4*. The work is written such that Chorus 1 sings verses 1 and 3; Chorus 2 sings verses 2 and 4; and both choirs join together in verse 5, which is the *sesquialtera* section. The concluding part carries the text above it: "Teutzsch *Gloria* zum Beschluss des Jubel Gesangs oder wo man sonst schliessen will." ("German *Gloria* for the conclusion of the joyful song, or where one otherwise wishes to conclude.")
4. "Nu sey dem Vater Danck."
5. This memorandum is found just before the Litany (Nr. 9) in the basso continuo partbook.

The conductor of the *Music* will surely know what to do in regard to placement and division of the first choir from the second. Should it be considered necessary to give a beat [i.e., to direct or conduct], it can be taken from the basso continuo, which is partitioned in its *tempora*.[6]

150. SCHÜTZ'S APPRAISAL OF CONSTANTIN CHRISTIAN DEDEKIND'S *AELBIANISCHE MUSENLUST* (DRESDEN, 1657) (21 SEPTEMBER 1657)

To
Herr Constantin Christian
Dedekind,[7]
Imperial Crowned Poet,
distinguished musician of the Electoral Saxon Court,
especially much favored gentleman and worthy friend!

I have learned among other things from your letter that you, out of steadfast trust in my person, made a request, asking me to give my opinion of the *Aelbianische Musenlust*, as you have mentioned above and provisionally entitled the work at hand. I have now given due consideration to that which concerns the music and found that the melodies are not only rendered and carried out technically in accordance with the musical rules [*regulis*] and modes [*modis musicis*] but, beyond this, pleasingly in their modulations. I am therefore wholly of the opinion that the gentleman should not forbear putting this small work into print and thus making it known to the world.

Thus I remind him kindly that he should not conceal the bestowed God-given gift but rather, in the name of God, publish these arias he has composed with the poetry for professionals and amateurs from which he then shall garner nothing but honor and praise. Moreover, I wish him every good fortune and commend him to divine protection, and furthermore remain

the gentleman's dutiful [friend] always,
Heinrich Schütz,
Electoral Saxon Kapellmeister.
Weissenfels, 21 September 1657.

---

6. The partitions are indicated by vertical strokes written into the part.
7. Also translated in *Spagn*. Nr. 11. Constantin Christian Dedekind (b. 2 Apr. 1628; d. 2 Sept. 1715) was a performer, composer, and poet. He studied with Christoph Bernhard at the Dresden Court, was appointed to the court cantorate as a bass singer in 1654 and named director of the *Hofkapelle* in 1666. He resigned in 1675 amid the animosities within the *Hofkapelle* to become a tax collector, and devoted the latter part of his life to his poetry. The *Aelbianische Musenlust* of 1657, a large collection of sacred and secular solo songs with continuo accompaniment, was his most significant published musical work.

151. JOHANN JACOB LÖWE VON EISENACH TO SCHÜTZ (5 MAY 1660)

Letter petitioning Schütz to intercede with August of Brunswick-Lüneburg on Löwe's behalf

[D-Wa: 1 Alt 25 no. 294, fols. 19r–20r]

[Address]

To the Noble, Steadfast and Right Worshipful, Gifted and Ingenious *Herr* Heinrich Schütz, Highly Ordained Electoral Saxon Kapellmeister, my especially Most Venerable *Herr* Father

[Text]

Noble, Steadfast, Highly Esteemed *Herr* Father.

I could not forbear notifying you through this letter of my intention to petition my Gracious Prince and Lord for permission to travel to my family in Vienna for a quarter year, inasmuch as I must still discuss with them much in regard to my patrimony, and the paid-down and still outstanding debts since my absence. I would also like to prevail upon my mother and brother to get out of the papacy and to Dresden one day, since we are owed a lot there, or to some other suitable Protestant region.[8] In view of these considerable reasons, I have no doubt that I shall receive this [permission] from my Gracious Prince and Lord, especially with the intercession of my *Herr* Father.

Secondly, whereas His Princely Serenity as a most-learned lord devotes so much to the library as well as other arts, thus I have in mind, insofar as I am able to obtain gracious permission, to bring along and present most humbly for His Princely Serenity's library the manuscripts of letters and poetry in Latin and Greek written by my late *Herr* father's first wife, the most-learned Elisabetha Johanna Westonia (to Emperor Rudolph, and other distinguished potentates, as well as most-learned people who lived during her lifetime),[9] likewise the manuscripts of letters and poetry by distinguished most-learned people which they sent to her. Also to be brought here for His Princely Serenity to see is an ingenious painting (which is an original I inherited by the most famous, artistic painter, Michael Raphuel [Raphael], appraised at 200 *Reichsthaler*), and insofar as it

---

8. *Spagn.* (299) omits the phrase "or to some other suitable Protestant region" ("oder an ein andern guten Evangelischen Orth").
9. *Spagn.* (297) transcribes the original text as *Wertonia*, read *Westonia*. Elisabetha Johanna Westonia was born Elizabeth Jane Weston (b. 1581/82), and in 1589 taken in by her colorful stepfather, Edward Kelley (b. 1 Aug. 1545; d. ca. 1597), to the Imperial Court in Prague where he enjoyed considerable personal success as an alchemist to Emperor Rudolph II (b. 18 Jul. 1552; d. 20 Jan. 1612). Kelley was first jailed for failing to produce gold in 1591 and died probably in 1597 as a result of a botched escape, and left behind his young family in desperate straits. Elizabeth took it upon herself to write letters to anyone who might help. Although she was already fluent in five languages as a teenager, she chose to write only in Latin. Because of her beautiful neo-Latin

might then please His Princely Serenity most graciously, it can be relinquished for the amount it was appraised at in the inheritance.

Finally, I will have copied at my own expense, for use in our Kapelle, the best musical compositions written by ingenious, famous masters in Vienna. I beseech my *Herr* Father dutifully whether he might promote me for this purpose and intercede most humbly with His Princely Serenity so that I might receive in full my one and a half years' salary, which was payable in January, that I might in some measure placate my ever-pressing creditors here, and also be left with money in hand for the journey. With that I commend my *Herr* Father to the protection of the Almighty, and remain

his ever dutiful and obedient son,
Johann Jacob Löwe of Eisenach, Kapellmeister.
Wolfenbüttel, 5 May 1660.

152. SCHÜTZ TO AUGUST THE YOUNGER, DUKE OF BRUNSWICK-LÜNEBURG (10 APRIL 1661)

Letter of congratulations and presentation of music in honor of the Duke's birthday

[D-W: Cod. Guelf 376 Nov, fols. 320r–321v][10]

[Address]

To the Most Serene, Most Noble Prince and Lord, Lord August, Duke of Brunswick and Lüneburg, my Most Gracious Lord

[Text]

Most Serene, Most Noble Prince, Most Gracious Lord.

My most humble services, unsparing diligence are always at the ready for Your Princely Serenity. Inasmuch as I recently received the gratifying news of Your Princely Serenity's hitherto continuing good health, and your princely welfare in addition to this, thus today, the tenth of April, I have not only greatly rejoiced humbly at this joyous birthday which

---

poetry, she quickly gained a reputation as a writer known as *Virgo Angla* ("English Maiden"), corresponded with and was admired greatly by some of the best minds and most influential figures of the day, and published two major editions of her work during her lifetime: *Poëmata* (Frankfurt/Oder, 1602) and *Parthenica* (Prague, ca. 1606). In 1603, Elizabeth married the German advocate Johannes Leo of Eisenach (i.e., Löwe), wrote less but gave birth to seven children in the ensuing nine years, and died in 23 November 1612 at the age of 31. See Weston, *Collected Writings*.

10. The document is in Schütz's hand and still bears his wax seal. Transcribed in *Schütz-GBr*, Nr. 106; *Spagn.*, Nr. 35; *Schütz-Dokumente*, Nr. 182.

Your Princely Serenity again attained and lived to see, but rather I am also occasioned out of most indebted devotion, along with others of your loyal servants, also for my insignificant person, though absent, to appear humbly with the present written congratulations of mine. Wishing from my heart and appealing to God that His divine omnipotence may graciously preserve Your Princely Serenity (as one whose world-famous name, as a radiant light among other distinguished potentates, shines forth throughout Germany, indeed all of Europe, in princely wisdom; laudable, prudent rule; most dignified age) in constant good health and all princely well-being, further lend many long years still for the protection of the Protestant Church and glory of your princely dynasty, as well as its welfare and prosperity.

In addition to this I report most humbly to Your Princely Serenity, that by command of His Electoral Serenity of Saxony, my Most Gracious Lord, I have had to stay here in Dresden into a ninth month on account of the composition and publication of the enclosed book, of which the present two copies, together with as many basso continuo parts for the organists, are sent to Your Princely Serenity and also to have this, in truth, slight work of mine looked upon. I am reminded of my bounden duty, begging you most humbly to accept the same in grace and, at your most gracious pleasure, to have one copy of it conveyed to your dearly beloved royal consort (a princess incomparably skilled in all other royal virtues, in particular in the laudable profession of music).

Furthermore I trust that Your Princely Serenity's *collegium musicum* is still to be found in good condition, well appointed in every way as I found and left it the last time I was there, and that Your Princely Serenity in your court city can be most graciously satisfied with its most humble service. As soon as I again arrive in Weissenfels from here and to my store of musical compositions of every kind by the most distinguished authors I have there at hand, without wishing to boast, as I hope to do as soon as possible, I am duly willing to offer the same [*collegium musicum*] all additional due assistance and, with utmost industry, to contribute that which perhaps might have been omitted hitherto.

With that I most loyally commend Your Princely Serenity together with his beloved family all and one to the mighty protection of the Almighty, and further most humbly recommend me and your princely *collegium musicum* to His enduring favor and affection from this time forward, and herewith remain to the best of my ability and means,

Your Princely Serenity's
bounden, most humble,
most obedient servant,
Heinrich Schütz, in his own hand.
Dresden, tenth day of the month, April 1661.

153. *BECKER PSALTER*, SECOND EDITION (DRESDEN, 1661): TITLE PAGE AND PREFACE TO THE READER

[Title page]

Psalms of David[11]
heretofore made into German verse
by
Dr. Cornelius Becker,
and subsequently,
with eleven old, and ninety-two new melodies
by the Electoral Saxon Kapellmeister
Heinrich Schütz,
put into print however
upon most gracious command
of the Most Serene Prince and Lord,
Lord Johann Georg
the Second
Elector of Saxony and Burgrave of Magdeburg,
besides
newly revised and expanded with melodies adapted to each psalm,
according to the common contrapuntal style,
for general use at church and in schools,
set for four voices
by the aforementioned author,
H. S.
Electoral Saxon Senior Kapellmeister at present,
together with
three useful registers appended at the end.
Printed in Dresden in Wolffgang Seyffert's Printing House
by Gottfried Seyffert,
1661.

[Preface]

Affectionate Reader.

For what reasons I was previously prevailed upon, and in fact rather a long time ago now, initially to set and have published only a few little melodies to the small

---

11. SWV 97–256; RISM A/I/8 S 2284. The D-W exemplar of the work (1.2.3 Musica 2°) has written at the bottom of the title page: "Mein Eigen Exemplar Henrich Schütz Mpp." ("My personal copy, Heinrich Schütz, in his own hand").

psalm book of the late Dr. Becker, but which subsequently appeared with ninety-two new and eleven old melodies, is to be found, among other things, in the first edition, printed in octavo at Freiberg by Georg Hofmann in 1628. But because after that time this, indeed, minor work of mine became rather well known and employed in various places, and so popular that the late Serene, Noble Prince and Lord, Lord Adolph Friedrich, Duke of Mecklenburg, etc., of most blessed memory,[12] caused the same to be re-published anew and quite elegantly brought out in quarto by Johann Jäger's Heirs in Güstrow in 1640. Furthermore, the currently reigning Illustrious Elector of Saxony and Lord, Lord Johann Georg II of Saxony, etc., and my Most Gracious Lord, at the beginning of his rule a few years ago (out of his well-known zeal to magnify God's glory through a distinguished Church Music in all manner of styles, following the example of the devout kings David, Jehoshaphat, Josiah, and others) conceived the princely Christian idea and resolved to make this book known in his electorate and land, and to have it introduced into churches and schools. Hence he most graciously urged upon me to look over the same once more and to improve upon it according to my judgment. Thus, in duty-bound acceptance of this most gracious command, I have obediently declared myself not only for the diligent revision of this early work of mine but rather, beyond that in the meantime, that I would take pains to provide individual melodies for all the remaining psalms, and those as well which might not yet have been vested with their own.

I succeeded to the extent of the talent bestowed upon me by God, as this present work will demonstrate, for which I for my part do not yearn for my own fame but rather would treasure it as my greatest pleasure if this work of mine might come into active use for the spreading of the glory and praise of our great and gracious God in heaven, in indebted gratitude for bestowing His daily and present grace and mercy upon our souls and bodies. Should ever there be anything found in this work that might be agreeable and endearing to one person or another, it is not to be attributed to my ability but rather to His Electoral Serenity's Christian direction and most gracious command alone, which occasioned me to this and prompted devoted, duty-bound obedience. Otherwise, to be quite honest, I would have rather preferred to spend the remainder of my brief life with revision and completion of various other and more artful *Inventions* started by me before this. I cannot pass over with silence, however, that after this work was already completed with all the melodies by me, I was given to understand, and in part have seen it in print and read it myself, how the poetry of this book has been engaged and assaulted to a considerable degree by some modern or present-day poets as being contrary in many places to the principles of this art, which then, truth be told, rather perplexed me and prohibited or held

---

12. In 1657, Adolph Friedrich I, Duke of Mecklenburg-Schwerin (b. 15 Dec. 1588; d. 27 Feb. 1658) married his daughter, Anna Maria (b. 1 Jul. 1627; d. 11 Dec. 1669), to August, Duke of Saxe-Weissenfels (b. 13 Aug. 1614; d. 4 Aug. 1680), the son of Elector Johann Georg I. Adolph Friedrich was a member of the literary society, the Fruchtbringende Gesellschaft, where he was known as *der Herrliche* ("the Magnificent").

back the release of this book for some time—until I was finally apprised by distinguished and prudent people that in suchlike church songs, our thoughts in this way would be held enraptured in a steadfast devotion not so much by the artful poetic constructions as by a spiritual paraphrase or exposition; and that if we did not pay such close attention to the poetry, if the text were not inconsistent with a proper German idiom, as with a rigid poetry [*Poesie*] in which the good German idioms would be repeatedly ignored, we could better allow ourselves to take pleasure in the singing.

Because this author or poet [i.e., Becker] has already obtained a singular praise in most evangelical churches in this case and, in truth, primarily, in that he would have his interpretation focused on our One Savior and Redeemer, Jesus Christ (to whom all the prophets and apostles, and indeed the entire Holy Scripture itself alluded), with total devotion and diligence. In addition to this, his psalms are well known everywhere besides, published in diverse formats, and would be in nearly everyone's hands and in use. Thus should I by no means be turned away from my intention but rather proceed with the composition of this work without further hesitation, in compliance with electoral direction. I was thereby moved to answer duly to the affecting counsel given to me, and to apply my hand once again, for a time withdrawn from it for the aforesaid reasons. To this I was also further encouraged, for I was at the same time reminded that these melodies of mine in all cases might equally be used quite nicely when set to other of today's (praise God) elevated German and Latin poetry and songs written in a similar poetic genre [*Genere Poeseos*] to these psalms, according to one's preference for one or the other.

This then is left to reside with the occasion. May the true God, in these afflicted times of late, let His holy, pure, true Word flourish, in the churches, the schools, and with each father in his home, as through pure, devout teachings, as also through spiritual and consolatory songs and psalms, until the longed-for future of His beloved son, our Savior and Redeemer, that we might await Him in love, patience and joyous hope, and be found always ready for that time. Amen.

AUTHOR.

154. *BECKER PSALTER*, SECOND EDITION (DRESDEN, 1661): SCHÜTZ'S REMARKS IN THE BASSO CONTINUO PARTBOOK

[D-W: 2.6.6. Musica][13]

For the organists,
on the melodies of
Dr. Becker's blessed psalms,

---

13. RISM A/I/8 S 2284a; *SA* 16–17; *NSA* 6. D-W possess the only extant print of this partbook. The part is printed economically in quarto format, with the verso of the title page used for Schütz's memorandum.

newly revised and enlarged
for four voices [*Quatuor Vocum*],
recently published in folio
in Dresden
by
Heinrich Schütz,
Senior Kapellmeister to
the Electoral Serenity of Saxony, etc.
Printed at Dresden by Wolfgang Seyffert, 1661.

To the Benevolent Reader.

In consequence of the diverse reports on my setting of melodies to the psalmbook of the late Dr. Becker, recently issued in Dresden in folio format, I have prepared for the organists a basso continuo which should appear at the same time. Thus it is with good intentions that I wanted thereby to issue a brief memorandum how I, in my humble estimation, have set these arias to the musical modes [*Modos Musicos*] and, indeed, most of them in their customary systems [*Systemate*] (the transpositions of which, with few exceptions, the learned musician [*musicus*] shall indeed recognize). Because, as we know, these modes must oftentimes be transposed for the sake of greater convenience for the cantorates, I have in the composition of this present continuo maintained such an order, and at the outset in fact shown each psalm in its system [*Systemate*] as it is found and indicated in the printed psalmbook, and subsequently one and another transposition indicated underneath.[14]

Whether or not this in truth seems a simple task and trifling thing, I am of the opinion nonetheless that today's thriving and very widely practiced displacement of the ancient modes out of their natural chord [structure] (namely, the alteration of ♭ minor [*moll*] into the ♯ or ♭ major [*dur*], and *vice versa*) may be seen to a considerable extent from these indicated transpositions of mine (out of which ancient mode the same [transposition] originates and with which formal cadences [*Clausulis formalibus*] these compositions are placed) and similar transpositions, and still more, may be easily created via other chords,[15] because I wanted to invoke here only that type which in performance of this work in one or the other place might not cause difficulty. May the benevolent

---

14. The print includes incipits of the bass lines in their transposed form, apparently to give inexperienced organists a start. Some of the more harmonically complicated are aimed specifically at more seasoned players. A transposition of Psalm 22: "Mein Gott, Mein Gott, Ach Herr," filled with sevenths, sixths, appoggiaturas, and suspensions, is labeled *a secundam inferiorem pro expertis*. Common descriptions might include *Ad 4 tam inferior. vel ad Tertiam inferiorem pro Exercitatis*, whereas upward transpositions are rare and never more than a second higher.

15. For an introductory discussion of transposition and tuning between keyboard instruments and voice, see Braun, *Deutsche Musiktheorie des 15. bis 17. Jahrhunderts: Zweiter Teil von Calvisius bis Mattheson*, 149–63.

reader look favorably upon this humble memorandum (to which I was occasioned mainly for the sake of filling up this small page) and farewell.

Author.

155. *BECKER PSALTER*, SECOND EDITION (DRESDEN, 1661): SCHÜTZ'S AFTERWORD TO ORGANISTS IN THE BASSO CONTINUO PARTBOOK

In conclusion:[16]

Young, beginning organists, who are inexperienced in transposing the basso continuo *ex tempore* from one key into another, are hereby reminded that they may prefer to take the added transpositions here for one and the other psalms, and to transcribe them into notes or into their [letter] tablature, into the same keys from which they intend to play (and best suits their choir or the congregation).

These transpositions for performances of this slight work (especially in those heavily figured systems) are oftentimes not only highly necessary but also convenient for the voices of the singers, and all the more pleasant for the ear. It was not necessary, however, to include each and every instance particular [*in specie*] to this print, considering that even moderately experienced organists will be able on their own to transpose and render these short and simple *continuos* from one key into another without difficulty.

156. SCHÜTZ'S RECEIPT FOR PAYMENT FROM THE WOLFENBÜTTEL COURT (21 MAY 1663)

[D-Wa: 1 Alt 25 Nr. 294, fol. 22r–v][17]

Deed of this my hand: that, by most gracious command of the Most Serene Prince and Lord, Lord August, Duke of Brunswick and Lüneburg, etc., 300 thalers were reimbursed and paid to me, the undersigned, on this date by *Herr* Stephan Daniel, distinguished merchant of Brunswick, in addition to most humble gratitude, is herewith acknowledged and thereupon duly receipted. Signed [at] Teplitz,[18] in the warm baths there, 21 May 1663.

Heinrich Schütz, in his own hand.

---

16. RISM A/I/8 S 2284a; *SA* 16–17; *NSA* 6.
17. The document is in Schütz's hand. Transcribed in *Schütz-GBr*, Nr. 107; *Spagn.*, Nr. 36; *Schütz-Dokumente*, Nr. 185.
18. Now Teplice, Czech Republic, a well-known spa or health resort approximately 70 km south of Dresden.

[On the verso, in a second hand]

Receipt of 300-thaler stipend of the Senior Kapellmeister *in absentia*, Heinrich Schütz. 21 May 1663.

157. SCHÜTZ TO THE ZEITZ COURT (14 JULY 1663)

Memorandum regarding musical improvements at the ducal court in Zeitz

[D-Dla: Loc. 8592/1 Acta / die an Herzog Moritz / zu Sachsen-Zeitz Durchl: von Anno 1663 / biss 1669. von fürstl: und anderen Personen / eingelaufenen, und wieder beantwortete Schreiben betr:, fol. 9r–v][19]

Most humble memorandum regarding the establishment
of the Court *Music* of His Princely Serenity,[20] Lord Moritz, Duke
of Saxony in the Residence City of Zeitz.[21]

1.

Regarding the two Merseburg *Kapellknaben* which apparently now reside with the former Cantor at Naumburg.[22]

Insofar as recently, already three weeks ago, I had His Serenity's Lord Superintendent of the Revenue contacted in writing in that regard, it would now be my well-considered most humble petition still that these two *Knaben* might be sent to me immediately and not begrudge the minor travel expenses and 1 thaler weekly for the provisioning of each, including tuition, seeing that the aforesaid *Knaben* should be among the Electoral [*Knaben*] as well as the other two discantists on hand who arrived previously, and could be brought to greater accomplishment [*perfection*] in two months here, it is hoped, than might scarcely happen down there [i.e., Zeitz] in four. All four could thus become

---

19. The document is in Schütz's hand. Transcribed in *Schütz-GBr*, Nr. 108; *Spagn.*, Nr. 41; *Schütz-Dokumente*, Nr. 186; *Spagn.*, 329–31.
20. *Spagn.* (332) translates the text as *Your Most Serene Highness*, and continues as though Schütz's memorandum were addressed directly to Duke Moritz. The memorandum is in fact not addressed to Moritz himself, but rather to an unnamed person intended to communicate the information to the Duke. The original text is *Ihrer* (not *Eurer*) *Hochfürstl Durchl*. The possessive pronoun *Ihrer* refers to the dative case of the feminine *die Durchlaucht* (i.e., *His Serenity*). Moreover, it would have been a complete breach of courtly etiquette for Schütz to write to the Saxon duke in such a perfunctory manner as this. *Schütz-Dokumente*, Nr 186 (409–12) also incorrectly claims that the memorandum is addressed directly to Duke Moritz.
21. The town of Zeitz, where Johann Georg I chose to establish a court for his son Moritz, lies some 43 km southwest of Leipzig.
22. Moritz brought Heinrich Gottfried Kühnel (d. 1684) from Naumburg when the Zeitz court was established. See Werner, *Städtische und fürstliche Musikpflege in Zeitz bis zum Anfang des 19. Jahrhunderts*, 82.

properly accustomed to each other here,[23] be provided with appropriate pieces, and hereafter be called upon and conveyed together with each other back from here, along with the Alto. Moreover, I also have in mind herewith: if I had these four discantists together here in order to see whether all of them are equally capable, perhaps a few substitutions with others who are present here might be variously tried and tested. And inasmuch as neglect of these four discantists constitutes the greatest part of the decline of a *collegium musicum*, thus the appropriate support and education of them will be attended to foremost and with utmost diligence, in which I for my part will indeed let nothing slide. It shall nevertheless prove arduous enough to bring the discant voice to the desired level of perfection.

2.

Regarding the new positif proposed by me for use instead of the organ, both in the church as well as at court:

That the completion of which might be most graciously and earnestly urged upon the organ builder by His Princely Serenity, inasmuch as this small work [i.e., instrument] must be employed as the foundation for all and sundry *Music* [making], and hence the organ builder, in the current manufacture of the large organ there, should build it [i.e., the portative] at the same time. I sent to the Kapellmeister beforehand the written notice regarding the keyboard, likewise [*item*] the stops, and convenience of transporting it in two pieces, in accordance with which the organ builder then [should] act, since this notice was written down in such a way upon sound consideration and advice. And insofar as the aforesaid organ builder can take the loud set of pipes from the *Brustwerk* (as they call it) out of the old organ, and then re-sell the same to his good advantage in another parish church, I just cannot see that he will be able to set a high price on this new positif, especially since not more than four stops should be built into it (more than which are unnecessary for a complete *Musick* [*sic*]).

Postscript regarding this second point.

Because I received the news with today's post, however, as if the organ builder had brought the previously negotiated positif already finished to Zeitz, one might leave off with the new one for a while, and for a time make do with the one brought along by the organ builder. The organ builder shall undoubtedly prefer this to starting the new one mentioned by me, which would prove difficult for him to install on account of some additional large pipes, though it would serve the music to far better effect, as his unfinished instrument is unable to do.

---

23. *Spagn.* (332) wrongly translates *zusammengewöhnen* as *to live together* rather than *to become accustomed to each other*.

3.

Regarding several new, required instruments currently being made here.

1. A bass viol [*Bassgeige*] to be used variously with the violas da gamba [*violen di gamba*] and otherwise in service at table as well, together with the case [*futral*],[24] at a cost of 16 thalers.

2. The large *violone*, which on good advice and with all possible thrift, except for the case still required for transporting it, was purchased and ordered by me for 24 thalers.

What the cost will be for the case required for it, together with the lock clasp, remains to be seen.

3. A spinet suitable for choir[25] was also re-ordered in Meissen in place of the previous one which was taken away by someone. I still do not know the price of it but believe that it, together with the case, should not run over 12, 13, or 14 thalers.[26]

4.

Regarding arrangements of additional monetary resources.

I also report that 50 thalers were indeed remitted to me by the Superintendent of the Revenue at the past Easter fair for the provisioning here of the two discantists and of the Alto. But because this sum for the aforementioned three persons is completely gone but for a paltry amount remaining, that is, since I duly pay the Alto 2 thalers weekly, beginning last Jubilate,[27] and likewise the 2 thalers weekly for the two *Kapellknaben* beginning at Easter, there is nothing left for their continued provisioning, nor for the payment of the ordered instruments (toward which I, from the little I possess, had to give something in the meantime to the master-builders at their urgent request). Hence I request in addition most humbly still for most gracious assistance and a similar new arrangement, together with my steadfast assurance that I shall use this money not other than with all possible thrift within the specified areas, shall keep a true account of it, and be prepared at any time to render it humbly before the Lord Superintendent of the Treasury.

Dated at Dresden, 14 July 1663.

---

24. *Spagn.* (333) transcribes the original text as *positif*, read *futral*.
25. *Spagn.* (334) translates "eine chormässige spinetta" as "a spinet tuned at normal pitch."
26. This is incorrectly translated by *Spagn.* (334) as "I still do not know the price of it but believe it to be comparable to that of the positif which should not exceed 12, 13, or 14 thalers."
27. Jubilate Sunday is the third Sunday after Easter. The other Sundays leading up to Pentecost are Quasimodogeniti, Misericordias Domini, Jubilate, Cantate, Rogate, and Exaudi.

158. SCHÜTZ TO MORITZ, DUKE OF SAXE-ZEITZ (29 SEPTEMBER 1663)

Memorandum concerning the proposed installation of the choir lofts in the palace church in Zeitz

[D-Dla: Loc. 8592/1 Acta die an Herzog Moritz zu Sachsen-Zeitz 1663–1669 von fürstlichen und anderen Personen eingelaufenen und wieder beantworteten Schreiben, fol. 33r–v][28]

[*Address*]

Most humble Memorandum to the Most Serene Prince and Lord, Lord Moritz, Duke of Saxony, my Most Gracious Lord

[*Text*]

Most Serene Prince, Most Gracious Lord.

Inasmuch it has reached my ears that the two newly built music lofts in Your Princely Serenity's palace church have not turned out as they should, certainly to my thinking, but that the musicians, because of the front columns, are hidden behind them and do not come properly into view when standing facing outwards, I therefore cannot conclude otherwise than that the resonance shall also flow forth all the less properly into the church to impart an agreeable effect. I am therefore occasioned (should we have the honor of this loft construction at all and want it used properly) to mention hereby most humbly and most diligently, may it most graciously please Your Princely Serenity, to consult yet with the architect in good time as to what extent these two lofts with ornate carpentry[29] and cabinet-work could perhaps be shifted out another one and a half *ells*[30] (as far as it might be done so that they would not need columns underneath) facing outwards into the church, in which way then, and no other, these lofts in my opinion would first attain to their perfection and proper praise, which I however ultimately submit most humbly to Your Princely Serenity's own most gracious resolution. Initially it was my suggestion that these two lofts should be set at the front on the two church pillars opposite each other, but ultimately I had to defer to the opinion of the architect.[31]

---

28. The document is in Schütz's hand. Transcribed in *Schütz-GBr*, Nr. 109; *Spagn.*, Nr. 43; *Schütz-Dokumente*, Nr. 188.
29. *Spagn.* (341) translates this as "with an ornate room and cabinet work." "Mit einer zierlichen Zimmer und Tischlerarbeit" follows a common form of abbreviation meaning "Zimmer[arbeit] und Tischlerarbeit."
30. *Ell* is one of several historical units of measurement. The German measurement *Ellenmass* is equated to the *mensura cubitalis*, roughly the distance between the elbow and the tip of the middle finger, which is approximately two-thirds of a meter. The term derives from Old High German *elina*, based on the Latin *ulna*.
31. It is difficult to imagine how this construction would not have taken up a very large part of the church in view of the location of the large structural columns referred to by Schütz.

And under these present conditions I consider the extent to which the organ builder shall correctly mount the present large organ in the one loft so that it properly catches one's eye in the church. However, I shall hope nevertheless that sound advice and prudence shall prevail herein. May Your Princely Serenity most graciously forgive me if I perhaps annoy you in this way out of excessive care. I remain your

most humble, obliging, loyal servant always,

Heinrich Schütz, in his own hand.

Dresden, on St. Michael's Day [29 September] 1663.

In connection to the shifting out of the aforesaid two lofts, they could also be decorated with ornate column-work similar to the musical choir over the altar in Dresden.[32]

159. CATALOG OF SCHÜTZ'S PUBLISHED WORKS SENT TO WOLFENBÜTTEL (UNDATED, PROBABLY SEPTEMBER 1663)

[D-W: Cod. Guelf 54 Extrav., fols. 225r–226v][33]

Index of my published musical works.

It is to be noted that whatever has been marked * has been sent to Wolfenbüttel

Opus 1*

Madrigals for five voices. Printed in Venice, 1611.

Opus 2

German Psalms, Motets and Concertos for eight and more voices, Part One. In folio. Printed in Dresden, 1619.

Opus 3

Historia of the Resurrection of the Lord. In German. Printed in Dresden, 1619.

Opus 4

Cantiones sacrae for four voices. Printed in Freiberg, 1625.

Opus 5

Dr. Becker's Little Book of Psalms. Printed in Freiberg, 1628.

Opus 6

Symphoniae sacrae, Part One, for 3, 4, 5, and 6 voices. Printed in Venice, 1629.

---

32. Ornamental palm trees on the sides of the two organs resemble the four large palms seen on other either side of the altar, seemingly projecting right through the balustrade. On either side of the altar are two large angels bearing festoons—one of wheat (bread), the other grapes (wine). Above these are more, smaller angels, two per side. Two draw attention to the crown and monogram of Duke Moritz, and the two on the other side similarly adorn the crown and monogram of the Duke's consort, Dorothea Maria of Saxe-Weimar (b. 11 Oct. 1641; d. 11 Jun. 1675).

33. In the hand of a copyist, edited by Schütz. Transcribed in *Spagn.*, Nr. 39; *Schütz-Dokumente*, Nr. 187.

Opus 7.

Musicalische Exequien. Printed in Freiberg, 1636.[34]

Opus 8.

[Kleine] geistliche Concerte, Part One, for 2, 3, 4, and 5 voices. Printed in Leipzig, 1636.

Opus 9.

[Kleine] geistliche Concerte, Part Two, for 1, 2, 3, 4, and 5 voices. Printed in Dresden, 1639.

Opus 10.

Symphoniae sacrae, Part Two, for 3, 4, and 5 voices. Printed in Dresden, 1647.

Opus 11.

Musicalia ad Chorum Sacrum or *Geistliche Chor-Music*, for 5, 6, and 7 voices. Printed in Dresden, 1648.

Opus 12.

Symphoniae sacrae, Part Three, for 5, 6, 7, and 8 voices. Printed in Dresden, 1650.

Opus 13.

Zwölf geistliche Gesänge for four voices. Published by *Herr* Christoph Kittel, Court Organist at Dresden, 1657.

Opus 14.

The revised and augmented arias on Dr. Becker's psalmbook. In folio, Dresden, 1661.

[the following in Schütz's hand]

Thus the still missing works are as follows:

Opus 2.

The large-scale Psalms and Concertos in folio, which I have diligently tried to obtain, and which shall be sent immediately.

Opus 3, the *Historia der Auferstehung Jesu Christi.*

Not a single copy of this is available, and the same, upon most gracious request, shall be copied out, improved, and sent.

Opus 5.

Dr. Becker's songbook in octavo.

Since this work has again been published for the second time in a revised and improved folio [edition] in 1661, it has been considered unnecessary to send this book.

Opus 14.

The newly revised and augmented arias or melodies on Dr. Becker's psalmbook in folio just mentioned, which, since they could not now be bound and made ready in such haste, though they are in preparation nevertheless, shall still be sent as quickly as possible.

Catalog of the published musical works of Kapellmeister Schütz.

---

34. It was actually printed in Dresden.

160. SCHÜTZ TO AUGUST OF BRUNSWICK-LÜNEBURG
(10 JANUARY 1664)

Letter regarding the delivery of his music to the Wolfenbüttel Court and his apology for its late arrival

[D-W: Cod. Guelf 376 Nov., fols. 322r–323v][35]

[Address]

To the Most Serene, Most Noble Prince and Lord, Lord August, Duke of Brunswick and Lüneburg, my Most Gracious Prince and Lord

[Text]

Most Serene Prince, Gracious Lord.

In consideration of the many and great princely kindnesses I have received from Your Princely Serenity hitherto, I am duly ashamed that until now I was so long delayed and negligent in submitting the most graciously requested published musical works of mine. However, I beg your most gracious forgiveness for my negligence and delay, and hence hope, as I have not be able earlier to gain access to these my printed compositions and to assemble these copies, after my return to Weissenfels from Dresden three weeks ago.

These works of mine now, however, as many of them as I could procure up to this time, shall have been safely delivered by Stephan Daniel (a well-known merchant from Brunswick, to whom I myself personally delivered the same along with an included catalog here at the present fair [i.e., Leipzig]) to Your Princely Serenity's court clerk hereby, it is hoped, and thus the same shall know then to appear with it according to Your Princely Serenity's most gracious ordinance.

And above all I offer Your Princely Serenity most humble, most profound gratitude that you intend most graciously to show this slight work of mine the honor and great favor most graciously to allow it yet a small space in your princely library, supremely famous throughout all Europe. In consequence I then had occasion to wish that, at the same time, I also could have sent along my residual works in my possession, copied by hand and (in my opinion) better than the foregoing elaborated work. This also could well have succeeded and I would have proceeded with the publication of the same had I not been without a publisher for it; and indeed according to my previously laid plan, I could have employed to that end Your Princely Serenity's stipend or annuity most graciously remitted to me previously, but up to now, owing to my meager income here, I must for the most part draw from it and use it for my own necessary sustenance and deliverance (where otherwise, from time to time, I live from hand to mouth and eke out a poor existence).

---

[35]. The document is in Schütz's hand. Transcribed in *Schütz-GBr*, Nr. 110; *Spagn.*, Nr. 38; *Schütz-Dokumente*, Nr. 189.

In this my most humble remembrance then, on account of so many great and princely kindnesses received by me from Your Princely Serenity up to the present, I declare myself bound all the more to you and your entire princely house, and as most humble requital offer myself most obediently herewith as much as I am able, above all to the continuing assistance to your princely estimable Court *Music*, should I still be considered qualified in future to do so.

With this I close, most loyally commending Your Princely Serenity to the powerful protection of Almighty God, for another freshly arrived blessed New Year, for constant good health and for the continuation and preservation of your life still for many long years, as well as all other princely welfare you desire for soul and body, and remaining

Your Princely Serenity's
most humble, most obedient,
and dutiful servant,
Heinrich Schütz, in his own hand.
Dated at Leipzig, 10 January 1664.

161. *HISTORIA VON DER GEBURT JESU CHRISTI* (DRESDEN, 1664): TITLE PAGE AND MEMORANDUM TO THE READER

[Title page]

Historia
of the joyful and blessed
birth of God's and
Mary's son,
Jesus Christ
our sole Mediator, Redeemer,
and Savior,[36]
as this,
upon most gracious command of His Electoral Highness
of Saxony, etc.,
Lord Johann Georg the Second,
is set vocally and instrumentally to music
by
Heinrich Schütz, Most Senior Kapellmeister
to the Electoral Highness of
Saxony, etc.

---

36. SWV 435; RISM A/I/8 S 2299; *SA* 17; *NSA* 1.

Printed in Dresden by Wolfgang Seyffert, 1664, and available there through Alexander Hering, Organist, as well as in Leipzig from the Cantor there.[37]

Brief memorandum informing the benevolent reader, to whom this print might come:

[1] That the complete work has been arranged by the author for two distinct choirs: namely, the choir of the Evangelist, and the choir of the concertists with the organ [accompaniment]. The choir of the Evangelist is comprised of three prints included here: one is intended for the vocal part, the second for the organ, and the third for the Bass *Geige* or *violone*. And the prudent director will know to select and employ for the Evangelist part a good, clear tenor voice, by whom the text might be sung only in accordance with the measure of a comprehensible speech (without giving a beat with the hand). And the author leaves it otherwise to prudent musicians to judge freely from it to what extent he has succeeded or failed in this novel [manner of] composition for the Evangelist in the recitative style [*stylo recitativo*], to his knowledge never seen in print in Germany before now, both as regards the melody [*Modulation*] above the text and the measure [*Mensur*]. It can still be mentioned hereby: should one prefer to make use of the old *choraliter* speaking style (in which the evangelists in the Passion as well as other sacred stories have customarily sung without organ up to now in our churches), this setting of his hopefully would not stray too far from the mark were he to continue in the following manner and proceed up to the end.

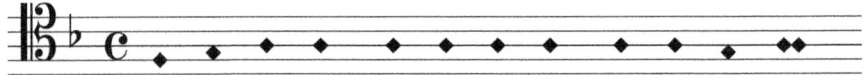

Es be-gab sich   a - ber zu der - sel - bi - gen Zeit,

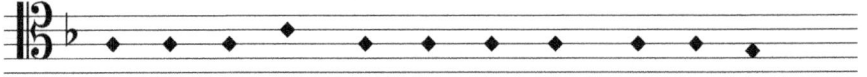

daß ein Ge-both   von dem Key - ser   Au - gu - sto etc.

With regard to the second concertizing choir with the organ [accompaniment], it encompasses ten *concertos* belonging to this drama [*Action*], the disposition of which can be gathered from the following specification. In particular, however, it is not to be passed by without comment that the author had misgivings about issuing the same [concertos] in

---

37. Sebastian Knüpfer (b. 6 Sept. 1644; d. 10 Oct. 1676) received his early musical training in Regensburg and took up residence in Leipzig in 1654. Though he lacked a university education, he was esteemed for his intellectual and scholarly interests as well as for his musical ability. Knüpfer succeeded Tobias Michael as Thomaskantor in 1657, which position he held for the rest of his life.

print, since he understands that, outside of princely well-appointed *Kapellen*, these inventions of his would scarcely achieve their proper effect elsewhere. It is left to each, however, may it perhaps please him to acquire a copy of the same, to contact either the Cantor in Leipzig [i.e., Sebastian Knüpfer] or else Alexander Hering,[38] Organist at the Kreuzkirche in Dresden where, for a small fee, these could be obtained with the permission of the author, together with the three copies for the choir of the Evangelist. Also on this account, he leaves it to the discretion of those, who might be inclined to use this evangelist [choir] of his for themselves, to compose these ten concertos (the texts of which are also to be found together with these prints) entirely anew in the manner preferred by them and for the available musical body [*corpus musicum*], or to have them composed by others. Finally this as a precaution: only on account of troublesome and extensive piracy would he have had rather few copies of this choir of the Evangelist put into print and furthermore withheld the same.

Detailed specifications of the ten concertos with organ, arranged by the author for this story.

The *Introduction* or preamble: "Die Geburt unsers Herren Jesu Christi, wie uns etc." à 9 in two large choirs, the one for four singing voices, and the other for five instrumental voices.

Intermedium 1. The Angel to the Shepherds in the Field: "Fürchtet euch nicht." A solo discant voice with two *violetten* [violins] and one *violone*. In the midst of which the Christ Child's cradle is introduced occasionally.

Intermedium 2. The Heavenly Host: "Ehre sey Gott." From eight [voices]. Six singing voices, two violins, with a complement of viols, according to taste [*ad libitum*].

Intermedium 3. The Shepherds: "Lasset uns nun gehen." Three alto voices, two recorders, and a bassoon.

Intermedium 4. The Magi: "Wo ist der neu geborne." Three tenor voices, two violins and a bassoon.

Intermedium 5. The High Priests: "Zu Bethlehem." Four bass voices and two trombones.

Intermedium 6. Herod: "Ziehet hin und forschet." A solo bass voice, two *clarini* or cornetti.

Intermedium 7. The Angel to Joseph: "Stehe auf." One discant voice, two viols, as above [*ut supra*] the cradle [music].

---

38. On the recommendation of Schütz, whose pupil he had been, Alexander Hering became organist at the Petrikirche in Bautzen on 25 April 1647. He resigned already on 31 August 1648 in order to go to Thuringia. In 1650, he was organist at the Dresden Kreuzkirche and joined together with Johann Klemm (*Schütz-GBr*, 111) to get into publishing. Hering was also one of the teachers of Johann Kuhnau, who was succeeded by J. S. Bach as Thomakantor in Leipzig in 1723. Hering died 16 December 1695. Additional information on Hering's activities can be found in Biehle, *Musikgeschichte von Bautzen bis zum Anfang des 19. Jahrhunderts*, 23–24.

Intermedium 8. The Angel to Joseph in Egypt: "Stehe auf Joseph." One discant voice, three viols. Cradle [music]

The *Conclusion*, in the disposition of the *Introduction*.

162. SCHÜTZ DIRECTED TO JOHANN GEORG II (3 MAY 1666)

Memorandum regarding outstanding payment of fees

[D-Dla: Loc. 7287/3, Einzelne Schriften, Kammersachen, insonderheit Besoldungsrückstände der Civil-, Militair und Hofdiener v. Bitten um deren Verabfolgung (new title page has "Verabschiedung") 1592–1677, fols. 218v and 219r][39]

Regarding the previously registered [matter of] my pay, hitherto in arrears, I cannot forebear most humbly calling to mind the fact that His Electoral Serenity, already three years ago, on 27 March 1663, had a most gracious command issued to the then President of the Treasury, the late Lord von Haugwitz,[40] that he would execute the ordinance, and in regard to this note see to the bookkeeper's settling of accounts with me, and should compensate and pay to me the remainder that might be found. At that time, however, owing to his many extraordinary duties, this was deferred so long by the aforesaid Lord von Haugwitz until finally he resigned this position, and thus this claim remains at present unpaid.

Whether now it might as yet most graciously please His Electoral Serenity to renew, through an additional command to the bookkeeper, the favor once granted to me, [this petition] is submitted most obediently for your most gracious consideration and pleasure.

Heinrich Schütz, in his own hand.
Dresden, 3 May 1666.

	50. T.—"—" Reminscere [Second week of Lent]
1660	50. T.—"—" Trinitatis [Trinity]
	50. T.—"—" Crucis [Feast of the Cross, 14 September]
	50. T.—"—" Luciae [Feast of St. Lucy, 13 December]
	50. T.—"—" Reminscere
1661	50. T.—"—" Trinitatis
	50. T.—"—" Crucis
	50. T.—"—" Luciae

---

39. The document is in a copyist's hand, dated and signed by Schütz. Transcribed in *Schütz-GBr*, Nr. 113; *Spagn.*, Nr. 16; *Schütz-Dokumente*, Nr. 193.

40. Johann Adolf von Haugwitz (b. 1607; d. 1666) was a senior member of the Upper Lusatian nobility and, at the time of his death, president of the Electoral Saxon Treasury. *NDB* 8, 93.

1662	50. T.—"—" Reminscere
	50. T.—"—" Trinitatis
	50. T.—"—" Crucis
	50. T.—"—" Luciae
1663	50. T.—"—" Reminscere
	50. T.—"—" Trinitatis

Signed at Dresden, 24 October 1663.
Tobias Berger
agrees with the original.[41]
Georg Eysoldt,[42] Notary Public,
Imperial and Electoral Saxon Prothonotary of the High Council, with the guarantee of the undersigned.[43]

163. SCHÜTZ TO THE SUPERINTENDENT AT ZEITZ (AFTER 1667)

Memorandum regarding compositions to be sent for use in the court and church at Zeitz

[D-WERa: MD, Rep. A 29d, I Nr. 19, fols. 22r–23r][44]

To His Honorable, Lord Superintendent in Zeitz, regarding my appended dutiful memorandum.

1.

That I should once again be willing, in accordance with His Princely Serenity's previous most gracious wishes, to contribute freely each and every one of my, in truth, modest musical works that might be considered suitable there for use by His Princely Court *Music*, and to forward them little by little. But as I have hitherto forwarded rather many divers compositions, about which my servant could give account, but which for the most part have gone missing, I should be displeased were the same not kept in secure custody by someone

---

41. *Concordat cum Originali.*
42. Written as *Georgius Eÿsoldus* in the document.
43. *Protosynedrii Protonotarius in fidem subscrpp.*
44. This document, in Schütz's hand, is undated and the intended recipient unnamed. If it was written after 1667, as proposed in *Schütz-GBr* (318), then the recipient must have been the poet and theologian, Johann Sebastian Mitternacht (b. 30 Mar. 1613; d. 25 Jul. 1679), who was appointed Senior Court Chaplain and Superintendent following the death of Philipp Saltzmann in November of that year. See *ADB* 22, 34. Also see Wollny, "A Source Complex in the Düben Collection," 173–91. Wollny (183) refers to *Schütz-GBr*, Nr. 56 (157–59), whereas the *Schütz-GBr* transcription of the document is in fact Nr. 115 (292–95). Transcribed in *Schütz-Dokumente*, Nr. 195.

for the Princely Kapelle.[45] Thus would I be induced hereby to take the liberty and to hear from you, for which discourtesy you will kindly forgive me, whether you might not do the singular honor in respect of the aforementioned work of mine, which I would send in stages, and receive them from me at first, and after that to commit them into the care of one of your musicians, and of the *Concertmeister* [sic] in particular,[46] if he would have them for use by the Princely Kapelle. I would then, God willing, be inclined to forward a double index divided into separate categories of that [work] which was already forwarded or might yet follow—the one [index] for the Lord Superintendent, the other for him into whose care these *concertos* would be committed. This is not only for the sake of showing my most humble indebtedness, but rather as well so that these compositions (should something of value be found in them) might remain safely and securely with the Princely Kapelle.

I have sent along with my servant a note regarding the various categories into which I shall arrange this index, and subsequently where each *concerto* or composition might possibly be entered into its [proper] place.

2.

Inasmuch as His Princely Serenity also intends most graciously to have the Becker psalms with my melodies introduced and circulated in his palace church (considering this also occurs in Dresden, Halle, and Merseburg) in particular for use in the weekly sermon services, I have obtained several exemplars of these psalms and had the enclosed three copies bound by the local bookbinder, and indeed with the intention that the two copies bound in gold should be reserved for His Princely Serenity and Her Ladyship, his consort, for use in their oratorium or *Kirchstüblein* [i.e., chapel], and the third to be used by the Lord Superintendent himself in church as a guide to when one psalm or the other might be sung. And to that end now, should His aforementioned Serenity once again be inclined to introduce these songs as soon as possible, I would request most humbly that it might be urged upon the Town Cantor[47] (by whose school cantorate these psalms must be sung, and not by the Princely *Music*) to get in touch with me when he has a chance. Thus I would give to him here an additional four copies: namely, for the four discant, alto, tenor, and bass voices, in order to make a start with it in the palace

---

45. *Spagn.* (343) transcribes the original text as *vorhanden*, read *von henden* (or possibly *von handen*), which consequently leads to her mistranslation of the text (346) suggesting that Schütz's compositions had been received rather than having been lost or gone astray.

46. Clemens Thieme (b. 7 Sept. 1631; d. 27 Mar. 1668), a German composer and instrumentalist, was initially trained under Philipp Stolle in Dresden, and then in 1642 was taken by Schütz to Copenhagen as a *Kapellknabe* in the Royal Danish Court. He joined the Electoral Saxon Kapelle in 1651 and, on Schütz's recommendation, was appointed to the Kapelle of Moritz, Duke of Saxe-Zeitz in 1663, where he rose to the station of *Konzertmeister*.

47. Johann Longolius was Cantor from 1663. Before taking on this position, he had spent a number of years as a student at the University of Leipzig and was active as a church musician in the city churches, likely under the supervision of the Thomaskantor at the time, Sebastian Knüpfer. Longolius continued as Cantor at Zeitz until his death in early 1680. See Werner, *Städtische und fürstliche Musikpflege in Zeitz*, 5.

church at any time, upon His Serenity's most gracious pleasure, and by order of the Lord Superintendent.

As it is the experience in Dresden, Merseburg, and Halle, however, that the listeners each time have looked at just copies of the text of these psalms, from which they can understand what is sung, and moreover can ultimately sing along as well, I have thus wanted hereby to send along copies of it as well, printed in the Lüneburg printing-house, in order to see if these might be considered suitable perhaps for use by one or the other listener, noble and lay persons at court. Should more of them be sent subsequently, I can cover the cost of the basic copy each time for 3 *gulden* apiece, and I am of the opinion that, should it please His Princely Serenity, the various copies that arrive should be bound, and each noble lady [*Frauenzimmer*], nobleman, and other court servants could initially be presented with a copy. The order, however, and at what point these psalms might perhaps be used, would properly rest with His Princely Serenity and the Lord Senior Court Chaplain, and for that reason I for my part await most gracious news.[48]

Index of the categories into which the register of new musical work shall be divided and maintained, which I shall remit immediately after this, God willing, to the princely Court *Music* (and indeed free of charge apart from my appointment):

1. Large-scale psalms, large-scale sacred *concertos*, *Te Deum laudamus* and similar full-voiced compositions with vocal and instrumental parts, to be used at any time according to circumstances.
2. Small[-scale] psalms and *concertos* or those designated with few voices, each time, some of which can be used now and then at the beginning of a princely *Tafelmusik*.
3. *Concertos* designated for the three principal holidays: Christmas, Easter, and Pentecost.
4. *Concertos* designated for the lesser holidays, such as New Year, the Three Magi, Purification [of the Virgin Mary—i.e., Candlemas], Ascension, Trinity, and other lesser holidays.
5. For the Sunday Gospels.
6. Secular and moral songs for a princely *Tafelmusik*.

Likewise I am also willing to aid the cantor, if he wishes, with the communication of various appropriate compositions for his municipal music [*Stadt Music*].

However, whatever might perhaps be produced as printed musical compositions, or perhaps as entire works transcribed by hand, such as sacred or biblical *historia* or other [works], shall be duly paid for and recompensed separately.

---

48. *Spagn.* (347) translates the passage incorrectly: "But [the decision regarding] the order and at approximately what times these Psalms should be used would stand deservedly with His Royal Highness and his Senior Court Chaplain, and I am for my part ready to provide a most gracious report on it."

164. SCHÜTZ TO CHRISTOPH BERNHARD (1670)

Upon receiving Christoph Bernhard's five-voice setting of Psalm 119 for performance at the Kapellmeister's funeral

[Johann Mattheson's, *Grundlage einer Ehrenpforte, woran der Tüchtigsten Capellmeister, Componisten, Musikgelehrten, Tonkünstler u. Leben, Wercke, Verdienste u. erscheinen sollen* (Hamburg, 1740), 322–23][49]

Second, that he in his advanced age, which he reached in excess of eighty-seven years, he wrote to his former student in Hamburg, Christoph Bernhard, with the request that he set the motto for his funeral sermon: "*Cantabiles mihi erant justificationes tuae in loco peregrinationis meae*" [Ps. 119:54],[50] in the Palestrina style of counterpoint, with 2 Cant., A, T, & B which motet he then received, in 1670, two years before his end, and was greatly pleased by it. He also praised the piece in his reply with these words: "My son, you have bestowed upon me a great kindness in sending the desired motet; I do not know of a single note in it that could be improved upon." It was also performed at his funeral [...]

165. CONSTANTIN CHRISTIAN DEDEKIND'S POEM COMMEMORATING THE COMPLETION OF SCHÜTZ'S TOMB (2 SEPTEMBER 1670)

[D-Dl: MB.8.1228, angeb.3, fols. 1r–2v][51]

The
Highly Esteemed, Eldest
Electoral Saxon
Kapellmeister,

---

49. Mattheson, *Grundlage einer Ehren-Pforte, woran der Tüchtigsten Capellmeister, Componisten, Musikgelehrten, Tonkünstler u. Leben, Wercke, Verdienste u. erscheinen sollen*. Johann Mattheson (b. 28 Sept. 1681; d. 17 Apr. 1764) was a German composer, theorist, lexicographer, and critic. Though active as a composer, Mattheson is best remembered for such critical works as *Der vollkommene Capellmeister* (Hamburg, 1739).

50. "Thy statutes have been my songs in the house of my pilgrimage."

51. Dedekind's poem, written two years before Schütz's death, is taken from the last page of a small commemorative publication: *Als Kuhr-Fürstl. Durchl. zu Sachsen Hooch-verdienter Capell-Meister / Der Edle / Veste und Sinnreiche Herr / Herr Heinrich Schüzze / im 88. Jahre seines Alters / durch einen unvermuhteten Zufall / diese Wällt geseegnet / und Derselbige / am 17. Winter-Monats 1672. welches der 24. Sonntag nach 3nit. war / zu seiner Ruhe-Stadt begleitet ward / sollte gleichfalls aus Schuldigkeit erscheinen / dessen Gehorsahmer / zu Ende benannt* (Dresden, ca. 1673). (As Highly Esteemed Kapellmeister to the Electoral Serenity of Saxony, the noble-hearted, respected and ingenious *Herr*, *Herr* Heinrich Schütz, in the eighty-eighth year of his life, through an unforeseen occurrence, passed away, and he, on 17 November 1672, which was the twenty-fourth Sunday after Trinity, was brought to his resting place, whose obedient friend named at the end, should likewise appear out of bounden duty.)

Herr Heinrich Schütz's
Christian
desire for a
blessed departure.

Come, Appointed Hour! I yearn to enter this chamber,
to set aside mortality, together with all earthly misery,
forever. HE, who conquered the world,
WHO triumphed most illustriously in this mortal struggle,
blissfully proclaims. HE shall seal you up, O Tomb,
until I shall greet HIM from within you on Judgment Day.
Come, Death. I await you, grant my desire,
for you transport me to the heavenly fold.

On 2 September 1670,
as the tomb was completed,
written at the request of the
Herr Kapellmeister by
Constantin Christian Dedekind.

166. SCHWANENGESANG (1671): PROPOSED TITLE PAGE OF SCHÜTZ'S UNPUBLISHED SETTING OF PSALM 119

[D-Dl: Mus. 1479-E-504][52]

NB. If this work should be issued in print, this or the enclosed handwritten title page might be used for it.[53]

One Hundred and Nineteenth
Psalm
of the King and Prophet
David
in
eleven pieces
together with the supplement
of the one-hundredth psalm: *Jauchzet dem Herrn*
and
a German Magnificat: *Meine Seele erhebt*

---

52. SWV 482–94; *NSA* 39. A facsimile reproduction of the title page is reproduced in *NSA* 39, xxiii.
53. The *nota bene* written at the top of the page is in Schütz's hand.

den Herren,
for eight voices
in
two choirs,
to the
customary church intonations.
Composed
and
presented to the Electoral Saxon Court Kapelle
in
praise of God
by Heinrich Schütz,
Electoral Saxon Senior Kapellmeister.
Cantus I. Chori
DRESDEN
Printed with Seyffert's fonts.
1671.

167. SCHÜTZ'S *CURRICULUM VITAE* WRITTEN BY MARTIN GEIER FOR THE COMPOSER'S FUNERAL (17 NOVEMBER 1672)

Schütz's curriculum vitae was written by Geier for presentation at the Kapellmeister's funeral

Brief Description of the arduous life of *Herr* Heinrich Schütz, Senior Kapellmeister of Electoral Saxony.[54]

The Senior Kapellmeister of Electoral Saxony, Heinrich Schütz, was born into this world in Köstritz, a small, well-known place on the Elster River belonging to the Most Noble Lord von Wolfframsdorff, in the year 1585, on the eighth day of October, at seven o'clock in the evening. His father was *Herr* Christoph Schütz, subsequently the *Bürgermeister* of the town of Weissenfels. His mother, *Frau* Euphrosina, was the rightful daughter of the late *Herr* Johann Bieger,[55] distinguished lawyer and *Bürgermeister* of

---

54. Facsimile edition of the original is available as Geier, *Kurtze Beschreibung des (Tit.) Herrn Heinrich Schützen / Chur=Fürstl. Sächs. Älteren Capellmeisters / geführten müheseeligen Lebens=Lauff*. An alternate English translation is available, including the sermon itself, by Leaver, *Music in the Service of the Church: The Funeral Sermon for Heinrich Schütz (1585–1672)*. An exemplar of the original print is housed in D-W: Stolberg Leichenpredigtsammlung, Nr. 20653. The biographical portion of the funeral book is found on fols. 20v–25r. Martin Geier (b. 24 Apr. 1614; d. 12 Sept. 1680) pursued his university studies in Leipzig, Strasbourg, Jena, and Wittenberg. After several years as Professor of Theology at the University and as Superintendent in Leipzig, he was summoned by Elector Johann Georg II to succeed Jacob Weller as Senior Court Chaplain and Church Councillor in Dresden.

55. Berger, according to Geier.

Gera. His grandfather, on his father's side, was Albrecht Schütz, Treasurer of the Town Council of Weissenfels; and his grandmother, on his mother's side, *Frau* Dorothea, was born in Gera to the venerable and well-known family named Schreiber. Owing here to the brevity of time, the writer shall modestly leave out further reports on his grandparents and relatives on either side of his family, but instead extol the fact that the venerable parents of the *Herr* Kapellmeister, out of Christian care, according to which they first aspired to the Kingdom of God for their newborn son, and so that he might become the undoubted heir to our Sole Redeemer, Jesus Christ, brought him forth for holy baptism on the following ninth [day] of that same month, where he was endowed through the power of the blood of Christ with the most precious merit of his Savior, and was received into the family of God with the name Heinrich. Through devout fostering and timely instruction in the knowledge of his God, his venerable parents faithfully instilled these blessed beginnings of his Christian faith, and most zealously sought how he, with waxing strengths, might go forth in true piety above all else, mature into a righteous Christian, and attain to those true gifts and graces of a clement and loving human being. Accordingly then, after his grandfather, Albrecht Schütz, the most worthy Treasurer of the Town Council of Weissenfels, died in accordance with God's will in 1591, his father as the surviving heir to the estate had to move to Weissenfels. He instructed him there together with his other siblings according to the well-laid foundation of piety always in pursuit of a virtuous conduct, tranquil life, good morals, useful sciences and languages, and subsequently to advanced studies not only through private instructors but through the instruction of other impressively learned people as well.

In the same way that the conceit for a thing is not easy to conceal, an extraordinary inclination toward the noble art of music was found straightway in *Herr* Schütz in his youth. He soon learned to sing securely and rather well, with a particular grace, which then was not an insignificant cause of his early advancement; for in 1598, after His Princely Grace, Lord Landgrave Moritz of Hesse-Kassel spent a night at his parents and heard him (who was such a small boy at the time) sing so pleasingly, His Princely Grace was moved to speak to his parents for permission to take him to his princely court, with the promise that he should be brought up in all the useful skills and laudable virtues. But as his parents were reluctant to having him leave them in his tender childhood, His Princely Grace persisted in writing in regard to his person. His parents noticed that he bore an inclination and desire to go out into the world, finally consented to it, and on 20 August 1599, he was led forth by his dear father and committed to the care of His Most Princely Grace, the Lord Landgrave. Taking heed of this opportunity he resided there several years and attended the stately court school, or rather a *Gymnasium*, together with counts, distinguished members of the nobility, and other eminent students, and was instructed in various languages, arts and practices [*exercitien*], in which his applied diligence and aroused disposition were also not in vain. He made astonishing progress in Latin, Greek, and French in a short time, and together with the other studies soon demonstrated similar success, so much so that his tutors and professors too, since he proved himself a success at everything, held him in very high regard, and each wished and prompted him to direct his studies toward his own particular profession.

After he had submitted everything to the will of the Most High, he finally chose for himself the study of law, which accordingly made him resolve to see something of the world and to advance his studies. He was not lacking opportunities for this, as it likewise came about that around 1607 his blessed parents had sent his brother Georg together with Heinrich Schütz,[56] the son of his blessed father's brother, to Marburg so that they could study there. When he heard this he obtained permission from His Most Princely Grace to set out for Marburg to join the aforementioned company. Having now obtained his wish, he applied himself most fervently to the continuation of his chosen study of law, and hence devoted himself diligently to the *Institutiones Juris*,[57] *Quaestiones Hoenonii*,[58] and other distinguished authors, and in a brief time demonstrated laudably through a disputation *de Legatis* that he had not made ill use of his time.

Soon after that, in 1609, it happened that His Most Highly Esteemed, Most Princely Grace, Lord Landgrave Moritz, came to Marburg, where he [Schütz] attended upon him according to his duty, on which occasion (I do not know by what fate) His Grace stated how he had understood that he [Schütz] devoted himself completely and principally to his study of law. But because he [Moritz] perceived in him a singular inclination toward the profession of the noble art of music, and since the world-famous musician *Herr* Giovanni Gabrieli in Venice was still alive, he would not be ill disposed to provide the financing and to send him there to pursue his musical study thoroughly, if he, *Herr* Schütz, were so inclined. Since young people seldom decline offers of this kind, he thus made his decision at that time and accepted this gracious proposition with most humble gratitude, thinking that, upon his return from Italy, he could take up the books again and continue his studies in greater depth. In the name of God, 1609, he left for Italy accordingly and, indeed, primarily to achieve his set goal, for Venice, where he soon committed himself to the instruction of the world-famous musician, Giovanni Gabrieli, and resided there into a fourth year, during which time he not only sought after the proper use of his *peregrination*,[59] he took great care of what was memorable about one place or another,

---

56. The future Kapellmeister was seven months older than his like-named cousin (b. 15 May 1586; bur. 15 Apr. 1621).
57. This may have been Hermann Vulteius (b. 16 Dec. 1565; d. 28 Apr. 1634), *Hermanni Vulteji [...] in institutiones juris civilis a Justiniano compositas commentarius: additi sunt in fine indices sex, operi ipsi accommodatissimi*, 3rd ed. (Marburg: Paulus Egenolphus, 1605). Vulteius (Vultejus) was a professor and rector at the University of Marburg.
58. This may have been Philipp Heinrich von Hoen (Hoenonius) (b. 23 Jul. 1576; d. 28 Apr. 1648), *Philippi Hoenonii [...] quaestiones seu controversiae juris illustres, ex libris quatuor institutionum Justinianii excerptae, [...] quibus accesserunt disputationes ejusdem ad celebrem titulum pandectarum postremium, [...]*, 3rd ed. (Herborn Nassau, 1609). Hoen (or Hoenonius) studied at the University of Marburg and subsequently became a Professor of Law at Herborn.
59. Leaver (62) observes the relationship of *Peregrination* to the text of the funeral sermon [Ps. 119:54], which was likewise the text used for the funeral motet by Bernhard.

diligently sought after learned and wise people, established good correspondence with the same, noted well what was worthy of imitation; and according to the teachings of the apostle, he reflected on "whatsoever things are true, whatsoever things are honest, whatsoever things are just, whatsoever things are pure, whatsoever things are lovely, whatsoever things are of good report; if there be any virtue, and if there be any praise" [Phil. 4:8].[60] He also, by the grace of God, distinguished himself in music above the others in his company at that time, and had a small musical work published in Venice, through which he was received with singular glory, respect and praise before one and all.

After his aforementioned teacher at Venice died, he set out from there in 1612, back to Germany to the aforesaid Lord Landgrave who immediately gave him 200 *gulden* until he might have a fixed appointment. Insofar as he was not content to remain in music in this manner, he preferred to take up his books once more in order to lay claim to those things in them which he had neglected in Italy, and to use music as an avocation in addition to this for further advancement. The Almighty, however, who perhaps singled him out in his mother's womb for music, pulled the books from his hands this time as well, as he was called in 1615 to Dresden (which thought never would have entered his mind) by the Most Serene Elector of Saxony, Duke Johann Georg I, of most blessed memory, for the christening of the second prince, the Most Serene Duke August, at present Administrator of the Archdiocese of Magdeburg. Because he had to heed this eminent favor, he traveled there with the permission of the Lord Landgrave, where His Electoral Serenity, at the princely baptism, immediately presented him with the office and the *Directorium* of the Electoral *Music*. As he now recognized in particular the finger of Almighty God in this, he did not decline this great occasion; on the contrary, insofar as he could be released by His Grace, the Lord Landgrave, he humbly accepted the opportunity. His Princely Grace, the Lord Landgrave, did not begrudge him this honorable fortune, and in a letter to His aforementioned Electoral Serenity discharged him quite willingly, and honored him with a chain and portrait, and a singularly gracious valedictory.

Now, after he, *Herr* Schütz, turned toward Dresden, with his fine qualifications and considerable erudition, he won much favor, love, and affection before his most gracious lordships one and all, with a thankful heart perceived God's merciful succor in his plans, and that everything there developed through God's grace to augment his state of well-being. The better to direct his situation here, he deliberated on an honorable marriage for himself. Consequently he fervently appealed to the true God chiefly for His fatherly guidance in his Christian purpose, then called upon the opinion of his beloved family, and since he felt a singularly honorable affection and heartfelt love for *Jungfrau* Magdalena, the dearly beloved daughter of the Electoral Saxon bookkeeper for land and beverage tax, the late, noble, and well-appointed *Herr* Christian Wildeck, he, in the name of the Almighty, with the good wishes and will of his beloved relatives, proposed this marriage

---

60. The biblical source of the passage was identified by Leaver, 57.

now, with due humility, to the esteemed parents of the aforesaid *Jungfrau* Wildeck, who then, having first appealed to God the Most High for their part, and after mature consideration between themselves and with their close relatives, betrothed and pledged their beloved daughter, in the name of the Holy Trinity, to the aforementioned *Herr* Schütz in consideration of his devout conduct, gentle heart and spirit, considerable erudition, knowledge, and other singularly praiseworthy qualities. This matrimonial and honorable engagement was then consummated in the customary manner in a clerical wedding ceremony on 1 June 1619. After this joyful and honorable light ascended for him, the good Lord increased this more and more, and blessed him and his wife with two daughters, named Anna Justina and Euphrosyne. But the sweetness of this agreeable marriage was transformed all too soon into a cup of bitterness, in that he, in the sixth year of his love, had to suffer his wife being torn from his side by an early death, on 6 September 1625, reducing him thereby to a state of great sorrow. Hence he then sent his two aforementioned daughters first to his beloved mother in Weissenfels, and after that to be raised by their close relative, the wife of the then tax bookkeeper, *Herr* Christian Hartmann.[61]

Since the pressures of the war increased more and more in these lands, which then impeded everything that had otherwise flourished in gentle times of peace, and at the same time created a considerable obstruction to his profession, he resolved to undertake a journey once again. After he acquired a letter of respite from His Electoral Serenity, now of most blessed memory, for a specific period of time, he left from here for Italy for the second time on 11 August 1628. But after his safe return [to Dresden], he had to learn painfully how his beloved father, Christoph Schütz (former *Bürgermeister* of Weissenfels) departed this world on 25 August 1631, and his beloved father-in-law, Christian Wildeck (former Electoral Tax Bookkeeper) on 1 October that same year, and thus he was constantly met with one affliction after the other. And with no end in sight to the wicked and troubled times of war, he traveled perpetually from place to place—always, however, with permission from his most gracious lordship—partly to become better skilled in his noble art of music, partly at the most gracious request of mighty royal and princely potentates; and thus he became famous far and wide, insofar as he had to prepare and direct the *Music* at the Royal wedding and other auspicious assemblies—in 1634 upon request of His Royal Majesty of Denmark to Copenhagen, in 1638 to Brunswick and Lüneburg, in 1642 again to Denmark. Dear God, however, upon Schütz's return, spoiled for him his happiness and high honor evermore with sorrow, as his brother Valerius Schütz died in 1632, his beloved mother in 1635, his mother-in-law in 1636, his brother Dr. Georg Schütz

---

61. There are errors in Geier's account as indicated by Moser, *Heinrich Schütz: His Life and Works*, 121–22. Schütz's wife died 6 September 1625, and according to the biographical entry in the funeral sermon, the daughters Euphrosyne and Anna Justina were entrusted to the maternal grandmother (Wildeck) until 1633, and subsequently given into the care of her aunt Maria, the wife of Michael Hartmann, the Electoral Saxon tax recorder. When Maria Hartmann died in 1643, Euphrosyne was taken in by the wife of the Electoral Saxon tax collector at Leipzig, Johann Hanitsch, her nearest cousin. She remained in their care until her marriage to Christoph Pincker in 1648.

in 1637, and his beloved daughter *Jungfrau* Anna Justina in Dresden in 1638, and he was reduced to an abiding sorrow and grief thereby.

In August 1647 the blessed deceased betrothed his sole surviving and youngest daughter, *Jungfrau* Euphrosyne, to the Most Honorable, Right Worshipful and Most Learned *Herr* Christoph Pincker, J. U. D.,[62] at the time a *Juris Practicum* [practicing lawyer], and currently Electoral Saxon Appellate-Counsel, Assessor of the Alderman's Chair at Leipzig, and *Bürgermeister* there, and subsequently on 25 January 1648 had this Christian betrothal consummated through a clerical ceremony, from which marriage he also derived particular comfort and pleasure, and also lived to see five grandchildren, of which only one by the name of *Frau* Gertraud Euphrosina survives, and who was married on 18 May 1670 to *Herr* Johann Seidel, canon at Wurzen[63] and alderman[64] at Leipzig, from whom he also lived to see two grandchildren (one of which soon died) and thus was made a great grandfather, and who now attends her blessed grandfather's funeral.[65]

In January 1655, however, his only living daughter in Leipzig, as the blessed departed arrived there to visit her, had been torn away by an early death, to his and his son-in-law's greatest sorrow. The blessed deceased, however, as a reasonable Christian never exalted himself in the honor and fortune so often sent his way; rather, on the contrary, let it be an additional incitement to proper and seemly Christian endeavor. In the misery and grief often sent his way, he did not turn from his true God but put his faith in Him ever with all his heart, and subjected all his deeds and plans to the Supreme Will, undoubting, that He who caused the wounds shall also heal them and that all turns out for the best. In this confidence he then applied his time no less in this Electoral Residence as in other places where he was born and raised, where he lived abroad, and with study and other laudable exercises gained universal praise and honorable Christian resonance. He penitently recognized himself at all times as a poor sinner, comforted himself of the rewards of true faith in his Savior and Redeemer, Jesus Christ. He diligently heard the Word of God, attended confession and most worthy Holy Communion, inasmuch as this occurred recently just a few weeks ago, on 15 September. And he moreover devoted himself faithfully to the duty of a good Christian in regard to his neighbors, since he conducted himself toward each person according to rank, with respect, with all discretion, friendship, and kindness; performed much good for his poor friends and people in need, and aided them as much as possible. Hence he then once again on account of his subtle conduct, keen mind, and singular dexterity thus in his senior probity was greatly loved and honored, extolled and exalted, by the High and the Humble, into his hoary old age. At all times too he enjoyed great favor of the Elector and Electoral Prince, who also would have the late *Herr* Kapellmeister accompanied in death by sending noble envoys, etc.

With regard to the illness and final farewell of the blessed deceased: his stamina and his hearing in particular had diminished greatly over the past several years, such that he was able

---

62. *Juris utriusque doctor*, doctor of both laws.
63. Wurzen is an ancient Saxon town on the Mulde, located about 25 km east of Leipzig.
64. *Ratsverwandter* (according to *DWB*) is equivalent to a *membrum senatus* or *alderman*.
65. Leaver (60) thinks it is the great granddaughter that attends the funeral; the reference is still to the granddaughter, Gertraud Euphrosina.

to go out but very little, nor could he listen to the Word of God. Instead he had to stay home for the most part, where he spent most of his time with reading of the Holy Scripture and books of other distinguished theologians, and also worked with great diligence toward completing the ever-splendid musical compositions on various psalms of David—the one hundred and nineteenth in particular—likewise the Passion according to three of the evangelists. He observed a strict diet and moderation, yet during this time suffered several attacks of severe rheumatism, which however he always resisted through the application of effective remedies.

This past November 6, he arose whole and sound, and dressed himself. But just after nine o'clock, as he wanted to look for something in the apartment, he was seized by a sudden weakness and a *Steckfluss*,[66] and was unable to prevent himself from sinking to the floor. His people came to him to help him up and immediately brought him to bed. And although he had recovered somewhat and spoke quite comprehensibly, this *Steckfluss* was indeed so hard upon him that after he let these words be heard—he submits everything to the gracious will of God—he no longer had the strength to speak. And though the physician was immediately summoned to come with precious medicines to help him, and applied his utmost efforts to restore his [Schütz's] strength, there was little that could be done for him. His father confessor was likewise summoned to him, who recited and shouted into his ear all manner of prayers and passages from the Scriptures. Then bowing his head several times and with his hands, he gave us to understand that he had Jesus in his heart, whereupon the father confessor blessed him, and he was gone as though in sleep, lying completely still, until finally his breathing and pulse subsided gradually and faded away, and as the clock struck four, amid the prayer and singing of those around him, peacefully and blissfully, without so much as a shudder, passed away, after he had been Electoral Saxon Kapellmeister for fifty-seven years, and had reached the age of eighty-seven years and twenty-nine days.

168. CHRISTOPH BERNHARD'S RHYMED PSALM 150 FROM THE *GEISTREICHES GESANG-BUCH* (DRESDEN, 1676)

Bernhard's numbered text corresponding to David Conrad's engraving of Schütz directing in the Hofkapelle

Psalm 150[67]
in the
Frontispiece

---

66. *Steckfluss* comes with a number of English names, including suffocating or suffocative catarrh, apoplexy of the lungs, and *angina pectoris*. Leaver translates the word as "stroke" (61). This is unlikely since *Steckfluss* was also an acknowledged cause of death amongst infants and children (sometimes accompanied by coughing and shortness of breath), and it is doubtful that Schütz would have been able to move his head, speak and comprehend as clearly as he seems to have done, and to gesture meaningfully and consciously with *both* hands up to the time of death.

67. Christoph Bernhard, *Geistreiches Gesang-Buch / An D. Cornelij Beckers Psalmen und Lutherischen Kirchen-Liedern mit ihren Melodeyen unter Discant und Basso, sammt einem Kirchen-Gebeth-Buche Auf Chur-Fürstl.*

Behold here the Temple of the King among Saxons,
of the *Ruta*-David,[68] how his splendor was enhanced
through magnanimity, art and diligence! Behold David himself (1) standing,
and preceding his Asaph (2) in the devotional procession.

Hark, how the choirs (3) praise the Lord in His sanctuary;
and how the angelic host (4) in its firmament above
exalt the Glory of the Lord, as His acts (5) surround Him
in His Majesty (6) with resounding sounds of praise.

Hark the sound of trumpets (7), the wafting sounds of harp and psaltery (8),
of drums' and dance's (9) celebration, the glorification of strings and pipes (10),
of cymbals' (11) sibilant sound, which pleasingly and sweetly ring;
Yea, whatever has breath (12)[69] to Him sings Halleluja!

[original]

Der CL. Psalm
Im
Kupfer=Titul:

Seht hier des GOttes=Hauss des Königs untern Sachsen/
Des Rauten=Davids/ an/ wie seine Zier erwachsen/
durch Kosten/ Kunst und Fleiss! Seht selbst den David (1) stehn/
und seinem Assaph (2) vohr—zur Andachts Folge—gehn.

Hört/ wie der Sänger=Köhr' (3) im Heiligthum GOTT loben;
und wie das Engel=Volk (4) in seiner Macht=Fäst' oben/
des HErren Ruhm erhöht; wie seine Tahten (5) Ihn/
in seiner Herrlichkeit/ (6) mit Lob-Getöhn umzühn.

Durchl. zu Sachsen u. Hertzog Johann Georgens des Anderen gnädigste Verordnung und Kosten / für die Churfl. Häuser und Capellen aufgeleget und ausgegeben / im Jahre 1676. In the Wolfenbüttel copy of this work (D-W: S 379.4° Helmst.), the engraving is found just inside the front cover, the main title page of the Bernhard is found after the prayer book, and the poem (unpaginated) immediately precedes the title page.

68. The *Raute* or *Immergrüne Raute* (English, *Rue*; Latin, *Ruta*) is an evergreen plant associated symbolically with the Dukes of Saxe-Wittenberg who renounced the ancestral homeland in Saxe-Lauenburg in the thirteenth century. The plant was incorporated into the coat of arms of the electoral Wettin family, where it appears as a rue garland in bend on the dynastic escutcheon. The rue symbolizes Saxony's growth, constancy, and blessedness.

69. The number 2 can be made out on Schütz's right shoulder, and the number 12 is written on the organ.

Hört der Posaunen Hall (7) des Harffe=Psalters (8) Schweiffen/
der Pauk= und Reygen (9) Lob/ den Ruhm der Säite= und Pfeiffen (10)
der Zimbeln (11) Lispel=Spiel/ das wohl= und lieblich klingt;
Ja/ was nuhr Odem hat (12) Ihm/ Halleluja! singt.

169. ANONYMOUS GENEALOGY OF THE SCHÜTZ FAMILY (1761)

[*Neueröfnetes Historisch=Sächss. Curiositäten CABINET aufs Jahr Christi 1761. Worinnen in allen 12. Monathen auf 24. Bogen abermahln viele alte und neue merkwürdige Historische, Philosophische, Geographische, Genealogische, Physicalische, Natur= und andere Begebenheiten Wie nicht weniger Biographien gelehrter und berühmter Männer zu lesen.* (Dresden [s.d.]), 297–304.][70]

No. LXV.
Account of the Schütz Family of Weissenfels.

Albrecht Schütz, who was City Magistrate as well as Council Chamberlain in Weissenfels, died in 1591. He had two spouses, namely: 1) Margaretha Fischer; 2) Dorothea, from the old and venerable Schreiber family in Gera. His children were:

I.) Christoph Schütz, *Bürgermeister* of Weissenfels. He died 25 August 1631.[71] He had two spouses, namely:
  1) Margaretha, daughter of Peter Weidemann, Senator in Gera
  2) Euphrosina, daughter of Johann Bieger, *Jur. Pract.*[72] and governing *Bürgermeister*, who died a widow in 1635.

His children were:
  A) Johann Schütz. He was born 24 June 1575, studied at Leipzig, then subsequently made a peregrination to Hungary under Emperor Rudolph II. Thereafter he was provincial judge for twelve years in Schleiz, in the Reuss dominion, whereafter he was tax-collector in Ziegenrück in 1621 and finally in Sachsenburg in 1633. He died 25 August 1652. He was married to Catharina, the widow of Paul Sonntag, and the daughter of *M.* Carl Wolff, Reuss-Plauen's Councillor and Secretary in Schleiz, whose brother, Heinrich Wolff, became school teacher [*Ludimoderator*] in

---

70. The genealogy is reproduced in full in Möller, Böcher, and Haustein, *"Ihr sollet Schatz und nicht mehr Schütze heissen": Gereimtes und Ungereimtes über Heinrich Schütz: Eine Quellensammlung 1613–1834*, 340–42, and found in D-Dl: Sign. Eph. Histor. 362a.
71. The date is incorrect, since the elder Schütz was buried 9 October 1631. Möller (2003), 342.
72. *Juris practicus*, legal counsel or representative; barrister at law.

Eisleben, 22 November 1602, and died in exile in Nordhausen, as it were, in 1686. With this spouse he fathered:

a) Johann Schütz, was collegiate syndic in Merseburg.

b) Dorothea, was married to Zacharias Thrun, court clerk, and subsequently tax-collector in Sachsenburg.

c) Euphrosina, married to Heinrich von Görmar, of Gorsleben,[73] Berga and Reinsdorf.[74]

d) Martha, was twice married, namely: 1) to Daniel Siegfried, court clerk in Heldrungen, who died miserably in the Pappenheim incursion in 1632,[75] and his wife barely saved herself and her infant daughter, 2) with Georg Ruprecht, tax-collector in Frandorf. Anna Maria, the daughter from the first husband, married Andrea Kramper, cloth-merchant in Frankenhausen.

e) Anna Maria, entered a marriage with Christoph Schreiber, the Schwarzburg administrative treasurer in Frankenhausen.

B) Heinrich Schütz, from the second marriage, was born 8 October 1585 in Köstritz on the Elster, the estate of Lord von Wolframsdorf. He was from his youth on guided toward formal study, and through his natural grace in singing, in which he received instruction at the same time, set himself in such favor with the Landgrave Moritz of Hesse that he himself took him into his *Hofkapelle* 20 August 1599, whereby he continued ardently to lay the foundation of his studies in the court school in Kassel. In 1607, he, with his brother Georg Schütz, together with his cousin Heinrich Schütz, traveled to the University of Marburg, and there studied law. In 1609 the Margrave [sic], at his own expense, let him travel to Italy to refine the *Music*, as he then resided in Venice to embrace *Music* completely under the famous *Musico*, Giovanni Gabrieli. In 1612 he returned, as the Landgrave then gave him a temporary annual allowance of 200 *gulden*. But in 1615 he became Director of the Kapelle to Elector Johann Georg I in Dresden, and was granted a gracious dismissal by the Landgrave. On 1 June 1619, in Dresden, he married *Jungfrau* Magdalena, daughter of Christoph [sic] Wildeck, the Bookkeeper for Land and Beverage Tax, who died 9 October 1631, and who in turn died 9 September 1625. In 1628 he obtained leave for a second journey to Italy,

---

73. The village of Gorsleben was the birthplace of the composer, music theorist, and Thomaskantor before Johann Hermann Schein, Sethus Calvisius (b. 21 Feb. 1556; d. 24 Nov. 1615).

74. Gorschleben (Gorsleben), Berge (Berga), and Reinsdorf are located in or near Kyffhäuserkreis, Thuringia.

75. Gottfried Heinrich, Count of Pappenheim (b. 8 Jun. 1594; d. 16 Nov. 1632), was a fearless and greatly admired military leader for the Catholic cause during the Thirty Years' War. He served with Tilly against Christian IV of Denmark, was involved in the sacking and destruction of Magdeburg in 1631, and died on the field at the Battle of Lützen, the same day as his opponent, Gustavus Adolphus, King of Sweden.

in 1634 to Copenhagen, Denmark, in 1638 to Brunswick-Lüneburg, and 1642 the second time to Denmark. In the end he died in Dresden, 6 November 1672, at the age of 88.[76] With his spouse he produced three [sic] daughters:[77]

1) Anna Justina, who died unmarried in 1638
2) Euphrosyne, born 28 November 1623. She was married 25 January 1648 to Christoph Pincker, Doctor of Laws, subsequently Electoral Saxon Appellate Counsel of the Alderman's Chair in Leipzig, and *Bürgermeister* there, and died in puerperium 1 [sic] January 1655.

C) Benjamin Schütz, jurist[78] of the law faculty, syndic and deacon at Erfurt. I am aware of a son by him, also named Benjamin Schütz, student of laws in Jena.

D) Georg Schütz, from the second marriage, Doctor of Laws, and subsequently Assessor of the Supreme Court of the Judicature Leipzig. He died in 1637. He was wed to 1) Anna, daughter of Friedrich Gross, bookkeeper in Leipzig; 2) with Anna Goldbeck, widow of Petrus Lenander, Privy Council and Vice-Chancellor to the County Solms, he was indeed engaged in 1637 but died affianced before the union, in 1637. From his marriage, he fathered

1) Christoph Georg Schütz, architect in Leipzig, who died at the age of seventy-four in 1696. In 1655 he became Councillor in Saumur and subsequently in Leipzig, in 1658, city magistrate in 1668, and architect in 1680. His spouses were 1) Anna Sabina, 12 November 1640, daughter of *L.* Antonius Kirchof,[79] Public Professor, and Rector of the Thomasschule in Leipzig. The wedding was 14 June 1659, but she died giving birth 20 June 1661. 2) Anna Salome, was born 14 August 1647, daughter of Dr. Heinrich Volkmar, Jr., of Hennigsberg, Public Professor[80] and Assessor of the Faculty of Law. The wedding was 19 April 1664. She died giving birth 7 July 1686. With these two spouses he fathered:
   a) Anna Salome, born 1666, was married to *Lic.* Hochschmidt, Public Professor of Theology in Leipzig, died 26 October 1685.
   b) Heinrich Schütz, born 1667.
   c) Margaretha, born 1670.
   d) Christoph Georg Schütz, born 1671.

---

76. Schütz was in his eighty-eighth year, but he was eighty-seven years old when he died.
77. Schütz had only two children: Anna Justina and Euphrosyne.
78. *JCtus* (*iuris consultus*), jurist or legal advisor.
79. *L.*(*Licentiatus*), licentiate. The *Licentiatus* is the next academic degree after *Baccalaureus*, comprising a faculty examination and inaugural disputation.
80. *P.P.* (*Publicus Professor*).

- e) *N.* Schütz, born 1672. He died a student in December 1684.
- f) Ludovicus Wilhelmus, born 1675.
- g) Friderich Wilhelmus, born 1677, Doctor of Theology and Pastor at St. Thomas in Leipzig, died in 1739. His daughter Wilhelmina Sophia, *vid. Tilleri*, died 19 March 1754.
- h) Johanna Elisabeth, born 1678.
- i) Regina Margaretha, born 1680.
- k) Gottfried Ludwig, born 1681.
- l) Johann Gottlieb, born 1683.
- m) Sophia Cristiana, born 1685.

2) Heinrich Friedrich Schütz, born 1631, was a constable in Old Dresden. He died in 1707 at the age of seventy-five. His spouses were 1) Sophia Magdalena, daughter of Johann Antonius, surgeon in Dresden, 2) Anna Maria, daughter of *M.* Daniel Petermann, *P.L.C.*[81] and Rector of the municipal school in Meissen, born 1649. The wedding was in 1677. She died in 1700. In this marriage he fathered:

Anna Magdalena, married name Brehm.

II) *N. N.*[82] Schütz, (I do not know whether this was perhaps *M.* Valerius Schütz who died in 1632).[83] His son, in the meantime:

Heinrich Schütz, who in 1607 studied in Marburg with the aforesaid Director of the Kapelle in Dresden, also named Heinrich Schütz.

---

81. *Poeta Laureatus Caesareus*, Imperial Poet Laureate.
82. *Nemini notus*, known to no one; or *Nescio nomen*, I do not know the name.
83. This information is incorrect. Valerius Schütz, born in 1601 and killed in a duel in 1632, could not have been the father of the Heinrich Schütz with whom the future Kapellmeister traveled to Marburg in 1607.

GLOSSARY

Denarius (pl. *Denarii*): *Pfennig* or penny

Groschen: A silver coin valued at one twenty-fourth of a thaler

Gulden: Originally a gold coin, synonymous with *floren* (*fl.*)

Herr (pl. *Herren*): (1) gentleman; (2) nobleman; (3) Lord (as noble title); (4) master, lord (as ruler); (5) Mr., Esq. (as title); (6) Sir (as a general form of address)

Historia (pl. *Historiae*): Since the Lutheran Reformation, a musical setting of a biblical story, most frequently on the Passion, Easter, and Christmas

Hofkapelle (pl. *Hofkapellen*): Court chapel, court ensemble

Hofmusik: Court musical establishment

Jungfrau: Maiden, or honorific used for younger women who have not yet been married

Kapelle (pl. *Kapellen*): (1) chapel, place of worship; (2) music ensemble or establishment

Kapellknabe (pl. *Kapellknaben*): Choirboy, boy who belongs to the chapel or *Kapelle*

Knabe (pl. *Knaben*): Boy; also used as an shortened form of *Kapellknabe*, etc.

Music, Musica, Musick, Musik: (1) music; (2) musical compositions; (3) music establishment. It is not always clear which meaning is intended, and sometimes more than one meaning might be understood simultaneously.

Musicus (pl. *Musici*): A learned musician or composer

Pfennig (pl. *Pfennige*): Coin of variable, but of less value, than a *groschen*; often made of alloyed silver and copper

Reichsthaler: A thaler that is current or passable throughout the domain or empire, as compared to other regional thalers

Sängerknabe (pl., *Sängerknaben*): Choirboy or a boy who sings

Tafelknabe (pl. *Tafelknaben*): Boy who sings at table

Tafelmusik: Banquet music, music at table

Thaler: Thaler; a silver coin of differing and regional value; originally an abbreviation of *Joachimsthaler*

Tischknabe (pl. *Tischknaben*): Boy who sings at table

BIBLIOGRAPHY

Ambrose. *Omnia quotquot extant D. Ambrosii Episcopii Mediolanensis Opera*. Basel: Froben, 1555.
Bepler, Jill. "Tugend- und Lasterbilder einer Fürstin: Die Witwe von Schöningen." *L'HOMME. Europäische Zeitschrift für Feministische Geschichtswissenschaft* 8, no. 2 (1997): 218–31.
Biehle, Herbert. *Musikgeschichte von Bautzen bis zum Anfang des 19. Jahrhunderts*. Leipzig: Kistner & Siegel, 1924.
Bieritz, Karl-Heinrich. *Das Kirchenjahr. Feste, Gedenk- und Feiertage in Geschichte und Gegenwart*. Rev. ed. Munich: Beck, 1994.
Braun, Werner. *Deutsche Musiktheorie des 15. bis 17. Jahrhunderts: Zweiter Teil von Calvisius bis Mattheson*. Geschichte der Musiktheorie, Bd 8/II, edited by Thomas Ertelt and Frieder Zaminer. Darmstadt: Wissenschaftliche Buchgesellschaft, 1994.
Bruch, Delores. "Fritzsche, Gottfried." In *The Organ: An Encyclopedia*, edited by Douglas E. Bush and Richard Kassel, 213–14. New York: Routledge, 2006.
Buelow, George J. "A Schütz Reader: Documents of Performance Practice." *American Choral Review* 27, no. 4 (1985): 1–35.
Dane, Werner. "Briefwechsel zwischen dem landgraflich hessischen und dem kurfürstlich sächsischen Hof um Heinrich Schütz 1614–1619." *Zeitschrift für Musikwissenschaft* 17 (1935–36): 343–55.
Frandsen, Mary E. "Allies in the Cause of Italian Music: Schütz, Prince Johann Georg II and Musical Politics in Dresden." *Journal of the Royal Musical Association* 125, no. 1 (2000): 1–40.
Frandsen, Mary E. *Crossing Confessional Boundaries: The Patronage of Italian Sacred Music in Seventeenth-Century Dresden*. Oxford and New York: Oxford University Press, 2006.
Frandsen, Mary E. "Gottfried Fritzsche (Frietzsche) at the Dresden Court, 1628–29." *The Organ Yearbook* 41 (2012): 91–114.

Frandsen, Mary E. "Music in a Time of War: The Efforts of Saxon Prince Johann Georg II to Establish a Musical Ensemble, 1637–1651." *Schütz-Jahrbuch* 30 (2008): 33–68.

Fürstenau, Moritz. *Beiträge zur Geschichte der königlich-sächsischen musikalischen Kapelle.* Dresden: Meser, 1849.

Geck, Karl Wilhelm. *Sophie Elisabeth, Herzogin zu Braunschweig und Lüneburg (1613–1676) als Musikerin.* Saarbrücken: Saarbrücker Druckerei und Verlag, 1992.

Geier, Martin. *Kurtze Beschreibung des (Tit.) Herrn Heinrich Schützen / Chur=Fürstl. Sächs. Älteren Capellmeisters / geführten müheseeligen Lebens=Lauff.* Fascimile reprint with afterword by Dietrich Berke. Kassel: Bärenreiter, 1972.

Gregor-Dellin, Martin. *Heinrich Schütz: Sein Leben, sein Werk, seine Zeit.* Rev. ed. München and Zürich: Piper, 1987.

Heinemann, Michael. , ed. *Schriftstücke von Heinrich Schütz.* Schütz-Dokumente, Vol. 1. Edited by Heinrich Schütz-Archiv der Hochschule für Musik Carl Maria von Weber Dresden. Cologne: Verlag Dohr, 2010.

Horace. *Odes and Epodes.* Edited and translated by Niall Rudd. Cambridge, MA: Harvard University Press, 2004.

Johnston, Gregory S. "Polyphonic Keyboard Accompaniment in the Early Baroque: An Alternative to Basso Continuo." *Early Music* 26, no. 1 (1998): 51–64.

Jerome. *Sancti evsebii hieronymi epistvlae, pars 1.* In Corpus Scriptorum Ecclesiasticorum Latinorum, edited by Isidorus Hilberg, 54. Leipzig: G. Freytag, 1910.

Jung, Hans Rudolf. "Ein neuaufgefundenes Gutachten von Heinrich Schütz aus dem Jahre 1617." *Archiv für Musikwissenschaft* 18 (1961): 241–47.

Jung, Hans Rudolf. "Zwei unbekannte Briefe von Heinrich Schütz aus den Jahren 1653–54." *Beiträge zur Musikwissenschaft* 14 (1972): 231–36.

Kittel, Caspar. *Arien und Kantaten: Dresden 1638.* Edited by Werner Braun. Winterthur, Switzerland: Amadeus, 2000.

Köhler, Siegfried. *Heinrich Schütz: Anmerkungen zu Leben und Werk.* Leipzig: VEB Deutscher Verlag für Musik, 1985.

Kobuch, Agatha. "Neue Sagittariana im Staatsarchiv Dresden. Ermittlung unbekannter Quellen über den kursächsischen Hofkapellmeister Heinrich Schütz." *Jahrbuch für Regionalgeschichte* 13 (1986): 79–124.

Kobuch, Agatha. "Neue Sagittariana im Staatsarchiv Dresden. Ermittlung unbekannter Quellen über den kursächsischen Hofkapellmeister Heinrich Schütz. Nachtrag." *Jahrbuch für Regionalgeschichte* 15/1 (1988): 118–24.

La Mara [Ida Maria Lipsius (1837–1927)]. *Musikerbriefe aus fünf Jahrhunderten. Nach den Urhandschriften erstmalig hrsg. von La Mara.* 2 vols. Leipzig: Breitkopf & Härtel, 1886.

Leaver, Robin A. "The Funeral Sermon for Heinrich Schütz." *Bach* 4 (1973): 3–17; 5 (1974): 9–22, 27–35.

Leaver, Robin A. *Music in the Service of the Church: The Funeral Sermon for Heinrich Schütz (1585–1672).* Church Music Pamphlet Series, edited by Carl Schalk. St. Louis: Concordia, 1984.

Lenz, Rudolf, ed. *Abkürzungen aus Personalschriften des XVI. bis XVIII. Jahrhunderts.* 3rd ed. Marburger Personalschriften-Forschungen, 35. Stuttgart: Franz Steiner, 2002.

Liliencron, Rochus, Freiherr von. *Allgemine deutsche Biographie.* Hrsg. durch die Historische Commission bei der Königl. Akademie der Wissenschaften. Vols. 1–56. Leipzig: Duncker & Humblot 1875–1912.

Lüdtke, Joachim. *Die Lautenbücher Philipp Hainhofers (1578–1647)*. Abhandlungen zur Musikgeschichte, 5. Edited by Martin Staehelin. Göttingen: Vandehoeck & Ruprecht, 1999.

MacClintock Carol, trans. and ed. *Readings in the History of Music in Performance*. Bloomington: Indiana University Press, 1979.

Mattheson, Johann. *Grundlage einer Ehren-Pforte, woran der Tüchtigsten Capellmeister, Componisten, Musikgelehrten, Tonkünstler u. Leben, Wercke, Verdienste u. erscheinen sollen*. Hamburg, 1740. Facsimile reproduction edited by Max Schneider. Kassel: Bärenreiter, 1969.

Möller, Eberhard. "Eine Hochzeit im Hause Schütz." In *Beiträge zur musikalischen Quellenforschung: Protokoll-Band Nr. 3 der Kolloquien im Rahmen der Köstritzer Schütz-Tage*, edited by Ingeborg Stein, 19–53. Bad Köstritz: Forschungs- und Gedenkstätte Heinrich-Schütz-Hause, 1995.

Möller, Eberhard, Friederike Böcher, and Christine Haustein. *"Ihr sollet Schatz und nicht mehr Schütze heissen": Gereimtes und Ungereimtes über Heinrich Schütz: Eine Quellensammlung 1613–1834*. Köstritzer Schriften, 3. Altenburg: Kamprad, 2003.

Moser, Hans Joachim. *Heinrich Schütz: Sein Leben und Werk*. 2nd rcv. cd. Kassel: Bärenreiter, 1954. First published Kassel: Bärenreiter, 1936.

Moser, Hans Joachim. *Heinrich Schütz: His Life and Works*. Translated from the 2nd rev. ed. by Carl F. Pfatteicher. St. Louis: Concordia, 1959.

Müller von Asow, Erich H. *Heinrich Schütz. Gesammelte Briefe und Schriften*. Regensburg: Gustav Bosse, 1931.

Norman, Gertrude, and Miriam Lubell Shrifte, comps. and eds. *Letters of Composers: An Anthology, 1603–1945*. New York: Knopf, 1946.

Opitz, Martin. *Weltliche Poëmata. Der Ander Theil. Zum vierdten mal vermehret vnd vbersehen herauß gegeben*. Frankfurt/Oder: Thomas Matthias Götz, 1644. Facsimile reprint edited by Erich Trunz. Deutsche Neudrucke. Reihe: Barock 3.Tübingen: Max Niemeyer, 1975.

Praetorius, Michael. *Syntagma Musicum II: De Organographia* (Wolfenbüttel: Elias Holwein, 1619). Facsimile ed. by Wilibald Gurlitt. Kassel: Bärenreiter, 1958.

Praetorius, Michael. *Syntagma musicum III* (Wolfenbüttel, 1619). Translated and edited by Jeffery Kite-Powell. New York: Oxford University Press, 2004.

Printz, Wolfgang Caspar. *Historische Beschreibung der Edlen Sing- und Kling-Kunst*. Dresden: Johann Christoph Mieths Buchh., 1690. Facsimile ed. by Othmar Wessely. Graz: Akademische Druck- u. Verlagsanstalt, 1964.

Prüfer, Arthur. *Johan Herman Schein*. Leipzig: Breitkopf & Härtel, 1895. Reprinted as *Johann Hermann Schein*. Kassel: Bärenreiter, 1989.

Rifkin, Joshua. "Schütz–Weckmann–Kopenhagen: Zur Frage der zweiten Dänemarkreise." In *Von Isaac bis Bach: Studien zur älteren deutschen Musikgeschichte. Festschrift Martin Just zum 60. Geburtstag*, edited by Frank Heidlberger, et al., 180–88. Kassel: Bärenreiter, 1991.

Rifkin, Joshua. "Towards a New Image of Henrich Schütz." Pts. 1 and 2. *Musical Times* 126, no. 1713 (November 1985): 651–58; 126, no. 1714 (December 1985): 716–20.

Roche, Jerome. "What Schütz Learnt from Grandi in 1629." *Musical Times* 113, no. 1557 (November 1972): 1074–75.

Rowen, Ruth Halle. *Music Through Sources and Documents*. Englewood Cliffs, NJ: Prentice-Hall, 1979.

Schäfer, Wilhelm. *Sachsen-Chronik für Vergangenheit und Gegenwart, oder Magazin für Ansammlung und Mittheilung der allseitigen Eigenschaften, Schicksale und Verhältnisse der sächsischen Gesammtlande*, 1st ser. Dresden: Julius Blochmann jun., 1854.

Schattkowsky, Martina. *Zwischen Rittergut, Residenz und Reich: die Lebenswelt des kursächsischen Landadligen Christoph von Loss auf Schleinitz (1574–1620)*. Schriften zur sächsischen Geschichte und Volkskunde, 20. Leipzig: Leipziger Universitätsverlag, 2007.

Schering, Arnold, and Rudolf Wustmann. *Musikgeschichte Leipzigs*. 3 vols. Leipzig: F. Kistner & C.F.W. Siegel, 1926–41.

Schütz, Heinrich. *Neue Ausgabe sämtlicher Werke*. Herausgegeben im Auftrag der Internationalen Heinrich-Schütz-Gesellschaft. Vols. 1–40. Kassel: Bärenreiter, 1955–2008.

Schütz, Heinrich. *Sämtliche Werke*. Edited by Philipp Spitta. 16 vols. Leipzig: Breitkopf & Härtel, 1885–94.

Schütz, Heinrich. *Stuttgarter Schütz-Ausgabe. Sämtliche Werke*. Edited by Günter Graulich. Neuhausen-Stuttgart: Hänssler 1971–.

Skei, Allen B. *Heinrich Schütz: A Guide to Research*. Garland Composer Resource Manuals, 1. New York and London: Garland, 1981.

Smallman, Basil. *The Music of Heinrich Schütz 1585–1672*. Leeds: Mayflower, 1985.

Smallman, Basil. *Schütz*. The Master Musicians, edited by Stanley Sadie. Oxford: Oxford University Press, 2000.

Spagnoli, Gina. *Letters and Documents of Heinrich Schütz 1656–1672: An Annotated Translation*. Studies in Music, edited by George J. Buelow, 106. Ann Arbor: UMI, 1990.

Steude, Wolfram. "Neue Schütz Ermittlungen." *Deutsches Jahrbuch der Musikwissenschaft für 1967* (1968): 64–69.

Strunk, Oliver W. *Source Readings in Music History*. Vol. 4, *The Baroque Era*. New York: W. W. Norton, 1965. First published 1950.

Thiele, Alfred. "Heinrich Schütz und Weimar." In *Festschrift zur Ehrung von Heinrich Schütz (1585–1672)*, edited by Günther Kraft, 62–82. Weimar: Buchdruckerei Uschmann, 1954.

Valentin, Caroline. *Geschichte der Musik in Frankfurt am Main vom Anfange des XIV. Bis zum Anfange des XVIII. Jahrhunderts*. Im Auftrage des Vereins für Geschichte und Altertumskunde zu Frankfurt am Main. Frankfurt a. Main: K. Th. Völcker, 1906.

Varwig, Bettina. *Histories of Heinrich Schütz*. Cambridge: Cambridge University Press, 2011.

Vollhardt, Reinhard. *Geschichte der Cantoren und Organisten von den Städten im Königreich Sachsen*. Berlin: Wilhelm Issleib, 1899. Reprint, Leipzig: Peters, 1978.

Wade, Mara R. *Triumphus nuptialis danicus: German Court Culture and Denmark: The "Great Wedding" of 1634*. Wolfenbütteler Arbeiten zur Barockforschung, 27. Wiesbaden: Harrossowitz, 1996.

Watanabe-O'Kelly, Helen. *Court Culture in Dresden: From Renaissance to Baroque*. Basingstoke; New York: Palgrave, 2002.

Weiss, Piero, and Richard Taruskin. *Music in the Western World: A History in Documents*. New York: Schirmer, 1984.

Werbeck, Walter. "Heinrich Schütz und der Streit zwischen Marco Scacchi und Paul Siefert." *Schütz-Jahrbuch* 17 (1995): 63–79.

Werner, Arno. "Musik und Musiker in Landeschule Pforta." *Sammelbände der Internationalen Musikgesellschaft* 8, no. 4 (1907): 535–50.

Werner, Arno. "Nachrichten über Johann Samuel Schein [Kleine Mitteilungen]." *Sammelbände der Internationalen Musikgesellschaft* 9, no. 4 (1908): 634.

Werner, Arno. *Städtische und fürstliche Musikpflege in Weissenfels bis zum Ende des 18. Jahrhunderts*. Leipzig: Breitkopf & Härtel, 1911.

Werner, Arno. *Städtische und fürstliche Musikpflege in Zeitz bis zum Anfang des 19. Jahrhunderts.* Bückeburg und Leipzig: C. F. W. Siegel (R. Linnemann), 1922.

Wessely, Othmar. "Zwei unveröffentlichte Heinrich Schütz-Dokumente." *Die Musikerziehung* 7 (1953–54): 7–10.

Weston, Elizabeth Jane. *Collected Writings.* Edited and translated by Donald Cheney and Brenda M. Hosington, with the assistance of D. K. Money. Toronto: University of Toronto Press, 2000.

Wollny, Peter. "A Source Complex in the Düben Collection." In *The Dissemination of Music in Seventeenth-Century Europe: Celebrating the Düben Collection: Proceedings from the International Conference at Uppsala University 2006*, 173–91, edited by Erik Kjellberg. Varia Musicologica, 18. Bern and New York: Peter Lang, 2010.

Zahn, Johannes. *Die Melodien der deutschen evangelischen Kirchenlieder, aus den Quellen geschöpft und mitgeteilt von Johannes Zahn.* 6 vols. Hildesheim: Georg Olm 1963. First published, Gütersloh: Bertelsmann, 1889–93.

Ziegler, Kaspar. *Von den Madrigalen. Mit einer Eingleitung und Anmerkungen von Dorothea Glodny-Wiercinski.* Ars poetica, 12. Frankfurt am Main: Athenäum, 1971.

Electronic Resources

Grove Music Online. Edited by Deanne Root. http://www.grovemusic.com. Accessed 4 June 2011.

Adrio, Adam, and Clytus Gottwald. "Calvisius, Sethus."

Baron, John H. "Kittel, Caspar."

Baron, John H. "Kittel, Christoph."

Baron, John H. "Nauwach, Johann."

Baron, John H. "Stolle, Philipp."

Baron, John H. "Ziegler, Caspar."

Baselt, Bernd, and Dorothea Schröder. "Michael, Rogier."

Baselt, Bernd, and Dorothea Schröder. "Michael, Tobias."

Beechey, Gwilym. "Strungk, Delphin."

Blankenburg, Walter. "Otto, Georg."

Brumana, Biancamaria, and Colin Timms. "Bontempi, Giovanni Andrea."

Buch, Hans-Joachim. "Thieme, Clemens."

Federhofer, Hellmut, and Steven Saunders. "Sansoni, Giovanni."

Fishback, Horace, and Gregory S. Johnston. "Vierdanck, Johann."

Klotz, Hans, and Dietrich Kollmannsperger. "Fritzsche, Gottfried."

Pyron, Nona, and Aurelio Bianco. "Farina, Carlo."

Rifkin, Joshua, and Eva Linfield, with Derek McCullough (work list) and Stephen Baron (bibliography). "Schütz, Heinrich."

Roche, Jerome, and Roark Miller. "Grandi, Alessandro."

Silbiger, Alexander. "Weckmann, Matthias."

Snyder, Kerala J. "Bernhard, Christoph."

Snyder, Kerala J. "Rosenmüller, Johann."

Snyder, Kerala J., and Gregory S. Johnston. "Schein, Johann Hermann." Walter, Horst. "Löwe von Eisenach, Johann Jakob."

INDEX

A

Adolph Friedrich, Duke of Mecklenburg-Schwerin, 3n5, 151n59, 156n66, 230, 230n12
Albrecht Friedrich, Duke of Prussia, 59n9
Albrecht V, Duke of Bavaria, 2n2
Albrici, Vincenzo (composer, organist), 186n116
Allegri, Lorenzo (composer, lutenist), 49n96
Altenburg (town), 9n16, 79n52, 196n142
Anna Sophia, Duchess of Brunswick-Wolfenbüttel, 121n127
Antonius, Johann (Dresden surgeon), 261
Appellate Court at Dresden, 106
Archdiocese of Magdeburg, 138n27, 151n60, 156, 184, 253
Augsburg (town), 15n25, 72, 72n28, 82–83, 83n71, 84, 131n14
August, Duke of Saxe-Weissenfels, 3n5, 43n76, 138n27, 155–57, 230n12
August, Duke of Saxony, 151n59
August, Duke of Saxony (Administrator of the Magdeburg Diocese), 156, 156n66, 253
August the Younger, Duke of Brunswick-Lüneburg, 10n19, 121n126, 211, 216, 226–28, 233, 240–41, fig 11, fig 14

B

Bach, J. S., 72n29, 243n38
bandora, 34, 34n53
baptism, 3, 43n76, 138n27, 149–50n49, 149–54, 156, 172, 184, 251, 253
baptism, music preparation for princely, 149–54
basso continuo, 24, 26–27, 34–35, 39, 96, 102–3, 105, 110, 144, 146, 162–66, 177, 180, 222–24, 224n5, 225, 228, 231–33
bassoon, 27, 47n86, 151, 170, 181, 243
Battle of Lützen, 87n77, 259n75
Battle of the White Mountain, 31n49
battles between Protestant and Imperial troops, 87n77
Baumann, Jacob (instrumentalist), 15n25
Bautzen (town), 130, 140n33, 141, 144, 243n38
Bautzen, Town Council of, 140, 140n33, 141–44, 170–71
Becker, Cornelius (theologian, poet)
  about, 47–48, 62–65, 65n17, 72n29, 229–32
  Becker Psalter (1628), 47n87, 62–66, 65n17, 216, 229–33, 238
  Becker Psalter (1661, 2nd edition), 229–33, 232n14–15, 239, fig 12
Berg, Gimel (Saxon Court Book-printer), 24, 26, 33, 110, 144, 163

Berlich, Burkard (Council and Chamber Secretary to the Elector of Saxony), 174–75, 174n92
Bernhard, Christoph (composer, singer, theorist)
   about, 193–94n132, 248, 256–58, fig16
   Geistreiches Gesang-Buch, 256–58, 256n67, fig 16
Bieger, Johann (Schütz's grandfather), 250, 258
Bodenschatz, Erhard (composer, music editor), 54n108
bombard, 170, 170n88
Bontempi, Giovanni Andrea (composer, singer, librettist), 181, 185–86n116, 186, 203n163
Breslau (Wrocław, Poland) (town), 31n49
Briegel, Wolfgang Carl (composer, Kapellmeister in Gotha), 158n71
Bruno (*Kapellknabe,* son of Hans Bruno, organist), 6, 6n10, 7–8
Bruno, Hans (instrumentalist), 6n10
Brunswick (town), 36n38, 122, 125, 146, 146n44, 163, 172, 211, 216–17, 220, 233, 254, 260

C

Caccini, Giulio (composer, singer), 7n13, 49n96
   Arien und Kantaten, 7n13
Calbe (Kalbe in Saxony-Anhalt) (town), 138, 138n27
Calvinists, 4n6
Calvisius, Sethus (theorist, composer, Thomaskantor), 18n32, 77n43, 259n73
   Exercitationes musicae duae, 18n32
Cantor of the Dresden Kreuzschule, 134n19
Carlo Emanuele I, Duke of Savoy, 49n96
Castelli, Francesco (Italian violinist), 66, 68, 72–73, 73n34, 74, 83
Castrato, 124, 185–86, 203
Catholic cause during Thirty Years' War, 259n75
Catholicism, 4n6, 38n66, 83, 172
Catholic potentates, 90
Charles, Duke of Nevers (Carlo I Gonzaga), 72n30
Chemnitz (town), 191n127
Chemnitz Palace, 8
chitarrone, 24, 26
Christian (V), Prince-Elect of Denmark, 79n51–52, 88, 90–91, 109, 145n41, 146n42, 147n45, 153n63

Christian I, Duke of Saxe-Merseburg, 187n119
Christian I, Elector of Saxony, 4n6, 10n19, 176n101
Christian II, Elector of Saxony, 4n6, 6n9, 10n19, 46n81
Christian IV, King of Denmark, 46n81, 79n52, 92n84, 93n89, 95, 111n117, 145n41, 153n63, 178, 259n75
Christina (Chretienne) of Lorraine, 58n8
cittern, 40, 40n71, 46, 49, 79
Colander, Anthonius (court musician), 15
Copenhagen, Denmark, 7n14, 79n52, 90–91, 93, 95n92, 111, 118, 126, 145, 153n63, 161, 194n137, 246n46, 254, 260
Copenhagen, Royal Danish Court at, 90–91
cornetto, 19, 27, 47, 47n86, 59, 151, 151n55, 243
counterpoint, 161, 164, 164n82, 165, 180, 248
Cracau, August (District Administrator), 7n12
Cremcovius, Valentinus (Valens) (rector at Magdeburg), 65, 65n18
   Cithara Davidica Luthero-Becceriana, 65
Cremona (town), 55

D

Daniel, Stephan (merchant in Brunswick), 216–17, 220, 233, 240
Dedekind, Constantin Christian (poet, composer)
   about, 225, 225n7, 248–49, 248n51
   Aelbianische Musenlust, 225
   commemorative poem, 248n51
Dixon, John (English musician), 78n46, 132, 151n56
Dresden (town), 78, 79n50, 80n55, 80n57, 81, 81n64, 82, 84, 85n74, 87, 87n77, 89, 92, 96–98, 101, 104, 106–7, 110–12, 115, 118, 128–29, 131, 134n19, 136–37, 138n27, 143–44, 146, 148–49, 153, 153n63, 157–59, 161, 161n76, 162–63, 163n81, 164, 168, 173–80, 184, 185n116, 188–90, 194, 194n132, 195–96, 196n144, 197–99–200, 202–4, 206, 208, 211, 213, 214n181, 215, 217–18, 221–22, 224–26, 228–29, 231–33, 236, 238–46, 246n46, 247, 250, 250n54, 253–56, 258–61
Dresden, Electoral Palace in, 203, fig 4
Dresden, Kapellmeister in, 23, 117

Dresden Court, 78–79, 79n51, 81, 94–95, 105, 119–20, 131–33, 154, 166–71, 172n89, 176–77, 186–88, 199, 208–9, 225n7
Dresden Court musicians, 112–13
Dresden *Hofkapelle,* 4n10, 15n25, 46n79, 48n90, 49n93, 80n63, 81n64, 114n119, 126, 134n18, 150n50–51, 189–90, 194–95, 197–99, fig 16
Dresden *Kapellverzeichnis,* 79n49
Dresden Kreuzkirche, 243n38
Dresden Kreuzschule, Cantor of the, 134n19

E

Eggenberg, Johann Ulrich von (Count in Adelsberg, Ruler of Pettau), 38, 38n66
Eichler, Moses (Schütz's servant), 92
Electoral Palace in Dresden, 203, fig 4
Electors of the Holy Roman Empire, 51, 69
Erbach, Christian (composer, organist), 131n14

F

Farina, Carlo (violinist), 48, 48n90, 50, 68, 73, 75
Ferdinand II, Archduke of Austria and Holy Roman Emperor, 13n23, 31n49, 38, 38n66, 109n115
Ferdinand III, Archduke of Austria and Holy Roman Emperor, 108, 109n115, 117–18
Fischer, Michael (trumpeter), 60
Florence (town), 49n96, 58, 67
Fontana, Agostino (singer), 153–55, 153n63
Förster, Kasper (Kapellmeister), 137, 137n14, 138, 160–61
Frankfurt am Main, City Council of, 28–29
Frederik II, King of Denmark, 46n80
Frederik III, King of Denmark, 111n117, 145n41
Freiberg, 37–38, 38n63, 39, 62, 64–65, 131n14, 149, 230, 238–39
Freiberg Petrikirche, 36n58
Friderich, Abraham *(Kapellknabe),* 80, 80n58
Friedrichsburg (town), 85
Friedrich Ulrich, Duke of Brunswick-Lüneburg, 121n127
Friedrich Wilhelm II, Duke of Saxe-Altenburg, 146n42
Fritzsche, Gottfried (organ builder), 35–36, 121n117

G

Gabrieli, Giovanni (composer, organist, teacher), 2, 2n2, 25, 70, 134n19, 160, 181n107, 182–83, 252, 259
Geier, Martin (Senior Court Chaplain and Church Councillor)
  about, 250, 250n54, 254n61
  Schütz's *curriculum vitae,* 250
Georg Friedrich, Margrave of Brandenburg-Ansbach, 23n38, 163n81
Georg II, Landgrave of Hesse-Darmstadt, 56n5
Gera (town), 16, 16n29, 17n31, 18–20, 96–97, 100, 139, 251, 258
Gera, Town Council of, 19–20
Gera castle, 139
Gera Rutheneum (Gymnasium), 18n32, 138–39, 138n19
Gesualdo, Carlo, Prince of Venosa, 84
Glückstadt (Lykstad), Lord Governor of, 91–92
Gonzaga, Carlo I (Charles, Duke of Nevers), 72n30
Gonzaga, Eleonora, Empress, 48n90
Gonzaga, Vincenzo, Duke of Mantua, 72, 72n30
Gonzaga, Vincenzo II, Duke of Mantua, 72
Görmar, Heinrich von, 259
Gotha (town), 158n72
Gottlieb, Johann, 161
Gottorp (Schleswig-Holstein), 93n89, 110
Gottorp, Duke of, 153
Grandi, Alessandro (composer), 181, 181n107
  Super Lilia Convallium, 181
Graz, *Hofkapelle* in, 23n38
Grohmann, Friederich *(Kapellknabe),* 80, 80n56
Gross, Friedrich (bookkeeper), 260
Grundt, Michael (trombonist), 79, 79n49, 80
Grünschneider, Tobias (violinist), 66–67, 67n21–22, 68
Gudeborn (town), 59
Gumpelzhaimer, Adam (composer), 72n29
Gumprecht, Jeremias (merchant), 159
Gumprecht, Martin, 131
Günther, Gabriel (Wilhelm Günther's son), 46–47, 46n82, 47, 47n84, 80
Günther, Johann Friedrich, 17n30
Günther, Wilhelm (instrumentalist), 15, 47, 47n84, 48, 50, 59, 79, 79n50

Gustavus Adolphus, King of Sweden, 87n77, 121n127, 159n75
Güstrow (town), 230
Güstrow court, 7n14

H

Habsburg, Maria von *(Infanta de España)*, 13n14
Habsburg, Maximilian II von, Holy Roman Emperor, 13n24
Habsburg, Maximilian von, Archduke of Austria, 13n24, 14
Habsburgs, 38n66
Hadersleben (Haderslev), Denmark, 91, 91n82
Hainhofer, Philipp (merchant, banker, political agent)
 about, 72, 72n28, 72n30, 82–84, 83n70
 Lautenbücher, 72n32
Halle (town), 3n5, 6n10, 37, 37n60, 43n76, 49n94, 79n52, 151–52, 156n66, 159, 199, 246–47
Hamburg (town), 6n10, 36n58, 37n60–61, 47n85, 79n51, 85, 85n74, 87, 91–92, 92n84, 93n89, 121, 148, 194n132, 248n49
Hanitsch, Johann, 254n61
Hanitzsch, Gottfried (revenue-department administrator), 82
Hartenstein, *Herr* von, 79n50, 151
Hartmann, Andreas, 201
Hartmann, Christian, 254
Hartmann, Maria, 254n61
Hartmann, Michael (Electoral Saxon tax recorder), 52, 52n102, 53, 254n61
Hasselt, Johann (Hans) (singer), 49, 49n92, 50, 81–82
Hassler, Hans Leo (composer, organist), 72n29
Hauptvogel, Nicoll, 15
Hedwig of Denmark, Electress, Duchess of Saxony, 46n81, 61–64
Hemmerlein, Daniel (instrumentalist), 79, 79n48, 80
Hempel, Georg, 77
Hering, Alexander (organist), 131n14, 141–44, 170–71, 242–43, 243n38
Hertel, Zacharias (instrumentalist), 132, 151, 151n55
Hesse-Kassel, Court of, 3–5, 8, 10–12, 22–23
Hestius, Zacharias (Vice-Kapellmeister), 80n57, 94, 172, 172n89

Hildesheim (town), 120, 122
Hirnschrötl, Sebastian (singer), 15, 49, 49n93, 50, 132, 150
Historische Beschreibung der Edlen Sing-und Kling-Kunst, xviin3
Hoen, Philipp Heinrich von, 252n58–59
Hoë von Hoënegg, Matthias (theologian, Court Chaplain), 75n36, 83, 136n20
Hoffmann, Georg (printer), 38, 62
Hofkapelle in Dresden, 4n10, 15n25, 46n79, 48n90, 49n93, 81n64, 114n119, 134n18, 150n50–51, 189–90, 194–95, 197–99, fig 16
Hofkontz, Johann Georg (tenor), 132–34, 134n18, 136, 155, 171–73, 173n90, 189–91, 189n125, 193
Hohenzollern, Georg Wilhelm von, Elector of Brandenburg, 40n72, 78n44, 121n127
Holk, Heinrich Graf von, 87n77, 191n127
homosexuality, 146n43
Horace, 70n25
Hoyer, Gregor (instrumentalist), 15
Hoym, Christoph von (Chief Overseer), 46, 46n83, 59, 175, 175n99
Huber, Johann (bellows treader), 132
Hubmeier, Hippolyte (Rector in Göttingen), 18n32
 Disputationes quaestionum illustrium, philosophicarum, musicarum, 18n32

I

Imperial printing patent of 1637, 117–18
Italian musicians at the Dresden Court, 199–200
Italy, 23n38, 25, 44–45, 46n79, 47n84, 55, 57–58, 61, 67n21, 68, 71–72, 72n28, 73–74, 74n35, 75–76, 81n64, 83, 86, 146, 164–65, 178, 182–83, 186n116, 200, 205, 252–54, 259

J

Jägerdörfer, Jonas (timpanist), 132
James I, King of England, 46n81
Johann Albrecht II, Duke of Mecklenburg-Güstrow, 121n126
Johann Georg I, Elector of Saxony, 3, 3n5, 4, 4n6, 5–13, 21–24, 31, 31n49, 40–45, 46n81, 47–48, 49n96, 52, 52n101, 52n103, 53–54, 54n106, 54n109, 56–58, 59n10, 60–62, 66–68, 67n21, 146n42, 253, 259, fig 3

Index

Johann Georg II, Elector of Saxony, 69, 115–17, 149n49, 154–55, 154n64, 161–64, 161n76, 174n92, 184n115, 185–86n116, 192n128, 204–6, 207n169, 230, 244–45, 250n54, fig 7

Johann Georg III, Elector of Saxony, 150n49

Johann Philipp, Duke of Saxe-Altenburg, 10n19

Johann Sigismund, Elector of Brandenburg, 121n127

K

Kaiser, Georg (singer), 192, 196–97, 196n144

Kapelle in Halle, 49n94, 79n52

Kapellknaben (choir boys)
  allowances and provisions for, 132, 236
  annual stipend for, 167
  assignment to locations, 77
  at the Dresden court, 7n14, 176
  fixed rehearsal each day, 135
  food, drink, clothing, and supplies for, 167, 169, 174–75, 177
  Friderich, Abraham *(Kapellknabe)*, 80, 80n58
  Grohmann, Friederich *(Kapellknabe)*, 80, 80n56
  Günther, Gabriel, 46–47, 46n82, 47, 47n84, 80
  instruction of, 19, 116–17, 119–20, 155, 174–75
  instrumentalist, 46, 49–50, 76, 79, 80n55, 133, 166, 168
  Italian and German singers, 205
  Kittel, Caspar, 7, 7n13, 15n26, 80, 83
  Kittel, Christoph (Court Organist), 132–33, 135, 173–77
  Klemm, Johann (Court Organist), 110, 114n119, 130–31, 130n11, 131n14, 132–34, 144, 150–51, 162, 243n38
  lodging, boarding, and expenses, 114–15, 131–32
  Michael, Augustin, 80, 80n60–61
  Michael, Simon, 80, 80n59, 80n61
  money for boarding, 53–54, 74
  morning and evening prayer, 48, 63
  Petermann, Andreas (Court Cantor), 134, 134n19
  Pitzsch, Christian, 80, 80n62
  skilled musicians trained in vocal and instrumental music, 217
  stipend and monetary expenses for, 43, 52–53, 71, 73, 236
  Tax, Thomas (instrumentalist), 15, 80, 80n63
  transportation for, 187
  two *Kapellknaben* residing with former cantor at Naumburg, 234–35
  Vierdanck, Johann (composer, organist, instrumentalist), 7, 7n14, 15n26, 59
  young, 7, 19, 77–78, 174, 263
  Zehm, Martin *(Kapellknabe)*, 46, 46n80, 56, 59

Kapellmeister in Dresden, 23, 117

Kassel (town), 5, 8–10, 12–13

Kassel Court, 8, 11, 11n11, 12, 22–23, 182, 183n111, 211, 259

Kelley, Edward (alchemist), 226–27n9

Kirchof, Antonius (Rector of the Thomasschule), 260, 260n79

Kittel, Caspar (Court Organist), 7, 7n13, 15n26, 55, 66–68, 72–74, 79, 80, 83
  Arien und Kantaten, 7n13

Kittel, Christoph (Court Organist), 132–33, 135, 166–170, 173–77, 208–09, 222–23, 239

Kittel, Jonas (singer), 132, 150, 150n51

Klee, Hans (instrumentalist), 15

Kleinhempel, Conrad (Excise Councillor, electoral agent), 150, 150n53

Klemm, Johann (Court Organist), 110, 114n119, 130–31, 130n11, 131n14, 132–34, 144, 150–51, 162, 243n38

Klemm, Johann Heinrich (son of Johann Klemm), 114, 114n119, 150

Klug, Joseph, 72n29
  Geistliche Lieder, 72n29

Knabe, Martin (singer, organist), 81n65–66, 139–40

Knüpfer, Sebastian (Thomaskantor), 242n37, 243, 246n47

Köckeritz, Johann (instrumentalist), 15, 49, 81, 81n64

Köckeritz, Martin (relative of Johann Köckeritz), 80, 80n54–55

Köhler, Siegfried, 187n118

Köstritz (Bad Köstritz) (town), 16n19, 250, 259

Kramer, Johann (singer), 49, 49n94, 50, 60

Kramper, Andrea (cloth-merchant), 259

Krause, Andreas (instrumentalist), 80n55

Kreichel, Christoph *(Kapellknabe)*, 176

Index

Krüger, Christian (instrumentalist), 60, 60n50, 80, 152
Kühnel, Heinrich Gottfried (cantor in Naumburg), 234n22
Kurfürstentage (Electoral Diet), 56n5

L

Langensalza (town), 5, 8, 22n36
Lebzelter, Friedrich (Privy Chamber Servant), 47, 47n85, 55–56, 59, 73–75, 83, 85–87, 90–92
Lehmann, Georg (court administrator), 53
Leipzig, 9n87, 16n29, 18n32, 29n46, 32, 32n50, 44, 65–67, 71, 72n29, 75, 77, 77n40, 77n42–44, 78, 78n44, 79, 79n47, 82, 87n77, 105, 110, 127, 130–31, 131n14, 140, 146, 146n43, 149–50, 150n53–54, 152, 157, 159, 163, 163n78, 174n92, 182, 201, 201n160, 216–17, 219, 221, 234n21, 239–42, 242n37, 243, 243n38, 246n47, 250n54, 254n61, 255, 255n62, 258, 260–61
Leipziger Bund (Protestant alliance), 78n44
Leipzig fairs, 42, 44, 48, 71, 75, 127, 216, 219, 236, 240
Lenander, Petrus (Privy Council and Vice-Chancellor), 260
Leopold Wilhelm of Austria (Catholic Administrator of Magdeburg), 152n60
Leo von Eisenach, Johannes (diplomat, advocate), 227n9
Leyserus, Polycarpus (Polykarp Leyser) (Protestant theologian), 77, 77n42
Longolius, Johann (cantor), 248n47
Loss auf Schleinitz, Christoph von (Imperial Treasurer), 6, 6n9, 8–10, 13, 45, 183
Löwe von Eisenach, Johann Jacob (Kapellmeister), 213–14n181, 214, 226–27, 227n9
Lübeck (town), 7n14, 93n89
Lübeck, Town Council of, 93n89
Ludwig, Gottfried, 261
lute, 17, 24, 26, 34, 40n71, 46, 49n96, 72
Luther, Martin, 63, 183, 193n130, 207
Lutheran Orthodoxy, 136n20
Lutheran Reformation, 263

M

madrigals, 1–2, 77n43, 84, 138, 147–48, 148n47, 183n112, 201, 201n159–60, 202, 238

Magdalena, Countess of Hohenlohe-Langenburg, 97n96
Magdalena, Countess of Schwarzburg-Rudolstadt, 97, 97n96
Magdalena Sibylle of Prussia, Electress of Saxony, 59n10
Magdalena Sybille of Saxony, 146n42
Magdeburg (town), 3n5, 36n58, 65, 65n18, 138n27, 151n60, 214, 259n75
Mantua (town), 48n90, 68, 68n23, 73n34
Mantuan court, 68
Mantuan Succession, 68n23
Maria Magdalena of Austria, Grand Duchess of Tuscany, 58, 58n8
Martinengo, Giulio Cesare (*Maestro di Cappella* at San Marco), 183n113
Mattheson, Johann (composer, critic, lexicographer)
  about, 248, 248n49
  Der vollkommene Capellmeister, 248n49
  Grundlage einer Ehrenpforte, 248, 248n49
Matthias, Holy Roman Emperor, King of Bohemia, King of Hungary, 13n22–13n23, 38
May, Hans, 15
Medici, Cosimo II de, Grand Duke of Tuscany, 58n8
Medici, Ferdinando II de, Grand Duke of Tuscany, 58n8
Meissen (town), 7, 22, 54n108, 62, 80n55, 80n57, 236, 261
Mensur, 147, 224, 242
Merkel, Adam *(Kapellknabe)*, 176
Merulo, Claudio (composer, organist), 2n2
Meuler, Jobst (string manufacturer), 30, 30n48
Michael, Augustin *(Kapellknabe)*, 80, 80n60–61
Michael, Rogier (Electoral Kapellmeister), 23n38, 44, 51, 77n43, 80n59, 163, 163n81, 189
Michael, Simon *(Kapellknabe)*, 80, 80n59, 80n61
Michael, Tobias (composer, Thomaskantor), 80n59, 146n43, 150, 150n54, 163, 242n37
Musicalische Seelenlust, 150n54
Mitternacht, Johann Sebastian (poet, theologian, Senior Court Chaplain and Superintendent at Zeitz), 245n44
modes, 70, 70n26, 102, 164, 164n82, 225, 232

Mölich, Michael (instrumentalist and citharist), 46, 46n79, 56, 59
Monteverdi, Claudio (composer)
  about, 72n30, 147–48, 148n47, 181n107, 183n113
  compositions, 148, 148n47
Moritz, Duke of Saxony, Duke of Saxe-Zeitz, 152n61, 187n119, 195n137, 214m181, 237–38, 246n46
Moritz, Landgrave of Hesse-Kassel, 3–4, 6n8, 8, 9n16, 43n76, 182–83, 192, 251–53, 259, fig 2
Morsius, Joachim
  about, 93–94, 93n89
  Stammbuch, 93, 93n85, 94n90
Moser, Wilhelm Ludwig (Court Chamber Secretary), xx, 29–30, 33–37, 36n57, 197, 197n146, 254n62, xxn14
Mühlhausen (town), 48, 50–52, 52n103, 56, 79n51
Mühlhausen, Electoral Assembly in, 48, 50–52, 52n103, 56
Müller, Johann (organist), 49, 49n95, 50

N
Naples (town), 82–84
Naples, music ordered from, 84
Naumburg (town), 54n108, 184n114
Naumburg, Cantor at, 234, 234n22
Naumburg, Council at, 209
Nauwach, Johann (composer, organist, theorbist)
  about, 15, 49, 49n95–96, 50
  Lieder, 49n96
Neander, Christoph *(Kreuzkantor),* 47n85
Neander, Peter *(Cantor figuralis* in Gera), 18n32, 138, 138n29
Nicolaus (instrumentalist), 15
Nuremberg (town), 29–30, fig 4
Nuremberg City Council, 30
Nusser, Philipp Jacob (singer), 49, 150, 150n50
Nykøbing (Nykøbing Falster, Denmark), 95, 95n92

O
Opitz, Martin (poet)
  about, 56n5, xviiin1
  Weltliche Poëmata, xviiin1

organ galleries in Zeitz, 237–38, fig 13
organist, 2n2, 3–5, 6n10, 7n13–7n14, 8, 10, 16–17, 26–27, 34, 39, 46n79, 49–50, 65, 79n51, 81n65, 102, 110, 114, 116, 121n128, 130–31, 131n14, 133–35, 137n24, 139–44, 146, 146n43–146n44, 152, 162–63, 166–67, 170–71, 173–75, 177, 180, 191, 209, 214n183, 223, 228, 231–33, 239, 242–43, 243n38
organ tablature, 39, 39n68, 166, 166n84, 223, 233
Osterhausen, Johann Georg von (Marshal of the Palace), 43, 55, 55n3
Otto, Georg (Kapellmeister), 22, 22n36, 183n11

P
Pachelbel, Johann (composer), 72n29
Palestrina, Giovanni Pierluigi da (composer), 248
Pappenheim, Gottfried Heinrich, Count of, 259, 259n75
Peltz (Beltz), Johann (instrumentalist), 40–41, 40n70, 49
Peranda, Marco Giuseppe (composer, Kapellmeister, singer), 49n95
performance practice, 15–17, 19, 26–28, 34–35, 34n53–n55, 39, 51, 61, 64–66, 77, 94, 101–03, 116–17, 123–24, 126, 147–48, 151–52, 155, 164–66, 165n83, 168, 179–81, 223–25, 232–33, 232n14–n15, 237, 242–43
Petermann, Andreas (Court Cantor), 134, 134n19
Petermann, Daniel (Rector in Meissen), 261
Pflugk, Georg (Marshal of the Palace), 55–56, 55n2, 59–60, 73–74, 81–82, 107
Pforta (town), 54, 54n108, 77n43, 184n114
Philipp, Duke of Schleswig-Holstein-Sonderburg-Glücksburg, 187n119
Pincker, Christoph (jurist, Schütz's son-in-law), 155–57, 159, 216n183, 254n61, 255, 260
Pincker, Gertraud Euphrosina (Schütz's granddaughter), 255, 255n65
Pirna (town), 14
Pitzsch, Christian *(Kapellknabe),* 80, 80n62
Pleissenburg (town), 87n77
Praetorius, Hieronymus (organist), 121n128
Praetorius, Jacob (composer, organist), 79nn51, 121, 121n128

Praetorius, Michael (composer, Kapellmeister, organist)
  about, 6n10, 9, 9n15, 12, 23n38, 36n58, 44, 51, 67n22, 121n127, 163n81, 189, fig 5
  Pommer and *Bombart,* 170n88
  Syntagma musicum II, 40n71, 67n22, 170n88
Pretzel, Johann (organist), 81n65
Price, John (English musician), 78n46
printing patents, 21–22, 47–48, 62, 104–105, 108–09, 117–18
Printz, Wolfgang Caspar (composer, historian, novelist), xvii
Profe, Ambrosius (music editor, publisher, composer, theorist), 32
  Ander Theil geistlicher Concerten und Harmonien, 32–33, 32n50
Protestant dioceses and administrators, 3n5, 78n44, 79n52, 138n27, 151n59–n60, 156, 156n66, 176n101, 184, 253
Protestant hymns, 9n15, 101–102, 155, 223
Psalter, 47n87, 62–66, 207, 229–33, fig 12

R
Raphael (Michael Raphuel) (painter), 226
recitative style *(stile recitativo),* 86, 242
recorder, 243
Reichbrodt von Schrenckendorf, Christian (Councillor and Privy Secretary), 153–54, 188–89, 191–97, 196n142, 198, 202–3
Reuss, Heinrich II, 97n97, 138, 138n28–29, 139, 139n32, 199–200
Reuss, Heinrich III, 97n97
Reuss, Heinrich IX, 97n97
Reuss, Heinrich Posthumus, 16–21, 16n29, 17n31, 18n32, 96–101, 138n28–29
Reuss, Heinrich X, 97n97
Reuss, House of, 97n97
Reuss, Magdalena, Countess of Hohenlohe-Langenburg, 97n96
Reuss, Magdalena, Countess of Schwarzburg-Rudolstadt, 97, 97n96
Reuss dominion, 258
Reuss family, 138n28
Richter, Christoph *(Kapellknabe),* 176
Rinuccini, Ottavio (librettist), 56n5

Rosenmüller, Johann (composer, organist), 146, 146n43
Rudolph II, Holy Roman Emperor, 226n9, 258
Ruprecht, Georg (tax-collector), 259

S
Sachsenburg castle, 76, 76n39, 258–59
Saint Martin's Church (Martinikirche) in Brunswick, 146, 163
Saltzmann, Philipp (Senior Court Chaplain and Superintendent at Zeitz), 245n44
Sängerknaben (choirboys), 116, 263. *See also* Kapellknaben
Sansoni, Giovanni (Imperial cornettist), 47, 47n86, 59, 151, 151n57, 161–62, 162n76
Sautor, Johann (Court Chamberlain), 52–54, 73
Scacchi, Marco (composer, writer on music)
  about, 137–38, 137n23, 160–61
  Cribrum musicum ad triticum Syferticum, 137–38, 160
Scacchi-Siefert dispute, 137–38, 160–61
Scheffer, Christian, 60, 60n12
Scheibe, Samuel (book seller), 163
Scheidemann, Heinrich (composer, organist), 79n51
Scheidt, Samuel (composer, organist, Kapellmeister)
  about, xvii, 36, 36n58–59, 37, 77, 79n52, 81n65, 151n55, fig 6
  Cantione sacrae, 37n61
  Ludorum musicorum secunda pars, 37n61
  Padouanen, 49n94, 151n55
  Paduana, galliarda, courante, alemande, intrada, canzonetto, 37n61
  Pars prima concertuum sacrorum...adiectic symphoniis et choris instrumentalibus, 37n61
  Tabulatura Nova, Parts 1 & 2, 37n60
Schein, Johann Hermann (composer, poet, Thomaskantor)
  about, xvii, 54n108, 77–78, 77n43, 130n12, 150n54, 163, 163n80, 184n114, 259n73, fig 8
  Geistliche Chormusik, 77n43
Schein, Johann Samuel (organist), 130–31, 130n12, 140–41, 150n54
Schirmer, Christian, 137–38
Schmalkaldic War, 22n37

Index

Schreiber, Christoph (administrative treasurer in Frankenhausen), 259
Schütz, Albrecht (City Magistrate and Council Chamberlain in Weissenfels), 251, 258
Schütz, Anna (née Goldbeck), 260
Schütz, Anna (née Gross), 29n46, 260
Schütz, Anna Justina, 216n183, 254, 254n61, 255, 260, 260n77
Schütz, Anna Magdalena (*Frau* Brehm), 261
Schütz, Anna Maria (*Frau* Schreiber), 259
Schütz, Anna Maria (née Petermann), 261
Schütz, Anna Sabina (née Kirchof), 260
Schütz, Anna Salome (née Volkmar), 260
Schütz, Benjamin (jurist), 260
Schütz, Catharina (née Wolff) (widow Sonntag), 258
Schütz, Christoph (*Bürgermeister* of Weissenfels), 25, 254
Schütz, Christoph Georg (architect in Leipzig), 260
Schütz, Dorothea (*Frau* Thrun), 259
Schütz, Dorothea (née Schreiber), 258
Schütz, Euphrosina (*Frau* von Görmar), 259
Schütz, Euphrosina (née Bieger) (Schütz's mother), 250, 258
Schütz, Euphrosyne (*Frau* Pincker), 26n77, 155–57, 156n67, 159, 216n183, 254, 254n61, 255, 260, xviiin1
Schütz, Friderich Wilhelmus (Pastor at St. Thomas in Leipzig,), 261
Schütz, Georg (Assessor of the Supreme Court), 29, 29n46, 65, 182n110, 254, 259–60
Schütz, Gottfried Ludwig, 261
Schütz, Heinrich (composer, Kapellmeister). *See also* works by Heinrich Schütz
  Agostino Fontana, appointment of Italian musician, 153–55
  Bautzen's organist vacancy, Alexander Hering for, 141–44
  Caspar Kittel, travel documentation for, 66–68
  Caspar Kittel and Augustus Tax, compensation for, 166–70
  Caspar Kittel in the Kapelle, role of, 208–10
  Caspar Kittel's return from Italy, money requested for, 55
  choir-desk in palace chapel, modifications to, 74–75
  Choir of the Evangelist, 34–35
  Christoph Bernhard and Johann Georg Hofkontz, roles of, 191–94
  Christoph Bernhard's five-voice setting of Psalm 119, 248
  Constantin Christian Dedekind's *Aelbianische Musenlust,* appraisal of, 225
  Court of Ernst "The Pious," Duke of Saxe-Gotha-Altenburg, introduction to, 157–59
  curriculum vitae by Martin Geier for Schütz's funeral, 250–56
  Danish Court, appointment to, 92
  Danish Court, second appointment to, 118–19
  Denmark, outstanding honorarium from the Royal Court in, 107
  Denmark, petition for leave to travel to, 87–89
  Denmark, request for assistance to travel to, 85–87
  Denmark, travel and security pass for, 95–96, 109–10, fig 9
  Denmark, travel to retrieve compositions in, 107
  Dresden, Imperial visit to, 13–15
  Dresden Court, boarding and expenses for *Knaben* at the, 131–36
  Dresden Court, continuation of service at, 12–13
  Dresden Court, departure of musicians from the, 194–95
  Dresden Court, his repeated absence from, 94–95
  Dresden Court, Italian musicians at the, 199–200, 204–6
  Dresden Court, organ music appraisal for, 36–37
  Dresden Court, payment request for musicians at, 56
  Dresden Court, requesting services at, 4–6
  Dresden Court, various music matters at the, 73–74
  Dresden Court musicians request his intercession regarding unpaid salaries, 112
  Dresden *Hofkapelle* with Schütz directing at the music desk, fig 16

Schütz, Heinrich (*cont.*)
- Dresden musical establishment, state of, 126–27
- ducal court in Zeitz, musical improvements at the, 234–36
- Duchess Sophie Elizabeth's progress in composition, 120–22
- Duke August the Younger's birthday, music in honor of the, 227–28
- engraving by Augustus John, fig 1
- engraving by Christian Romstet, fig 15
- fees, outstanding payment of, 244–45
- financial circumstances, distressed, 52–53
- Francesco Castelli, support for, 74–75
- Friedrich Sultz and his two sons, appointments of, 186–88
- Georg Kaiser's and Friedrich Sultz's departure from Dresden owing to non-payment of salaries, 196–97
- Giovanni Andrea Bontempi, proposed appointment of, 181–86
- Hamburg, arrival in, 91–92
- Hans Hasselt, re-acquisition of the bassist, 81–82
- Hildesheim, intention to spend time in, 120–22
- *Hofkapelle*, decline of the, 194–95
- *Hofkapelle*, petition to the Duke of Saxony regarding the suffering members of the, 189–94
- Imperial patent of 1637, petition for extension of, 117–18
- index of musicians proposed for travel to Mühlhausen, 48–50
- instrumentalists, appointment of four, 115–17
- Italian musicians at the Dresden Court, 199–200, 204–6
- Italy, late return from, 66–68
- Italy, musical purchases in, 74–75
- Italy, payments and advances following his trip to, 75–76
- Italy, request for money upon arrival in, 60–62
- Italy, request to travel to, 44–45, 57–58
- Johann Georg II, letter of recognition and gratitude drafted on behalf of, 161–62
- Johann Hermann Schein, elegy on the death of, 77–78
- Kapelle, complaint about practices and conditions in the, 202–3
- Kapelle, planned changes to the, 76–77
- Kapelle, restoration of the, 129–30
- Kapelle's demise and the need to fill positions, 113–15
- *Kapellknabe*, runaway, 6–7
- *Kapellknaben*, boarding of, 74–75
- *Kapellknaben*, voice changes in two, 46–47
- *Kapellknaben* at the Dresden Court, introduction of four, 176
- *Kapellknaben* in care of Christoph Kittel, compensation for the four, 176–77
- *Kapellknaben* in care of Christoph Kittel, costs and conditions of, 174–75
- Kapellmeister in Dresden, 23, 117, 259–60
- Kassel Court, apology for delay in return to, 11–12
- Kassel Court, letter requesting his return to, 8, 22–23
- Kleine geistliche Concerte I & II, presentation copies of, 105–6
- *Knaben* assigned to court musicians for board and training, 119–20
- letter to August the Younger, Duke of Brunswick-Lüneburg, fig 14
- Marco Scacchi's *Cribrum musicum ad triticum Syferticum*, response to, 137–38
- marriage in Dresden, 23, 23n38
- Marshal of the Court's intervention in matters of the musicians of the *Hofkapelle*, 197–99
- musical establishments of the Church, Court, and Town of Gera, appraisal of, 16–21
- musical works from Naples, re-ordering, 82–84
- musicians travelling to Leipzig, 79–81
- organ builder Gottfried Fritzsche, 35–36
- organ purchase, 120–22
- payment for arrears to his income, 54
- Peter Neander in Gera, recommendation for replacement of, 138–40
- petition for outstanding salaries, 41–42
- poem commemorating Schütz's tomb, 248–49
- princely baptism, attendance at, 150–52
- printing patents petitions, electoral, 21–22, 47–48, 104–5, 108–9

property acquisition near Weissenfels and request for back pay, 42–44
Psalm 133, composition of, 29
psalm book of Dr. Cornelius Becker, 62–66
published works sent to Wolfenbüttel, 238–41
release from service, request for, 8–9
retirement, desire for, 126–27, 189, 203–4
retirement and pension request for, 181–86, 206–10
retirement due to age and failing health, request for, 209–11
retirement in Weissenfels, 127–30, 208–10
Royal Court in Denmark, honorary appointment to, 126–27
Royal Danish Court in Copenhagen, 90–91
salaries and pawned possessions, musicians sought access to their, 212–13
Scacchi-Siefert Dispute, assessment of, 160–61
Sophie Elisabeth, payment for Schütz's service by, 218–21
steel strings from Nuremberg, order of, 29–30
St. Petri's vacant organist position, recommendation for, 140
tenor for the court, recruitment of a new, 76–77
Teutoniam dudum belli, text to, 32–33
transportation of musicians and instruments from Dresden to Leipzig, 78
travel by musicians, 188–89
unpaid salaries, list of, 51–52
vacant organist position in Bautzen, recommendation for, 140
Venice, money request to settle debts from, 71
Venice, travel pass and letter of introduction, 58
violinists, appraisal of two, 66–68
wedding of Euphrosyne Schütz and Christoph Pincker, 155–57, 159
Weissenfels, move to, 208–9
Weissenfels, sale of property in, 199–200
Wolfenbüttel, contract *in absentia* as Kapellmeister in, 216–18
Wolfenbüttel, published works sent to, 238–41

Wolfenbüttel Court, appointment of an unidentified falsettist, theorbist, and painter at the, 219–21
Wolfenbüttel Court, appointment of Johann Jacob Löwe and other music matters at the, 213–16
Wolfenbüttel Court, payments received from, 233–37
Wolfenbüttel Court, unknown musician of interest to, 125
Wolfenbüttel Court's musical establishment, 123–24
Zeitz, choir lofts in palace church in, 237–38
Zeitz, compositions for the court and church at, 245–47
Schütz, Heinrich Friedrich (constable), 261
Schütz, Johann (collegiate syndic in Merseburg), 259
Schütz, Johann (provincial judge), 258
Schütz, Johanna Elisabeth, 261
Schütz, Ludovicus Wilhelmus (pastor), 261
Schütz, Magdalena (née Wildeck), 23n39, 63, 156n67, 253, 259
Schütz, Margaretha, 260
Schütz, Margaretha (née Fischer), 258
Schütz, Margaretha (née Weidemann), 258
Schütz, Martha, 259
Schütz, N. (student), 261
Schütz, N . N., 261, 261n82
Schütz, Regina Margaretha, 261
Schütz, Sophia Cristiana, 261
Schütz, Sophia Magdalena (née Antonius), 261
Schütz, Valerius, 17, 17n30, 254, 261, 261n83
Schütz, Wilhelmina Sophia, 261
Schütz family genealogy, anonymous, 258–61
Schweissken, Christian, 53
shawm, 170, 170n88
Sibylla Maria (eldest daughter of Johann Georg II), 149n49
Siefert, Paul (composer and organist)
about, 137, 137n23–24, 160–61
Anticribratio musica, 160
Siegfried, Anna Maria (*Frau* Kramper), 259
Siegfried, Daniel (court clerk), 259
Silberling, David *(Kapellknabe),* 176
Simson, Thomas (instrumentalist), 15
Sonntag, Paul, 258

Sophie Eleonore, Duchess of Saxony, 56n5, 184n115, 207n169
Sophie Elisabeth, Duchess of Brunswick-Lüneburg, 120–22, 121n126, 125, 211, 213–16, 218–21, fig 10
Sophie Hedwig, Duchess of Saxe-Zeitz, 187n119
Starschedel, Otto von (Court Advisor), 9, 9n16, 10, 10n18
St. Maria Magdalena Church, Hamburg, 36n58
Stolle, Philipp (instrumentalist), 79, 79n52, 80, 115–17, 120, 150, 194n137, 246n46
St. Peter's Church, Hamburg, 121
Sultz, Friedrich (instrumentalist), 49, 186–88, 194, 194n136, 196–97, 197n147
Sultz, Jacob (instrumentalist), 187
Sultz, Ludwig (instrumentalist), 187

T

Tact, 34, 34n55, 65, 148
Taube, Heinrich von (Marshal of the Court), 175, 175n98, 176, 197, 197n149, 202–3
Tax, Augustus (instrumentalist), 15, 15n25, 48, 50, 79n52, 80, 114–17, 132–33, 151, 166–70
Tax, Thomas (instrumentalist), 15, 80, 80n63
tax collector, 7n11, 209, 225n7, 254n61, 258–59
theorbo, 7n13, 72, 116, 150, 218–221
Thieme, Clemens (composer, instrumentalist), 169, 194–95, 194n137, 214n181, 246n46
Thirty Years' War, 4n6, 15n27, 75n36, 154n64, 158n71, 178, 259n75
Thrun, Zacharias (court clerk), 259
timpani, 132
Tischknaben, 19, 73–74, 264
Torgau (town), 22, 22n36–37, 36n58, 49n96, 52, 56, 56n5, 59n10, 77n40, 78, xviin1
transposition, 102, 232–33, 232n14–15
Traubell, Hans Christoph (theorbist), 15
trombone, 19, 27, 27n42, 49n91, 79–80, 146n43, 151–52, 170, 181, 243
Trost, Ernst (trombone player), 49, 49n91, 50
trumpet, 60, 60n12, 257

V

Venice (town), 1–2, 2n2, 43, 58, 60–62, 66–67, 67n11, 68, 68n23, 69–71, 74, 93n88, 134n19, 137, 146n43, 147–48, 148n47, 149, 181n107, 182–83, 183n112, 185n116, 186, 238, 252–53, 259

Vierdanck, Johann (composer, organist and instrumentalist), 7, 7n14, 15n26, 59
viol, 51, 103, 116, 151, 170, 236, 243–244
viola da gamba, 34–35, 236
violin, 27, 55–56, 67, 67n22, 79, 116, 144, 145n40, 146, 148, 170, 177, 181n107, 243
violone, 96, 103, 144, 148n48, 236, 242–43
Voigt, Andreas (instrumentalist), 15
Volkmar, Jr., Heinrich (Public Professor), 260, 260n80
Vopelius, Johann (military captain), 87, 87n77
Vulteius, Hermann (professor and rector), 252n57
Institutiones Juris, 252

W

war
  about, 32, 51n98–99, 68n23, 85, 88, 91, 98–100, 106–7, 254
  "Music in a Time of War" (Frandsen), 151n56, 162n76
Watzdorf, Volrad von, 70
Weckmann, Matthias (instrumentalist, court organist), 79, 79n51–52, 80, 115–16, 120, 121n128, 152
Weidemann, Peter (Senator in Gera), 258
Weissenfels (town), 42–43, 43n76, 81n65, 127–29, 131, 135, 137, 139, 141, 143, 157, 159, 172–73, 182, 184, 184n114, 189, 199, 199n156, 200, 206, 208–9, 216, 225, 228, 240, 250, 254, 258
Weissenfels, Town Council of, 251
Weissensee (town), 52, 52n103
Weisshahn, Adolph, 15
Weixer, Daniel (organist), 110, 131n14
Weller, Tobias (organ builder), 132
Weller von Molssdorf, Jacob (Senior Court Chaplain), 133–36, 133n17, 135–36n20, 136n21, 173, 193, 202–3, 250n54
Werner, Christian (cantor), 137, 151n57
Werner, Friedrich (instrumentalist), 115, 117, 151, 151n57, 162
Werner, Hans (instrumentalist), 15
Westonia, Elisabetha Johanna (Elizabeth Jane Weston) (spouse of Johannes Leo of Eisenach), 226, 226n9, 227
Wildeck, Christian (Book-keeper for Land and Beverage Tax), 23n39, 253–54, 259

Wildvogel, Georg (Privy Chamber Secretary), 82, 82n67
Wilhelm IV, Landgrave of Hesse-Kassel, 22n36
Wolfenbüttel (town), 36, 36n58, 40n72, 121n126, 122, 146n43–44, 211, 216–17, 219, 238
Wolfenbüttel Court, 123–25, 213–14, 219–20, 233–34, 240
Wolff, Carl (Counselor, Secretary), 258
Wolff, Heinrich (school teacher), 258
Wolffersdorff, Gottfried von (Councillor of the Treasury), 184, 184n114
Wolframsdorf, Lord von, 259
works by Heinrich Schütz. *See also* Schütz, Heinrich
  Becker Psalter (2nd edition, 1661), 229–33, 232n14–15, 239, fig 12
  Becker Psalter (1628), 47n87, 62–66, 65n17, 216, 229–33, 238
  Cantiones sacrae (1625), 37–39, 37n62, 149, 238
  Dafne (1627), 22n37, 49n96, 56n5, xviin1
  Da Pacem Domine (1627), 48n89, 50n97, 56n5
  Geistliche Chormusik (1648), 77n43, 131n14, 161n75, 162–66, 239
  German Psalms, Motets and Concertos for eight and more voices, 238
  Historia der Auferstehung Jesu Christi (1623), 33–35, 149, 238–39
  Historia des Geburts Jesu Christi (1664), 241–44
  Il primo libro de madrigali (1611), 1–3
  Kleine geistliche Concerte I (1636), 104n108, 105–6
  Kleine geistliche Concerte II (1639), 105, 105n109, 110–11
  Musicalische Exequien (1636), 16n29, 18n32, 96–103, 96n94–95, 149, 239, 239n34
  Psalmen Davids (1619), 24, 24n40
  Schwanengesang (1671), 249–50
  Symphoniae sacrae I (1629), 69–70, 69n4, 93n88, 147, 149, 238
  Symphoniae sacrae II (1647), 131n14, 144–49, 148n48, 180, 239
  Symphoniae sacrae III (1650), 177–81, 239
  Teutoniam dudum belli (1621), 32–33
  Zwölf Geistliche Gesänge (1657), 222–25, 239

Z

Zehm, Martin *(Kapellknabe)*, 46, 46n80, 56, 59
Zeitz (town), 152n61, 214n181, 234–38, 234n21, 245–47, 246n47, fig 13
Zeitz, palace church in, fig 13
Zeitz Court, 234–37
Ziegler, Caspar (composer, jurist, poet), 201–2, 201n160

CPSIA information can be obtained at www.ICGtesting.com
Printed in the USA
BVOW08s2253110716

455189BV00002B/3/P

9 780190 628475